INTRODUCTION
to
INDEXING and ABSTRACTING

INTRODUCTION to INDEXING and ABSTRACTING

Third Edition

Donald B. Cleveland
Professor
University of North Texas

and

Ana D. Cleveland
Professor
University of North Texas

2001
Libraries Unlimited
A Division of Greenwood Publishing Group, Inc.
Greenwood Village, Colorado

LIBRARIES UNLIMITED
A Division of Greenwood Publishing Group, Inc.
7730 East Belleview Avenue, Suite A200
Greenwood Village, CO 80111
1-800-225-5800
www.lu.com

Library of Congress Cataloging-in-Publication Data

Cleveland, Donald B., 1935-
    Introduction to indexing and abstracting / Donald B. Cleveland and Ana D. Cleveland.--
3rd ed.
        p. cm.
    Includes bibliographical references and index.
    ISBN 1-56308-641-7 (cloth)
        1. Indexing. 2. Abstracting. I. Cleveland, Ana D., 1943- II. Title.

Z695.9 .C592 2000
025.3--dc21
                                                                              00-041236

This text is dedicated to the hundreds of students who have gone through our indexing course, many of them now successfully indexing on a daily basis as a part of their professional work.

Contents

Preface xiii

Chapter 1—INTRODUCTION 1
Making an Index 1
The Need for Indexes. 2
The Nature of Indexes 4
Makers of Indexes 5
A Brief Historical Perspective 6
A Note to the Neophyte Indexer. 9

Chapter 2—THE NATURE OF INFORMATION 11
The Information Age 11
A Natural Phenomenon. 13
The Study of Information. 18
A Basic Resource 18
Mechanisms for Information Preservation and Transmittal 19

Chapter 3—THE ORGANIZATION OF INFORMATION 22
The Information Cycle 22
The Basic Information Retrieval Model 23
    The Information Is Created and Acquired for the System. . . . 24
    Knowledge Records Are Analyzed and Tagged by Sets
        of Index Terms. 26
    The Knowledge Records Are Stored Physically and the
        Index Terms Are Stored into a Structured File. 26
    The User's Query Is Tagged with Sets of Index Terms and
        Then Is Matched Against the Tagged Records 27
    Matched Documents Are Retrieved for Review 27
    Feedback May Lead to Several Reiterations of the Search. . . . 28
Classification and Indexing 29
The Relationship of Indexing, Abstracting, and Searching 31
Using Indexes and Abstracts 33

Chapter 4—VOCABULARY CONTROL. 35

The Purpose of Controlled Vocabulary. 35
The Nature of Indexing Languages. 37
Authority Lists 38
Generic Vocabularies 39
The Thesaurus. 40
Thesaurus Construction 41
    Term Relationships 43
    Term Forms 45
Thesaurus Evaluation. 46

Chapter 5—TYPES OF INDEXES AND ABSTRACTS 48

Types of Indexes. 48
    Alphabetical Indexes. 48
    Author Indexes 49
    Book Indexes. 49
    Citation Indexes 49
    Classified Indexes 51
    Coordinate Indexes 51
    Cumulative Indexes 51
    Faceted Indexes 51
    First-line Indexes 52
    Hypermedia Indexes. 52
    Internet Indexes 52
    Multimedia Indexes 53
    Periodical Indexes 53
    Permuted Title Indexes 54
    String Indexes 54
    Word Indexes 55
Types of Abstracts. 55
    Indicative Abstracts 56
    Informative Abstracts 57
    Critical Abstracts 57
    Classifying Abstracts by Use 58
    Classifying Abstracts by Author 58
    Structured Abstracts. 59
Examples from Indexing Tools 61
Examples from Abstracting Tools 74
Examples of Thesauri 91

Chapter 6—THE INDEXING PROCESS. 97

Aboutness 98
Steps in Indexing 99
    Recording of Bibliographic Data 100

Content Analysis 101
    The Title. 101
    The Abstract. 101
    The Text Itself. 102
    The References Section 102
Some Key Points 103
    Subject Determination 103
    Locators 104
    Term Selection 104
    Entry Points 104
Depth of Indexing 105
    Exhaustivity 105
    Specificity. 106
    Making Choices. 106
Display of Indexes 107

Chapter 7—THE ABSTRACTING PROCESS 108
The Purpose of an Abstract 108
Coverage 109
    Economic Constraints 109
    Significant Material 109
    Publication Source 109
    Subject Interest of the Users. 110
Steps in Abstracting 110
    Step One 110
        The Title. 110
        The Author 111
        Author Affiliation. 111
        Funding Agency. 111
        Publication Source 112
        Foreign Languages 113
        Other Information. 113
    Step Two 113
    Step Three 115
    Step Four 117
    Step Five 117
Editing 118
Evaluation of Abstracts 119
The Writing Process 119

Chapter 8—INDEXING AND ABSTRACTING A DOCUMENT . . 121
Example of a Technical Paper. 121
Abstracting the Document. 129
Indexing the Document 131

Chapter 9—BOOK INDEXING 137

   The Nature of Book Indexes. 137
   Steps in Indexing. 139
      Step One 139
      Step Two 139
      Step Three 139
      Step Four 139
      Step Five 139
   Index Terms 140
   Name Entries. 142
   Subject Entries 144
   Additional Details 145
   Ninety-Nine "Dos-and-Don'ts" 146

Chapter 10—BOOK INDEXING EXAMPLE. 150

   Example Book Chapter. 150
   Indexing the Chapter. 160

**Chapter 11—INDEXING SPECIAL SUBJECT AREAS
              AND FORMATS.** 165

   Background. 165
   Special Subject Areas 166
      Science 166
      Social Sciences 168
      Humanities 169
   Special Formats 171
      Newspapers. 171
      Nonprint Forms 174
      Images. 174

Chapter 12—EVALUATION OF INDEXING 179

   Background. 179
   The General Problem 180
   Beginning with the User. 182
   Relevance. 183
   Recall and Precision 185
   Effects of Exhaustivity and Specificity 187
   Index Quality. 187
   Evaluating Abstracts. 189
   Standards. 189
   Editing 190

Chapter 13—INDEXING AND ABSTRACTING SERVICES 192

Background. 192
Bringing in the Computers. 193
Types of Databases. 194
Online Services. 195
Searching the Database 196
The Future 199

Chapter 14—THE USE OF COMPUTERS 200

The Computer Tool 200
    The Script. 204
Indexing with a Computer. 206
Types of Indexing Software 207
Indexing Software 209
Automatic Indexing and Abstracting 211
    Indexing. 211
    Abstracting 213

Chapter 15—INDEXING AND THE INTERNET 215

Background. 215
Searching the Web 216
Organization of Information 220
    Metadata and the Web 223
    Dublin Core. 224
    OCLC CORC 226
        CORC Resource Record Database 226
        CORC Authority Database 226
        CORC Pathfinder Database. 226
        CORC Web Dewey 226
Digital Object Identifiers (DOIs) 227
Summary 227
Promises and Pitfalls. 228

**Chapter 16—NINETY-NINE WEB RESOURCES FOR
                INDEXERS AND ABSTRACTORS** 231

Online Bookstores 231
Search Services. 232
Indexing Services. 233
Dictionaries and Dictionary Directories 234
Multireference Resources and Tools 234
E-Mail Reference Sites. 236
Virtual Libraries 237

Chapter 16—NINETY-NINE WEB RESOURCES FOR INDEXERS AND ABSTRACTORS (*continued*)

Special Formats and Subjects Indexing 238
Standards 238
Indexing Software 239
Publishers. 239
Indexing Organizations 240
Indexing-Related Discussion Groups 240
Indexing and the Web 241

Chapter 17—THE PROFESSION 242

Education and Training 242
Job Opportunities 243
The Role of Research 245
The Future 249
The Final Word 249

Glossary 251

Bibliography 261

Index 277

Preface

With the third edition of this book, the authors wish to express their gratitude to the many students, instructors, librarians, and colleagues in academia and the publishing world who made the first two editions successful in the marketplace. We hope this third edition will prove equally as useful.

Like its first two editions, this book is aimed at the neophyte indexer and the practitioner as a guide to the fundamentals of indexing and abstracting. In this new edition chapters have been rewritten and new materials have been added, including discussions of indexing on the Internet and image indexing, because this is where major developments are now occurring.

As in previous editions no knowledge of indexing and/or abstracting is assumed and the step-by-step examples and explanations are given with this in mind.

Introduction

MAKING AN INDEX

Anyone who can read, knows the alphabet, and has a modicum of horse sense can make an index. There are, however, good indexes and bad indexes. Making a good index requires more than common sense. It requires an understanding of the empirical knowledge base of indexing that has developed over the centuries and an appreciation for the methods that work. It also requires an understanding of who uses indexes, how they use them and for what purposes, as well as a respect for the nature of the professional activity itself.

Mark Twain informed us that writing is simply arranging words in rows on paper and that anyone can do it because all the words are in the dictionary. The same might be said for indexing. All the keywords are in the document. All we have to do is make a list of them. Mark Twain, however, knew quite well that it is not quite that simple. Writing and indexing are artistic crafts that must be studied intensively and practiced. How we arrange the words on those rows is a critical issue.

Indexing and abstracting are practical arts and this book was planned, organized, and written entirely on that premise. The goal is to tell you what you must know, what you must do and how to do it.

What is a good index? It is an index that leads a user to the exact information that is needed with no hurdles, no false paths, and no irrelevant materials. The perfect index always leads a user to totally pertinent information, seldom leads to trivial information and never, ever leads to nonpertinent information. The perfect index reduces to an absolute minimum the need for cross-references because the first term you look up is the right one and it points to all the information needed. If that term leads to such perfect information there is no need to flip around chasing down cross-references. Perfect indexes in the future will have no need for cross-references or scope notes. Of course such a perfect index is yet to be created, and probably never will be; still, we strive for it every time we turn to the task of indexing.

When a user picks up an index, several things can happen, some of them good and some of them bad. The legendary football coach at the University of Texas, Darrel Royal, was asked once why he was not particularly fond of the pass as a play, and he said that, when you throw a pass, three things can happen and two of them are bad. For you nonfootball fans, the three things are:

1. The receiver drops the ball.
2. The pass is intercepted.
3. The pass is completed.

When you use an index, four things can happen and three of them are bad:

1. You do not find any information although it is there.
2. You find information, but it is not what you thought it would be.
3. You find a part of the available information.
4. You find information and it is exactly what you need.

An indexer tries to minimize numbers one through three and to maximize number four. All four outcomes should be acutely in the indexer's mind as s/he works.

Indexing is the process that makes an index and an indexer is the person who does the indexing. But, what does that entail? Simply put, indexing produces entries in an index. This process involves the steps of analyzing the content of the information item, expressing the *aboutness* of the item in some abbreviated form and indicating the location of the information. Along with abstracting, indexing creates surrogates of information items. According to Webster a surrogate is something that serves as a substitute. The surrogate stands in the place of longer items in an information retrieval system. It is an image of the real thing. When we make an index, we create an abbreviated and orderly image of the knowledge record. Good indexers are creative and imaginative people who make such artful images.

THE NEED FOR INDEXES

The information superhighway and all the less exotic information country roads need maps and road signs. That is exactly what indexing and abstracting can do: provide detailed and accurate maps and road signs. The Information Age and the incredible information technology explosion are giving power and prestige to the humble art of indexing although we often have to disguise ourselves with new jargon words. Nowadays we do not just create indexing systems; instead we create robots, spiders, and meta-search tools. The organization of information has moved beyond the traditional library walls into the streets of society. The astute observer and participant in these exciting times realizes that the only thing that can keep our information stores from becoming information chaos is an organized system of content analysis and information guides.

The function of an index is to give users systematic and effective shortcuts to the information they need. In most cases, without an index, the retrieval of information would be impractical. If we had a million documents we could rent an aircraft hangar, buy hundreds of tables, and stack the books, telling the users that our system is random searching. These types of systems are not impossible, but they are impractical. An index is needed.

The mass corpus of print and nonprint material in the world would be virtually inaccessible without indexes. Documents needing indexes cover a vast range. In the most obvious information depository, a library, there are books, journals, government documents, technical reports, microforms, electronic stores, etc. A library is just one small example of an information system.

Indexes are not luxury items. They are essential to social order. The business world, the government, education systems, etc., all depend on complex and extensive information stores and only effective indexing systems can make these information structures accessible.

Indexes are needed for any information collection, except the very smallest. Thousands of indexes exist, and are used daily, but users seldom think of them as such. How many people, when they want to make a telephone call, say that they are going to consult the telephone yellow index? Don't they say, "telephone yellow pages"? It never occurs to them that this is an index. Actually, a telephone directory is a two-part index consisting of a personal name index and a classified subject index. What if there were no indexes in the world? Society would come to a standstill. Telephones and the Internet would be useless. Every time a search bottom is clicked in a navigator, some type of indexing, from rudimentary to sophisticated, is evoked.

Not all indexes are the traditional type. For example, software that simply checks a query term against every word in a text is in a sense a "virtual index." The structure, logic, and end results of the software are mechanisms for automatic, real-time indexing. Designing these indexing devices requires little knowledge of indexing principles and these devices are simple to use, and the results reflect a lack of intellectual effort and procedural endeavor. Unsophisticated input brings unsophisticated output. These types of systems are well meaning, although their designers cannot understand what they have done wrong. What they have done wrong is to underestimate and misunderstand the nature of indexing, and the entire problem of content analysis and surrogation.

But, what exactly does an index do? If a user wants to be absolutely sure that she has not missed anything, then she would need to examine every item in the hypothetical aircraft hangar mentioned above. One by one she would go through the files and glance at the contents. Every book on the tables would be pulled and examined. This is not usually practical, and the best way to save time is to use an index. Indexes cut down dramatically on the amount of items that have to be looked at. That is the heart of the matter. An index separates the wheat from the sheaf and then sorts the wheat down to a handful of desired grains.

Thus, an index has two general purposes: to minimize the time and effort in finding information, and to maximize the searching success of the user. Both purposes are accomplished by choosing the best words that will match a user's language and by having a system of accurate and complete cross-references to related information.

Indexes and abstracts give added value to a document. If not, then why index it? The index will help users find documents thus ensuring increased usage of the documents. With this in mind, a good index will be designed according to the user's way of thinking. An index results in a user being able to find information and information is essential to survival. We should feel no shame in giving this lofty importance to professional indexers and the work that they do.

THE NATURE OF
INDEXES

In order to understand the nature of indexes we might think of abstract informational spaces. Let us visualize information items in an abstract space, and then let us visualize indexes and abstracts also in this space. Indexing and abstracting transform document space into an index/abstract space. In an ideal situation the document space and the indexing space are very similar. There is a great reduction in the number of words in the documents themselves for the indexing space, but the spirit and soul of the document space is replicated in the index space. The goal is to ensure that both spaces exist in the same subject space. An index is metadata, which is data about data. Metadata indicates the characteristics and relationships of the information in the data items and other data items that are similar.

The index space reflects two states of concern about the documents indexed. The first state is what is *included* in the index and the second state is what is *excluded* from the index. The inclusion state may have information that is important and information that is trivial and unimportant. The exclusion state may have the same. Important information may have been omitted. Hopefully, trivial and unimportant information remains in the exclusion state. At the operational level, this depends on the decisions of the indexer. When important information is left out, we can say that information was lost during the indexing process. That information may be virtually lost forever unless some browser stumbles across it.

An index is not an alphabetical list of nouns and gerunds in a text. It follows, therefore, that the process of indexing is more than simply extracting all nouns in the text and attaching locators to them.

An index is not a list or an appendage or a rearranged table of contents. It is a distinct knowledge record with its own internal validity and consistency. Ideas are intricately connected to each other. That is why we say that this self-contained knowledge record gives added value to the information item being pointed to.

Indexes come in many forms and formats and serve many purposes. Some indexes are printed, some are electronic, and some are both. There are name indexes, subject indexes, and map indexes, artifacts indexes, and many others. There are indexes to books, to periodicals, to images, to databases, numerical data, and so on. Some indexes are created entirely manually and some are created entirely by a computer. And many are created with a varying combination of manual and computer methods. Whatever the production methods, a good index is the result of utilizing the collected experience of indexers over the years and following the instincts of educated common sense.

MAKERS OF INDEXES

What does an indexer do? The indexer analyses a document and tags it with subject and other designators based on her perception of what a user would search under. The indexer's agenda is quite clear: What does the user need? At a different level the indexer may compile sets of index entries into a format for dissemination. The indexer may actually be involved in the larger aspects of establishing formats and policies for an indexing operation, large or small, in a library or other information center, or in an organization devoted to creating and distributing indexes and/or abstracts. Even if the indexer is a free-lancer working alone, the indexer will set up policies and infrastructure for operating a business. Indexing always exists in a larger environmental context.

Most indexers are doing good work. They take pride in what they do and they strive to do it well. They are professionals who do indexing according to professional standards and ethics. Indexers come from many diverse educational and experiential backgrounds. Some get into the work early, in their twenties and some later, even after retirement. Some work full time at indexing and some work part-time. Some work in organizations or businesses and others work as freelancers or consultants. Some teach indexing and some write indexing books. Some build personal reputations in the field by criticizing indexing books. All of this is important work.

Indexing is not a full-time activity for most indexers. Several surveys indicate that the majority of indexers spend approximately half of their work time indexing. Some work in libraries, publishing offices, research institutes, universities, and other organizations related to information dissemination. Some writers index their own works, but would never consider themselves to be indexers. Actually some of these "amateurs" do quite well, especially in highly specific subject areas where they know what users are seeking.

Indexers are often loners and feel comfortable working alone, since that is generally how they work. Self-discipline and an affinity for detail are two highly important qualifications. A good memory is an asset, although indexing software is a great help with this. Being a good, fast reader is also a real plus for an indexer, especially if the indexer hopes to make a living out of it.

Makers of indexes are also censors. And many times they are very powerful censors. Perhaps not intentionally (and the indexer may vigorously deny it), but unrecognized bias, prejudice, and personal agendas are not uncommon in the work of information professionals. For example, Joseph Goebbels was a very effective information professional. He did his horrible work quite well; but it was certainly biased, prejudiced, with personal agendas and vendettas. We hope most of us are not like that; still, since we are human, the censor elements can be there.

An indexer should have an inquisitive and imaginative mind because indexing involves answering obvious questions and in asking the right nonobvious questions. For example, what does a particular sentence in the text really mean? If I choose this or that individual term, will my index user be likely to select this term when searching for information? Is this paragraph trivial information to the reader? The good indexer becomes the surrogate of the *reader*. The indexer becomes the stand-in for the reader and understands that role as s/he moves through the text, underlining words.

A BRIEF HISTORICAL
PERSPECTIVE

At the point in time when mankind developed the skill to recognize symbols as a communication device, civilization had its beginning. The first evidence we have of the beginning of such communication is the paintings on the walls of caves. The next step was to systematize the pictorial images into more complex messages. The hunter goes out of the cave and follows the beast and spears the beast and everybody has a barbecue around the fire. The tribe's recorder draws these events on the wall of the cave. For at least 5,000 years such systems existed. Then came the use of symbols to represent language itself with meanings, ideas, and the vocals of natural language expressed through symbols and purposeful positioning of these symbols with each other. Abstract thought could now be recorded with symbols. Nonpictorial writing developed in various parts of the world, independently of each other as far as we know.

The history of indexing and abstracting is closely related to the history of writing and the collection of information records. The first evidence of the systematic gathering and organizing of written records occurs in Sumer around 3,000 B.C. Egyptian and Sumerian writing were done on clay tablets and papyrus. For more than 3,000 years clay tablets and cuneiform scrip were used in the Mesopotamian valley and elsewhere. In China and India, around 2,000 B.C., record keeping became a part of the society. These early people realized that it is not possible to have an orderly society without an orderly memory of what has occurred. Early on societies passed laws requiring that business transactions, at any level, be recorded and authorized. This requirement often spread to include other social activities, such as births, marriages, and deaths.

This was a giant step forward. Societal events and agreements between friends and among enemies could be recorded. Business people, government workers, religious officials, scholars, school children, all needed to store the written records they were creating on a daily basis. Theological records were kept in a sacred place and access was limited to the high and mighty. The scribes who wrote and read these records were key people in the society.

Indexing and abstracting have their distant origins somewhere and at some time when someone realized that written records need to be organized so that access is easy. It is certainly conceivable that early on scribes started making scribbles on records to mark their content, which is what indexing and abstracting is. It is a natural impulse.

The problem of the storage of information is quickly followed by the problem of how to retrieve the information stored. These early civilizations proposed schemes of knowledge classification and document arrangement. Some of the problems they solved are still the legacy of these pioneers to our information retrieval systems in the twenty-first century.

So surrogates to information stores are as old as writing and have existed in different forms in virtually every language. It often surprises the modern day librarian to learn that some of our basic processes were not invented by the librarian giants of the last 100 years, but actually were practiced hundreds of years B.C. Subject arrangement and abstracting are prime examples.

An index must have some order of presentation. We are accustomed primarily to an alphabetical order, but it can be arranged by classification groups, numerical or chronological. Alphabetical arrangement of information was not automatic from the beginning. It evolved over time, with examples here and there scattered over the centuries.

As a matter of fact we are not sure how the letters of the alphabet obtained their arrangement. Early on the Greeks appeared to be using some sort of alphabetic order for long lists of things, but how the order evolved is not clearly understood. We have an example of an alphabetical index in the fifth century, although this was a fascinating anomaly and not a current trend. We know that around 900 A.D. an encyclopedia was arranged in alphabetical order, but most such works had classified arrangements. Although elementary alphabetic subject indexes have been traced as far back as the fifth century A.D., alphabetical ordering was not the precise procedure that we demand in modern times. It was considered adequate to order on the first one to three letters.

The early indexes were limited to personal names or were indexes to the occurrence of words in the text. That is, they were concordances rather than topical subject indexes. Marginal summaries were around as early as the ninth century.

Indexing took a major step forward with the development of the codex form of the book. For the first time a book index became practical. Using an index to a papyrus roll would entail a lot of rolling and unrolling. Think of that the next time that you use a microfilm machine.

The changing nature of scholarship in the Middle Ages created a need for indexes. During the latter part of this era debate became a major pedagogical method in the universities. The primary areas of study, such as theology, law, and natural sciences, lent themselves to the use of vigorous debate as a teaching technique. Clearly, debate relies on the ability to cite the recognized experts in the field. Thus, a need for alphabetical indexing rose quite naturally. Shortly after the invention of printing a number of decent book indexes were created, and the practice slowly built over the years that followed. The concept of what a book index should be steadily advanced. Chapter headings are as old as books themselves and content lists were introduced early, but the rapid growth of printing and the proliferation of books increased the need for book indexes.

One practice that developed was the idea of binding blank pages at the beginning or end of the book. There the reader could write comments or note subjects of importance to him. Lawyers filled in the pages with extensive alphabetical lists of statutes in which they were interested. Clerics used the blank pages in their Bibles to write in references to scriptures. These were do-it-yourself indexes. When we examine material during these centuries it is obvious that indexing was far from being a common practice and that our concept of indexing still lay in the future. The index was usually in the front of the book, lifted verbatim from the text and did not always match our idea of what would be the proper keyword of that particular text. These indexes were simple but not very easy to use.

The sixteenth century brought an evolution to better quality book indexes and the seventeenth century brought a new type of information tool: periodicals. When periodicals began to proliferate, indexes became essential. At first indexes to individual titles proved mostly adequate, but by the middle of the nineteenth century it became obvious that this procedure seriously limited scholars who needed access to information across the literature.

Throughout the centuries abstracting had been developing, and, as a matter of fact, preceded indexing. Abstracting, as we know it, probably began with writings on the outside of clay envelopes several millenniums B.C. In classical times summaries began to be placed at the beginning of records to facilitate searching.

The Greek abstracts often contained comments or literary criticism at the end of the summary. So critical abstracting goes back a long way. These early abstracts summarized, clarified, and often evaluated the item. Abstracting is closely related to annotating and often the line between the two was somewhat blurred.

For almost two hundred years between the invention of the printing press and the rise of the journal, scholars had limited methods for scholarly communication. They published books and wrote letters to each other. That changed dramatically with the advent of the scholarly journal.

Along with the development of the learned journal was the development of abstract journals. In January 1665 the first published abstract journal was issued, called the *Journal Des Scavans*. Approximately half of each page was devoted to a single item, usually a new book, along with details of its author, title, and place of publication. The scholar now had a bibliographic control device in the form of a serial publication that covered mainly periodical articles published far and near. The abstract serial covered, to some extent, books and related material, but mainly focused on periodicals. With such a journal in hand, scholars could feel they had a chance to keep up to date with intellectual developments. We had begun to do something to make information in written records more accessible, either by arranging the important features in a known order, or by condensing long documents into convenient abstracts or epitomes.

By the 1700s other abstract journals began to appear. For example, in 1703, the German abstract journal *Monatsextracte* started publication in Leipzig. During the eighteenth century this type of publication was begun in England and France as well. Many of these were similar to the *Journal Des Scavans* in format and purpose. They served as a basic method of intellectual exchange among the diverse and scattered peoples of Europe.

The abstract journal began to proliferate in the nineteenth century, with a trend toward the development of specialized publications. Already the growth of the primary journal had people concerned about the so-called information explosion. In the *American Eclectic* for September 1841, a German writer (W. Menzel) protested against the increasing number of scientific periodicals in Germany:

> Of medical journals, there are forty-three in Germany. It must be granted that different modes of practice require different periodicals . . . but forty-three journals are an astonishing number. What physician who practices daily can read them all, and to what physician who does not practice can they be useful?

There is a lot of wisdom hidden in this long-ago observation. The good German physician was not likely thinking in terms of indexes and abstracts, but that was what he was talking about.

In the 1850s W. F. Poole published an index that cut across many journals to begin the modern concept of a single publication indexing numerous issues of many periodicals. The importance of this event to the development of indexing cannot be overstated.

In 1900 H. W. Wilson first published *Readers' Guide to Periodical Literature.* This index was especially notable for the emphasis it placed on subject access and good cross-referencing. Each article in a periodical was indexed under its author and its specific subject. There were numerous cross-references to link up each subject with related subjects and with aspects of the subject.

Also, at the end of the nineteenth century scholars began to demand improved bibliographic access to their literature. With this in mind, Paul Otlet and Henri La Fontaine founded the International Institute of Bibliography, which had the purpose, among other things, to improve indexing approaches to the scholarly literature. Out of their work, title-word indexing was proposed, which eventually led to modern keyword and free-text indexing.

In the meantime book indexing continued to improve. From indexes with simple lists of terms, indexes began to have subdivisions of terms and, slowly, cross-references began to appear.

The presence of an index in a book was generally taken for granted, its absence generally ignored and its quality rarely the subject of comment by publishers, critics, or readers. Indexing was done, if at all, by any available personnel, often clerks without training or skill.

Post-World War II brought us the modern *information explosion* and the attempt to use computers to control the explosion. By the 1950s computers had entered the indexing and abstracting arena and efforts were begun to evaluate indexing using quantitative methods. Hans Peter Luhn of IBM introduced a mechanized form of derived title-word indexing schemes where ambiguity could be reduced by showing terms in the context of their occurrence. About the same time, serious testing of the effectiveness of indexing techniques began, and the profession became a battleground for competing philosophies, methods, and techniques for indexing.

The 1960s brought the *third generation* computers, which centered on large-scale storage devices. Indexes and abstracts began to be published with computers using batch processing methods. By the 1990s the random-access devices had been perfected to the point where computer-stored indexes could be directly keyword searched. The latest development is the Internet and its worldwide ubiquity.

As the twentieth century closed, it was evident that indexing had outstripped the ideas of previous ages. We have progressed from indexes to individual works, through indexes to several volumes, to cooperative indexes, to massive database indexes, and now we have the World Wide Web with many formidable indexing challenges to face.

A NOTE TO THE NEOPHYTE INDEXER

Indexing cannot be learned and fully understood as an isolated subject. It is best understood if it is considered as a part of an infrastructure for organizing information. The student of indexing should have a basic understanding of the general concepts of information and how information is created, disseminated, and used. Good indexers understand library cataloging and classification and information access work and how people search books, libraries, and other complex information systems.

Indexing has always been and will forever be primarily an art. This does not mean that we cannot take advantage of empirical research to understand and refine what we do. Defining indexing, in an empirical sense, is not unlike trying to define art in an empirical sense. We may not be able to precisely define what a good index *is*, but we can recognize one when we see one. This presents a problem when we turn to the instruction of indexing. At the present time there seems to be an endless supply of people ready to tell others how it should be done, and we all have our rigid views of what that method should be. There is some hope in the yeoman attempts of colleagues to establish official standards for indexing, although standards have to be accepted, interpreted, and implemented by those who index. This is not an infallible process. The neophyte's most formidable challenge is knowing who and what to believe, given the ubiquitous presence of dogmatic pronouncements. As you go through this book (or read any other writing on indexing) you should believe what makes sense. Indexing is a commonsense art.

It is not completely understood how indexers carry out their work; thus we are not completely sure how to teach indexing. Like any other art it is based on fundamental principles, intuition, insight, imagination, and practice, practice, practice. The first (fundamental principles) can be taught, and the last (practice) depends on the discipline of the learner. All the other elements (intuition, insight, and imagination) are intangible.

The literature is full of rules, procedures, steps, theories, etc. A lot of good advice can be distilled from these writings. At the same time, however, there is an abundance of dogmatic contradictions. The best we can do is to try to find the rational and workable concepts that have been generated over the years.

What follows in this text is some of the thinking and approaches that have evolved from a wonderful history of indexing. The goal of this book is to introduce the field and point the direction for those who might want to practice the arts of indexing and abstracting. This book will focus on synthesizing the thinking and experience of indexers and abstractors over the years and will not dwell on narrowly focused research papers. Of course the discussion will be based on the research and practical experience gained in the past, but the purpose of this third edition, as in the previous editions, is to present the practical knowledge necessary to become a professional indexer. Reading this book will not make an indexer out of you. No book or indexing class can. You have to do that on your own. We hope there are some useful guidelines in what follows.

Having introduced the basic background of indexing, it is time to set to work. The next chapter will discuss the general concept of information and the role of indexing and abstracting in the information processing world.

The Nature of Information

THE INFORMATION AGE

Information is not only the most basic aspect of our society, but is one of the most essential. Our survival is dependent on the effective transfer of information at every level. It is an indispensable aspect of modern society and information processing has always been an integral part of every activity that humans undertake, from passing genes, to telling a joke, to smelling a rose, to building a bridge, to everything in our lives, both awake and asleep.

We are being told, rather frequently, that this is the Information Age and that the key to success and a happy life is knowledge access and connectivity, preferably through electronic devices. Librarians and indexers are only one part of a large group of professionals who produce, organize, and disseminate information.

The concept of the Information Age is now universal. Several decades ago librarians talked about an "Information Age," then this terminology was picked up by the computer world, then the government, and finally it became ubiquitous in the business world. The Information Age has changed our ways of living: in medical care, education, and most notably, in the way we entertain ourselves. It has changed the whole fabric of our careers and the types of skills and training we need.

It should first be made clear that past generations were very much concerned about information, that information played a significant role in their lives, and that there were problems with its storage and retrieval. Information is a universal concept that knows no boundaries of time or place. The profession of handling information was not invented in the last hundred years. It goes back in time to at least the point where humankind developed writing systems to record their thoughts.

During and after World War II, there was an increasing recognition of the central role of information in individual, social, economic, and cultural affairs, which brought on an interest in the concept of information itself. During this period of time, the Information Age was fueled by a revolution in information technologies, but over the decades that followed, it was realized that computers and communication devices were only one dimension of the information world. The phenomena of information rests on a broad range of biological and behavioral attributes that we are only beginning to understand.

It is popular to say that the Industrial Society gave way to the Information Society. This may be a rather poor concept. The Industrial Society is still a gigantic enterprise and very much alive and has not been replaced by anything. It is true, of course, that the Industrial Society depends more on information than ever before, but it still is turning out automobiles and washing machines and selling them. The Information Society is a different, independent facet of our society, influencing the entire society, but not replacing everything else wholesale. The creation, processing, and distribution of information is a major industry. Most all industries are rapidly realizing that accurate, readily accessible information is the key to success, no matter what the enterprise.

The designation "Information Age" means that the idea of information is recognized as a natural phenomenon and the study of its nature is a prime concern. Also, the new age has brought a major shift in the products and services industries. There is a high concentration of people and resources involved in the fundamental tasks of creating and disseminating information.

There are a number of factors that characterize the Information Age. The obvious one is the sheer growth in the amount of information. Closely related to that is the increasing amount of information in new forms which cannot be handled with traditional techniques. One example of this is the Internet with its potpourri of multimedia.

In the 1950s the term *information explosion* appeared to describe the exponential increase in information generation. Hardly any paper on information written since World War II has failed to warn that something must give since the handling of information is at a crisis stage. Information is exploding, with the implication that information systems likewise are going to blow up. As we know, the information profession turned to computers as promising tools for coping with the so-called *explosion*. This age of information explosion (or, as some people like to say, this age of information pollution) cannot be controlled unless information is properly organized for retrieval. A major tool for doing this is indexing.

Why is information so important? Because it is the way we control our lives. Information has always been considered a means for control and the Information Age has intensified this concept. The word *control* has many negative connotations. We think of science fiction novels, of manipulative bosses we have worked for, of totalitarian governments, and so forth; but the idea of control has many more positive connotations. For example, a steering wheel controls the wheels of a car.

The concept of information for control has other endless examples, going back into the twilight of humankind's appearance. Early humankind learned the habits of animals and nature's secrets for when and what kind of plants to gather and later how to raise their own animals and plant their own crops. In this way they used information in order to control their destinies.

Several years ago when one of your authors was told that he had cancer, he wanted as much information as possible because he wanted to control his life. If he was going to die in two days, he wanted to be in control. If he were going to live two years, then he needed the information to plan his two remaining years. He suddenly wanted total and absolute control of his life, and information was the key. Never before had the concept of information become so personal.

The idea of using information for control spans from the amoebae to the ultimate force of the universe. One of the tragedies of the human condition is that we lack the information we need to optimize our place in the scheme of things. Control is, therefore, a defining force in the rise of the Information Society and the Information Age. When electronic mechanisms became available, the power to control, in both the good and bad connotations of the word, increased to an incredible degree. Thus came *the Information Age-revolution-explosion-society*.

As we move through the early years of the twenty-first century, we can look back at the incredible distance we have traveled in the information field during the twentieth century. In terms of automated systems we began the century with punched cards and ended the century with practically the entire world wired.

As the new millennium dawned, we hit the ground running.

A NATURAL PHENOMENON

Information should be thought of as the most natural thing in nature, fundamental to the continuing existence of every living cell in the universe. Information is a fundamental phenomenon that is transferred in civilization with a common system of symbols by living organisms, mechanical devices, or a combination of the two. It was not until the twentieth century that information was considered to be a scientific term, partly as a result of the rise of electronic information technology.

So, what is it? Basic definitions of information are difficult, but this may not be a major concern. Basic definitions of nature are never easy. What is electricity? Or gravity? We have formulas which describe the behavioral properties of electricity and gravity, and on this behavioral knowledge we have built televisions, computers, flying machines. We may not be able to exactly define gravity, but if we jump off the Eiffel Tower, we will surely be able to describe the *properties* of gravity.

Trying to define the word *information* is a valuable intellectual exercise that makes for interesting talk, but probably has little practical value. What we are interested in are the *properties* of information so that it can be created, organized, and disseminated. Just as we have been able to build elaborate applications without knowing what electricity is, we are able to build elaborate information systems without fully understanding what information is. Having said that, let us try for a working understanding of what information is, although no formal definition will be attempted.

Information is input into a system—then it has the potential to affect or reduce a state of uncertainty and thus allow decisions to be made or communication to occur. The best working definition of the word information is simply the ordinary way people use the word. *Information is learning something I did not already know.* Learning something new comes through a variety of receptors: fellow humans, other living organisms, computers, the comic page, TV, radio, touch, smell. Some of it comes already highly organized and some of it comes in seemingly chaotic bits and pieces. Our brain has an incredible organizing power. It constantly churns away on many nonlinear levels to put things into order and find meaning. This occurs not only in our brain, but individual cells in all parts of the body constantly process information, all the way down to the individual DNA codes, the most fundamental information storage and retrieval devices.

Information is found in neurons, in electromagnetic fields, in DNA, in chemical molecules. Information holds together the universe, or, perhaps, blows it apart when a star explodes. For a good while physicists have talked about the physical world in terms of it being a mass-energy information-processing system. Information to a physicist studying the information processing mechanism in mass-energy is quite different than information as perceived by a librarian. They are talking about the same phenomena, but in vastly different application terms.

If we wish, we can elaborate in the attempt to find theoretical understanding of what happens when we "learn something we did not know" but trying to shoot the moving target of defining information may be less important than just getting about our business.

Everyone recognizes the importance of information. The parent receives information from the cry of a baby. On a different level a general knows he needs accurate and updated information to plan his battle. Most of what doctors do involves gathering information, including information on the patient, information concerning the illness, information concerning the physical condition (blood tests, X-rays, blood pressure), information concerning the appropriate treatment, and feedback information on the success of the treatment. Information is fundamental to all decision making structures, from the daily personal decisions to the most global international enterprises.

Throughout the day hundreds of situations occur requiring information: wake-up calls, the newspaper, the empty gas gauge on the car, etc. At work we ask the receptionist what mood the boss is in and throughout the day we read reports, write reports, search computers, make phone calls, read a lunch menu, and on and on. Information removes uncertainty, and in formal information theory, mathematics formulae measure this uncertainty and maintain that this is the measure of information. These formulae do not measure meaning in the information, but they measure what *potential* message was likely to have been sent.

Our personal information system never shuts down. Even when we sleep an information system is alert and hears the smoke alarm or the snoring of our bed companion. All organisms receive information through their senses, but humans have developed advanced systems of language that can be recorded and stored as physical symbols. For centuries these symbols were stored on analog devices, such as chiseled stones, papyrus rolls, and prints. In the last century the power of digitized media was added to the repertory, bringing the concept of information into a new era.

Information has three major continuums:

1.   Created.
2.   Shared.
3.   Used.

Human information, which indexers are concerned with, is shared knowledge and actually exists only in the organism. Records, in whatever form they exist, are only symbols that mean nothing unless the organism processes those symbols. These symbols are external storage for the mind.

In addressing the nature of information it needs to be pointed out that information transfer is a process and that process is carried out by a system. A system is a mechanism for carrying out a process. An information system is a mechanism for obtaining, analyzing, categorizing, and disseminating information. A process is a time dependent event. It begins, it develops, and it ends. If I call my broker to see about the sinking ship that did not come in, I pick up the phone, I dial, I tell him to sell, and I hang up the phone. This is a time-dependent process, which has a beginning, middle, and an end. It was spatial. The information system was the telephone and the company that allowed me to make the call.

As information professionals we are concerned more with the carriers of information rather than with what information is. By *carriers* we mean the multitude of mechanisms that gets information from point A to point B (e.g., language, print, pictures, body language, mechanical devices, electrical devices, DNA, etc.).

To the indexer the heart of the matter is how language carries information. That is crucial to the indexer's work and basic research in indexing needs to focus on this. The indexer must first examine the information contained in an information object and then make the difficult determination of what information is conveyed in the information object. In other words, what is the information *about*? There is a fine, but critical distinction between the concepts of *contained* and *conveyed*. This *aboutness* issue will be discussed in Chapter 6.

Information may be structured by evolving complexity:

Symbols are the beginning of formalized communication.

Words and *numbers* are symbols combined to convey meaning at a higher level.

Data express discrete occurrences.

Information is the result of processing data and giving meaning to it.

Knowledge is the result of the information being absorbed and causing some change.

Wisdom results in proper decisions being made with the newly formed knowledge.

Shannon and Weaver, in a classical monograph published in 1949 titled *The Mathematical Theory of Communication*, suggested that communication can be conceptualized on three levels:

1. The technical.
2. The semantic.
3. The influential (effectiveness) levels.

Shannon and Weaver's work consists of a set of theorems developed to describe the transmission of a coded signal in a noisy channel and originated in the context of telecommunications research, but it is directly applicable to a wide variety of information-related tasks (data encryption, for example), and, in a broad sense, to the indexing problem.

The technical level is concerned with the physical transfer of discrete symbols from a sender to a receiver. How accurate is the transference of the information? The second, the semantic level, deals with the meaning of the message. At this level we are concerned with the ambiguousness in language and meaning. The third level deals with the reaction or results. This level is concerned with the relevance of the information. How does the receiver react to the message?

If I send you this message: X2#$ % & * then you will be puzzled. There has been a breakdown in the physical transfer of symbols. My handwriting is so poor that your receptors cannot read it. If I try again and very carefully write the word *base*, then the physical transfer is complete. But am I discussing with you a number system? Chemical materials? Fort Knox? Baseball? Tiffany lamps? The problem now is *semantic.*

Suppose that when I write *base* on the board in the classroom, a student in the back of the room throws a book against the wall and storms out of the room. It turns out that the student has just finished a bitter divorce with an army sergeant at Fort Knox. The word *base* hits where it hurts. Now, we are talking about reaction to the information, or effectiveness.

Information professionals have dealt very well with the first level, as evidenced by the gigantic information resource we have managed to store in libraries and computers around the world. The physical information is there and can be clearly read.

Unfortunately, we have not been as successful as we need to be on the other levels. On the semantic level, we have developed methods of cataloging and indexing, but we have room for improvement and new challenges are presented daily. On the third level we are just beginning to understand how people search for and use information.

These three levels are not independent of each other and in a communication structure they must be addressed as interrelated to each other. This model is appropriate to indexing and abstracting. At the technical level, an index must be in an appropriate language, must have an understandable format and a clear procedure for using the index. At the technical level, the signal must get through with a minimum of noise. At the semantic level is the heart of the indexing problem. Words must convey meanings without ambiguity. At the third level, the index must correctly identify relevant information, that is, it must be effective.

Another dimension of the nature of information is the types of literature media, or the *forms* in which information is transferred. There are two general forms: *primary* information and *secondary* information. Primary information comes directly from the creator of the information (for example, from the author of a research article in a scientific journal or from the writer of a diary or autobiography). Items in the primary literature may also be primary sources. Secondary forms reflect further digestion, analysis, description, or synthesis, usually from an intermediary between the creator of the information and user of the information.

The following is an outline of the major traditional forms of the literature:

A. Conventional primary media
1. The scholarly journal
2. Alternatives to the journal
   a. Preprints (copies in advance of regular presentation or dissemination)
   b. Reprints
3. Report literature (research that does not appear in scholarly journals before being distributed by some other means to interested users)
4. Informal exchange groups (groups that distribute correspondence, newsletters, and manuscripts, sometimes through some sort of central agent)

B. Nonconventional primary media (e.g., audiotapes and disks, videotapes, microforms)

C. Secondary media
1. Standard reference books
2. Bibliographies
3. Reviews
4. Indexing journals
5. Abstracting journals

D. Electronic forms (both primary and secondary)
1. Cable
2. Radio
3. Television
4. Videotext
5. Telecommunication (Internet, videoconferencing, distributed education)
6. Electronic publishing

Indexing and abstracting cuts across all these forms and formats.

THE STUDY OF INFORMATION

The study of information is called *information science*. This term first appeared in the literature over forty years ago and since that time has been interpreted from a number of different angles. In a broad sense, it represents the study of information across a number of academic disciplines. When it is related to computer science, it is looked at as the study of the phenomena of information for those who use computers as information processors. Within the framework of libraries, information science deals with applications of new tasks and technology to traditional practices of librarianship. When information is considered in a narrow sense, it is considered a new area of study from an integration of concepts from many different academic points of view, with special interest in communication theory and technological applications, along with the utilization of standard research methods to study theory and applications.

The information science field continues to have the problem of confusion in terminology and definition and given the dynamics of the field, it is doubtful if the confusion will abate any time soon.

The problem is not new. How can we expect a definition for information science when we have never found one for *library science?* Or is it *library service?* There have been many, many definitions of library science, but probably the best one is "library science is what librarians do." Perhaps information science is what information scientists do.

Since the study of information is interdisciplinary, it involves input from disciplines such as mathematics, philosophy, the physical and biological sciences, cognitive sciences, library science, and other social sciences. Given the interdisciplinary nature of information none of these disciplines has a proprietary ownership of the concept of information science. Each of these disciplines study information science from a particular facet of application.

A true information science would address information in a global context, but in the study of indexing we concentrate on a narrow slice of information science: that which deals with the human processing of information.

A BASIC RESOURCE

Information is recognized as a major resource both at the personal level and in society in general. More and more it is being referred to as national resource. The quality and availability of information determines the strength of a nation and the social welfare of its people.

It is a basic resource, as is energy, food, water, and trees. In many ways information helps save other resources, such as energy, manual labor, time, and people. Medical information saves people's lives and financial information helps them save money and perhaps get rich.

Economists are beginning to understand that information is the most important national resource that we have. They continue to talk about the emerging information economy. The output of information economy all over the world is over $2 trillion a year and in the United States since the 1980s telecommunication services have grown by some 800 percent. In the United States alone it is estimated that over 60 percent of the work force consists of jobs directly involved in information products and services. The Information Age is related basically to the cultural change in the concept of information and to the spectacular improvement in technology. As a result of these factors there has been the dramatic growth in the number of people whose occupation is the information field. And all of this has had a powerful impact on the economics of the world.

This concept of information as an economic entity has developed in the past few decades. At first there was an attempt to describe information in terms of classic economics, but this soon proved to be an unsatisfactory model because of fundamental differences in information as an economic commodity. For example, information grows rather than being consumed when it is used. One of the basic usages of information is to acquire more information. That is why we say that information is never diminished by being shared but most likely grows. And information cannot be exchanged; it can only be shared.

Information occurs as a basic resource at the national and global level in two fundamental ways: as a potent economic factor and as the prime ingredient for public policy decisions.

When we think of information as an economic factor, we must remember that there is no such thing as free information. A library book is not free. Someone, somewhere paid for that book and pays for the operation of the library system. Someone, somewhere pays for the information on the Internet.

There is one fact of life that is clearly emerging. Information is necessary for survival and in order to access that information, information skills are necessary for all our people. This means much more than computer skills. It means teaching people to find and evaluate information. Indexes and abstracts are a major resource for this.

MECHANISMS FOR INFORMATION PRESERVATION AND TRANSMITTAL

The evolution of society brought forth formal mechanisms for information preservation and transmittal. Long ago humans began to draw pictures on the walls of caves. For around 40,000 years humankind has tried to record and share its experiences and feelings through recorded knowledge. Pictorial representation of events was the beginning of recorded knowledge.

Libraries, educational systems, societies of scholars, and professionals all date back into antiquity, and all had the primary objective of protecting and transmitting information and knowledge from generation to generation. All of these mechanisms had a common approach: to gather information and store it in a warm and dry place until someone expressed a desire for a particular record, at which time the record of interest was retrieved. It is a simple but powerful idea.

For century upon century the traditional library as we know it carried out this idea without serious difficulty, but in the 1940s we entered an age of information proliferation which put a critical strain on the traditional mechanisms. We developed into a society of specialists with everybody taking a little tidbit of knowledge, becoming an expert, and as a result demanding in-depth analysis of the information recorded. General pointers to information stores were no longer sufficient. We were not satisfied to have millions of documents; we needed rapid, effective analysis of the informational contents of those documents. We became impatient with traditional library techniques.

Paralleling this shift in informational needs was a technological change. We developed microform technology, data communication devices, television, computing machines, and reproduction devices. The documentation movement spread to this country from Europe, and here it attempted to wed the new information technology with our traditional library approaches. Being a people susceptible to gadgetry, we lived for a while with an innocent dream, believing that all we needed was a readable microform device and larger, faster computers. Now we have very large and unbelievably fast computing machines, but we still have problems in information handling. In many instances it was found that computers simply allowed us to make the same old mistakes at an incredible speed. Why? Because there are deep intellectual complexities involved which we are only beginning to understand and appreciate: problems concerning users and their *individual* needs, the realization that relevance of a particular document is the judgment of a single individual, not a universal constant. It is no longer acceptable to build systems geared to a mythical average user who has never existed and never will. There are problems concerning indexing, classification, and information seeking behavior. How do scientists look for information? How do nonscientists search? Slowly, we are realizing that an information system is concerned with more than just documents and their contents. Much involved is human behavior.

The fundamental problem, which is common to all information retrieval mechanisms, is to give the best possible match between the description of a subject provided by a user to the pertinent documents in the system. The mechanisms for this are complex, but the first, basic step begins with subject analysis by the information professional and this professional is often an indexer.

The early decades of the Information Age were characterized by innovative mechanisms of information processing. Libraries shifted from independent entities to formal networks with an emphasis on resources sharing. The realities of economic constraints and the changing information needs of users are making the traditional library model obsolete. No library is an island to itself and survival means getting connected. In the old model constraints of time and distance made it necessary for libraries to concentrate on building collections and interlibrary loan was an exceptional and often reluctant choice. Now materials at great distances are only nanoseconds away.

One of the most important quiet revolutions in retrieval mechanisms came in the latter half of the nineteenth century when information retrieval moved from the general to the specific. Requests for information had traditionally been filled by providing a user with a stack of documents that hopefully fell within the scope of the user's need. The idea of users demanding answers was a new type of information request. For example, if a user needs to know the exact days of the Battle of Gettysburg she does not want to be handed a stack of books on the Civil War. Instead, the user wants the librarian to relay the dates, no more, no less. The concept of a reference librarian and a reference desk arrived.

The twenty-first century will need even more innovation with an emphasis on cybernetworking, which goes beyond the library world. The nodes of this information store will be an incredible conglomeration of library and nonlibrary resources in every nook and corner of the world. This will not be easy. Political, social, economic, and financial problems will be formidable.

Modern mechanisms must deal with huge information stores with millions of items. This requires constant file maintenance with thousand of record changes within a day or two. Also, modern mechanisms must have sophisticated input/output capabilities because rapid input/output (I/O) is demanded and users continue to press for better systems for doing this.

Modern mechanisms focus more and more on digitized information. Lately there has been a growth in the use of digital scanners to store images in digitized form. While these devices take a large amount of storage, they offer a whole new world for processing and disseminating information.

The Internet has brought us a new mechanism called the *virtual library*. This is an abstract idea describing networks of vast databases scattered throughout the world and brought to one access point by a computer and telecommunication technologies. This is not just another name for Web searching. A virtual library will look like a library, with resources organized in a way similar to how they are arranged in a four-wall library. Online catalogs, encyclopedias, governments documents, abstracts, indexes, electronic journals, bibliographical and numeric databases, full-text documents, and so forth, will be available with the click of an icon.

A basic challenge with virtual libraries is deciding what local libraries will physically have and what will be accessed outside of the walls. Also, the organizations that support and maintain the virtual library (e.g., an academic library), must have something to offer to cyberspace. Somewhere, somebody must generate, process, store and make available information. Also, somebody must pay for it. There is the danger that too many people will believe in information sharing as long as it is the other guy who is doing the sharing and footing the bill.

If one word could be picked to describe the modern revolution of information mechanisms, the word would be *dynamics*. These dynamics begin with user needs, which vary widely across different environments and are characterized by moment by moment changes. For example, at the center of the dynamic information infrastructure mechanism is the problem of vocabulary. Changing vocabulary has always been the indexer's nemesis, but the modern information environment has intensified the problem.

In the Information Age, data, information, knowledge and wisdom become corporate and societal memory rather than being in the brains of the village elders. Such corporate memory must have effective access mechanisms and this introduces issues such as how do we know and meet the needs of users? How do people search for information? How do they evaluate it and how do they do follow-up searching? There are endless problems of language and how to represent information.

These problems are what indexing is all about.

The Organization of Information

CHAPTER 3

THE INFORMATION CYCLE

The access of information is determined by the degree of its successful organization. Unorganized or badly organized information invites chaos as the size of the information store increases. How to best organize information stores is a continuing challenge and it has many aspects. Among these aspects are fundamental classification theory and techniques, principles of vocabulary control, and the relationship of information organization to users and their searching culture.

The process begins when information is created and ends when the information is put to use and often times this process repeats itself, building on what was done before. Information creation and distribution form a distinct, repetitive pattern known as the information cycle (see figure 1), where information builds on previous information, both in scientific and nonscientific activities. Very few people have an absolutely original and totally creative thought. Invention begins within a framework of existing reality. New ideas are created out of old ideas and the cycle continues through time.

The information specialist is directly involved in at least four of the eight activities shown in the figure, namely in bibliographic control, storage, user queries, and the retrieval of the item. Clearly, bibliographic control is crucial to this cycle.

It would be inappropriate to say that any node in the information cycle is more important than any other node. If any of the nodes are removed then the entire cycle degenerates. We can, however, say that the information professional is involved in most of the nodes, and is sometimes a part of all the nodes. The cycle represents a large and diverse enterprise, involving a vast range of people and other resources.

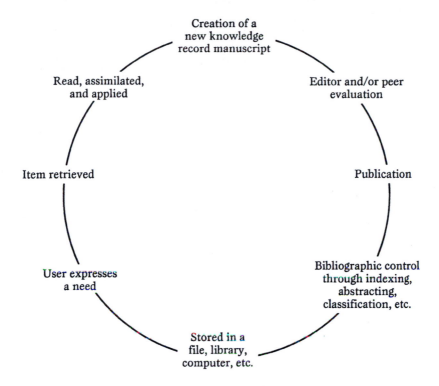

Fig. 1. The information cycle.

THE BASIC INFORMATION RETRIEVAL MODEL

Information retrieval is a generic term, loosely used and meaning different things to different people. For example, to data processing people it generally means the management of unique data records as required in a data processing cycle. That is, exact records of data are known, are stored at specific places in a storage medium and are retrieved on demand. The only intellectual problems involved are those concerned with structuring files and developing addressing methods that will minimize time and maximize computer efficiency. Information scientists call this operation *data retrieval* and suggest that information retrieval is a more complex activity involving uncertainty as to which records are appropriate. The exact record is not known and must be inferred as closely as possible. For any given query, more than one of these unknown records may be pertinent.

Information systems can take many different physical forms, ranging from paper files to totally digitized collections. Organization and searching techniques are also varied, but the fundamental problem that is common to all information systems is that of providing for the nearest possible coincidence between the description of a topic by a user and the description of the topic in the system's database.

First, the information must be organized. This may be a manual process, an algorithmic procedure invoked by the computer, or a combination of both. Once the information store is organized, the system uses a search procedure to locate the information in the database.

In short, an information retrieval system is a mechanism for carrying out the information retrieval process. There are a number of basic functions involved in this process:

1.   The information is created and acquired for the system.

2.   Knowledge records are analyzed and tagged by sets of index terms.

3.   The knowledge records are stored physically (books on shelves, reports into a file cabinet, computer data on storage devices) and the index terms are stored into a structured file, either manual or computer.

4.   The user's query is tagged with sets of index terms and then is matched against the tagged records. In computer-based systems the terms are usually matched using Boolean operators.

5.   Matched documents are retrieved for review.

6.   Feedback may lead to several reiterations of the search.

Let's look at each of these processes in more detail.

The Information Is Created and Acquired for the System

First, information records are created using some physical medium. This may involve complex procedures including a series of editing and feedback, production, and final distribution. A large segment of the information industry is centered on these activities. Once the information is made available, then it is acquired at the local level, based on the purpose of the information system and the kinds of uses that will be made of the information. From the global mass of recorded information minute portions of it are acquired by individual organizations. This is a critical step in the process, because no information system can retrieve relevant information if it does not have access to such information. The two driving forces at this point are user needs and economic constraints. User needs are considered, information is identified, and the budget is checked. Often written acquisition policies play a major role in the decision making.

Information retrieval systems cost money and as with everything else in life a balance must be found between what we would like to have and what we can afford. Cost is calculated in several ways:

1.   The actual money we pay to acquire the information.

2.   The cost to the individual or organization if a specific unit of information is not acquired for the system.

3.   The wasted cost if the information is acquired too late.

When acquiring information for a system, several factors are of concern. First, what type of retrieval will the system support? Modern information retrieval systems can be broadly divided into three categories:

1. Data retrieval.
2. Reference retrieval.
3. Text retrieval.

Data systems give specific answers to questions; e.g., who won the 1951 World Series? Another example of data retrieval would be to present a table showing the numbers of cats in each city in the United States, whereas reference retrieval might be citations to journal articles providing the actual articles with statistics and discussion.

Reference systems indicate where the answer might be found and/or give overall reviews of the general subject areas. Reference systems are usually bibliographic lists and sometimes have abstracts of potential useful documents. Also, the abstract may have the answer to who won the World Series in 1951. Incidentally, in 1951 Bobby Thomson's "Shot Heard 'Round the World" gave the New York Giants a victory over the New York Yankees.

Text retrieval presents all or most of the original item. This is sometimes known as *document delivery*. Understandably, document delivery is often an issue with the users of information retrieval systems.

A major concern when acquiring information for a system is the critical one of user needs and a system's designer should focus on the user's needs, both on the individual level and on the needs of the organization or institution as a whole. There are two general categories of information needs. First, the user may need a copy of a particular document for which the author or title is known. This is known as *item retrieval*, and is fairly simple for the system. Second, the user may need documents that deal with particular subjects or that are capable of answering particular questions. This is known as *subject retrieval*.

Subject needs can be divided into two general areas. First, the user may want current awareness services. The user's interests and professional needs may require keeping up with the latest developments in the field, therefore, the user may turn to the information retrieval system to provide this need. Typically, an automated system will set up a profile of the user's needs and will use an alerting module aimed at the individual users. If not, the user will search the system periodically to see what's new. Librarians are familiar with the users who pop in for a while to scan the professional journals.

Secondly, the user may need the system for specific problem solving. The user's daily work produces information problems that need solutions. In turn, problem solving needs can be divided into three general areas:

1. The need for a single item of factual data.
2. The need to have one or more documents discussing a particular subject.
3. The need for a comprehensive search.

For example, in studying for an exam, the user may want to know the dates of the American Civil War, or may want to learn all about the Battle of Gettysburg, or may want to be totally immersed in the Civil War.

Knowledge Records Are Analyzed and Tagged by Sets of Index Terms

Once the item is received, the processing begins. Information records need a proxy to represent them in the system's storage and searching structure. No one can read all the items in an information store in order to determine what is needed. Therefore, it has become necessary to create ways of representing documents with proxies. This reduces the number of actual documents that have to be examined by the user. Cataloging, classifying, indexing, and abstracting do this proxy representation. Scanning a document to decide what it is about is the key operation in subject analysis, yet it is the least reducible to rules.

In any retrieval system success or failure depends on the adequacy of the indexing and the related searching procedures. At the analysis stage the *aboutness* of the item is determined and it is decided how the item will fit into the system's database. The index terms are selected and are systematically added to the index file, while the item itself is placed into a different file. The terms are assigned to the documents by human indexers or automatic methods. In some systems indexing is implied, in that every term in the document is assumed to be an index term and the computer searches everything from top to bottom when a request is made to determine which documents are relevant.

Once the index terms are selected, they are coded (e.g., numbers, letters, or a combination of the two). Coding is representation on another level. In its purest form coding is not concerned with representing information content. The indexing terms have already accomplished this. Coding is concerned with symbolically representing the information content concepts already determined.

The Knowledge Records Are Stored Physically and the Index Terms Are Stored into a Structured File

These two files (the index file and the item file) form the storage part of an information retrieval system. In systems with large databases, a technique called *inverted files* is used to speed up the operation. Each record in the inverted file contains an index term and then the fields in the record indicate all the information items in the database that have been indexed with that term. A familiar example of an inverted subject file is the library subject catalog. A search under "cats" will produce a sequence of entries describing all the cat books in the library.

The User's Query Is Tagged with Sets of Index Terms and Then Is Matched Against the Tagged Records

This is the searching stage, in which the user's needs are expressed with the same representation language and also are coded by the same process. The documents (or their surrogates) are examined in order to determine which most nearly satisfy the query. The cognitive processes involved in query formulation is an aspect of the process that is receiving a great deal of attention at the present time by researchers.

If the documents were indexed with a thesaurus, then the query is indexed with the same thesaurus. Most information systems utilize what is known as a Boolean search strategy. Boolean algebra is the formalization and algebrazation of logic. Of particular interest to the problems of information retrieval is the algebra of sets, which describes the inclusion or exclusion of elements from a defined class, aggregate, or collection of elements. This mathematical model lends itself well to the procedures of information retrieval, since when users request information they create a class of subjects, e.g., *cats and dogs.* The searching procedure is then aimed at identifying informational units that fall into these classes. Boolean operators are used to create the exact class of information needed. If we need information dealing with *cats* that one term will sort out articles dealing with cats into a set of cat articles. If we add *house* to the term a new class is formed and now only those articles that deal with *house cats* will be sorted out. In any case, at the searching stage there is a binary decision. This article is or is not about cats.

There are some fundamental weaknesses in this type of search, but for the present we must realize that this is the major searching model and it should be understood, since most document systems are based on this matching of the terms in a document with the terms selected by the inquirer. From a mathematical point of view, Boolean algebra is a beautiful exercise in thought and a challenge to the aesthetic aspects of human inquiry. For the average, everyday librarian, it offers a technique that is both simple and practical.

Matched Documents Are Retrieved for Review

The results are presented to the user for her judgment of usefulness. It is at this point that ambiguity sets in because determining relevance is a moving target. The designer of an information retrieval system and the indexer who prepares the documents try to guess what a user will consider relevant to her task, but the user brings to the system a wide-ranging set of variables, including cognitive, psychological, educational, social, and cultural variables. All of these variables affect the user's judgment of the usefulness of the retrieved document.

There are many reasons why the user finds a search unsuccessful:

1. The user found no sources of information.
2. The user found a source, but could not find information in the source.

3. The user did not find enough information.
4. The information needed to be more in-depth.
5. The user was not sure if the information was correct.
6. The information found was not relevant.
7. The information found was too complex.
8. The user wanted a different viewpoint.
9. Too much information was found.
10. The information was outdated.

Feedback May Lead to Several Reiterations of the Search

A current area of research in information retrieval is directed at the idea of making adjustments to the system using feedback input from the user. Feedback is a crucial and central element in an information retrieval system.
The process can be graphically represented in figure 2:

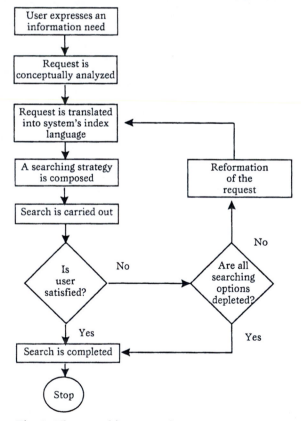

Fig. 2. The searching procedure.

Is an information retrieval process simple? No, because the operation is more than mechanical. In theory the process is simple: The user's request is converted to index terms and is matched against terms in the index file and the appropriate documents are pulled from the file. The concept is simple but the implementation is complex.

Understanding this simple model is essential to understanding the function of an index. The index in the model is a *black box* to the user, but the indexer is responsible for the content of the black box and ultimately must take a great deal of the responsibility for the success or failure of the system.

In the last analysis the user will decide if the system is working for her, regardless of any evaluation methods developed by the system's engineers. The concept of relevance is totally specific to each and every user.

Finally, information retrieval systems also can be characterized in terms of their application and purpose. For example, an online library catalog is a category of application which has the purpose of pointing to library resources. A medical records system is a category of information systems that has the purpose of keeping the medical history of individuals.

Each of the above functions has been studied in order to improve retrieval systems, although indexing has always received the lion's share of attention. In any retrieval system success or failure depends on the adequacy of the indexing and the closely related searching procedures.

CLASSIFICATION AND INDEXING

An information store is just an attic full of documents until the documents have been organized for access and made available for use. The traditional means for doing this are: descriptive cataloging, subject cataloging, and classification.

Indexing systems using strict vocabulary control have a process that is similar, in principle, with these traditional processes. Indexing includes a number of steps, such as analyzing content, assigning content indicators, adding location indicators, and assembling the resulting entries. The indexer must carefully determine the appropriate level and type of indexing to be done.

While indexing and classification are not equivalent concepts, they are certainly first cousins. In fact, indexing, in a sense, is a type of classification. Documents are tagged with index terms and then documents fall into classes created by those index terms. In other words, classes are created by sets of index terms. Modern classification systems and modern indexing systems developed parallel to each other and have a lot in common.

On a conceptual level the two have the common goal of organizing and storing recorded knowledge in a way that will make it retrievable in an effective and efficient manner. They both involve the process of analysis of document content, conceptualization of the analysis, and translation into a surrogate of the information in the document, either as an index term or a classification slot. Their common goal is to give users shortcuts to finding information. Thus, their usage and functions intermingle and their relationships to one another play an important role in information organization and retrieval.

Classification is the systematic arrangement of entities into groups or categories according to established criteria. It is as old as human thought and is a natural activity of the human mind. When faced with a new idea or physical situation we immediately begin to try to understand by finding something it is similar to in our mind's knowledge base. We look for known characteristics in the new thing. We believe everything belongs to some class of things. Therefore, classification is a familiar concept to turn to when we need mechanisms for bibliographic control. We want to quickly and effectively identify small groups of useful items out of the millions in the database. Why not group information items that are similar and then find the group or groups that are needed? It is not being facetious to say that we would have a hard time making it through the day without classification systems.

At the operational level there are some perceived differences between the two procedures. Classification is viewed as being a highly controlled and structured operation. Authority lists and rigid rules dictate exactly how information is to be organized and sometimes this is a problem because an object might fit into many categories. For example, in a classification scheme a leopard might be in a section dealing with the derivatives of cats in the animal kingdom, but it might also be considered from a different viewpoint when placed in a classification section dealing with the manufacture of leopard skin coats. The same cat could be represented as one part of an almost totally different organization of a collection of information. This cat might have nine classification lives. Faceted classification systems help with this problem. Of course, there is no single way to organize the entire universe of information into an orderly and well-structured pattern of relationships that is best for *all* users.

Generally classification systems tend to isolate books and other information items into fixed niches. Of course, that is the point. The accompanying limited number of subject headings attempt to identify items that cut across subject areas. Indexing, on the other hand, attempts to make the pigeonholes of items much more flexible by making classes of items easily adjusted to overlapping classes at the same time.

Classification means to put similar things into groups with some designation tag that generally captures the essence of the group. Some people become confused in that in general in numerate classification systems the categories pre-exist and items are dropped into the proper category. With indexing, many terms are assigned to the information item. Some see this as a different activity. Procedurally it is; theoretically it is not. The term is a classification category and when the indexer selects a term she drops the item into that category. The difference is that in indexing the item goes into many more categories than it generally does in a classification system.

The relationship between classification and indexing can be found in the ultimate goal: examining something to determine the characteristics and processes that would best allow the user to retrieve what is desired. A classifier's job is to examine the piece as a whole and assign a classification identifier so that the object can be collated with like objects and then be located. An indexer's job is very similar in this respect. The indexer must study the individual words and concepts of that object and make those individual words and concepts readily accessible.

THE RELATIONSHIP OF INDEXING, ABSTRACTING, AND SEARCHING

When considering indexing and abstracting it is always essential to consider searching. John Denver sang of the difficulties of finding answers when you do not know the questions. If John had been an indexer, he would have sung about how can you index something if you do not know how the users will pose questions.

Good indexing is closely related to the searching stage of information retrieval. When a user brings a query to a system, the question needs to be indexed using the same indexing language that was used to index the target document. If the user says that she needs information on *cats* and the document was indexed with the term *felines*, then the indexing language will replace *cats* with *felines*. The concept holds with any index, including book indexes. It is done with some type of cross-referencing. Thus indexing and searching must be addressed as inseparable in any information retrieval system.

An index and an abstract are devices for searching. They exist for no other purpose. Woe to the indexer or abstractor who forgets this cardinal rule. One of the puzzles of the information retrieval field is how little indexers and professional searchers communicate with each other in the literature, in the invisible colleges, in conferences and in the workplace. Hopefully, the Web, with its ubiquitous communication possibilities, will change this.

The goal of indexing and abstracting is to accurately represent the content of an item with terms that are explicit to the information searchers. Of course, the complexity and ambiguity of natural language makes this a nontrivial task. Just as indexing and abstracting must be carefully done to reflect as closely as possible the content of an information item, so must searching. The user (or the user's agent) must form a query that reflects as closely as possible the content of the searching question or information problem. In a perfect, ideal system, the searcher would follow the same logical analysis and come to the same conclusion about the correct index terms that the indexer did when she indexed the item. The same terms would be selected and there would be no disappointments.

The relationship of indexing, abstracting and searching can be illustrated with the diagram in figure 3 on page 32.

The broken lines indicate the path taken by the user, who essentially works backward in the indexing and abstracting path illustrated. One thing not shown in the illustration is that the user may also use index tools, such as thesauri or classification lists, to facilitate the use of the index. Note the user line from the index to the abstract. Abstracts are often approached by an index, especially if the abstracts have a classified arrangement.

The model is still oversimplified. Implied are attributes of accessibility, communication and the management and use of information resources. Also involved are human communication and information behavior and the systems and technologies that enhance communication and learning.

And principles of management are a vital part of the model. Information systems must be analyzed, designed, and evaluated by people working together in organizational, social, and technical environments.

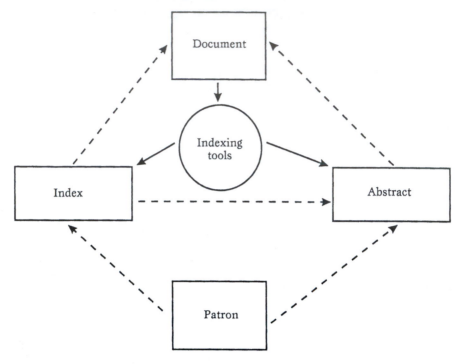

Fig. 3. Relationship of indexing, abstracting, and searching.

It should be apparent that indexing and searching cannot be separated either abstractly or pragmatically. When we formulate a search query, we index an information question or information problem. The indexer cannot know ahead of time how the searcher will act. Which terms will actually be chosen and how will the searcher react to the meaning given the terms? *Knowing the user* is a phrase we hear all the time, and it is a critical and difficult moving target.

Searchers have one major advantage over the indexer. If the searcher does not find what is needed, the search process can begin again. The indexer cannot back up and start again if she indexes wrong. What the indexer tries to do is help minimize the searcher's need to back up by anticipating needs and building in appropriate cross-references. Cross-references, in particular, help the searcher back up and start again.

If we could understand the user's cognitive processes when the user searches, it would be priceless in designing index languages, in indexing, and in searching.

USING INDEXES AND ABSTRACTS

Professionals in many fields are having a problem coping with the information explosion. Many are overwhelmed by the availability of information in their areas and at the same time they are concerned about the consequences of not reading widely. Often they lack effective strategies to deal with the situation, although many effective strategies are available. One of these strategies could be the efficient and effective use of indexes. Many do have these skills and do use them effectively, but we need to further promote an awareness that the excellent tools that exist can allow the scholar to circumvent the size of the many databases that they use.

When we think of users of indexes and abstracts, we usually think of a library patron searching for journal articles, or perhaps standing in the stacks, flipping through book indexes, but index users are more than scholars and students in a library. Almost everyone in any situation of needing information uses indexes. Indexes and abstracts are cornerstones in the global information infrastructure. And their importance is increasing manifold as cyberspace fills up with information and with users who need access to this information. An index or abstract should help a user find what she is interested in. The indexer's obligation is to utilize professional techniques and common sense to assure that the unsophisticated index user finds needed information. The mechanics of the index should be transparent to the user. No user should be required to understand indexing theory in order to use an index.

Indexes and abstracts are not ends in themselves but are tools, which help users find the information they need to solve their problems. Indexes point to possible useful information. Abstracts allow efficient judgment of the relevance and pertinence of that information. The general users of these tools have little or no interest in the tools themselves, the mechanics or details of how they were compiled or how they work. They want to minimize what they need to know in order to find information. In general, they use indexes and abstracts to find:

1. A particular known item suggested to them by a reference or a colleague.
2. Application of some new procedures or discovery in their field.
3. Recent trends or ideas in the field.
4. A comprehensive overview of a field, subfield, or concept in the field.
5. Background of a problem.
6. Other works by an author recently discovered by the user.
7. A piece of data that might be in an abstract.

Abstracts are also surrogates and complement indexes by summarizing the actual content of the knowledge record. They can range from being too brief to being too long, almost as long as the original document. And, of course, if abstracts are to be used, they need to be indexed themselves. Users need to be able to find the abstracts.

The Information Age is like an exploded nova that seems to expand and rush off into cyberspace. As we turned the millennium it was evident more than ever how essential it is to expand our horizons on the importance of indexes and the importance of putting resources into this endeavor. Our profession is and always has been basically concerned with the organization of information. The concept has its antecedents in the ancient days, when people realized that the only way to retrieve information was to be sure that it was properly organized.

Of course, at the heart of properly organizing information is the ability to find pointers and surrogates to the information. The use of an index or an abstract is a compromise in the sense that neither an index nor an abstract can fully represent the document itself. Documents contain more significant information than can ever be conveyed by a surrogate to that document. Attempting to make the index or abstract a 100-percent surrogate leads to self-defeat. An index and an abstract are not exact mirrors of the document; they are surrogates. The goal is to make them surrogates in terms of the user and the purpose she has in using the index or abstract.

An index is a bridge over troubled information explosion waters for seekers of information. It is a device that connects a potential user of information to a potentially useful information store. A good index allows a swift and quiet trip over the troubled waters.

In a perfect system every relevant document would be retrieved when a search was made without the retrieval of a single irrelevant document. Many factors are involved in trying to reach this utopia, but it all begins with content analysis and the representation of that analysis.

Chapter 4 begins the discussion of these basic issues.

Vocabulary Control

A controlled vocabulary is a consistent set of words, along with rules of usage, to be followed when indexing. At the search stage a request is stated using the same consistent word list. In indexing parlance a controlled vocabulary is the terms or classification groups that have been created in order to make indexing consistent, while a natural language uncontrolled vocabulary uses the words directly from the text of a document as written by the author of the item.

THE PURPOSE OF
CONTROLLED VOCABULARY

When librarians became concerned with subject approaches to their stored knowledge records, they quickly came face-to-face with a stubborn fact of life: the complexity, variability, and richness of natural language, rather ironically, leads to ambiguity. An abundant vocabulary allows a depth of expression that gives humans the ability to communicate at a high level, but it also has a semantic complexity that opens the door to faulty understanding. Simply allowing any word in the language to represent content produces problems that are not immediately obvious. Using an unlimited, or an uncontrolled set of words or phrases, to index and to search a library leads to wasted effort and a certain degree of searching failure due to the enormous range of word choices. It is true, of course, that no two words in a language mean exactly the same thing. There are no true synonyms, although words are often very close in meaning, and more often, are not clearly understood. The inconsistent use of words can lead to failure or to partial failure in searching, for the simple reason that users are unlikely to choose all the terms that might be used by the indexer or the writers of the documents. In many cases, the user might choose the terms used by the indexer but with a different understanding of their meanings.

As a result, many forms of controlled vocabularies have been developed over the years, such as classification schedules, subject authority files, and thesauri. When someone suggested that computers could be used to index, a debate soon arose over *free text vs. controlled vocabulary*. The computer types did not understand why the indexing work could not be turned over to computers, like any other menial job. The extreme ends of the debate spectrum are 1) a highly structured indexing or classification system is necessary for optimum retrieval and 2) essentially any word in the text itself is an index term that will do the job. If we boil down all the discussion, research, and stubborn stances, the truth is that both have their place in an information retrieval system. Each approach has strengths and weaknesses and there are trade-offs in terms of effectiveness and in economics. Dubois (1986) adroitly summed up the research in the area and lists some useful advantages and disadvantages of the two approaches:

> Free text is low in cost and simplifies searching. Also, the full context is searched and every word has equal retrieval value. Further, there are no human indexing errors and there is no delay in incorporating new terms. On the other hand, free text puts a greater burden on the searcher, implicit information may be missed, there is an absence of specific to generic linkage, and the vocabulary of the discipline must be known by the user.
>
> Controlled vocabulary solves many semantic problems, permits generic relationships to be identified and maps areas of knowledge. On the other hand, it is costly, has the possibilities of inadequacies of coverage, has human error, vocabulary is possibly out of date, and there is always difficulty in systematically incorporating all relevant relationships between terms.
>
> A free text, natural language system may take index terms directly from titles, abstracts, or full text. The words of the author are used directly, with no distortion or indexer interpretation. There is little room for indexing error and new terms can be immediately incorporated into the vocabulary.

The trade-off is that the burden of accurate retrieval comes at the searching stage because of the problems of synonyms and generic relationships, which a controlled vocabulary attempts to overcome. A controlled vocabulary brings together like concepts into the same index term so that these concepts will not be scattered throughout the index under many synonymous or equivalent terms.

A controlled vocabulary is an artificial language that puts an information specialist between the text and the user. Users must then conform to this new language rather than to their day-by-day practitioner's language. Hopefully, the controlled vocabulary will be closely related to their natural vocabulary. Controlled vocabulary systems characteristically involve an information professional, with the goal of enhancing conceptual accord between the indexer and the index user.

The indexer examines a document, mentally filters the author's intent, and then chooses terms from the controlled list that represent the appropriate concepts and relationships as the indexer interprets them. The user approaches the index with personal concepts and terms. The function of the control mechanism is to eventually lead both the indexer and the user to the same point.

A controlled vocabulary is characterized in the following ways:

1. It represents the general conceptual structure of a subject area and presents a guide to the user of the index.
2. The terms are derived as nearly as possible from the vocabulary of use, that is, they closely reflect the literature vocabulary and the user's own technical usage.

3. It employs a considerable number of pre-coordinated phrases to re-
    duce false drops to a minimum. For example, by pre-coordinating
    Venetian blind there will not be a false drop of *blind Venetian* papers
    from the document file.

4. It supplies a standard vocabulary by controlling synonyms and near-
    synonyms in order to increase consistency. This is a primary func-
    tion, and provides a mechanism that will ensure that only one term
    from a list of similar terms will be used in indexing a given concept.

5. Where necessary it defines ambiguous terms.

6. Through cross-references it shows horizontal and vertical relation-
    ships among terms.

THE NATURE OF INDEXING LANGUAGES

Problems of language are the focal point of the indexing activity. These
language problems may vary widely, encompassing a native language such as
English, the special jargon of academic areas such as psychology, or the selected
words used exclusively in the system of concern. One of the exciting and primary contributions from other disciplines to library and information science
comes from linguistics, and the approaches used in this field are a key area for
research efforts in information science.

An indexing language is much more than a list of index terms that are acceptable to users. An indexing language also contains mechanisms for structuring and using those terms. The purpose of the structuring mechanisms is to
minimize the ambiguity of isolated vocabulary terms that may be totally out of
context. In the ideal situation, the mechanisms reduce the obscurity and redundancy of a general vocabulary. At the same time, they do not reduce the effectiveness of the user's personal vocabulary.

An indexing language helps users discriminate between terms and reduces ambiguity in the language. The index language designer cannot simply
report on usage, but must guide or dictate usage. We are concerned that the role
of an indexing language in an information retrieval system should be to assist
both indexers and searchers in using and manipulating the system.

There are some problems associated with controlled indexing languages.
For example, human beings find it difficult to confine themselves to constrained definitions in their native tongue or technical jargon. Habits of language persist, and arbitrarily imposed limitations are resented. Issue is often
taken with the way an authority list collapses several words into one; it is
argued that each word is distinct and that the generic word is inappropriate.
When constraints are applied to a vocabulary, human beings become uncomfortable, since deductive reasoning and creativity are directly related to the
flexibility and extent of human vocabularies. Also, relationships between an
indexing vocabulary and the complete vocabulary of the collection are not easy
to determine, and the retrieval power of certain words with respect to a group
of users is difficult to ascertain and keep current.

Indexing languages can be categorized into a number of fundamental
types. An initial breakdown would include *assigned-term* and *derived-term*

systems. In the former, an indexer must assign terms or descriptors on the basis of subjective interpretation of the concepts implied in the document, and in so doing will have to use some intellectual effort. Indexers determine the subject matter of the document and then filter the subject through their vocabulary store to decide what terms are appropriate. The indexer determines the subject matter of the document at hand, and assigns descriptors from a controlled vocabulary, which identifies concepts expressed by the document's author.

In derived-term systems, all descriptors are taken from the text itself. Thus, author indexes, title indexes, citation indexes, and natural language indexes are derived-term systems, whereas all indexing languages with vocabulary control devices such as subject heading lists, thesauri, and classification schemes are assigned-term systems. Since there is more intellectual effort involved with assigned-term systems, this will normally involve greater time and effort and therefore will cost more at the indexing stage of the operation.

Derived-term systems are sometimes called natural language or free-text indexing, because the system allows the indexer to select the terms to be used directly from the text being indexed, or, in automatic systems, the computer selects the terms. Since the terms are picked out of the text itself, this approach may also be called indexing by extraction. The uniterm systems developed in the early days of information retrieval are examples of this. The rationale for this approach is based on the idea that the authors are using words that conform to the subject field under discussion. They are communicating directly to the reader in a commonly understood language. Such a language is dynamic and constantly in vogue, and anything else is a contrived, artificial language that may constitute an unnecessary communication barrier between the author and the reader. Derived-term systems are generally thought of in terms of mechanical devices, such as the computerized title keyword in context (KWIC) indexes, which allow the whole process to be reduced to a clerical task.

The primary use of free-word vocabularies occurs in coordinate indexes and their derivatives. Such vocabularies begin from scratch, so to speak, and are accumulated. Indexers optionally select words, and when they are indexing the first document, they can freely choose all of the words they believe are necessary to convey the intended meaning and subject content of the document. Indexers must rely upon their own backgrounds and knowledge of the meanings of the words in the text, or they might use standard dictionaries and general thesauri for definitions. This means that the vocabulary tends to grow of its own accord as new documents are added to the system.

AUTHORITY LISTS

An authority list is a related group of words or phrases adopted by a particular group of people to be used in an indexing activity. A controlled vocabulary is implied, meaning that indexers must adhere to the list when preparing a document.

An authority list is a formal list of the words in the controlled vocabulary, showing the formal relationships between words and spelling out how they are to be used. Ambiguity is solved by referring to the authority list as the final arbitrator in vocabulary control. If indexers or searchers are unsure of what terms are to be used, they consult this authority list for direction. This is a guiding record of usage and formal decisions concerning usage. The structures can range from a few cross-references scattered here and there in a list of words to highly structured and complex usage rules. The most commonly recognized general types are classification schemes, subject heading lists and thesauri. All such lists attempt to effect a common bond of understanding between the creator of information and potential users of that information.

Where do authority lists come from? How are they generated? There are two ways to form and build vocabularies. Both are carefully planned and follow logical lines of development. First is the *evolutionary vocabulary*, which is edited or planned after the fact. This is the result of stopping the free vocabulary evolution at some point and trying to make some order out of the chaos. In the second case, the vocabulary is generated as the result of a special study or inquiry and a consensus of experts who predetermine what the vocabulary should be for an area of knowledge. This is called an *enumerated vocabulary*. Thus, the exact methods of vocabulary development depend on which type of vocabulary generation is used.

The evolutionary vocabulary consists of raw material supplied by indexers. After sufficient documents are indexed, alphabetic listings of words selected by indexers are surveyed in preparation for editing and acceptance procedures. Each term in the vocabulary, whether it be a single descriptor or a compound, becomes a candidate for inclusion in the list. The candidate word must be accepted on the basis of one or several criteria.

A new word common to the language or area of study may be a candidate if it can be defined well enough from any one of a number of points of view. Suppose the word *base*, defined from a military point of view, is added to a system. The specific definition of *base* is "the locality or installation on which a military force relies for supplies or from which it initiates operations." But, this word can have other meanings, depending on the viewpoint. In math, *base* is "the number with reference to which a number system or a mathematical table is constructed" and in chemistry it is defined as "any of various typically water soluble and acrid or brackish tasting compounds capable of reacting with an acid to form a salt, etc."

The word *model* may enter the system as a synonym for pattern, form, idea, measure, image, reproduction, mannequin, or paragon. It is necessary to decide whether there is a single dominant and most often used word, such as *paragon,* that may contain all document references.

Users' search query terms should be considered as a source for the vocabulary generation. Also, we need to consider specialized vocabularies, other indexing languages and experts' contributions. It is assumed that users' terminology is included in the vocabulary, and that the list is subject domain oriented.

GENERIC VOCABULARIES

Generic vocabularies show vertical arrangements of words within classes. Words may appear in several classes. Generic vocabularies also indicate synonymous relationships, near synonymous relationships, and related word groups. *Cat equals feline* would be considered synonymous in some systems, but in others, *feline* is broader than *cat*. In a general index, *feline* might mean approximately the same, but in a book on biology, especially taxonomical zoology, there would be a clear understanding of the different meanings of the terms.

Generic vocabularies allow terms that *should* be seen together to actually *be* seen together, whereas in an alphabetical index, they might very well be scattered. Generic vocabularies allow terms to be seen immediately in their context in scanning up or down in the display. For example:

Weapons
    Nonconventional
        Blowpipes
        Boomerangs
        Spears
        Big rocks

    Conventional
        Guns
        Rifles
        Pistols
        Shotguns
        Bowie knives

THE THESAURUS

One of the results of active attempts to overcome the problems involved in using uncontrolled vocabularies in indexing was the evolution and subsequent development of the thesaurus. Thesauri are not an entirely new, radical approach to bibliographic control, but grew out of continued attempts at vocabulary control. Classification schemes, subject headings, and thesauri are all authority control devices, but there are some differing characteristics. For example, classification schemes are generally hierarchical with secondary alphabetical indexes, while thesauri are generally alphabetical with hierarchical structure built in by the use of cross-references. The relationships between terms in the thesaurus are more specific. In thesauri, descriptors are often dependent on these terms and are intended to be combined with other terms, whereas in a classification scheme or a subject heading list the terms can stand alone. Terms in a thesaurus may be dependent on other terms. They are meant to be combined with other terms to express more specific concepts. In other words, we have on one hand pre-coordinated systems (e.g., classification and subject headings) and on the other hand, post-coordinated languages (e.g., descriptors and combinations).

A thesaurus controls the vocabulary in a variety of ways. In the first place, it determines the specifics of the language by giving the terms that can and cannot be used, thus restricting vocabulary. The more specific the language, the higher the precision will be in the documents selected.

In a sense a thesaurus is a specific language, with words, relationships of words and its own grammatical rules for usage. It is a controlled, collected subset of natural language. Its purpose is consistency in indexing and searching. Its first purpose is the control of synonyms, although it has many other functions, such as related words, more specific words, and broader words.

At one time indexers believed that there was a clear distinction between a thesaurus and a traditional classification. As a matter of fact they deliberately insisted that a thesaurus was a unique tool and not a classification device. The early thesauri were usually relatively simple alphabetical lists of terms showing exact relationships with straightforward codes. These thesauri were to be used in post-coordinate systems, while classification systems were to be used with pre-coordinate systems. However, over the years thesauri have evolved into much more complex tools, showing hierarchical relationships and/or fully faceted classification characteristics. Now, thesauri are used in pre-coordinated systems, and classification schemes are playing a role in post-coordinate systems.

Indexing students often have trouble with the concept of adhering to a thesaurus when indexing. They quickly understand the value of a thesaurus for helping them find the right words, but they have trouble understanding why, if the *right word* is not there, they cannot just supply the word directly from the text. It's frustrating to see the *right word* in the text and they are being told they cannot use it.

The answer to the dilemma is common sense: if we are *laissez-faire* and can divert from the thesaurus whenever we feel like it, then there is no controlled vocabulary. If a needed word is missing, then we should remember that the thesaurus can be revised and updated.

THESAURUS CONSTRUCTION

It should go without saying that a thesaurus should be based on what is relevant to users, but this is easier said than done. Bates (1989) has given us some characteristics of a user-focused thesaurus:

1. Includes a list of all terms in use in the database.
2. Carefully distinguishes terms actually used in a given database from those that are not.
3. Provides scope notes for problems likely to be encountered by end users.
4. Uses self-explanatory names for terms or relationships.
5. Includes a vast entry vocabulary, geared to end user requirements. This feature is particularly important.

As with any authority list, the construction of a thesaurus follows a basic approach. It begins with a free list of natural-language words from which groups of synonyms are gradually formed, representing as nearly as possible single concepts. This may be done in one of two fundamental ways, either by building top-down with a theoretical, enumerative approach, the same way traditional classification schemes are created, or by building bottom-up with an empirical approach. The latter begins with the literature and the users of the literature and often includes such quantitative methods as a count of the frequency of word use in the subject area.

In reality, the construction of a thesaurus is often somewhere in between the theoretical approach and the empirical one, with a committee working on the thesaurus using both approaches.

In the first approach, the committee is usually made up of subject specialists who provide words they think are appropriate, drawing the terms from their own expertise, from previously constructed indexing languages, from dictionaries, and from other such basic reference tools in the field. The alternative method is to go directly to the current literature, the subject literature itself, accumulate representative samples of the kinds of items that are likely to be indexed, and compile a list of words with which to work. This is an empirical approach and has the advantage of identifying the actual terms now being used by the writers themselves. As with any empirical approach, it has the disadvantage of being limited to a particular point in time, and we can say nothing about the relative permanence of its representation. The jargon of a particular subject area can be ephemeral and trendy, and serve little useful purpose in a thesaurus authority list.

If the first approach is adopted, a number of tools may be used. For example:

1. *Classification schemes and subject headings.* These schemes and lists, especially those designed for special collections in the fields to be covered by the thesaurus, are very valuable sources. A good classification scheme is particularly useful, for the obvious reason that it shows hierarchical relationships. It must be remembered that obsolescence is a weakness in classification, and care must be taken not to bring this into the thesaurus.

2. *Review articles.* Review articles are generally definitive works covering a broad field or a specific subfield. The advantage of review articles is that they provide current terminology and are relatively exhaustive.

3. *Monographs.* Monographs, particularly in science and technology, serve as periodical synthesizers of the primary literature. These publications, especially textbooks, introduce and define basic terminology in a field.

4. *Basic reference tools.* Handbooks, dictionaries, encyclopedias, and other such reference tools deal with terminology in a subject field. Again, one must be cautioned against obsolescence when using these tools. It is assumed that thesaurus builders will become familiar with the quality and coverage of any such tools they may consult.

Whichever approach is used, it must be remembered that a thesaurus is neither a dictionary nor a classification scheme. Dictionaries serve as a record to standard usage of words and terms, but a thesaurus is the *result* of the understanding of proper usage.

STEPS IN THESAURUS CONSTRUCTION

The following general steps are suggested for constructing a thesaurus:

1. Identify the subject field. The boundaries of the subject field should be clearly defined and the parameters set to indicate which areas will be emphasized and which will be given only cursory treatment.

2. Identify the nature of the literature to be indexed. Is it primarily journal literature? Or does it consist of books, reports, conference papers, etc.? Is it retrospective or current? If it is retrospective, then it will be more complex to make changes in the thesaurus. Will most of the material be on the Web?

3. Identify the users. What are their information needs? Will they be doing their own searching or will someone do it for them? Will their questions be broad or specific?

4. Identify the file structure. Will this be a pre-coordinated or post-coordinated system?

5. Consult published indexes, glossaries, dictionaries, and other tools in the subject areas for the raw vocabulary. This should not be done necessarily with the idea of copying terms, but such perusal can increase the thesaurus designer's understanding of the terminology and semantic relationships in the field.

6. Cluster the terms.

7. Establish term relationships.

Term Relationships

One of the key points of a thesaurus is that it indicates the relationships among terms. The thesaurus structures three basic types of relationships: equivalence, hierarchical, and associative. This is achieved by showing under each term the broader, narrower, and related terms, indicated by BT, NT, and RT, placed alongside the words being considered. For example:

INTELLIGENCE
    BT: Ability
    NT: Comprehension
    RT: Talent
    RT: Aptitude

The *broader term* reference shows hierarchical relationship upward in the classification tree. It differs from the *use for* reference in that both the basic term and its broader term are descriptor terms and both can be used.

The *narrower term* reference is similar to the broader term reference, except it goes down in the classification tree.

The *related term* reference refers to a descriptor that can be used in addition to the basic term but is not in a hierarchical relationship. By having the related terms displayed, both the indexers and the searchers are in a better position to cover the full range of options that may be possible in either indexing or searching. *See also* is used to refer to a related term.

Another important guide in a thesaurus is the *use* concept. The *use* reference refers to a preferred descriptor from a nonusable term. In a sense it is reciprocal of a *use for* (UF) term, which is discussed below. For example:

Pecan trees
   USE TREES

Oak trees
   USE TREES

The *use for* reference deals primarily with synonyms or variant forms of the preferred descriptor. It is also used to lead the indexer to more general terms. For example:

TREES
   UF   Pecan trees

Another example:

PROMOTION POLICIES
   UF   Automatic promotion

         and

Automatic promotion
   USE: PROMOTION POLICIES

The UF instruction will enable the thesaurus to control vocabulary size by posting specific terms on the more general term. In some cases, UF references are also used to deal with synonyms and near-synonyms.

Another useful cross-reference in the thesaurus is the *scope note* (SN). A scope note is used to restrict the usage of a descriptor or to clarify one that is ambiguous. For example, it may be used with homographs to declare which word is intended, or it may support the use of narrower terms.

As a rule, scope notes are given in a thesaurus to avoid ambiguities. They serve to explain the scope of a term as well as to delimit it. These indicators are not necessarily straight dictionary definitions, but are more like brief descriptions of the sense or framework in which the terms should be used. For example:

CULTURAL BACKGROUND
   SN: The total social heritage and experience of an individual or
         group including institutions, folkways, literature, mores, and
         communal experience.

Thus, a thesaurus provides the control of terminology by showing a structural display of concepts, supplying for each concept all terms that might express that concept, and presenting the associate and hierarchical relationships of the vocabulary. Generally, the result is an alphabetical list of all the words and phrases making up the controlled vocabulary.

Term Forms

A distinction should be made between types of index terms:

Keywords are the raw words that come from the literature.

Descriptors are terms that have been defined for use by the thesaurus.

Identifiers are proper nouns. Identifiers are unique entities, not general concepts, and when they appear in documents, they must be used in the index as they are. Examples include:

- ▲ Names of people.
- ▲ Names of organizations.
- ▲ Project names.
- ▲ Nomenclatures.
- ▲ Identification numbers.
- ▲ Place names.
- ▲ Trademarks.
- ▲ Abbreviations and acronyms.

Preferred terms are the words chosen for the thesaurus to represent a class of synonymous words. By definition, hierarchical languages do not have synonyms and they are not in subject heading or fixed keyword languages. Of course, in any of these word lists, near-synonyms are possible, since it is a subjective opinion as to whether or not two terms are synonyms. Control over the synonyms in these languages is accomplished by use of the dictionaries, with careful definition of terms. A free keyword language makes control of synonyms very difficult.

Entry terms are words that allow the user to enter the vocabulary structure. If the entry term is not an allowable descriptor, it will refer the user to a term that is acceptable. Good indexing languages have good entry vocabularies. Entry vocabulary is the door to properly entering an index and the usefulness of an index is highly dependent on the entry vocabulary. A scant, obscure entry vocabulary will short circuit the user in the preliminary check into the list, leading away from the path needed. A strong, full entry vocabulary will enhance the user's chances for finding the right words in the search.

There are a few general rules for deciding on the form of terms used in the thesaurus. There may, of course, be exceptions to the rules, but in most cases:

1. Descriptors should be nouns, either single nouns, noun phrases, or nouns with qualifiers indicated in parentheses.

2. Multiword terms may be either pre-coordinated or formed by post-coordination of existing terms.

3. Generally, the singular form of the word is used for processes and properties and the plural is used for *classes* of people who do the actions involved. For example:

Processes
    Liquidation
    Indexing

Classes
    Teachers
    Preachers
    Candlestick makers

4. Multiword terms should be entered in their natural word order with *see* cross-references to the inverted forms.

5. Abbreviations should be used if the users know their meanings.

At this point in the thesaurus construction, consideration should be given to combining terms into multiword forms as necessary. The important issue here is to draw a fine line between how much pre-coordination will be done and how much will be left to the thesaurus user, who may be either the indexer or the searcher. Although the objective of the thesaurus is vocabulary control, too much control will make the device nonmanipulative and thus defeat its purpose, if the purpose of the thesaurus is to have a manipulative system. Careful rules must be laid down as to how terms are to be combined and defined. Criteria must be established for handling synonyms and related terms, both vertical and horizontal. The handling of cross-references must be described. Then the list must be alphabetized with a consistent alphabetizing procedure.

THESAURUS EVALUATION

Thesauri must be evaluated. Some general criteria are:

1. Authority.
2. Proven usefulness.
3. Regular revision.
4. Ease of use.

On the surface, the evaluation of a thesaurus is rather straightforward. How well does it help indexers and users select the exact terms they need and how well does it shows structural relationships between vocabulary terms? Unfortunately, like other aspects of information retrieval, the final judgments are usually subjective, despite the quasi-quantitative methods of recall and precision.

A thesaurus can be used at the indexing stage or the searching stage. Generally, indexers use the thesaurus to select approved terms to represent the document concepts, and the user of the index uses the thesaurus to find the correct term that will give entry into the index. In the ideal situation the terms will be broad enough to pull together relevant related information, but specific enough not to produce nonrelevant information. Seldom is this situation totally realized because of the many variables involved in the indexing and retrieval process, but the degree of effectiveness can be satisfactorily evaluated.

Although user satisfaction (or the lack of it) may be helpful in determining the quality of a thesaurus, it is essential that certain criteria be established beforehand. When deciding what criteria are to be used, it is important to remember exactly what it is that the tool is designed to do. A thesaurus is a device to control indexing. We attempt to establish a link between concepts and terms by grouping natural-language words into sets of similar words and selecting a preferred term to stand for the meaning of the entire group. Because of the ambiguity of language and its use, this can never be absolutely accomplished, but the degree of correspondence is an indicator of the quality of a thesaurus. Some questions that might be asked are:

1. How good is the subject coverage of the concepts displayed? Is it adequate to allow proper indexing and searching?

2. How well does the thesaurus handle broader terms, narrower terms, and related terms? In other words, are all the structural relationships between terms treated adequately?

3. How adequate is the display of the thesaurus? Is it easy to see, understand, and follow through on? Does it lead to efficient and effective indexing and searching?

Most of the failures of a thesaurus can be linked to these three basic areas. Another pragmatic factor to be considered in evaluating a thesaurus is its cost. Creating and maintaining a thesaurus is costly, and the question is whether or not its benefits equal or exceed that cost. In maintaining a thesaurus, a key point to keep in mind is that as more specificity is allowed the word list grows in size, which in turn complicates the structure and thus costs more to maintain. Exactly how specific the thesaurus will be is a basic construction decision, and cost cannot be ignored while making this decision.

Constructing a thesaurus is a complex, labor-intensive job, and the work on a particular thesaurus is never finished. We have learned a lot about these valuable tools in the past few decades and we have a long way to go before they are perfect tools.

Types of Indexes and Abstracts

CHAPTER 5

TYPES OF INDEXES

Indexes can be categorized many ways; for example, by arrangement or by searching structure or by specific subject fields or by purpose. A few general types will be discussed in the following section.

Alphabetical Indexes

Indexes may be in chronological order, classified order, evolution order (e.g., geological indexes), or canonical order (such as Scripture), but the general form of modern indexes is a single alphabetical index with names and subject entries interfiled. Indexers have promoted this idea over the years. A general purpose index is probably best ordered this way. There are still sensible reasons for having divided indexes. Works in science and law, for example, are better served with multiple indexes.

The term *alphabetical index* covers a number of different kinds of indexes. The arrangement of an index in alphabetical order is the most common method, because it is more convenient and follows a familiar pattern. It is not, however, the only method that can be used. The index may follow a classified arrangement or be both alphabetical and classified at the same time. Generally, any classified arrangement will need an alphabetical approach as a supplement, either separate or built in, to make it efficient to use.

An alphabetical index is based on the orderly principles of letters of the alphabet and is used for the arrangement of subject headings, cross-references, and qualifying terms, as well as main headings. All entry items are in one alphabetical order, including subject terms, author names, and place names. Even chemical formulas are placed in order by alphanumerical arrangement.

The major drawbacks with the alphabetical arrangement are the problems of synonymy and scattering of entries. If we want information on pecan trees, do we look under *Pecan Trees* or under *Trees*? Scattering means that subcategories of a subject are not drawn together under the generic term but are frequently cross-referenced from the *wrong* terms to the preferred term, but now users are slowed in their search because they chose a *wrong* term.

Author Indexes

Author indexes are not the most common type of indexes, but the author approach to information is not a rarity. Author indexes are those whose entry points are people, organizations, corporate authors, government agencies, universities, and the like. Users are guided to titles of documents by way of authors.

Authors can also be used as an indirect subject approach. Workers in a discipline are generally well aware of the leading writers in a field and will often approach the literature from the avenue of these known authors. Cleveland (1976) demonstrated that in certain kinds of retrieval systems authors are strong indicators of subject content in a cluster of documents. This quantitative study supports the intuitive feeling of the importance of authors as subject indicators.

To maintain consistency in author indexes, a number of decisions have to be made, such as the number of names to be allowed per entry when a document has multiple writers, the method of alphabetizing to be used for titles and prefixes, use of full name or initials, delineation of authors with common names, and so forth. Author indexes must be constructed under carefully established guidelines.

Book Indexes

When the word *index* is mentioned, most people think of a book index. The reading public is quite familiar with book indexes, which are lists of words, generally alphabetical, at the back of a book, giving a page location of the subject or name associated with each word. Just as indexes to library collections make it unnecessary for a user to read all the million or more documents in a library to find a few useful ones, a book index pinpoints information so that the reader will not have to read, or reread, the entire book. Once again, the index is not a substitute for the information in the book but is a pointer to the information included.

It remains an unexplainable mystery why everyone cannot understand the importance of indexes in books. Any book that ever serves as a reference in any sense of the word should have a quality index to make its information quickly and completely available. Unfortunately, too many books are published with poor indexes or no indexes at all. Such books are incomplete. Readers are handicapped and penalized and, in a way, have been cheated. When they buy a book they should expect an index, with some notable exceptions, such as most fiction.

Citation Indexes

A citation index consists of a list of articles, with a sublist under each article of subsequently published papers that *cite* the articles. In other words, given a particular paper, a citation index shows who cited that paper at a later point in time. In addition to this basic index there may be supplementary indexes arranged by author or keyword subject terms, but such approaches are not considered to be the primary approach to a citation index. Basically, this kind of index implies that a cited paper has an internal subject relationship with the papers that cite it, and we use this relationship to cluster related documents.

The premise of citation indexing is that citations reflect document content and that an author's citations can therefore be substituted for the judgment of indexers. Citations link together papers on a specific topic, and a citation index is built on the basis of this internal structure of subject literatures. It is not a recent idea; over a century ago the legal profession developed such an index, *Shepard's Citations,* which gives accounts of legal decisions and later citations. This is a fundamental searching tool for the law profession because of its reliance on precedent. Citation indexing, however, is relatively new as a general reference tool.

The primary advantage in using a citation index is that it leads the user to the latest articles; that is, unlike conventional indexes it goes forward in time rather than backwards. At a certain point, the user can discover how the ideas in a certain paper were received and what later developments were reported. Another advantage is that only the author's judgment of relevancy is involved, and therefore the production can be entirely mechanized.

The primary disadvantage of such an index is that it is based on the assumption that the authors of the papers are consistent and knowledgeable in their citations; this is mostly true, although not always.

Citation indexing is more than an aid to users seeking information. It is also a research tool for studying the behavioral characteristics of the literature and, indeed, for studying the structural growth of science itself.

Eugene Garfield (1979) has written:

> Although it was developed primarily for bibliographic purposes, and in spite of its recognized utility as a search tool, the most important application of citation indexing may prove to be nonbibliographic. If the literature of science reflects the activities of science, a comprehensive, multidisciplinary citation index can provide an interesting view of these activities. The view can shed some useful light on both the structure of science and process of scientific development.

Garfield believes that this use of citation indexing offers some "intriguing possibilities" for the study and management of science. Current generations of Information Science students need to be very well aware of Garfield's work over the years. He has opened many, many doors for research and applications in our field.

Citation indexing does not depend upon index words at all, thus avoiding the intellectual problems of meaning and the interpretation of meaning by conventional indexing. The underlying assumption of a citation index is that we rely on the author of a document to tell us what the subject is, rather than on an indexer, who must decide without consulting the writer. With citation indexes we see that authors are the most qualified persons to define and delineate material most relevant to their subjects. Because the citation index is not based on index term assignment and needs no interpretation or any kind of terminology, it gives a clear channel between the author and the user, without the introduction of artificial language.

Classified Indexes

A classified index has its contents arranged systematically by classes or subject headings. Classifiers love anything that is classified, including classified indexes. Classified indexes have an important role to play, especially in scientific indexing, but general indexes that are classified mystify the general user, primarily because they do not understand how they are constructed. Indexes should be user-oriented and most users find classified indexes difficult to use. Their mind set is alphabetical order, even for experts in a field who should be familiar with a hierarchical breakdown of their professional vocabulary; however, the usefulness of such indexes must not be underestimated because the indexes are very valuable in the appropriate environment.

Coordinate Indexes

Coordinate indexes allow terms to be combined or coordinated. Strictly speaking, this is really a process, although the term *coordinate index* is used quite frequently in the literature, the thought being that coordinating produces an index. Modern era coordinate indexes began with the idea of punching or notching a card and then using a mechanical device, such as long needles, to *drop out* cards containing the combination of index terms of interest. Combining two or more single index terms to create a new class creates coordinating indexes. For example, if the individual index terms *Pecan* and *Trees* are combined we have a new class of things: *Pecan Trees*.

When we started to use computers in information retrieval systems, the coordinated cards concept migrated to machine-readable form. At first glance, we might brush aside the idea of such indexing systems as archaic and only of historical interest, but the truth is that this concept still is the basis for modern retrieval systems, including most of the World Wide Web search tools now in vogue.

Cumulative Indexes

A cumulative index is a combination or merging of a set of indexes over time. Such indexes for established works can often cover many decades.

Generally, such indexes apply to journals and to large, important works and are published as separate volumes. Cumulative indexes are complex and usually are done by teams of indexers. Also, it should be noted that they cannot be done effectively by simply interfiling all the entries from the individual indexes. They require a good deal of editing because of duplications, terminology changes and a need to adjust the depth of indexing.

Faceted Indexes

Facet, by definition, means one side of something that has many sides. In other words, in a faceted indexing system, any subject is not a single unit but has many aspects; thus a faceted index attempts to discover all the individual aspects of a subject and then synthesize them in a way that best describes the subject under discussion.

A faceted scheme is a type of synthetic classification and is often called an analytic-synthetic system. Facet analysis is a tightly controlled process by which simple concepts are organized into carefully defined categories by connecting class numbers of the basic concepts. This is in contrast to enumerative classification systems, such as the Dewey Decimal Classification (DDC), which are mostly pre-structured. Enumerative systems are fixed and can accommodate new knowledge in limited ways, whereas faceted systems are much more flexible. A faceted system is pre-coordinated at the time of indexing and is arranged in classification order, rather than in straight alphabetical order. It differs from enumerative classification systems in that its terms are not exhaustive, but are intended to be used as building blocks.

The philosophical basis is that a paper is a new creation in which an author looks at a subject in a different way, or brings out new ideas or a new discovery. Since each paper is in a sense a new way of exploring knowledge, it cannot truly fit into a pre-existing category, as with the traditional classification schemes. The contents of the new document cannot be accurately revealed in a classification scheme built on previous knowledge; rather, a dynamic scheme is needed to reflect the dynamic nature of the knowledge itself. With a faceted system, we put together (on the spot, so to speak) the class most closely representing the informational concepts in the new document.

First-line Indexes

First-line indexes generally refer to poems. In these indexes all the words in the first line of a poem are listed in their alphabetical position in the index. These types of indexes are rather common and appear in various types of reference sources.

Hypermedia Indexes

Hypermedia is text and nontextual material in an electronic form that allows users to search nonlinearly by associations. This type of indexing allows users to thread their way to what they want through electronic nodes and links between those nodes. The indexing aspects are transparent to the user, but someone has analyzed the information and has made indexing decisions in establishing these nodes and connections.

Internet Indexes

Internet indexes are undefinable, but they are out there. They exist in traditional forms, in hypermedia forms, in automatic forms, and in implicit forms. They rarely are called *indexes* although that is what they are. The challenge for indexers is to rise to the occasion and lead the way in developing these indexes.

Multimedia Indexes

These indexes integrate images, sounds, and textual material. In an age when audio and visual media are playing an increasing role in all kinds of communication systems, there is a rapidly growing need to develop and refine the indexing to these media. Indexing this material is presenting new problems and challenges to the indexing profession.

Periodical Indexes

The growth of modern science, in large part, owes a debt to the rise of the journal. A *journal* can be generally defined as a continuing publication issued in successive parts with numerical or chronological designations. The medium may be paper, electronic, videos, or any other medium.

Journals have proven to be a vital key to the science communication process as it now exists. The periodical is an amazing innovation. Its format is convenient and it is easily distributed. Primary research is reported in the journal literature, and in fact, it is the source of most information that later finds its way into books. It follows that the role of a periodical index is critical—not just to science but to all scholarship.

There are two types of periodical indexes: *individual indexes* to individual journals and *broad indexes* to a group of journals. In the first case, the publisher of the journal prepares an index, usually for a volume at the end of a year's run of the journal. These indexes are prepared under the direction of the editor of the journal. The approach to this kind of indexing can range from a simple, uncontrolled vocabulary to a complex indexing system with a thesaurus.

The indexing of the world periodical literature is a major enterprise. One of the landmark events in indexing was the conceptualization and implementation of indexes that cut across many titles and specific subject areas. Early on indexes were created to individual issues and annual accumulations. One index for information over a large set of journals was a revolutionary jump in information retrieval.

Whereas one or two people write most books, there are thousands of authors in an index to periodicals. Periodical indexes are based on the same principles and have the same general objectives as book indexes, but because their scope is broader, they present a number of unique problems. For example, preparing a book index is a well-defined operation, with a beginning and an end. It focuses in most cases on a general topic, and it can usually be prepared entirely by one person. On the other hand, periodical indexes are open-ended projects, usually done by a number of people, covering perhaps years, with shifts in subject emphasis and indexing objectives. Consistency, a vital key to quality indexing, becomes a paramount challenge. Each issue of a periodical may deal with unrelated topics by several different authors, written in different styles, and aimed at different users. The periodical index must bring order out of this divergence.

Permuted Title Indexes

Title indexes work reasonably well for highly specific searching, provided the titles are highly specific. Permuted title word indexes are created by systematically rotating information-conveying words in the title as subject entry points into the index. The premise of a permuted title index is that titles effectively indicate the content of documents. Because it reflects the content of a document, a permuted title index helps users decide if that document would satisfy their information needs. The best argument for creating permuted title indexes is simple: it can be done quickly, with a minimum of cost, and entirely by computer. There is little delay because of indexers, index editors, and production backlog. On the other hand, a permuted title index is not as useful as a subject index based on analysis of the major portions of a document. The main drawbacks of permuted title indexing are:

1. The titles may not accurately reflect content.
2. The limited number of terms in the titles restrict complete subject indication.
3. Most of the indexes are unappealing to the eye and are difficult to scan.
4. The lack of vocabulary control can increase the retrieval of irrelevant documents.

Since permuted title indexes are concordances, they suffer from the weaknesses of concordances, such as the scattering of synonyms and generic terms, causing user frustration and missed entries. There is little, if any, controlled consistency, since the indexes reflect content only as much as the title words represent conceptual subjects.

String Indexes

Although string indexing is a modern term, its antecedent of trying to bring out the best in a classified scheme goes back many years. Historical links can be traced to the theoretical work of Farradane, Ranganathan, Cutter, and others.

The idea is to display a series of rotating index entries from a basic list of index terms that make up the *string*. The objective is to give the user an entry point for all index terms and to display them in context with each other.

A string index is usually, but not necessarily, output by a computer. Except for basic keyword in context (KWIC) indexing, string indexing is generally not a fully automated process. A computer follows strict rules to create permutations of the index tags, but a human indexer analyzes the document in the usual way and then codes the master string of terms. The computer finishes the job by making each coded term an access point.

Researchers, who use index terms to find information, need to know the correct terms to use and the correct relationships that exist between the terms. String indexing was invented to make sure that the latter is given proper attention. Index users run the risk of missing useful entries by failing to search the most specific subject of interest. String indexing is a method that attempts to minimize this by presenting the single entries, one by one, in an alphabetical list. That is, string indexes provide that every concept becomes linked to its directly related concept in the hierarchy system. As it turns out, the terms form a citation pattern in the string from general to specific, and all terms or subject names for which an item can be indexed are included.

This type of indexing is highly mechanical, which relieves the indexer of a lot of decision making.

Word Indexes

Word and name indexes, which are sometimes called concordances, are indexes to the individual names and words that the author used, and in one sense most closely represent the information and ideas the author had in mind when creating the manuscript. These indexes are the exact term or word within the context of the document which pinpoint the subject discussed and its location.

There are limitations to the usefulness of these kinds of indexes, but in certain cases they perform a needed function. An example of word indexes is a Bible concordance. The main drawback with this type of index is that it complicates searching in several ways. Searching becomes more difficult and uncertain, since this type of index spreads similar entries over many synonymous terms, ignores misspellings, and confuses any general-specific term relationships that certainly exist in the implied indexing language being unconsciously used.

TYPES OF ABSTRACTS

Abstracts are written to decrease the time and effort it takes to search the overwhelming output from research and scholarship around the world. An inestimable number of new papers are published each year, with the number increasing annually. It is unlikely that practitioners in any field come even close to reading this outpouring in their own field of interest, no matter how specialized. That is exactly the point in using an abstract. It is quite likely that the users neither need nor want to read everything. They are concerned with finding that minute portion of the bulk that relates to their current activity or individual interest at a given point. Their specialty may be turtles, but of the hundreds of turtle articles published they want only a few dozen, perhaps, and the rest do not fill any information need. An abstract helps them to decide. Instead of obtaining and examining a 3,000-word paper, they can read a 150-word abstract and then either request the paper or forget about it. Occasionally the abstract will carry all the information a user needs and, as a result, it serves an additional function.

Abstracts satisfy users' needs for both current and extensive retrospective information. Users simply scan abstracts as they are published to see what new papers have been written and then turn to older abstracts when they want to go back through the literature.

On the other hand, information professionals sense a growing need for new techniques that will allow more complex and in-depth analysis and synthesis of information. Information funding agencies continue to call for research in this direction. Indexes identify locations where information may be found, but indexes do not deal with validity, fairness or the morality of that information. Over the past fifty years there have been numerous times when researchers and practitioners have raised the issue of *quality filtering*. Can retrieval systems be designed that will give users the best information out of the total database? Or more to the point, can indexes be constructed that aid in such a filtering process? Abstracting would seem to be a logical place to try to develop such filters.

Such techniques will need to include more and more qualitative evaluation at the indexing and abstracting stages of bibliographic control. The future necessity for critical abstract writing is very strong with the overflow of information on the Internet. There is a need for new, more sophisticated methods to filter out quality information from the junk at all levels. The traditional, bland ("just-state-the-facts-Ma'am") type of abstracting must be carefully rethought in this new millennium. It is time to open the discussion on the totally ridiculous idea that abstracts should not make critical comments. Why not? Users are very busy people and they want a strong, respected opinion from information handlers about what is valid and what is not. Professional information handlers must not continue to avoid this serious responsibility.

Not all people agree with the idea that an abstract can properly take the place of reading the paper. Many feel that it is presumptuous to think that a 150- to 250-word abstract can carry enough information from a well-written 3,000-word paper to be of much use except as a guide. The inclusion of an abstract merely serves to let the user have a better indication of what will be found in the paper. It alerts users to the existence of new data and gives them an indication of what that data is like, but it is not to be used as an original source.

In the literature, types of abstracts are defined in various ways in an attempt to categorize them. Although this is useful, the ambiguity that exists is due to the fact that in reality abstract writers tend to ignore the gray lines of formal definition and write abstracts that are a combination of the arbitrarily defined *different types*.

Traditionally, abstracts have been classified in several different ways: by the way they are written, by their use, and by who writes them.

Indicative Abstracts

Indicative or *descriptive* abstracts disclose that significant information and specific data can be found in the document. For example, an indicative abstract might state that "the number of onions grown in California was determined and reported in this article." An indicative abstract simply describes what type of record is being abstracted and what it is about. In most cases, the indicative abstract is somewhat shorter, is written in general terms, and does not give the user a progressive account of the paper's development. It has often been described as an alerting device and is never expected to replace the paper itself. It guides users to the paper by telling them what can be found there. To accomplish this, the abstract cannot be too general. At the minimum it must give essential information, such as the purpose of the paper and the results.

Informative Abstracts

An *informative* abstract actually presents the specific data. In this case, the abstract would read: "According to this article, a billion seventy-five onions were grown in California." An informative abstract tries to present as much quantitative and qualitative data as it can. This type is the most useful for documents reporting on experimental investigations. It abridges the principal ideas and facts and contains actual data. Informative abstracts have been compared to a skeleton with all the flesh missing—the viewer is given enough detail to accurately reconstruct what the departed soul must have looked like. The user often does not have to retrieve the paper for further information, since such things as formulas, statistical results, and parts of tables are often included in the abstract.

An informative abstract should cover four essential points:

1. Objective and scope of the work.
2. Methods used.
3. Results.
4. Conclusions.

Item 1 is important because it may allow users to determine, without reading any more of the abstract, that they have no use for the paper. Number 2 above must cover equipment used and all the methodological details so that the user will gain a good understanding of the investigation.

Critical Abstracts

A *critical* abstract makes a value judgment or editorial comment on the paper. In our example, the abstract would now state: "This article reports on the number of onions grown in California, but since it doesn't indicate which years, the information is not of much value." The critical abstract is generally recognized as a third type of abstract, although it is questionable if it is indeed a third category. If it is heavily editorial it cannot convey much basic information and is really a review of the document rather than a true indicator of document content. Some abstractors feel strongly that a good abstract avoids the bias and personal viewpoint of critical comment, and that the abstractor, whose job is solely to reveal content, should be remote and invisible in the final product. It is difficult enough to keep bias out; why deliberately introduce it?

Critical abstracting can be a powerful tool. The key, of course, is that the abstractor is sufficiently knowledgeable of the subject and the methodologies in the paper so that she can make quality judgments. This kind of abstract is generally used on general papers with broad overviews, on reviews, and on monographs, but is also used for single papers.

Although many abstracts are clearly either indicative or informative, in actual practice they are often combined and perform both an indicative, informative, and critical function. Indexing and abstracting services often indicate that the abstracting will be indicative, informative, or a combination of both, according to the nature of the material being abstracted.

All three type of abstracts serve a useful purpose, although the most popular one, and probably the most important one, is the informative type. A vast majority of abstracting results in informative abstracts, since a majority of abstractable materials lend themselves to this form. On the other hand, reviews, books, essays, and the like lend themselves to indicative abstracts and occasionally to critical ones. Once again, the type of material and the eventual users are the basis for a decision on which type of abstract should be used.

Classifying Abstracts by Use

Another way to classify abstracts is by purpose: discipline-oriented, mission-oriented, or slanted. Any one of these may be indicative, informative, or critical in its internal construction.

When an abstract is written for a specific area of knowledge (e.g., mathematics), it is said to be *discipline-oriented*. When it is written to support application activities that may or may not be interdisciplinary in nature, it is a *mission-oriented abstract*. A mission-oriented group is defined in terms of an assignment, rather than a subject area. The *slanted* abstract is often a form of the mission-oriented abstract and is one that highlights or concentrates on a selected portion of a document's subject content. For example, a paper that discusses disease in dogs, cats, and chickens might have only the part about dogs abstracted if the user group is doing research on diseases in dogs.

Classifying Abstracts by Author

Three fundamental groups of people may write abstracts: authors of the papers, subject area experts, or professional abstractors. The ideal abstractor would probably be the author of the paper who is a recognized expert in the subject and has training and years of experience in writing abstracts. Obviously, such rare individuals write relatively few abstracts.

On first thought, it might appear that an author would be the best person, since presumably the author knows more about the paper than anybody else does. Authors do not necessarily make good abstractors. It is somewhat analogous to a playwright who takes the lead part in her own play, although someone else might be a much better interpreter of the writer's work. On the positive side, author-prepared abstracts are on time, since they generally accompany the manuscript, and they are less expensive, since no additional expense is necessary if the author's abstract is used. A number of indexing and abstracting services give their abstractors the option of using author abstracts published with the papers if they judge them to be satisfactory. On the negative side, authors generally are not versed in the procedures and methods for writing good abstracts and do not have the experience required to do a good job. Equally serious, authors often are too close to the paper to give it an objective treatment. Authors can fail to see that what they think is important may not necessarily be the most important information for the user. Authors as abstractors have been known to use their abstracts to promote the paper; this can create a misleading abstract and is unfair to the user. The upshot has been that author-prepared abstracts vary considerably in quality.

Many abstracting journals rely on subject specialists, who are not professional abstractors but are professionals in their subject, to write abstracts. If these experts are trained and experienced in the procedures and methods of abstracting, they generally produce excellent, high-quality abstracts. An outstanding example is *Excerpta Medica,* which relies extensively on experts in the health sciences field.

A few cautions are in order, however, in using subject experts. The expert may not be absolutely expert in all the ramifications of an area, especially if she is assigned topics across a wide range of the subject. For example, there are specialized areas of mathematics that other highly competent mathematicians know absolutely nothing about, and they would be unable even to follow a proof in that area. Also, it must be remembered that since experts represent the establishment in a subject area, they may be intellectually reluctant to accept an offbeat new idea from an upstart young author. It is also possible that the author is a professional opponent whose views are diametrically opposite to those of the abstractor. Such factors can affect the results.

The third group consists of full-time professional abstractors. It is easier for a subject expert to be trained in abstracting than to make a professional abstractor competent in a subject field, but professional abstractors, as a group, produce high-quality abstracts, especially if they are assigned to areas with which they have become familiar. Although professional abstractors demand higher wages, they do the work on time, often have foreign language expertise, and can cover areas in which subject experts cannot be found.

Structured Abstracts

Attention is being given to how we can improve abstracting to help professionals cope with the information deluge. For example, one concern has been inaccuracy in abstracts. Pitkin (1999) found that from 18 percent to 68 percent of the abstracts in leading general medical journals had data that were either inconsistent or were not in the text of the article. This has researchers worried.

One device developed in the attempt to improve abstracts was the structured abstract. A structured abstract follows a set form of subheadings and the abstract writer fills in the blanks. This type of abstract has been promoted in the medical field for more than a decade and has made inroads into other fields. The form of a structured abstract can vary according to need, but a type example is:

Background

Aim

Method

Results

Conclusion

Proponents of structured abstracts believe that such abstracts contain more pertinent information, are of a higher quality and facilitate peer review. Today, many journals require that authors submit structured abstracts to insure that critical information dealing with purpose, methodology and results appears in an organized fashion.

Productive scientists and other scholars have come to recognize the value of information in their work, and they consider the publication, storage, and retrieval of this information an integral part of their activities, not as something incidental. As a result, they have learned to depend upon bibliographic control to expedite their work.

Two points should be kept in mind. First, the abstracts themselves can vary in quality from worthless to superb. They can be affected by errors, policy, omissions, and abstractor bias, or they can be so poorly written that they are difficult to use. Second, not all users are equally proficient in using abstracts and other bibliographic tools, and the user imposes a self-limitation on the tools.

And it must be remembered that users do not depend solely on libraries for information. Scientists turn first to colleagues, then to their own journals, books, and reports and to conference information and the *invisible college* (personal network of unpublished information that flows back and forth). The abstractor must keep this in mind and strive for a product that will be a priority choice of information seekers, which at present is not true.

Abstracts, like all devices for bibliographic control, are imperfect. There are, however, many excellent abstracting tools.

The rest of this chapter will show examples of indexes, abstracts, and thesauri selected to show the range of these tools in the world and to illustrate how certain tools have different complementary indexes. The reader is strongly encouraged to study the many hundreds and hundreds of indexes, abstracts, and thesauri available to get an in-depth feeling for the structure and arrangement of these tools.

EXAMPLES FROM INDEXING TOOLS

Index by Categories

GEOGRAPHIC BREAKDOWNS

BY CENSUS DIVISION

Communications and Transportation
Travel to US, spending by world area of residence, and economic impact, by spending category and State, 1996, annual rpt, 2044–49

Energy Resources and Demand
Electric power plants production, capacity, sales, and fuel stocks, use, and costs, by State, 1997-98, annual rpt, 3164–11

Health and Vital Statistics
Births and birth and fertility rates, by parent and birth characteristics and location, 1993, US Vital Statistics annual rpt, 4144–1

Natural Resources, Environment, and Pollution
Wildlife-related recreation, hunting, and fishing economic impacts, by species and region, 1996, 5506–16.2

Recreation and Leisure
Fishing (black bass) participation, by location and participant characteristics, 1996, 5506–16.3

Veterans Affairs
Hospital capacity, use, services, and mgmt, for VA compared to community hospitals, by location, 1975-97 with projections to 2010, GAO rpt, 26121–765

BY CITY

Agriculture and Food
Peaches production, prices, and use by State, and terminal market prices in selected cities, 1998, annual rpt, 1311–12
Sweetpotato production, acreage, shipments, and prices, for North Carolina and other producer States, 1970s-98, annual rpt, 1311–33
Watermelon production, acreage, shipments, prices and arrivals by city, by State, 1998, annual rpt, 1311–35

Communications and Transportation
Truck rates for fresh vegetables, by crop, growing area, and market, periodic situation rpt with articles, 1561–11

Energy Resources and Demand
Heating oil addition to Strategic Petroleum Reserve, costs and benefits under alternative plans and policies, with data on supply, demand, and movements, 1975-2010, 3338–16

Government and Defense
State and local govt productivity measures, with output, employment, and financial data, for 11 govt services, 1967-92, 6828–34

Health and Vital Statistics
Births and birth and fertility rates, by parent and birth characteristics and location, 1993, US Vital Statistics annual rpt, 4144–1

Industry and Commerce
Foreign-controlled US manufacturing establishments, employment, and rankings, by country, BEA economic area, and whether newly built or acquired, 1992, 2702–1.113
Northern Mariana Islands economic census, 1997: employment, firms, payroll, and receipts, by SIC 1- to 4-digit industry, 2597–1
Retail trade economic census, 1997: establishments, employment, sales, and payroll, by NAICS 3- to 7-digit kind of business, MSA, county, and city, State rpt series, 2397–1
Wholesale trade economic census, 1997: establishments, employment, finances, and operations, by NAICS 3- to 8-digit kind of business, MSA, county, and city, State rpt series, 2405–1

Law Enforcement
Methamphetamine abuse, arrestees testing positive in selected cities, and related deaths, by selected characteristics, 1990-98, 236–6.5
Police employment, spending, and operations, for State, city, county, and special district agencies, 1997, 6068–308

Natural Resources, Environment, and Pollution
Flood risk relation to housing prices, and Corps of Engineers flood evacuation activities and costs, 1984-93, 3758–13
Water quality, chemistry, hydrology, and other characteristics, local area studies, series, 5666–27
Water supply and quality in streams and lakes, and groundwater levels in wells, by drainage basin, 1996, annual State rpt series, 5666–16
Western US land use by location, and irrigation in Idaho Upper Snake River basin by crop and county, 1974-95, 5308–42

BY COUNTY

Agriculture and Food
Census of Agriculture, 1997: farms, farmland, production, finances, and operator characteristics, by county, State rpt series, 1661–1
Census of Agriculture, 1997: farms, farmland, production, sales, expenses, and govt payments, by commodity for leading States and counties, 1663–2
Farm finances and other characteristics, and agricultural sales and trade, with summary economic indicators by metro-nonmetro location, State fact sheet series, 1546–6

Education
Head Start enrollment, funding, child and family characteristics, staff, and services, FY97, biennial rpt, 4584–15

Energy Resources and Demand
Hydroelectric power plants undeveloped capacity, dam status, and environmental suitability, by site and river basin, 1998, State rpt series, 3306–7

Health and Vital Statistics
Births and birth and fertility rates, by parent and birth characteristics and location, 1993, US Vital Statistics annual rpt, 4144–1
Mines (metal and nonmetal) quartz dust exposure of miners, by mine and mine characteristics, 1992-98, 6668–14

Industry and Commerce
Retail trade economic census, 1997: establishments, employment, sales, and payroll, by NAICS 3- to 7-digit kind of business, MSA, county, and city, State rpt series, 2397–1
Wholesale trade economic census, 1997: establishments, employment, finances, and operations, by NAICS 3- to 8-digit kind of business, MSA, county, and city, State rpt series, 2405–1

Law Enforcement
Police employment, spending, and operations, for State, city, county, and special district agencies, 1997, 6068–308
Wiretaps authorized, costs, arrests, trials, and convictions, by offense and jurisdiction, 1998, annual rpt, 18204–7

Natural Resources, Environment, and Pollution
Rio Grande River upper basin water supply and use, agricultural impacts, and water project funding, 1980s-94, 5308–40
Water quality and pollution in streams and lakes, and environmental and health impacts, by drainage basin, series, 5666–30
Western US land use by location, and irrigation in Idaho Upper Snake River basin by crop and county, 1974-95, 5308–42

Population
Appalachia population, migration, employment, income, and infant mortality, by State and county, 1990-97, 9088–45
Income (personal) per capita and total, by State, MSA, BEA economic area, county, and metro-nonmetro location, 1995-97, annual article, 2702–1.114

BY FOREIGN COUNTRY

Agriculture and Food
Dairy industry cattle inventory, milk production, and operations, by State and selected country, 1991-96, 1396–1.2
Europe agricultural production, consumption, and trade, and impacts of new EU member accessions, by commodity and country, 1988-98 and projected to 2005, 1528–374
Swine inventory by State and selected country, and industry mgmt and health issues, 1990-95, 1396–2.3

Example 5.1. *American Statistics Index* supp. 5 (June 1999) p. 101 (index by categories). Reprinted by permission of CIS © 1999.

Index by Titles

Titles are listed alphabetically in natural word order, as they appear in the Abstracts Section. Titles beginning with numbers (e.g. "1990 Census . . .") appear at the end of the Index. Where appropriate, alternative word-orders of titles have also been provided.

In addition to publication titles, individual report titles within a publication series are indexed, as are the titles of all periodical articles receiving individual abstracts.

Boldface numbers in parentheses, before ASI accession numbers in quarterly supplement issues, indicate the 1999 Monthly Supplement abstracts issue number that you should look in to find the text of the referenced abstract.

Abstracts of Reports and Testimony: FY98, **2610**4–17.1

Accelerating Cleanup: Paths to Closure, 3378–2

Accountability Report, FY98: U.S. Nuclear Regulatory Commission, 9634–20

Addenda to 1996 National Survey of Fishing, Hunting, and Wildlife Associated Recreation, 5506–16

Additions and Resident Patients at End of Year, State and County Mental Hospitals, by Age and Diagnosis, by State, U.S., 4094–2

Advance Data from Vital and Health Statistics of the Centers for Disease Control and Prevention/National Center for Health Statistics, 4146–8

Advanced Structural Ceramics: Vast Potential Has Yet To Be Realized, 9882–16.105

Affordable Housing Advisory Annual Report, 1998: Federal Home Loan Bank of Topeka. Building Foundations, 9304–31

Against the Tide: Malcolm Bryan and the Introduction of Monetary Aggregate Targets, 9371–1.102

Aging Baby Boom: Implications for Employment and Training Programs, 6408–78

Agricultural Chemical Usage, 1616–1

Agricultural Chemical Usage: 1998 Field Crops Summary, 1616–1.3

Agricultural Pesticide Use in the Great Lakes Basin: Estimates of Major Active Ingredients Applied During 1994-95 for the Lake Erie, Michigan, and Superior Basins, 9238–86

Agriculture and European Union Enlargement, 1528–374

Aircraft Evacuations onto Escape Slides and Platforms II: Effects of Exit Size, 7506–10.292

Analysis of Balance Sheets of Local Farm Supply and Marketing Cooperatives, 1128–85

Analysis of Financial Statements: Local Farm Supply, Marketing Cooperatives, 1128–85

Annual Environmental Reports on DOE Facilities, 3324–2

Annual Epidemiologic Surveillance Reports on DOE Facilities, 3324–7

Annual Report on Carcinogens, 4044–15

Annual Report on Pipeline Safety, 1993, 7304–5

Annual Report on Pipeline Safety, 1994, 7304–5

Annual Report to Congress 1998: Energy Information Administration, 3164–29

Annual Report, 1997: Office of the Chief Financial Officer, Small Business Administration, 9764–12

Annual Review of Aircraft Accident Data, U.S. General Aviation, 1996, 9614–3

Another Look at the Low Taxable Income of Foreign-Controlled Companies in the U.S., 8006–3.69

Applied General Equilibrium Model of Moroccan Trade Liberalization Featuring External Economies, 2626–12.60

Aquaculture Studies: National Animal Health Monitoring System (NAHMS), 1396–4

ARC Socioeconomic Data: Regional Statistics and Reports, 9088–45

Are Stocks Overtaking Real Estate in Household Portfolios?, 9385–11.103

Baseline Reference of 1998 Equine Health and Management, 1396–6.2

Beef Studies: National Animal Health Monitoring System (NAHMS), 1396–5

Biennial Report to Congress on the Status of Children in Head Start Programs, FY97, 4584–15

Black Bass Fishing in the U.S., 5506–16.3

Boating Statistics, 1995, 7404–1

Boating Statistics, 1996, 7404–1

Bosnia Peace Operation: Pace of Implementing Dayton Accelerated as International Involvement Increased, 26123–590

Brookhaven National Laboratory: Epidemiologic Surveillance Report for 1993, 3324–7.5

Brookhaven National Laboratory: Epidemiologic Surveillance Report for 1994, 3324–7.5

Brookhaven National Laboratory: Epidemiologic Surveillance Report for 1995, 3324–7.5

Building Foundations. Federal Home Loan Bank of Topeka: 1998 Annual Report of the Affordable Housing Advisory Council, 9304–31

Bureau of Labor Statistics Press Releases, 6726–1

Bureau of Land Management 1998 Annual Report: Your Lands, Your Legacy, 5724–19

Bureau of Reclamation, FY98 Annual Report, 5824–1

Cable Industry Prices, 1998, 9284–27

Can Occupational Labor Shortages Be Identified Using Available Data?, 6722–1.117

Canned Deciduous Fruit Situation in Selected Countries, 1925–34.113

Carcinogens, Annual Report, 4044–15

Carcinogens Report, 8th Edition: Summary, 4048–45

Cases Decided by the U.S. Merit Systems Protection Board, FY98, 9494–2

CBO Memoranda, 26306–8

CBO Papers, 26306–3

CDIE Impact Evaluation Reports, 9916–1

Census of Agriculture. Volume 2, Subject Series, Part 3: Ranking of States and Counties, 1663–2

Census of Agriculture, 1997. Volume 1: Geographic Area Series, 1661–1

Census of Agriculture, 1997. Volume 2. Subject Series, Part 2: Ranking of States and Counties, 2333–3

Census of Manufactures. Industry Series, 2493–1

Census of Retail Trade. Geographic Area Series, 2397–1

Census of Transportation, Communications, and Utilities. Commodity Flow Survey, U.S. (Preliminary), 2575–1

Census of Wholesale Trade. Geographic Area Series, 2405–1

Center for Economic Studies Discussion Papers, 2626–12

Changes in the U.S. Beef Cow-Calf Industry, 1993-97, 1396–5.4

Changes in the U.S. Dairy Industry: 1991-96, 1396–1.2

Changes in the U.S. Pork Industry, 1990-95, 1396–2.3

Checking Accounts: What Do Banks Offer and What Do Consumers Value?, 9373–1.103

Chief Financial Officer's Annual Report, 9624–29

Chief Financial Officer's Annual Report (Audited), 1996, 8434–8

Chief Financial Officer's Annual Report (Audited), 1997, 8434–8

Cognitive Style and Learning: Performance of Adaptors and Innovators in a Novel Dynamic Task, 7506–10.294

Colorado Cooperative Snow Survey Data of Federal-State-Private Cooperative Snow Surveys, Water Year 1995, 1264–14.3

Colorado Cooperative Snow Survey Data of Federal-State-Private Cooperative Snow Surveys, Water Year 1996, 1264–14.3

Colorado Cooperative Snow Survey Data of Federal-State-Private Cooperative Snow Surveys, Water Year 1997, 1264–14.3

Colorado River Basin Study, 5308–41

Combination Vaccines for Childhood Immunization: Recommendations of the Advisory Committee on Immunization Practices (ACIP), the American Academy of Pediatrics (AAP), and the American Academy of Family Physicians (AAFP), 4206–2.171

Commodity Flow Survey, U.S. (Preliminary), 1997. 1997 Economic Census, Transportation, 2575–1

Example 5.2. *American Statistics Index* supp. 5 (June 1999) p. 109 (index by titles). Reprinted by permission of CIS © 1999.

Index by Agency Report Numbers

Agency report number practices vary from agency to agency, and from publication to publication within an agency. Sometimes a number is noted on the publication, sometimes it is not. In the following list an attempt is made to include every agency report number available in the form in which it appears on the publication.

Those publications covered that did not have identifiable assigned numbers are not included in the list.

Boldface numbers in parentheses, before ASI accession numbers in quarterly supplement issues, indicate the 1999 Monthly Supplement abstracts issue number that you should look in to find the text of the referenced abstract.

EXECUTIVE OFFICE OF THE PRESIDENT

NCJ-172873	236–6.4
NCJ-175677	236–6.5

DEPARTMENT OF AGRICULTURE

AC97-A-10	1661–1.10
AC97-A-11	1661–1.11
AC97-A-12	1661–1.12
AC97-A-13	1661–1.13
AC97-A-14	1661–1.14
AC97-A-15	1661–1.15
AC97-A-16	1661–1.16
AC97-S-2	1663–2
AER-760	1528–375
AER-764	1598–308
AgCh 1(99)	1616–1.3
Da 1-2(99)	1627–4
FHORT (nos.)	1925–34
MtAn 1-1(99)	1623–8
MtAn 8(2-99)	1623–11
N186.995	1396–2.1
N200.696	1396–1.1
N201.696	1396–2.2
N206.996	1396–3.1
N211.996	1396–3.2
N231.597	1396–1.4
N233.697	1396–5.1
N235.597	1396–4.1
N238.598	1396–5.4
N246.897	1396–4.2
N247.198	1396–5.3
N280.898	1396–6.1
N281.998	1396–6.2
N298.199	1396–6.3
N212.1196	1396–1.3
N245.1097	1396–1.5
N248.1097	1396–2.3
RBS Res. Rpt. 154	1128–85
Res. Paper RMRS-RP-8	1208–636
SB-959	1641–12
SB-960	1641–26
SB-964	1614–5
SpCr 3(5-99)	1618–28
TB-1859	1548–452
TB-1865	1528–374
TBS-(nos.)	1561–10
VGS-(nos.)	1561–11

DEPARTMENT OF COMMERCE

Census CES 97-15	2626–12.59
Census CES 97-16	2626–12.60
Census CES 97-17	2626–12.61
Census EC97M-3118G	2493–1.39
Census EC97M-3121C	2493–1.50
Census EC97M-3261I	2493–1.204
Census EC97X-CS1	2311–1
Census EC97TV-AK	2573–1.2
Census EC97TV-AL	2573–1.1
Census EC97TV-AR	2573–1.4
Census EC97TV-AZ	2573–1.3
Census EC97TV-CA	2573–1.5
Census EC97TV-CO	2573–1.6
Census EC97TV-CT	2573–1.7
Census EC97TV-DC	2573–1.9
Census EC97TV-DE	2573–1.8
Census EC97TV-FL	2573–1.10
Census EC97TV-GA	2573–1.11
Census EC97TV-HI	2573–1.12
Census EC97TV-IA	2573–1.16
Census EC97TV-ID	2573–1.13
Census EC97TV-IL	2573–1.14
Census EC97TV-IN	2573–1.15
Census EC97TV-KS	2573–1.17
Census EC97TV-KY	2573–1.18
Census EC97TV-LA	2573–1.19
Census EC97TV-MA	2573–1.22
Census EC97TV-MD	2573–1.21
Census EC97TV-ME	2573–1.20
Census EC97TV-MI	2573–1.23
Census EC97TV-MN	2573–1.24
Census EC97TV-MO	2573–1.26
Census EC97TV-MS	2573–1.25
Census EC97TV-MT	2573–1.27
Census EC97TV-NC	2573–1.34
Census EC97TV-ND	2573–1.35
Census EC97TV-NE	2573–1.28
Census EC97TV-NH	2573–1.30
Census EC97TV-NJ	2573–1.31
Census EC97TV-NM	2573–1.32
Census EC97TV-NV	2573–1.29
Census EC97TV-NY	2573–1.33
Census EC97TV-OH	2573–1.36
Census EC97TV-OK	2573–1.37
Census EC97TV-OR	2573–1.38
Census EC97TV-PA	2573–1.39
Census EC97TV-RI	2573–1.40
Census EC97TV-SC	2573–1.41
Census EC97TV-SD	2573–1.42
Census EC97TV-TN	2573–1.43
Census EC97TV-TX	2573–1.44
Census EC97TV-UT	2573–1.45
Census EC97TV-VA	2573–1.47
Census EC97TV-VT	2573–1.46
Census EC97TV-WA	2573–1.48
Census EC97TV-WI	2573–1.50
Census EC97TV-WV	2573–1.49
Census EC97TV-WY	2573–1.51
Census EC97TCF-US(P)	2575–1
Census EC97M31R-NL	2628–10
Census EC97R44A-WY	2397–1.51
Census EC97W42A-WY	2405–1.51
Census OA97-E-7	2597–1
Census P-23, No. 198	2546–2.183
NIST Spec. Pub. 932	2214–7
NOAA TM ERL	
GLERL-107	2148–69

NOAA TR NMFS 138	2168–15
NOAA TR NMFS 139	2168–15

DEPARTMENT OF DEFENSE

IWR Rpt. 98-PS-2	3758–1

DEPARTMENT OF EDUCATION

NCES 1999-179	4826–2.60
PLLI 98-8055	4818–17

DEPARTMENT OF ENERGY

DOE/EH-98006266	3324–7.6
DOE/EH-98007132-Rev.2	3324–7.5
DOE/EH-99001563	3324–7.4
DOE/EH-99001921	3324–7.5
DOE/EIA-0109(yr./nos.)	3162–6
DOE/EIA-0173(98)	3164–29
DOE/EIA-0348(98)/1	3164–11.1
DOE/EIA-0478(98)	3164–65
DOE/EIA-0560(98)	3164–99
DOE/EM-0362	3378–2
DOE/FE-0376-(no.)	3338–16
DOE/FE-0376-1	3338–16.1
DOE/FE-0376-2	3338–16.2
DOE/ID-10430(AK)	3306–7.2
DOE/ID-10430(AL)	3306–7.1
DOE/ID-10430(AR)	3306–7.4
DOE/ID-10430(AZ)	3306–7.3
DOE/ID-10430(CA)	3306–7.5
DOE/ID-10430(State)	3306–7
ER-B-99-08	3006–5.107
PPPL-3337	3324–2.7
SLAC-R-525	3324–2.8

DEPARTMENT OF HEALTH AND HUMAN SERVICES

MMWR Vol.(nos.)/No.	
RR-(nos.)	4206–2
NHSDA Series: H-5	4096–3.7
NHSDA Series: H-8	4096–3.7
NIH 98-0824	4044–16.1
NIH 98-4318	4478–226
OEI-03-98-00490	4006–11.54
PHS 99-1100	4144–1
PHS 99-1250, No. 304	4146–8.304
SMA 98-3200	4096–3.7
SMA 99-3295	4096–3.7

DEPARTMENT OF INTERIOR

BLM-BC-GI-99-	
001+1300	5724–19
BLM-WO-GI-98-	
015+1120	5724–22
FHWAR Rpt. 96-1	5506–16.1
FHWAR Rpt. 96-2	5506–16.2
FHWAR Rpt. 96-3	5506–16.3
USGS Circ. 1144	5666–30.1
USGS Circ. 1150	5666–30.2
USGS Circ. 1151	5666–30.3
USGS Circ. 1155	5666–30.20

Example 5.3. *American Statistics Index* supp. 5 (June 1999) p. 117 (index by agency report numbers). Reprinted by permission of CIS © 1999.

Department of Energy   3164–112.1

Glossary. (p. 292-307).
Previous report, for 1994, is described in ASI
1998 Annual (or 1998 Monthly Supplement 9)
under this number. That report included data on
transmission system capital stock of individual
utilities.
ASI coverage began with report for 1986 (see
ASI 1990 Annual Supplement under this number).

TABLES:
[Data are for 1996, unless otherwise noted.]

**3164–92.1: Wholesale Electricity Transac-
tions**
[Tables show volume and related costs or reve-
nues from firm, nonfirm, and other transfers of
electricity. Data are shown for transactions between investor-owned utilities and all utilities
by ownership type, by NERC region, unless
otherwise noted.]
8-9. Purchases and sales for resale. (p. 19-26)
10. Exchanges. (p. 27)
11. Noninvestor-owned utility exchanges. (p.
29)
12-13. Wheeling by and to investor-owned
utilities. (p. 30-31)
14. Purchases by cooperative borrowers. (p.
32)
15-16. Receipts and deliveries within and between NERC regions [by transaction type,
from all ownership classes combined]. (p. 33-
42)
17. Transactions in Alaska and Hawaii. (p. 43)
18. U.S. trade with Canada [by Province] and
Mexico [not by utility type]. (p. 44)

3164–92.2: Individual Utilities
[Tables show data for individual utilities, arranged by State.]
INVESTOR-OWNED UTILITIES
19-20. Purchases and sales for resale. (p. 46-
103)
21. Exchanges. (p. 104)
22. Purchases not reported to the FERC. (p.
109)
23-24. Wheeling by and to investor-owned
utilities. (p. 110-121)
PUBLIC UTILITIES
25-30. Purchases and sales for resale. FY96.
(p. 123-198)
31. Purchases not reported on Form EIA-412.
(p. 199)
32. Exchanges and wheeling [receipts and
deliveries; value not shown]. (p. 204)
COOPERATIVE UTILITIES
33-34. Purchases by the power supply segment and distribution segment of cooperative
borrowers. (p. 209-238)
35. Purchases not reported to the Rural Utilities Service. (p. 239)
36. Exchanges and wheeling [receipts and
deliveries; value not shown]. (p. 241)

✓ 3164–112   **RENEWABLE ENERGY
ANNUAL 1998, with Data
for 1997**
Annual.   Dec. 1998.
vi+85 p.
DOE/EIA-0603(98)/1.   GPO.
Internet: EIA home page.
ASI/MF/3

Fourth annual report, for 1998, on supply, use,
and trade of renewable energy resources, with
data for selected years 1993-97. Report also covers solar thermal and photovoltaic collectors
manufacture, and geothermal heat pump shipments. Data are primarily from responses of EIA
industry surveys reported on Forms 63A/B and
902, and EIA secondary and private sources.
Contents: highlights, with 1 chart and 1 summary table (p. 1-3); overview, with 11 charts and
40 tables, listed below (p. 5-41); data sources and
limitations, with 3 methodological tables (p. 43-
52); facsimile survey form (p. 53-61); list of Internet addresses (p. 63-69); directory of State energy agencies and utility regulatory commissions
(p. 71-80); and glossary (p. 81-85).
Previous report, for 1997, is described in ASI
1997 Annual under this number.
ASI coverage began with report for 1995 (see
ASI 1996 Annual under 3164-109). Report is
first described under this number in ASI 1997
Annual.

TABLES:
[Renewable energy sources include conventional
hydroelectric, geothermal, biomass, solar thermal and photovoltaic, wind, municipal solid
waste and landfill gas, and wood and wood waste.
End-use sectors are residential and commercial, industrial, transportation, government, and
electric utility.]

**3164–112.1: Renewable Energy Use and
Equipment Manufacture**
OVERVIEW
[Data are for 1993-97, unless otherwise noted.
Tables 1-8 show data by renewable energy
source.]
1. U.S. [total] energy consumption by energy
source. (p. 5)
2. Renewable energy consumption by [select-
ed] sector. (p. 7)
3. [Industrial and electric utility] renewable
energy consumption for electricity generation
[and imports and exports]. (p. 8)
4. [Industrial and electric utility] electricity
generation from renewable energy [and imports and exports]. (p. 9)
5-6. Renewable electric utility net and
nonutility gross generation [by State], 1997.
(p. 10-11)
7. U.S. electric generating capacity [and from
nonrenewable sources]. (p. 12)
8. Biomass energy consumption by [selected]
sector and census region. (p. 13)
9. Residential wood energy consumption
[quantity and Btu, by census region], 1997. (p.
14)
10. U.S. utility net electric generation from
solar energy [by selected utility], 1997. (p. 18)
11. Annual photovoltaic [cells and modules],
and solar thermal [collectors] shipments,
1978-97. (p. 19)

SOLAR THERMAL COLLECTOR SHIPMENTS
[Data are for 1996-97, unless otherwise noted.]
12. Annual [total, import, and export] shipments [and number of companies], 1987-97.
(p. 20)
13. Annual shipments [and average per manu-
facturer] by type, 1987-97. (p. 21)
14. Shipments ranked by top 5 [domestic] origins and destinations [and percents of U.S. to-
tal]. (p. 21)
15. Shipments by [State and outlying area]
destination [and total exports], 1997. (p. 22)
16. [Percent] distribution of U.S. exports by
country, 1997. (p. 23)
17. Distribution of shipments [to wholesale
and retail distributors, exporters, installers,
and end users and others]. (p. 23)
18. Quantity, value, and average price [of
shipments, by type of collector]. (p. 25)
19. Shipments by market sector, end use, and
type. (p. 26)
20. Shipments of complete systems [and number of companies and value of systems]. (p. 26)
21. Number of companies expecting to introduce new products [by type], 1998. (p. 27)
22. Percent of shipments by the 10 largest
companies, 1987-97. (p. 27)
23. Companies involved in solar thermal activities by type. (p. 28)

PHOTOVOLTAIC MODULES AND CELLS
[Data are for 1995-97, unless otherwise noted.]
24. [Companies, by] solar-related sales as a
percentage of total sales, 1996-97. (p. 28)
25. Annual shipments. (p. 28)
26. Annual [total, import, and export] shipments [and number of companies], 1986-97.
(p. 29)
27. Distribution of [shipments to wholesale
and retail distributors, exporters, installers,
end users, module manufacturers, and others].
(p. 30)
28. Shipments by type. (p. 30)
29. [Value and average price of] shipments by
type, 1996-97. (p. 31)
30. Shipments by market [end-use] sector,
[specific] end use, and type, 1996-97. (p. 32)
31. Export shipments by type, 1996-97. (p.
33)
32. Destination of U.S. export shipments by
country, 1997. (p. 34)
33. Shipments [and value] of complete [mo-
dule] systems. (p. 35)
34. [Person-years] employment [and number
of companies] in the photovoltaic manufacturing industry, 1991-97. (p. 35)
35. Companies expecting to introduce new
products [by type] in 1998. (p. 35)
36. Number of companies involved in photo-
voltaic-related activities [by type], 1996-97.
(p. 35)

GEOTHERMAL HEAT PUMPS
37-38. Shipments and capacities by model
type, 1994-97. (p. 38)
39. Shipments by census region, and [exports,
by] model type, 1996-97. (p. 39)
40. Shipments [to wholesale and retail distributors, installers, end users, and others] by
model type, 1996-97. (p. 40)

Example 5.4. *American Statistics Index* supp. 1 (June 1999) p. 19 (abstracts).
Reprinted by permission of CIS © 1999.

Index by Subjects and Names

Media

Market research
Food (kosher) foreign market conditions in selected countries, 1994-98, 1928-14
Food advertising nutrition claims, health warning disclosures, and consumer perceptions, 1997, 9406-1.68
see also Consumer surveys
Market shares
see Economic concentration and diversification
Marketing
see also Advertising
see also Agricultural marketing
see also Competition
see also Consumer protection
see also Consumer surveys
see also Direct marketing
see also Economic concentration and diversification
see also Market research
see also Packaging and containers
see also Price regulation
see also Prices
see also Retail trade
see also Wholesale trade
see also under names of specific commodities or commodity groups
Marketing quotas
see Agricultural production quotas and price supports
Marriage and divorce
see also Births out of wedlock
see also Families and households
see also under By Marital Status in the "Index by Categories"
Marshes
see Wetlands
Martin, Frank D.
"Developing the Capital Market in Kenya and Morocco", 9916-1.95
Maryland
Farm finances and other characteristics, and agricultural sales and trade, with summary economic indicators by metro-nonmetro location, 1998 State fact sheet, 1546-6.65
Medicaid reimbursement of hospitals, State allocations of low-income patient share adjustments by hospital type, for 6 States, FY96, GAO rpt, 26121-768
Population, migration, employment, income, and infant mortality, for Appalachia by State and county, 1990-97, 9088-45
Trucks, by detailed characteristics and type of product carried, 1997 survey, State rpt, 2573-1.21
Water quality and pollution in streams and lakes, and environmental and health impacts, 1992-95, 5666-30.16
Water quality and pollution in streams and lakes, and environmental and health impacts, 1992-96, 5666-30.14
Watermelon production, acreage, shipments, prices and arrivals by city, by State, 1998, annual rpt, 1311-35
see also Baltimore, Md.
see also under By State in the "Index by Categories"
Mass media
Asia financial crisis, stock returns relation to economic news items, for 9 countries, 1990-98, technical paper, 9366-7.488
see also Advertising
see also Motion pictures

see also Newspapers
see also Periodicals
see also Radio
see also Television
Mass transit
see Airlines
see Buses
see Railroads
see Subways
see Urban transportation
Massachusetts
Farm finances and other characteristics, and agricultural sales and trade, with summary economic indicators by metro-nonmetro location, 1998 State fact sheet, 1546-6.66
Trucks, by detailed characteristics and type of product carried, 1997 survey, State rpt, 2573-1.22
Water quality and pollution in streams and lakes, and environmental and health impacts, 1992-95, 5666-30.20
see also Boston, Mass.
see also Cape Cod, Mass.
see also Lawrence, Mass.
see also Worcester, Mass.
see also under By State in the "Index by Categories"
Maternity
Developing countries maternal and child health and nutrition programs, AID evaluations, working paper series, 9916-26
DOE contractor facility workers, injuries, illnesses, and absences, by sex, age, occupation, and diagnosis, annual site rpt series, 3324-7
Drug, alcohol, and cigarette use, by selected characteristics, 1997 survey, annual rpt, 4096-3.7
Parity, reproduction rates, and other characteristics of births, 1993, US Vital Statistics annual rpt, 4144-1
see also Birth defects
see also Births
see also Births out of wedlock
see also Birthweight
see also Breast-feeding
see also Family planning
see also Fertility
see also Infant mortality
see also Midwives
see also Obstetrics and gynecology
see also Prenatal care
see also Teenage pregnancy
Maternity benefits
see also Women, Infants, and Children (WIC) Special Supplemental Food Program
Mathematic models and modeling
see also Economic and econometric models
Mathematics
Compensatory education activities and participation, and student achievement, by program and grade, 1991-92, annual rpt, 4804-44
Discrimination in education, enrollment and performance indicators by student characteristics, and Education Dept enforcement activities, 1971-96, 11046-9.1
Higher education engineering enrollment, persistence, and outcomes, and student and instn characteristics, by sex, 1982-93, 4818-17

Minority group, women, and disabled persons employment and education in science and engineering, by field and other characteristics, 1980s-96, biennial rpt, 9624-20
R&D funding by Fed Govt, total and for higher education instns, by field and agency, FY70s-97, annual rpt, 9627-37
R&D funding by source and performer, and science and technology employment, by field, 1950s-98, 9627-34
see also Computer sciences
Mattrick, Keith
"Trends in Public Infrastructure Spending", 26306-3.171
Mays, R. W.
"Southeastern U.S. Deepwater Reef Fish Assemblages, Habitat Characteristics, Catches, and Life History Summaries", 2168-158
McCormick, Alexander C.
"Credit Production and Progress Toward the Bachelor's Degree: An Analysis of Postsecondary Transcripts for Beginning Students at 4-Year Institutions. Postsecondary Education Descriptive Analysis Reports", 4826-2.60
McGuckin, Tom
"Water Management Study: Upper Rio Grande Basin", 5308-40
McLaughlin, Diane K.
"Do Rural Youth Attain Their Educational Goals?", 1502-7.102
McLean, Garnet A.
"Aircraft Evacuations onto Escape Slides and Platforms II: Effects of Exit Size", 7506-10.292
Measures
see Industrial standards
see Instruments and measuring devices
see Weights and measures
Meat and meat products
Agriculture census, 1997: farms, farmland, production, finances, and operator characteristics, by county, State rpt series, 1661-1
Consumption per capita of meat, 1980-99, annual rpt, 1614-5.1
Production, prices, receipts, and disposition for meat animals, by species and State, 1993-97, 1641-12
Production, prices, receipts, and disposition for meat animals, by species and State, 1998, annual rpt, 1623-8
Retail trade economic census, 1997: establishments, employment, sales, and payroll, by NAICS 3- to 7-digit kind of business, MSA, county, and city, State rpt series, 2397-1
Wholesale trade economic census, 1997: establishments, employment, finances, and operations, by NAICS 3- to 8-digit kind of business, MSA, county, and city, State rpt series, 2405-1
see also Oils, oilseeds, and fats
see also Poultry industry and products
Mecklenburg County, N.C.
Water quality, chemistry, hydrology, and other characteristics, 1998 local area study, 5666-27.83
Media
see Mass media

Example 5.5. *American Statistics Index* supp. 5 (June 1999) p. 61 (index by subjects and names). Reprinted by permission of CIS © 1999.

Animal and Plant Science

9725014:   14th Annual Meeting of the Aquaculture Association of Canada

10-13 Jun 1997

Quebec (Canada)

Sponsor: Ministry of Agriculture, Fisheries, and Food; Department of Fisheries and Oceans

ORDERING NFORMATION: Aquaculture Association of Canada, PO Box 1987, St. Andrews N.B., Canada E0G 2X0. Phone: 506-529-4766; Fax: 506-529-4609, Full papers available.

98-000002. Future of breed improvement programs with fish and fish farming. *Gall, G.A.E.* (Univ. California, Davis, CA, USA).

98-000003. Transgenic fish: Balancing the potential and the problems associated with implementation into aquaculture. *Devlin, R.H.; Biagi, C.A.; Smailus, D.E.* (Fisheries and Oceans Canada, West Vancouver Lab., West Vancouver, B.C., Canada, V7V 1N6).

98-000004. Consumer perceptions of genetically engineered food products. *Hallman, W.f.* (Dep. Human Ecology, Cook Coll. Rutgers Univ., New Brunswick, NJ 08903-0231, USA).

98-000005. Walleye culture in Ontario: Pond production methods. *Flowers, D.D.* (Ontario Minstry Natural Resources, While Lake Fish Culture Stn., Sharbot Lake, Ontario, K0H 2P0).

98-000006. Intensive culture of walleye. *Summerfelt, R.C.* (Dep. Animal Ecology, Iowa State Univ., Ames, IA 50011-3221, USA).

98-000007. Selective breeding of walleye: Building block for closed system aquaculture. *Mille: _.M.; Hove, M.; Senanan, W.; Kapuscinski, A.R.* (Dep. Veterinary PathoBol.. Univ. Minnesota, St. Paul, MN, USA).

98-000008. Yield - Maximazing stocking density of 'curimbata', *Prochilodus marggravil,* for fishculture. *Paixao, A.M.* (1 Aquae Consultoria em Aqueicultura e Desenvolvimento Ambiental Ltda, Condominio Retiro das Pedras, Rua Ipe Roxo nc. 2, Belo Horizonte, MG, Brasil).

98-000009. Current status and future outlook of global salmon markets: Implications for canadian salmon farmers. *Kenney, E.A.* (Kenney and Associates, Vancouve: 3C, B6J 3K1).

98-000010. Marketing in the face of competition. *Barnett, J.* (Canadian Association Fish Exporters, Ottawa, Ontario, Canada K2C 0P8).

98-000011. Competing successfully in the US retail market. *Kramm, J.*

98-000012. Competing successfully in the US food service market. *Hennessey, F.* ((Red Lobster and Olive Garden Restaurants) Darden Restau-

Example 5.6. *Conference Papers Index* vol. 26, no. 1 (Jan. 1998) p. 1 (arranged by subject and conference). Reprinted by permission of Cambridge Scientific Abstracts; © Cambridge Scientific Abstracts 1998. All rights reserved.

ACC-synthase antisense tomato fruit, Inhibition of 98-002130
(Acerinae, Percidae) and first report of an unusual 98-004944
Acetabularia acetabulum, *KURKKU* may encode a stable 98-001739
Acetabularia acetabulum, Nightstick may encode an 98-001704
acetabulum, *KURKKU* may encode a stable cytoplasmic 98-001739
acetabulum, Nightstick may encode an activator of 98-001704
Acetaldehyde and ethanol on postharvest physiology of 98-004751
Acetate for advancing ovulation in cyclic mares 98-006247
Acetate in rats, rabbits, horses, pigs and flounders after 98-001164
Acetate increases anthracyclines activity on canine breast 98-001086
Acetate, Sustained-release bioadhesive lozenge containing 98-006081
Acetate (TA), Controlled enhancement of drug incorporation 98-006344
Acetolactate synthase inhibitor LGC-40863, Toxicokinetics 98-001375
Acetyl-Coenzyme A carboxylase, Link between light and fatty 98-001730
Acetylcholine-activated potassium channel in chronic 98-007713
Acetylcholine alters cyclic AMP, cyclic GMP and O_2 98-007984
Acetylcholine and nitroglycerin as assessed by continuous 98-009377
Acetylcholine, Frequency of provoked coronary arterial spasm 98-008902
Acetylcholine? Immunodetection of acetylcholinesterase and 98-002265
Acetylcholine in patients with coronary artery 98-008308
Acetylcholine increase during the progression of heart 98-008363
Acetylcholine-induced release of nitric oxide is impaired 98-006996
Acetylcholine-induced vasoconstriction of epicardial 98-006998
Acetylcholine relates with the long-term prognosis of 98-009360
Acetylcholine to ergonovine test in patients with rest 98-009456
Acetylcholinesterase and acetylcholine receptor in leaf 98-002265
Acetylsalicylic acid (ASA) versus molsidomine in PTCA - A 98-009202
Acetyltransferase by CDPK, Regulation of recombinant soybean 98-002822
Acid (13-OTDA) converted from alpha-linolenic acid via 98-002377
Acid/5-hydroxyferulic acid *O*-methyltransferase gene 98-003007
Acid 8' hydroxylase activity, *In vitro* assay for 98-001689
Acid A on taxane biosynthesis in yew cuttings, Effect of 98-001468
Acid a risk factor for all-cause and coronary mortality? 98-009298
Acid accumulation, Activation of plant defenses and 98-002893
Acid activation of slow anion channels in *Vicia faba* 98-002869
Acid, Activity and metabolism of 8',8',8'-trideuteroabscisic 98-002242
Acid after heart transplantation, Immunosuppressive effects 98-007658
Acid after local delivery in porcine coronary 98-006942
Acid analogues, Inhibition of cultured roots by jasmonic 98-002280
Acid analysis using precolumn derivatization with 98-001817
Acid and indole-3-acetic acid in *Pisum sativum* 98-002212
Acid and its physiological role in *Dunaliella* 98-002260
Acid and lipid metabolism in marine fish embryos and 98-000046
Acid and oxalate-producing fungi, Expression of oxalate 98-002593
Acid and poly(N-vinyl pyrrolidone), Release properties of 98-006019
Acid and the inhibition of endothelial activation: An 98-009163
Acid as modifying agents, Controlled release formulations of 98-006244
Acid (ASA) versus molsidomine in PTCA - A double-blind 98-009202
Acid assimilating enzymes of tomato fruits during 98-001762
Acid based biopolymers, Ricinoleic acid based 98-006148
Acid beta-oxidation alters Arabidopsis inflorescence 98-002381
Acid-binding protein as early marker of acute myocardial 98-007907
Acid binding protein type II suggests a mechanism of 98-006852
Acid biosynthesis in animals, Transformation of tomato with 98-002982
Acid biosynthesis in maize, Tryptophan-independent 98-002200
Acid biosynthesis in microspore-derived embryos of 98-002244
Acid biosynthesis in tobacco, Benzaldehyde as an 98-002589
Acid biosynthesis, VP14 of maize catalyzes the carotenoid 98-002243
Acid carriers in *Ricinus communis*, Expression analysis 98-002403
Acid characterization of different lipid fractions for 98-003928
Acid, Charge density study of 98-006902
Acid:CoA-ligase genes and their roles in the biosynthesis 98-002329
Acid content of *Larrea tridentata* and *Hilaria* 98-002773

Example 5.7. *Conference Papers Index* vol. 26, no. 1 (Jan. 1998) p. su-1 (subject index). Reprinted by permission of Cambridge Scientific Abstracts; © Cambridge Scientific Abstracts 1998. All rights reserved.

Abrahamsson, B. 98-006058,
    98-006059,98-006060,98-006061,
    98-006062
Abrahamsson, P. 98-007429,
    98-007431
Abramov, D. 98-007094
Abramov, Yu.A. 98-006455,
    98-006901
Abrams, G.D. . 98-001604,98-001635,
    98-001689,98-002135,98-002244
Abrams, S. 98-002280
Abrams, S.R. .. 98-001635,98-001690,
    98-002244
Abreu, M.C. 98-009551
Abrysch, F. 98-007465,98-008442,
    98-009372
Absolon, R.F. 98-000830
Abt, G. 98-003115
Abtew, W. 98-004677
Abu-Hamdeh, N.H. 98-004183
Abu-Zreig, M. 98-004652
Abulaban, A. 98-004454
Acar, C. 98-007921,98-007922
Acar, J. 98-008587
Acar, P. 98-008821,98-008827
Acedo, M.S. 98-009292
Aceituno, E. 98-008001
Acevedo, M. 98-008091
Achakri, H. 98-007217
Achenbach, K. 98-007830
Achenbach, S. 98-008343,
    98-008345,98-008680,98-008715,
    98-009000
Achenbachd, K. 98-007961
Acher, R. 98-004835
Achilli, F. 98-008243
Achremczyk, P. 98-007608
Achuta, S. 98-002056
Acker, W. 98-000700
Ackerman, S. ... 98-002767,98-002768
Ackermann, K. 98-007228,
    98-007229,98-007230
Acock, B. 98-002531
Acogido, G. 98-004844
Acs, F. 98-010713
Acuna, E. 98-004836,98-004837,
    98-004838
Adechi, O. 98-006676
Adachi, T. 98-002079,98-008884
Adam, A. 98-008123
Adam, J.F. 98-009091
Adam, L. 98-003017
Adamantidis, M. 98-009190
Adambounou, L.T. 98-000092
Adamian, K.G. 98-007167
Adamidi, C. 98-003051
Adamopoulos, S. 98-008385,
    98-008958,98-009223
Adamopoulou, C. 98-003116
Adamowicz, E. 98-009457
Adamowicz, M. 98-007858
Adams, H. 98-001720,98-002658,

Adeniyi, R. 98-000099,98-000100,
    98-000101,98-000102,98-000103,
    98-000491
Adenwalla, S. 98-006517
Adewale, A.S. 98-004847
Adewolu, M.A. 98-000063
Adeyeye, C.M. 98-006025
Adgey, A.A.J. 98-007471
Adhiya, J. 98-002003
Adina, B. 98-001588
Adjou, K.T. 98-001411
Adkison, M. 98-000492
Adkison, M.A. 98-000204
Adler, A. 98-007753
Adler, J. 98-005960
Adler, K. 98-003117
Adler, Y. 98-008649,98-008984
Adlercreutz, H. 98-007382,
    98-008303
Adnagulov, E.V. 98-003118
Adnot, S. 98-008308,98-008921
Adolph, S.A. 98-003644
Adolph, S.C. 98-004840,98-005529
Adomi, A. 98-010140
Adragao, P. 98-008210,98-008634
Adzamli, K. 98-008668
Aebersold, P. 98-005192
Aebi, U. 98-006960
Aebischer, N. 98-008230
Aerts, A. 98-007728,98-007730,
    98-007731
Aerts, J.-M.P. 98-004706
Aerts, M.A.E. 98-001236
Aerts, P. 98-003416,98-003807
Aeschbacher, B. 98-009269
Aeschbacher, B.C. 98-008237,
    98-008795
Aessopos, A. 98-009586
Aevarsson, A. 98-006621
Affrime, M.B. 98-008888
Afzal, T.M. 98-004443
Agabiti Rosei, E. 98-007990
Agabiti-Rosei, E. 98-007687,
    98-008283,98-008816
Agamalian, M. .. 98-006458,98-006526
Agapitos, E. 98-009583
Agapitos, N. 98-009587
Agapov, A.A. 98-008657
Agarie, S. 98-002507,98-002509,
    98-003004
Agarwal, R. 98-007555
Agassian, A. 98-003119,98-003120
Agate, G. 98-009744
Agee, C.S. 98-001831,98-001832
Ageev, F. 98-009102
Ageeva, M.V. 98-001472
Agelopoulos, G. 98-009272
Ageyeva, N.V. 98-008613
Aggelakas, S. .. 98-007777,98-006806,
    98-009609
Aggeli, C. 98-007279,98-008356,
    98-008686,98-008687,98-008986,
    98-009316,98-009513

Example 5.8. *Conference Papers Index* vol. 26, no. 1 (Jan. 1998) p. au-1 (author index). Reprinted by permission of Cambridge Scientific Abstracts; © Cambridge Scientific Abstracts 1998. All rights reserved.

Aarnio, Aulis. "Law and Action: Reflections on Collective Legal Actions" in *Actions, Norms, Values*, Meggle, Georg (ed), 37-54. Hawthorne, de Gruyter, 1999.

This paper deals with collegial judicial decisions as a form of human action. The scope is limited to three questions: (i) What are the structure and status of the general theory of action? (ii) Is this theory applicable to such performative acts as judicial decisions? (iii) Are the 'actions' of collective agents actions in the proper sense? The author defends the thesis that general theory of action is applicable not only to individual, but also to collective actions; difficulties are not due to the structure of that theory or to its "individualistic character", but to the notion of a "collective will". This kind of "will" is epistemologically always a result of political procedures, and to speak of the "collective will" presupposes the analysis of these procedures.

Abad, Manuel and Fernandez, Alicia and Meske, Nelli. Free Boolean Correlation Lattices. *Rep Math Log*, 30, 3-11, 1996.

In this paper we study some algebraic properties of the variety of Boolean correlation lattices. We give a characterization of congruences and simple algebras of the variety and we describe the algebra with a finite set of free generators.

Abbey, Ruth. Mediocrity Versus Meritocracy: Nietzsche's (Mis) Reading of Chamfort. *Hist Polit Thought*, 19(3), 457-483, Autumn 98.

This article challenges the claim that Friedrich Nietzsche is a good reader of the French moralist, Chamfort, when it comes to Chamfort's politics. Chamfort is a meritocrat rather than the bitter egalitarian Nietzsche portrays him to be. Moreover, the moralist's meritocratic beliefs, his hopes for a new social order and the emergence of a new aristocracy resemble many of Nietzsche's own values. Had Nietzsche read Chamfort as a meritocrat, he could have found much to stimulate and clarify his own thoughts about the aristocracy of the future.

Abbott, Barbara. Water = H2O. *Mind*, 108(429), 145-148, Ja 99.

This paper defends the position that water is H2O. La Porte in 1998 points out that many kinds (babies, tomatoes) contain a higher proportion of water than the Great Salt Lake, yet we do not call them 'water'. I reply that this is because babies, tomatoes, etc. form separate kinds of things, which the nonwater parts are crucial in constituting, while the nonwater parts of the Great Salt Lake are simply impurities. The alternative view must either deny the truth that babies have a high proportion of water in them, or must make the unsupported claim that 'water' is ambiguous.

Abe, Jair Minoro. Some Recent Applications of Paraconsistent Systems to AI. *Log Anal*, 40(157), 83-96, Ja-Mr 97.

In this paper we present some applications of paraconsistent logics that are being established powerfully over the past years. This work does not intend to be complete, nor go to in technical details, restricting and focusing primarily some developments made recently.

Abe, Masao and Fredericks, James L (trans). The Problem of "Inverse Correspondence" in the Philosophy of Nishida: Comparing Nishida with Tanabe. *Int Phil Quart*, 39(1), 59-76, Mr 99.

Abram, David. Nature at Arm's Length. *Res Phil Technol*, 15, 177-180, 1995.

Abram, David and Light, Andrew and Lovekin, David (& others). Discussion of David Rothenberg's *Hand's End*. *Res Phil Technol*, 15, 199-207, 1995.

Abrusci, V Michele and Maringelli, Elena. A New Correctness Criterion for Cyclic Proof Nets. *J Log Lang Info*, 7(4), 449-459, O 98.

We define proof nets for cyclic multiplicative linear logic as edge bicolored graphs. Our characterization is purely graph theoretical and works without further complication for proof nets with cuts, which are usually harder to handle in the noncommutative case. This also provides

Example 5.9. *The Philosopher's Index* vol. 33, no. 2 (second quarter 1999) p. 151 (author index). Reprinted by permission of Philosopher's Information Center, © 1999.

A PRIORI
see also Synthetic A Priori
"Devitt's Naturalism: A Priori Resistence to the A Priori?" in *The Maribor Papers in Naturalized Semantics*, Jutronic-Tihomirovic, Dunja (ed). Rey, Georges.
"Is Logical Space an A Priori Framework of the Life-World?" in *Phenomenology: Japanese and American Perspectives*, Hopkins, Burt C (ed). Okamoto, Yukiko.
"Responses to the Maribor Papers" in *The Maribor Papers in Naturalized Semantics*, Jutronic-Tihomirovic, Dunja (ed). Devitt, Michael.
A Defence of Teaching General Thinking Skills. Higgins, Steven and Baumfield, Vivienne.
Do Locke's Arguments against Innate Ideas Apply to Kant's Doctrine of the *A Priori*?. Klaassen, Johann A.
Historicismo y apriorismo. Montero, Fernando.
On Wright's Characterization on *The A Priori*. Fred, Ivette.
Persons and Bodies. Corcoran, Kevin J.
¿Es la teoría del lenguaje de Humboldt una alternativa a la filosofía de su época?. Navarro Pérez, Jorge.

ABDUCTION
Abductive Anti-Realism: Saving the Technology. Richmond, Alasdair M.
Between Abduction and the Deep Blue Sea. Richmond, Alasdair M.
Hermeneutical Philosophy and Pragmatism: A Philosophy of Science. Heelan, Patrick A.

ABE, M
The Problem of "Inverse Correspondence" in the Philosophy of Nishida: Comparing Nishida with Tanabe. Abe, Masao and Fredericks, James L (trans).

ABELARD
Die angesehene Meinung: Studien zum *endoxon* im Mittelalter. Von Moos, Peter.
Evolution, Sociobiology, and the Atonement. Williams, Patricia A.
On the Dating of Abailard's *Dialogus*: A Reply to Mews. Allen, Julie A.

ABORIGINAL
La cuestión indígena y la reforma constitucional en México. Blanco Fornieles, Víctor.

ABORTION
"Abortion Bypass? A New Technology and an Old Debate" in *Technology, Morality and Social Policy*, Hudson, Yeager (ed). Mahowald, Mary B.
"State-Sponsored Abortion in a Property Rights Framework" in *Technology, Morality and Social Policy*, Hudson, Yeager (ed). Rowan, John.
Nature et personne. Baertschi, Bernard.
Understanding the 'Conservative' View on Abortion. Wendler, Dave.

ABRAM, D
Feet on the Ground: Responses to *Hand's End*. Rothenberg, David.

ABSOLUTE
Absolute Idealism. Sprigge, Timothy L S.
Being Hegelian After Danto. Hilmer, Brigitte.
Husserl et l'absolu du Monde en phénoménologie. Paquette, Éric.
The Viewpoint of No-One in Particular. Fine, Arthur.
~~Why Everything Is Not Relative. Siegel, Harvey.~~

ABSOLUTISM
Conceptual Relativism. Brueckner, Anthony.
Toward a Credible Form of Moral Absolutism: Or How to Derive Moral Absolutism from Consequentialism (Together with a Relevant Theory of Human Value). Haber, Joram Graf.

ABSTRACT
Heidegger and 'The Way of Art': The Empty Origin and Contemporary Abstraction. Fóti, Véronique M.

ABSTRACT ENTITY
Cuestiones abiertas en el Platonismo de Gödel: La contraversia Chihara-Maddy. Caba, Antonio.

Example 5.10. *The Philosopher's Index* vol. 33, no. 2 (second quarter 1999) p. 1 (subject index). Reprinted by permission of Philosopher's Information Center, © 1999.

Ach, J (ed) and Quante, M (ed). *Brain Death and Organ Transplantation*. Stuttgart, Frommann-Holzboog, 1997.
Leist, Anton. *Bioethics*, 13(1), 69-73, Ja 99.

Adler, Franklin Hugh. *Italian Industrialists from Liberalism to Fascism: The Political Development of the Industrial Bourgeoisie, 1906-1934*. New York, Cambridge Univ Pr, 1995.
Gottfried, Paul. *Telos*, 107, 196-200, Spr 96.
Woods, Dwayne. *Telos*, 105, 159-164, Fall 95.

Adorno, Theodor W. *Frankfurter Adorno Blätter (Theodor W. Adorno Archiv, Bd. IV)*. München, Adorno Archiv, 1995.
Wagner, Gerhard. *Z Krit Theor*, 3, 132-134, 1996.

Adorno, Theodor W and Weber Nicholson, Shierry (trans). *Hegel: Three Studies*. Cambridge, MIT Pr, 1993.
Harris, H S. *Phil Soc Sci*, 29(1), 155-157, Mr 99.

Aertsen, Jan A. *Medieval Philosophy and the Transcendentals: The Case of Thomas Aquinas*. Leiden, E J Brill, 1996.
Tomarchio, John. *Thomist*, 63(1), 146-151, Ja 99.

Aguirre, Mariano. *Los días del futuro—La sociedad internacional en la era de la globalización*. Barcelona, Icaria-Antrazyt, 1993.
Piris, Alberto. *Rev Int Filosof Polit*, 9, 173-177, Je 97.

Aguirre Oraa, Jose Maria. *Raison critique ou Raison herméneutique? Une analyse de la controverse entre Habermas et Gadamer*. Paris, Cerf, 1998.
Schouwey, Jacques. *Rev Theol Phil*, 130(4), 448-449, 1998.

Aguirre Sala, Jorge F. *Ética del placer*. México, Univ Iberoamericana, 1994.
Soto, Diego. *Estud de Filosof*, 10, 183-186, Ag 94.

Akama, Seiki (ed). *Logic, Language and Computation*. Dordrecht, Kluwer, 1997.
Abbott, Barbara. *Phil in Rev*, 18(5), 313-314, O 98.

Alba Rico, Santiago. *Las Reglas del Caos*. Barcelona, Ed Anagrama, 1995.
Rendueles, César. *An Seminar Metaf*, 31, 251-253, 1997.

Alighieri, Dante, Imbach, Ruedi (ed) and Ricklin, Thomas (ed & trans). *Das Gastmahl: 1. und 2. Buch, italienisch-deutsch: Philosophische Werke 4/I u. II*. Hamburg, Meiner, 1996.
Rudolph, Enno. *Arch Gesch Phil*, 80(2), 224-226, 1998.

Allen, R E (ed & trans). *The Dialogues of Plato, Volume III: Ion, Hippias Minor, Laches, Protagoras*. New Haven, Yale Univ Pr, 1996.
Gocer, A. *Ancient Phil*, 18(2), 473-477, Fall 98.

Allison, Henry E. *Idealism and Freedom: Essays on Kant's Theoretical and Practical Philosophy*. New York, Cambridge Univ Pr, 1996.
Wood, Allen W. *Phil Rev*, 106(4), 601-605, O 97.

Almond, Brenda. *Exploring Ethics: A Traveller's Tale*. Cambridge MA, Blackwell, 1998.
Kupperman, Joel J. *J Applied Phil*, 16(1), 103-105, 1999.

Alston, William P. *A Realist Conception of Truth*. Ithaca, Cornell Univ Pr, 1996.
Bertolet, Rod. *Dialogue (Canada)*, 37(3), 648-650, Sum 98.
Schmitt, Frederick F. *Phil Rev*, 106(4), 617-619, O 97.

Altham, J E J (ed) and Harrison, Ross (ed). *World, Mind, and Ethics: Essays on the Ethical Philosophy of Bernard Williams*. New York, Cambridge Univ Pr, 1995.
Skorupski, John. *Phil Rev*, 106(4), 579-583, O 97.

Example 5.11. *The Philosopher's Index* vol. 33, no. 2 (second quarter 1999) p. 301 (book review index). Reprinted by permission of Philosopher's Information Center, © 1999.

Aavitsland P. Bioterrorisme—trussel og beredskap.
Tidsskr Nor Laegeforen 1999 May 10;119(12):1730
(Nor)
Aaziz R, Tepfer M. Recombination in RNA viruses and in
virus–resistant transgenic plants. J Gen Virol 1999 Jun;80
(Pt 6):1339–46 (85 ref.)
Abad A, Baraia–Etxaburu J, Muñoz J, Santamaría JM.
Enfermedad de Kikuchi en un paciente con síndrome de
la inmunodeficiencia adquirida.
Enferm Infecc Microbiol Clin 1999 Apr;17(4):193–4
(Spa)
Abad A, Baraia–Etxaburu J, Zubero Z, Santamaría JM.
Neumonía por Bordetella bronchiseptica y síndrome de
inmunodeficiencia adquirida. Rev Clin Esp 1999 May;
199(5):330–1 (10 ref.)
(Spa)
Abad C see Martinez C
Abad C see Pastor MT
Abad MJ, Bermejo P, Gonzales E, Iglesias I, Irurzun A,
Carrasco L. Antiviral activity of Bolivian plant extracts.
Gen Pharmacol 1999 Apr;32(4):499–503
Abad MJ, Bermejo P, Sanchez Palomino S, Chiriboga X,
Carrasco L. Antiviral activity of some South American
medicinal plants. Phytother Res 1999 Mar;13(2):142–6
Abad P see Piotte C
Abad V see Weise M
Abad Díez JM see Siles Gutiérrez M
Abad–Zapatero C see Schluckebier G
Abade A see Alvarez M
Abade A see Manco L
Abadeh S see Tse WY
Abades J see Puebla G
Abaïtova NE see Karpov NIu
Abajo P see Vargas–Díez E
Abakumova OIu see Lokhov PG
Aballa TC see Lynne CM
Abanes–De Mello A see Pogliano J
Abásolo Galdós RM, Aizpuru Barandiarán F, Mar Medina
J, Ruiz de Gauna López de Heredia R, Domingo Rico C.
Hipertensión de bata blanca e hipertensión non–dippers en
pacientes recientemente diagnosticados de hipertensión
arterial ligera. Aten Primaria 1999 Apr 15;23(6):332–8 (Eng.
Abstr.)
(Spa)
Abass MT see Youssef SK
Abassi O see Bouderka MA
Abastado JP see Rovira P
Abatangelo G see Leonardi A
Abatangelo G see Tavolini IM
Abate B see Liu C
Abate G see Di Iorio A
Abate J see Tetzlaff JE
Abate L see Cantrell CL
Abate M see Corsetti MT
Abate N see Chandalia M
Abati A see Fetsch PA
Abati A see Gamelin E
Abba R see Albani G
Al–Abbad AJ, Malleson PN, Petty RE, Cabral DA. Apparent
medium vessel vasculitis associated with a spinal
meningioma [letter] J Rheumatol 1999 May;26(5):1211–2
Abbal M see Cantagrel A
Abbal M see Rostaing L
Abballe X see Namour F
Abbara S see Müller BT
Abbas F see Van Winkelhoff AJ
Abbas NA, Pitt MA, Green AT, Solomon LR. Successful
treatment of hepatitis B virus (HBV)–associated
membranoproliferative glomerulonephritis (MPGN) with
alpha interferon. Nephrol Dial Transplant 1999 May;
14(5):1272–5
Abbas S see Khan P
Abbasi K. Free the slaves [editorial] BMJ 1999 Jun 12;
318(7198):1568–9
Abbasi S see Cole CH

Example 5.12. *Index Medicus* vol. 40 no. 9 part 2
(Sept. 1999), p. 2269 (author section). Reprinted
courtesy of National Library of Medicine.

ABNORMALITIES

CHEMICALLY INDUCED see ABNORMALITIES, DRUG-INDUCED

DIAGNOSIS

MULTISCAN—a Scandinavian multicenter second trimester obstetric ultrasound and serum screening study. Jørgensen FS, et al. **Acta Obstet Gynecol Scand** 1999 Jul;78(6):501–10

Neonatal pelvic mass. Neonatal ovarian torsion. Kurzrock EA, et al. **Clin Pediatr (Phila)** 1999 Jul;38(7):415; discussion 415–6

The probability of abnormal preimplantation development can be predicted by a single static observation on pronuclear stage morphology. Tesarik J, et al. **Hum Reprod** 1999 May;14(5):1318–23

[Prenatal diagnosis of fetal abnormalities: importance of a prognostic evaluation] Dommergues M, et al. **Arch Pediatr** 1999;6 Suppl 2:243s–245s   (Fre)

[Notification of abnormalities and handicaps before and after birth] Francoual C, et al. **Arch Pediatr** 1999;6 Suppl 2:249s–251s   (Fre)

EPIDEMIOLOGY

Gestational diabetes mellitus (class A): a human teratogen? Kousseff BG. **Am J Med Genet** 1999 Apr 23;83(5):402–8

Artefactual increasing frequency of omphaloceles in the Northern Netherlands: lessons for systematic analysis of apparent epidemics. Reefhuis J, et al. **Int J Epidemiol** 1999 Apr;28(2):258–62

Maternal factors associated with severity of birth defects. Sheiner E, et al. **Int J Gynaecol Obstet** 1999 Mar; 64(3):227–32

Birth defects recognized in 10,000 babies born consecutively in Port Moresby General Hospital, Papua New Guinea. Dryden R. **P N G Med J** 1997 Mar;40(1):4–13

[The role of prenatal diagnosis on decreased incidence of congenital defects in the pediatric population of the Czech Republic 1990–1996] Sípek A, et al. **Ceska Gynekol** 1999 Jan;64(1):3–6 (Eng. Abstr.)   (Cze)

ETIOLOGY

Pregnancy outcome in long-term survivors of childhood cancer. Blatt J. **Med Pediatr Oncol** 1999 Jul;33(1):29–33 (32 ref.)

GENETICS

[Gene diagnosis in the hand of the physician] Knauer RII. **Fortschr Med** 1999 May 30;117(15):37–8   (Ger)

MORTALITY

Why do preterm infants die in the 1990s? Doyle LW, et al. **Med J Aust** 1999 Jun 7;170(11):528–32

PREVENTION & CONTROL

Can birth defects be prevented? [editorial] Dryden R. **P N G Med J** 1997 Mar;40(1):1–3 (12 ref.)

ABNORMALITIES, DRUG-INDUCED

see related
TERATOGENS

DIAGNOSIS

Atrioventricular septal defect with separate right and left atrioventricular valvar orifices in a patient with foetal hydantoin syndrome. Grech V, et al. **Cardiol Young** 1999 Jan;9(1):73–4

Example 5.13. *Index Medicus* vol. 40 no. 9 part 1 (Sept. 1999), p. 3 (subject section). Reprinted courtesy of National Library of Medicine.

EXAMPLES FROM ABSTRACTING TOOLS

LINGUISTICS

HISTORICAL

1501. DeLancey, S. and V. Golla. THE PENUTIAN HYPOTHESIS: RETROSPECT AND PROSPECT. International Journal of American Linguistics. 1997, 63(1)(January):171-202.

The name "Penutian" was coined by A. L. Kroeber and Roland B. Dixon in their ambitious and influential classification of California Indian languages as a label for the genetic relationship that they proposed among five Central California "stocks"—Costanoan, Miwok, Maiduan, Yokuts, and Wintuan. This grouping was based primarily on lexical evidence; the term "Penutian" derives from two stems for the numeral 'two' (*pen* and *uti*), one or the other of which Dixon and Kroeber found in all five stocks. In the final presentation of their material Dixon and Kroeber published a list of 171 "cognate stems" and some other lexical resemblances, from which they derived a set of rudimentary sound correspondences.

1502. Fitzgerald, S. HISTORICAL ASPECTS OF COEUR D'ALENE HARMONY. International Journal of American Linguistics. 1997, 63(3)(July):362-384.

Although the synchronic analysis of a language is often presented with little or no reference to the language's history, there are cases in which knowledge about the development of the language can provide valuable insight into its synchronic processes. The analysis of Coeur d'Alene harmony is such a case; the interaction of stressed vowels and faucal consonants can be better understood by the investigation of comparative data. In this paper, I discuss three aspects of Coeur d'Alene harmony which are of both synchronic and diachronic interest. A comparison of Coeur d'Alene with five other Interior Salish languages—Columbian, Kalispel, Spokane, Okanagan, and Shuswap—reveals at least partial answers to questions concerning the synchronic facts of harmony in Coeur d'Alene.

1503. Keating, E. HONORIFIC POSSESSION: POWER AND LANGUAGE IN POHNPEI, MICRONESIA. Language in Society. 1997, 26:247-268.

Mental categorization schemes, such as noun classification systems, can be productive sites for examining how experience is meaningfully and culturally structured through metaphorical and metonymic associations. Pohnpeian possessive classifiers not only constitute cultural categories of rank and power relations, but dynamically re-sort or re-classify these categories through honorific speech. Linguistic and interactional data are here combined with ethnographic data about Pohnpeian society and cultural beliefs, particularly notions about the meaning and construction of ranked social relationships, to show how micro-interactions which index status are linked both to larger cultural ideologies about power and, metaphorically, to the experiential domain.

1504. Kendall, D. L. THE TAKELMA VERB: TOWARD PROTO-TAKELMA-KALAPUYAN. International Journal of American Linguistics. 1997, 63(1)(January):1-17.

Takelma was a single language consisting of at least two, probably more, distinct dialects. It was spoken in southwestern Oregon and has been extinct for about fifty years. Almost all the extant Takelma data were collected by Edward Sapir and published in Sapir. The Sapir material is from the dialect now termed Lower Takelma. Other materials, though fragmentary, are

Example 5.14. *Abstracts in Anthropology* (1999) p. 435 (abstracts). Reprinted by permission of Baywood Publishing Co., Inc., © 1999.

Aborigines, 1677
Abstract art, 1656
Academia, 2223
    community, 1605
    freedom, 1637, 2056
    governance, 1628
    tenure, 1651
Acculturation, 2030
Acetylcholine receptors, 1795
Achebe, 1664
Achievement goals, 1636
Acorns, 1874
Activism, 2245
Addictions, 1831, 1862, 1908
Addiction treatment, 1939
Adhesion binding, 1868
Adolescent alcohol use, 1631
    pregnancies, 1801
Adolescents, 1620, 1777, 1846, 2160,
    2182
Adult health, 1896
    psychotherapy, 2142
Adults, 1573, 1728
Africa, 1507, 1637, 1724, 1727, 1744,
    1821, 1971, 2033, 2039, 2088,
    2198, 2205
African Americans, 1805, 1976, 2000,
    2016, 2019, 2030, 2040, 2215
    culture, 2193
    philosophy, 2206, 2209
    slaves, 2085
    universities, 1637, 2056
    women, 2212
Africans, 2014
Age differences, 1870
Ageing, 1864, 1871
Agency, 1612
Agoraphobia, 2125, 2141
Agrarian conflict, 1748

Agricultural policy, 1686
    production, 1700
Agriculture, 1682, 1719, 1721, 2039
    industry, 2070
Agromedicine, 1734, 1741, 1742, 1758
Ahmose Tempest Stela, 1679
AIDS, 1672, 1792, 1815, 1941, 1946, 2038
Al-Hiba, 2234
Alaska, 1595
Albania, 2077
Alcohol, 1901, 2155
    refusal, 1631
    use, 1774, 1908, 2134
Alcoholic families, 1617
Alcoholics, 2132, 2137, 2152
Alcoholics Anonymous, 2216
Alcoholism recovery, 2216
Alternative development, 1689
    medicine, 1957
    publishing, 1639
Alzheimer's disease, 1952, 2053
Amazonia, 1818
America, 2014
American anthropology, 2229
    Civil Liberties Union, 2073
    culture, 1655, 1676
    indians, 2004
    Museum of Natural History, 2229
Americans, 2162
Amino acids, 1827, 1967
Amish culture, 2130
Analgesic activity, 1795
Anglophones, 2090
Animacy maximization, 1547
Anorexia nervosa, 1890, 2155
Antecedents, 1526, 1619
Anthropological epistemology, 1589
    paradigms, 2235
    studies, 2224

Example 5.15. *Abstracts in Anthropology* (1999) p. 635 (subject index).
Reprinted by permission of Baywood Publishing Co., Inc., © 1999.

Berglund, S. et al., 1801
Bergman-Evans, B., 1997
Berkovits, R., 1550
Berman, A., 1643
Berman, S., 1596
Bernardi, G., 1706
Besnier, N., 1998
Biddle, J. E., 1732
Bierschenk, T., 2069
Bird-David, N., 1707
Birkelund, G. E., 1822
Black, J. S., 2225
Blaxter, M., 1802
Blustein, J., 1920
Bodenhorn, B., 1595
Bodnar, A. G. et al., 1803
Boillot, F., 1919
Bond, P., 1927
Boon, G. C., 1708
Bourdet, Y., 1709
Bovasso, G., 2163
Braddee, R. W., 2070
Braga, L. S., 1644
Brand, C., 1999
Brand, E. F., 1596
Brandell, J. R., 2117
Braslow, J. T., 2118
Braun, A. R. et al., 1804
Bricher, M., 2119
Broman, C. L., 2000
Brome, D. R., 2042
Brown, C. M., 1805
Brown, E. J., 1944
Brownson, R. C., 1806
Buechner, J. S., 2044
Bullinaria, J. A., 1508
Bunnell, H. T., 1519
Burdon, W. M., 2001
Buring, D., 2002
Burres, B., 1645
Burstein, P., 2119
Buschman, R. F., 1710
Bux, D. A., 1867
Byrd, D., 1551, 1552

Caldwell, P., 1807
Callaghan, C. A., 1553
Callahan, J., 1597
Callary, E., 1598

Campbell, R., 1599
Campos-Outcalt, D. et al. 2004
Canetto, S. S., 1771
Caplan, D., 1554
Caplan, L., 2246
Caputo, R. K., 2120
Carmel, S., 1809
Carr, G. L., 1646
Carroll, M. C., 1944
Carter, R. T. et al., 2005
Castaneda, X., 1810
Castle, N. G., 1811
Castle, S., 1840
Center for Public Integrity, The, 1812
Chaichian, M. A., 2175
Champagne, J., 1647
Chaney, J. M., 1910
Chang, H.-C., 2164
Chapin, F. S. III et al., 1685
Chapple, M. J., 2006
Charles, J. O., 1772
Chater, N., 1508
Chen, C.-J., 1980
Cheng, T.-j., 1711
Cheung, A. B. L., 2072
Cheung, F., 2121
Chiepe, G. T. K., 1600
Chiriboga, D., 2233
Chirwa, W. C., 2176
Chowder, K., 2073
Christopher, M., 2074
Cieslak, P. R. et al., 1813
Civic, D., 1814
Clapp, J. D., 1815
Clark, A., 1556
Clark, S., 1763
Clynes, R., 1816
Cnaattingius, S., 1817
Cobb, R. W., 1601
Cobb-Clark, D. A., 2177
Coffey, W. J., 2247
Cogan, J. C. et al., 2007
Cohen, A., 1602
Cohen, E., 2032
Cohen, J. H., 1648
Coimbra, C. E. A. et al., 1818
Coleman, B. J., 1819
Coleman, R., 1721
Colonna, F., 2190
Connerley, M. L., 1603

Example 5.16. *Abstracts in Anthropology* (1999) p. 625 (author index).
Reprinted by permission of Baywood Publishing Co., Inc., © 1999.

COMMUNICATION PROCESSES

1344

Arestova, O., Babanin, L., and Voiskounsky, A. Psychological research of computer-mediated communication in Russia. Behaviour & Information Technology 18(2):141-147, March/April 1999.

COMPUTER-MEDIATED COMMUNICATION. RESEARCH TRENDS. RUSSIA.

This article is devoted to the earliest Russian research carried out in the computer-mediated communication field. The most important modern directions of psychological research in the computer mediated-communication field in Russia also are described. The first research direction deals with the educational effects of children and adults participating in computer-mediated communication. The newest direction of psychological and sociological research is concentrated on analyzing the dynamics of the networks' users population growth and change. This project is also devoted to the psychological results of computer-mediated communication. The structure of human activity, its orientation basis, emotional, and motivational regulation were investigated. A special series of investigations is devoted to the gender differences in computer networking in Russia. Trends of future research in the computer-mediated communication field are also described.

1345

Caplan, S. E. and Greene, J. O. Acquisition of message-production skill by younger and older adults: effects of age, task complexity, and practice. Communication Monographs 66(1):31-48, March 1999.

AGE DIFFERENCES. AGING. MESSAGE PRODUCTION. TASK ANALYSIS. TASK PERFORMANCE.

This study investigated the impact of age, task complexity, and practice on adult message-production-skill acquisition and performance. Participants (30 older adults and 30 college students) learned a sequence for describing geometric arrays and then employed this organizing sequence in a series of 90 performance trials. Half of the participants learned a six-step (high task-complexity) sequence, while the remaining participants learned a three-step (low task-complexity) sequence for describing the arrays. The results suggest that overall message-production speed is characterized by a complexity effect (i.e., an interaction between age and task complexity such that younger adults exhibited superior performance relative to their older counterparts, and this difference was more pronounced under complex-task conditions). Complexity effects were also found for initial message-production-skill performance and rate of acquisition than younger adults, and this difference was even more pronounced when learning a complex skill. Finally, the results indicate a significant main effect for age on variation in overall task performance in that older adults' learning curves, regardless of task complexity, were characterized by greater variability in performance quality from trial to trial. These effects are consistent with changes in processing speed and working-memory capacity that have been suggested to accompany advancing age. The current findings may be seen to have direct implications for older-adult-skills training.

NOTE: Numerical entries refer to abstract numbers

Adams, K. H., 1398
Agard, R., 1646
Agrawal, B. C., 1541
Akkerboom, H., 1445
Albarran, A. B., 1368
Alexander, M. S., 1399
Alreck, P. L., 1625
Amin, H. V., 1620
Anderson, P. H., 1653
Andres, S. N. V., 1476
Andsager, J., 1400
Ansu-Kyeremeh, K., 1651
Antecol, M., 1561
Arant, M. D., 1562
Arestova, O., 1344
Arredondo, I., 1521
Attewell, P., 1401
Audigier, F., 1402

Babanin, L., 1344
Back, L., 1376
Bagozzi, R. P., 1657
Ball, S. J., 1522
Banning, S. A., 1563
Barnett, G. A., 1373
Baroody, J. R., 1564
Barreto, A. A., 1446
Barrett, M., 1523
Bartels, D., 1629
Battle, J., 1401
Bean, C., 1447
Beard, F., 1403
Becker, C., 1524
Behnke, R. R., 1347
Benoit, W. L., 1448
Berry, V. T., 1601
Bertrand, Y., 1404
Besser, D., 1405
Bielby, D. D., 1602
Bielby, W. T., 1602
Binik, Y. M., 1630
Blair, E., 1677
Blaney, J. R., 1448
Bliss, S. J., 1667
Bodendorf, F., 1616
Bowers, P. J., 1579
Boyd-Barrett, O., 1565, 1566, 1588
Bradley, P., 1567
Brain, M., 1526
Braithwaite, D. O., 1606
Brandon, D. P., 1406
Branham, R. J., 1449
Brashers, D. E., 1434
Braun, K. A., 1658
Broaddus, D. C., 1377
Brookes, R., 1568
Brown, J., 1451
Brown, M., 1570
Brown, W. J., 1407

Bruckman, A., 1408
Bruning, 1506
Buhr, T., 1456
Bunton, K., 1569
Burke, J., 1518
Burleson, B. R., 1357
Buzzanell, P. M., 1437

Cantor, J., 1422
Caplan, S. E., 1345
Carlson, K. C., 1477
Cassidy, M., 1409
Caughlin, J. P., 1348
Chabram-Dernersesian, A., 1647
Chan-Olmsted, C., 1368
Chandra, A., 1508
Cheney, G., 1370
Clarke, J. N., 1435
Colomb, J., 1410
Cone, S., 1571
Conti, D. B., 1369
Conville, R. L., 1349, 1350
Conyers, D., 1654
Coombs, W. T., 1504
Copeland, D., 1572
Corbett, J. B., 1411
Cowell, A., 1378
Crigler, A., 1456

Daly, J. A., 1351
David, G., 1412
Davis, C. N., 1478
de Arruda, M. C. C., 1659
de Arruda, M. L., 1659
De Cillia, R., 1450
Demers, D., 1573, 1574
Dhar, R., 1660
Dillard, J. P., 1352, 1454
Dillon, T. W., 1625
Dimmick, J., 1525
Dooley, P. L., 1575
Downing, J. D. H., 1479
Dozier, D. M., 1535
Dunwoody, S., 1379
Durkin, K., 1537

Eaton, L. G., 1436
Edge, S., 1576
Eisinger, R. M., 1451
Elasmar, M. G., 1526
Ellingson, L. L., 1437
Endersby, J. W., 1561
Englander, F., 1482
Englander, V., 1482
Engstrom, E., 1527
Eveland, W. P., Jr., 1452

Faber, R. J., 1516

Farrell, A. E., 1528
Fell, H. J., 1346
Ferrell, O. C., 1648
Ferri, A. J., 1527
Finn, A., 1539
Finn, J., 1606
Fisherkeller, J., 1413
Flanagan, P. S. L., 1619
Fleming, D., 1414
Floyd, K., 1353
Forbes, D., 1577
Fotsch, P. M., 1380
Fournier, J.-M., 1415
Friedland, L. A., 1578
Frost, R., 1418
Fuenzalida, V., 1670

Gaines, S. O., Jr., 1550
Gandy, O. H., Jr., 1381
Garay, R., 1453
Gaski, J. F., 1661
Gastil, J., 1454
Gaudino, J. L., 1417
Gaziano, C., 1382
Gaziano, E., 1382
Geiser-Getz, G. C., 1603
Gher, L. A., 1620
Giffard, C. A., 1580
Gilbert, E. M., 1624
Giles, R., 1529
Giroux, H. A., 1383
Gittings, C., 1505
Glasser, T. L., 1579
Goby, V. P., 1384
Goldberg, D. T., 1530
Golding, P., 1372
Goldstein, M., 1621
Gole, R. W., 1480
Goodall, H. L., Jr., 1636
Gopinath, M., 1657
Gordon, C. G., 1497
Gordon, W. T., 1631
Gosling, J., 1673
Grant, C., 1509
Grassl, W., 1662
Green, K., 1632
Greene, J. O., 1345
Gregory, J., 1633
Griffin, R. J., 1379
Griswold, W. F., 1416

Haas, S. M., 1434
Haggins, B. L., 1531
Hale, M. L., 1473
Hall, B. I., 1417
Hansen, K. A., 1581
Harker, D., 1510
Harrington, C. L., 1602
Harris, R. W., 1607
Harshman, C. L., 1498

Example 5.18. *Communication Abstracts* vol. 22 no. 5 (Oct. 1999) p. 792 (author index), copyright © 1999 by Sage Publications, Inc. Reprinted by permission of Sage Publications, Inc.

NOTE: Numerical entries refer to abstract numbers.

Aboriginal Australians, 1387, 1646
Academia, 1478
Academic Performance, 1401
Academic Specialization, 1634
Academics, 1634, 1641
Acculturation, 1385
Acquired Immunodeficiency Syndrome, 1434
Adolescents, 1355, 1413
Adults, 1353
Advertising, 1509, 1510, 1516, see also
    headings under Children, Negative,
    Political, Television
Advertising Agencies, 1512
Advertising Content, 1520
Advertising Education, 1648, 1650
Advertising Effectiveness, 1518
Advertising Effects, 1509, 1520, 1656, 1658
Advertising Ethics, 1508, 1648, 1649, 1650,
    1659, 1661, 1667
Advertising Recall, 1519
Advertising Regulations, 1510
Advertising Research, 1512, 1514, 1518
Affect, 1353
African Americans. See Blacks
Age Differences, 1345, 1532
Agenda Setting, 1600
Aggressive Behavior, 1546
Aging, 1345
Alternative News Agencies, 1580
Alzheimer's Disease, 1443
American Revolution, 1567
Antitrust Laws, 1491
Antiwar Movement, 1470
Anxiety, 1347
Arab States, 1620
Architecture, 1609
Argentina, 1476
Argumentation, 1463
Asia, 1374
Attitude Change, 1607
Attitude Formation, 1607
Attitudes, 1625
Audiences, 1463, 1545, 1570
Australia, 1387, 1510, 1511, 1539, 1590, 1592
Austria, 1450
Authoritarian Government, 1457

Babbling, 1346
Banks, 1511
Baseball Players, 1495
Behavioral Analysis, 1353
Betrothal, 1354
Bias, 1459, 1472
Blacks, 1380, 1531, 1538, 1551
Book Publishing, 1515
Book Trade, 1515
Brady, Robert A., 1467
Brand Management, 1662, 1663
Breast Cancer, 1437

Broadcasting, 1541, 1543, see also headings
    under Public, Religious
Broadcasting History, 1453, 1458, 1538, 1544,
    1557, 1571, 1671
Broadcasting Regulations, 1488, 1651
Business Communication, 1588
Business Markets, 1663

Cable Television, 1525, 1544, 1549, 1553
Call Centers, 1675
Canada, 1421, 1446, 1488, 1505, 1510, 1539,
    1561, 1590
Candidate Information, 1460
Career Development, 1527
Celebrities, 1529
Censorship, 1476, 1483, 1496, 1516, 1536
Children, 1355, 1408, 1444, 1452, 1469
Children and Advertising, 1666
Children and Television, 1422, 1537, 1546, 1673
Chile, 1626
China, 1638
Chinese, 1385, 1628
Choice Behavior, 1660, 1664, 1665
Chronic Illness, 1439
Citizen Participation, 1615
Citizenship, 1615
Civics Education, 1402
Civil Rights Movement, 1551
Civil War, 1593
Cognitive Processes, 1367, 1404, 1653, 1664
Cold War, 1458, 1571
Collective Memory, 1502
College Students, 1347, 1400, 1403, 1405
Comic Books, 1536
Commodification, 1587
Communication, 1346, 1354, 1361, 1380, 1386,
    1452, 1603, 1631, 1634, 1635, see also
    Telecommunications, headings under
    Business, Computer- Mediated, Couples,
    Digital, Environmental, Health,
    Intercultural, Interpersonal, International,
    Marital, Nonverbal, Oral, Online,
    Organizational, Political, Relational, Risk,
    Satellite, Science, Teacher-Student,
    Technical, Visual
Communication Apprehension, 1351
Communication Avoidance, 1351
Communication Behavior, 1358
Communication Education, 1417, 1419, 1430
Communication Ethics, 1612
Communication History, 1467, 1631
Communication Patterns, 1348
Communication Processes, 1353, 1363, 1372
Communication Research, 1348, 1352, 1357,
    1364, 1516, 1633, 1635, 1639
Communication Studies, 1355
Communication Styles, 1384
Communication Technology, 1371, 1373, 1374,
    1420, 1609, 1612, 1616, 1622

Example 5.19. *Communication Abstracts* vol. 22 no. 5 (Oct. 1999) p. 795 (subject index), copyright © 1999 by Sage Publications, Inc. Reprinted by permission of Sage Publications, Inc.

ADMINISTRATIVE STRUCTURE AND PROCESS

Organization and Process

0783

Allen, Lew, et al. A guide for renewing your school: lessons from the League of Professional Schools. San Francisco: Jossey-Bass, 1999, 105 pp.

CASE STUDIES. EDUCATIONAL ADMINISTRATION. EDUCATIONAL REFORM.
    SCHOOLS.

This work is based on years of practical experience, case examples, and empirical studies from the League of Professional Schools. The book guides school practitioners through the essential steps of a reform process: (1) designing a covenant to guide teaching and learning; (2) creating a shared governance process to promote democratic leadership and decision making; and (3) implementing action research to assess the reform process. The book also addresses the challenges of change, such as how to create a school climate that will foster implementation of the framework and how to determine the type of facilitation and staff development needed to sustain this work. It contains sample governances, charters, mission statements, worksheets, forms, and other tools, and the work presents a framework and a strategy for promoting school-wide renewal and improvement. Its thesis is that a school community's decision to implement the League's framework must include the knowledge that the community is about to turn the traditional norms of its schools upside down. To do otherwise would not result in lasting, sustainable change in the schools, and, therefore, would have little substantive impact on the achievement of the students.

0784

Beck, Lynn G. Metaphors of educational community: an analysis of the images that reflect and influence scholarship and practice. Educational Administration Quarterly 35(1):13-45, Feb. 1999.

ACADEMIC PERFORMANCE. ORGANIZATIONAL CULTURE.
    SCHOOL-COMMUNITY RELATIONS.

The idea that schools should function as communities is popular in education circles. It is also confusing, for the term "community" means different things to different people. This article argues that efforts to reduce ambiguity by linking the concept to clearly defined indicators may be short-sighted. Multiple meanings linked with the notion of community reflect the richness of this concept, the author contends, and these meanings should be explored and understood—not reduced or eliminated. Analyzing language used by academics and practitioners writing about community in school settings, the author attempts to demonstrate that the concept is both complex and reasonably coherent. Recognizing that this is so can only assist scholars who desire to better understand this phenomenon, the author argues. Similarly, knowledge of the ways one make sense of being in and out of community can provide guidance to people seeking to create and sustain communal schools.

Example 5.20. *Educational Administration Abstracts* vol. 34 no. 4 (Oct. 1999) p. 411 (classified abstracts), copyright © 1999 by Sage Publications, Inc. Reprinted by permission of Sage Publications, Inc.

NOTE: Numerical entries refer to abstract numbers

Academic Aptitude, 1032, 1033, 1035, 1037
Academic Disciplines, 0810
Academic Performance, 0784, 0807, 0811, 0819,
    0829, 0830, 0831, 0833, 0858, 0860, 0867,
    0873, 0877, 0884, 0901, 0902, 0928, 0929,
    0930, 0931, 0932, 0934, 0935, 0936, 0938,
    0939, 0940, 0941, 0945, 0946, 0947, 0948,
    0949, 0950, 0960, 0971
Academic Standards, 0787, 0788, 0794, 0808,
    0843, 0951, 0954, 0955, 0956, 0957, 1040,
    1048
Accelerated Learning, 0893
Accountability, 0794, 0952, 0963, 1034
Administrative Roles, 0797, 0800
Administrative Skills, 0979
Administrative Techniques, 0798, 0803
Administrator Education, 0914, 0915, 0916, 0917
Administrator Roles, 0802, 0988
Adolescents, 0827, 0856, 0906, 0909, 0961,
    0965, 0978, 1043, see also headings under
    Female, Male
Adorno, Theodor, 1054
Adult Education, 0836, 0958, 0959
African Americans. See Blacks
Age Differences, 0880
Agency Theory, 1059
Agenda Setting, 0915
Aptitude Tests, 0902
Arabs, 0982
Arendt, Hannah, 0845
Arithmetic, 0894
Art Education, 0862
Articulatory Phonetics, 0883
Arts Education, 1031
Assistant Principals, 0800
Attachment Behavior, 0827, 0909
Attitude Change, 0814
Attitudes, 0819, 0873
Australia, 0832, 0840, 0963, 1005

Bilingual Education, 0847
Bisexuals, 0911
Blacks, 0856, 0977, 0980, 0981, 0984, 0989,
    0990
Body Weight, 1023
Bullying, 1043

Calculators, 0894
Calculus, 0849
California, 0973, 1008
Cambodians, 1028
Canada, 0887, 0919, 0922, 0983, 1039, 1040
Career Counseling, 0972
Case Studies, 0783, 0969
Chicago, 0805
Child Development, 0967
Child Rearing, 0959, 0961, 0965, 0966, 0967
Children, 0875, 1012
Children and Television, 0864
Children's Literature, 0855

Children's Television, 1001
Citizen Participation, 0981
Civil War, 0996
Classroom Management, 0814, 0815, 0816, 0817,
    0937, 0994
Cognitive Development, 0966
Cognitive Processes, 0878, 0882, 0888, 0896,
    0966, 1024, 1042, see also Learning
    Processes
Collective Bargaining, 0818
College Students, 0835, 0904, 0907, 0908, 0910,
    0953, 0980, 1023
Colleges, 0811, 0824, see also Community
    Colleges, Universities
Colonialism, 0986
Commission Studies, 0858
Communication Education, 0881, 0920
Communication Skills, 0810
Community College Students, 1030
Community Colleges, 0973, see also Colleges,
    Universities
Community Services, 1039
Competitive Behavior, 0873
Computer-Assisted Counseling, 0913
Computer-Assisted Evaluation, 1019
Computer-Assisted Instruction, 0847, 0863, 0873,
    0875, 0876, 0884, 1011, 1016, 1018, 1021,
    1022
Computer Programming, 1021
Computer Use, 0880
Computers, 0829
Confirmatory Factor Analysis, 1057
Constitution, 1004, 1005
Constructivism, 0815, 1015
Cooperative Education, 0958
Coping Behavior, 0813, 0905
Cost Analysis, 1060
Counseling, 1027
Course Prerequisites, 0849
Courseware Design, 1016, 1019
Critical Analysis, 0852
Critical Thinking, 0810
Cross-Cultural Communication, 0916
Cross-Cultural Comparison, 0987, 0993
Cross-National Comparison, 0789, 0825
Cultural Literacy, 0842
Curriculum, 0850
Curriculum Design, 0839, 0842, 0843, 0845,
    0848, 0851, 0861, 0862, 0866, 0867, 0918,
    0977, 1019, 1031
Curriculum Development, 0837, 0838, 0841,
    0844, 0846, 0854, 0857, 0859, 0871, 0899,
    0903, 0981, 1056, 1058, 1061
Curriculum Diversity, 0840

Dallas Value-Added Accountability System,
    0930, 0946, 0947, 0949, 0950
Debate, 0837
Decision Making, 0786
Deconstructionism, 1052, 1058

Example 5.21. *Educational Administration Abstracts* vol. 34 no. 4 (Oct. 1999) p. 542 (subject index), copyright © 1999 by Sage Publications, Inc. Reprinted by permission of Sage Publications, Inc.

NOTE: Numerical entries refer to abstract numbers.

Abdal-Haqq, I., 0408
Abrahams, S., 0978
Abramovich, S., 1011
Abwender, D.A., 0482
Adalbjarnardóttir, S., 1002
Adams, A., 0593
Adamson, B.J., 0170
Addison, J.T., 0423
Addonizio, M., 1045
Adejokun, A., 0015
Adlam, R., 0395
Afflerbach, P., 0103
Agee, J., 0119
Agostino, V.R., 0449
Aguirre, J.K., 0440
Agyeman, J., 0326
Aho, S., 0038
Airasian, P.W., 0151, 0927
Al-Samarraik, S., 0715
Alao, S., 0606
Alban-Metcalfe, J., 0573
Albiston, S.K., 0050
Albright, M.H., 0742
Alcock, M.W., 0293
Alder, J.G., 0933
Alexander, P.A., 0349, 0350
Allen, G., 0089
Allen, L., 0783
Allen-Brown, V., 0001
Almog, T., 0895
Alspaugh, J.W., 0042
Altermatt, E.R., 0294
Altmann, A., 0848
Amada, G., 0391, 0904
Anderson, G.L., 0266
Anderson, L., 0417, 0520
Anderson, M.D., 0461
Anderson, R.D., 0837
Andreassen, R., 0607
Anjaneyalu, K.S.R., 0226
Annunziata, J., 0142
Antis, J., 0318
Aoki, T.T., 0976
Ardizzone, P.M., 0090
Ariar, T., 0123
Arkes, J., 0683
Armstrong, G.M., 0849
Armstrong-Stassen, M., 0218
Arnhold, N., 0996
Arora, C.M.H., 0565
Arthur, N., 0312
Ashman, A.F., 0579
Ashworth, J., 0178
Ashworth, P., 0759
Asthana, S., 0386
Athanassopoulos, A.D., 0667
Attewell, P., 0829
Audigier, F., 0850
Aunola, K., 0966
Avasalu, M., 0933

Babcock, L., 0547
Bacnik, A., 0334
Badgett, J., 0884
Badgett, J.L., 0372
Bailey, P., 0842
Baker, B D., 0721
Bakkenes, I., 0551
Baldauf, B., 0282
Ball, P., 0716
Balli, S.J., 0307
Band, S., 0283
Bane, K.D., 0646
Bankston, C. III, 0433
Barge, G., 0060
Barnes, A., 0632
Barnette, H.J., 0769
Barr, N., 0240
Barrow, M., 0751
Barton, A.C., 0061
Basso, R., 0828
Battle, J., 0829
Bauknight, S.H., 0724
Baur, L.A., 0171
Bautista, A., 0633
Beach, R., 0851
Beasley, R.E., 0219
Beauboeuf-Lafontant, T., 0977
Beaumatin, A., 0970
Beccegato, L.S., 0574
Beck, L.G., 0784
Bedard, G.H., 0653
Bedi, A.S., 0684
Beerman, K., 0091
Bees, C., 0501
Behrman, J.R., 0685
Beijaard, D., 0023
Belfiore, P.J., 0308
Bell, E.D., 0914
Bempechat, J., 0978
Benavides, A.H., 0979
Bencze, L., 0062
Bennell, P., 0179
Bennett, T.R., 0575
Beresford, J., 0146
Berg-Cross, L., 0392
Bernache, C., 0436
Bernal, D.D., 0706
Berninger, V.W., 0590
Berry, T., 0662
Bertelli, R., 0351
Bertrand, Y., 0882
Bevevino, M.M., 0369
Beyer, J.A., 1006
Bezmen, T., 0016
Bezzina, C., 0012
Bhola, H.S., 0668
Biddle, B.J., 0794
Bielaczyc, K., 0958
Biemans, H., 0023

Biemiller, A., 0309
Bierema, L.L., 0785
Biesta, G.H.H., 0760
Bigum, C., 0220
Bijstra, J.O., 0905
Binder, M., 0686
Bisanz, G.L., 1042
Bisanz, J., 1042
Bishop, D.M., 0194
Bizzari, J.C., 0502
Blair, K.D., 0804
Blake, B.E., 0852
Blase, J., 0512
Blase, J., 0512
Blass, N., 0655
Blatchford, P., 0296
Blocher, C.C., 0482
Bock, K., 0180
Bond, L., 0641
Bonesronning, H., 0621
Boone, M.B., 0737
Borish, S., 0246
Botelho, A., 0181
Bouissou, C., 0959
Boulton, P., 0276
Boulton-Lewis, G., 0094
Bound, J., 0687
Bourcet, C., 0906
Bowell, B., 0639
Bowen, G.L., 0830, 1029
Bowen, N.K., 0830, 0960
Bowen, W.G., 0705
Bowman, F., Jr., 0462
Boylan, C., 0821
Boyle-Baise, M., 0707
Bracher, D., 0561
Bradshaw, L.K., 0915
Brady, M.P., 0786
Brandes, G.M., 0051
Brasington, D.M., 0622
Braten, I., 0607
Braten, I., 1024
Brent, B.O., 0509
Breuvart, J.-M., 0761
Brewer, D.H., 0688, 0690
Bridges, D., 0004
Brindis, C., 0492
Brindley, S., 0593
Brint, S., 0450
Britton, B.K., 0352
Brock, B., 0912
Brooker, R., 0052, 0120
Brostrom, S., 0825
Brown, D.T., 0111
Brown, G., 0091, 1011
Brown, G.D.A., 0227
Brown, L., 0147
Brown, M.B., 0111
Brown, M.H., 0634
Brown, S.D., 0907

Example 5.22. *Educational Administration Abstracts* vol. 34 no. 4 (Oct. 1999) p. 547 (cumulative author index), copyright © 1999 by Sage Publications, Inc. Reprinted by permission of Sage Publications, Inc.

NOTE: Numerical entries refer to abstract numbers.

Aboriginal Australians, 0709
Academia, 0556, 0700
Academic Aptitude, 0040, 0106,1032, 1033, 1035, 1037
Academic Attitude, 0314, 0336
Academic Behavior, 0316
Academic Careers, 0188
Academic Departments, 0014
Academic Disciplines, 0051, 0810
Academic Failure, 0093, 0175, 0573, 0574, 0576, 0578, 0580, 0581, 0622, 0657, 0744
Academic Freedom, 0540
Academic Grades, 0089, 0384
Academic Incentives, 0388
Academic Journals, 0018
Academic Major, 0705
Academic Performance, 0025, 0028, 0035, 0040, 0042, 0043, 0044, 0047, 0049, 0056, 0070, 0076, 0088, 0089, 0100, 0106, 0201, 0230, 0278, 0294, 0296, 0306, 0307, 0308, 0309, 0310, 0311, 0314, 0317, 0318, 0327, 0336, 0345, 0349, 0373, 0380, 0382, 0383, 0386, 0387, 0389, 0433, 0438, 0439, 0447, 0448, 0485, 0489, 0504, 0550, 0562, 0573, 0574, 0575, 0576, 0578, 0580, 0581, 0583, 0584, 0621, 0622, 0623, 0624, 0625, 0644, 0659, 0663, 0664, 0665, 0669, 0675, 0709, 0719, 0744, 0745, 0754, 0784, 0807, 0811, 0819, 0829, 0830, 0831, 0833, 0858, 0860, 0867, 0873, 0877, 0884, 0901, 0902, 0928, 0929, 0930, 0931, 0932, 0934, 0935, 0936, 0938, 0939, 0940, 0941, 0945, 0946, 0947, 0948, 0949, 0950, 0960, 0971
Academic Standards, 0099, 0113, 0161, 0211, 0255, 0268, 0290, 0313, 0344, 0345, 0520, 0550, 0621, 0623, 0661, 0666, 0787, 0788, 0794, 0808, 0843, 0951, 0954, 0955, 0956, 0957, 1040, 1048
Academic Suspension, 0317
Academic Tenure, 0540
Accelerated Learning, 0813, 0893
Accidents, 0499, 0566
Accountability, 0457, 0513, 0562, 0644, 0659, 0663, 0794, 0952, 0963, 1034
Accounting Education, 0758
Accounting Standards, 0758
Acculturation, 0253, 0438
Action Research, 0062, 0323, 0762, 0763, 0782
Administrative Centralization, 0580
Administrative Reform, 0019
Administrative Roles, 0012, 0797, 0800
Administrative Skills, 0979
Administrative Techniques, 0798, 0803
Administrator Certification, 0397
Administrator Development, 0141, 0408
Administrator Education, 0118, 0646, 0647, 0914, 0915, 0916, 0917
Administrator Evaluation, 0515
Administrator Performance, 0150
Administrator Recruitment, 0511

Administrator Roles, 0802, 0988
Administrator Turnover, 0514
Adolescence, 0567
Adolescent Parents, 0492, 0493, 0494, 0495, 0496
Adolescent Pregnancy, 0428, 0431, 0492, 0494, 0730
Adolescent Violence, 0237, 0238
Adolescent Violence Survey, 0237
Adolescents, 0198, 0308, 0421, 0431, 0497, 0569, 0570, 0571, 0675, 0679, 0719, 0827, 0856, 0906, 0909, 0961, 0965, 0978, 1043, see also headings under Female, Male
Adorno, Theodor, 1054
Adult Education, 0054, 0145, 0287, 0289, 0304, 0315, 0423, 0424, 0508, 0510, 0527, 0528, 0536, 0586, 0588, 0589, 0591, 0668, 0836, 0958, 0959
Advanced Teachers, 0162
Affect, 0544, 0584, 0614
Africa, 0130
African Americans. See Blacks
Africans, 0015
After-School Programs, 0491
Age Differences, 0086, 0102, 0306, 0346, 0880
Age Stereotypes, 0716, 0717
Ageism, 0716, 0717
Agency Theory, 1059
Agenda Setting, 0915
Air Pollution, 0346
Alcohol Abuse, 0390
Algebra, 0354, 0387
Alphabet, 0364
Alternative Teacher Certification, 0396
Analogical Reasoning, 0354
Analogy Problems, 0350
Analogy Tests, 0354
Ancestry, 0773
Anglo-Americans, 0443, 0575, 0702
Anglo-Australians, 0709
Antidrug Campaigns, 0680
Antiracist Education, 0435
Antitheory, 0766
Antiviolence Intervention, 0498
Anxiety, 0233
Apprenticeships, 0008, 0017, 0052, 0055, 0057, 0059, 0187, 0189
Aptitude Tests, 0117, 0350, 0902
Arabs, 0982
Arendt, Hannah, 0845
Arithmetic, 0894
Arithmetic Division, 0063
Arkansas, 0215
Art Education, 0329, 0330, 0347, 0862
Art Museums, 0347
Articulatory Phonetics, 0883
Arts Education, 0596, 1031
Asia, 0179, 0430
Asian Americans, 0135, 0183, 0201
Asians, 0183

Example 5.23. *Educational Administration Abstracts* vol. 34 no. 4 (Oct. 1999) p. 555 (cumulative subject index), copyright © 1999 by Sage Publications, Inc. Reprinted by permission of Sage Publications, Inc.

49.4053 ADAMS, James — An assessment of voting systems under the proximity and directional models of the vote. *Public Choice* 98 (1-2), 1999 : 131-151.

I evaluate five single-winner voting systems according to their tendency to elect Condorcet candidates under alternative models of issue voting derived from behavioral research. These behavioral models posit that voters have both issue and nonissue motivations ; within this framework, I study the effects of both the directional and proximity voting models, with varying degrees of issue voting. Under the proximity metric, all voting systems are most efficient when voters attach little importance to issues, while the opposite is generally the case under directional voting. In contrast to previous results, voting systems tend to be more efficient for large than for small electorates. All voting systems — including the widely-criticized plurality method — are extremely efficient when voters in mass elections are inattentive to issues. [R]

49.4054 ANTER, Andreas — **Georg Jellineks wissenschaftliche Politik. Positionen, Kontexte, Wirkungslinien (Georg Jellinek's scientific politics : content, context, effect/ La politique scientifique de Georg Jellinek : positions, contexte, effets).** *Politische Vierteljahresschrift* 39 (3), Sept. 1998 : 503-526.

Georg Jellinek's political science marks a new start in the history of the discipline, which was in a state stagnation at the turn of the century. The essay shows the spectrum of his positions, evaluates their theoretical background, and follows their impact on the political science of the 20th c. Jellinek legitimates the political science, formerly pursued in Germany as a part of the *Staatslehre*, as an independent science, and persists at the same time on the close interrelations between both of the disciplines. He conceptualizes political science as *praktische Staatswissenschaft* and drafts the *Staatslehre* as a political science of the tasks of the state. The essay shows the relation between Jellinek's theory of the purposes of the state, his theory of value judgment and his concept of the political, and discusses his thesis of the " normative power of the factual " in the context of his view of dominion, order, state and law. [R]

49.4055 APPIAH, Kwame Anthony — **Patriotas cosmopolitas (Cosmopolitan patriots/Des patriotes cosmopolites).** *Revista brasileira de Ciências sociais* 36, Feb. 1998 : 79-94. [Résumé en Français]

The author examines the logical relationships between the values and ideas which support cosmopolitanism, patriotism and liberalism, stating that these ideas and feelings are not at all inherently contradictory. They should be used freely by contemporary men and women who seek an identity to protect their liberty, autonomy and commitments to the democratic and individualistic order. [R]

49.4056 ARANSON, Peter H. — **The new institutional analysis of politics.** *Journal of Institutional and Theoretical Economics* 154 (4), Dec. 1998 : 744-753.

I consider those aspects of the new institutional analysis of politics that are based on the theory of rational choice and are strongly informed by the new institutional economics of organization. This is the single most important recent development in political science and public choice. I discuss four general aspects of this field. (1) I ask whether there is something distinctively " new " about it and in doing so compare it to the new institutional economics. (2) I attend to the problem of specifying a null hypothesis to compare allocative and distributive consequences of choices made under different institutions or the supposed absence of institutions. (3) I

Example 5.24. *International Political Science Abstracts* vol. 49 no. 4 (May 1999) p. 445 (abstracts). Reprinted by permission of International Political Science Association © 1999.

A

Aborigines
  land rights : 1327
  Asia : 1398
  Australia, land rights : 1327
    cases, and liberalism : 2999
  Canada : 5177
    land : 5291
    opposition to militari-
    zation : 1377
  Latin America, and democracy : 4043
  Mexico : 2509
  see also Indigenous peoples
Abortion policy
  Canada, House of Commons, free voting :
    684
  Spain, and Constitutional Court : 4371
  USA
    1965-1972 : 3148
    debate : 725
    New York State, 1965-1972 : 3148
    Pennsylvania, 1965-1972 : 3148
Abstention *see* Electoral participation
Action
  free : 119
  libertarian theory : 84
  views of L. Wittgenstein : 1325
Activists
  Italy, political parties : 4782
  USA : 674
    feminism : 566
    political parties, 1972-1992, and re-
    ligion : 4733
    recruitment : 4667
Administration
  accountability : 1446
  and citizens : 2693
  and civil society : 1452
  and clients : 2371
  and democracy : 4137
  and environmental problems : 1397
  and ethics : 4291
  and policy-making : 2833
  and politics : 50
  and sustainable development : 2793
  contracts : 1452, 1554
  decentralization : 181
  effectiveness : 4244
  efficiency : 4234
  future : 1321
  large projects : 4083
  learning process : 1263
  local : 189
  management, and policy analysis :
    4149

(Administration)
  managerialism : 4, 114, 136, 2670
    and oversight : 1469
  participation : 415
  professionalism : 1498
  reform : 19, 30, 1308, 1489, 3178, 4089
    and time : 1463
    managerialism : 4, 2829
  reform proposals : 96
  size
    and corruption : 2750
    and economic openness : 2894
    and media voter model : 2753
  EU : 3510
  EU countries : 455
    and EU Commission expert commit-
    tees : 4968
    and EU law : 3590
  developing countries
    accountability, and market
    economy : 1364
    and economic growth : 1363
  Africa, and structural adjustment
    programs : 4399
  Algeria : 1667
  Argentina, reform : 1762
  Asia (South), reform : 3220
  Asia (South East), reform : 397
  Australia
    reform : 3164
    Victoria , reform : 4
  Bangladesh : 1822
    reform : 3220
  Canada, reform, and consultants : 3179
  Caribbean, reform : 19, 327
  Denmark, and gray zones : 391
  Europe (Eastern), reform : 4425
  Finland, reform : 4577
    and parliament : 3175
  France
    and EU : 4435
    reform : 1308
  Germany (FR), reform : 419, 3080
    reform proposals : 1727, 4534
  Greece, and EU : 886
  India, reform : 3220
  Iran, reform : 4418
  Ireland, reform : 49
  Israel
    managerialism, and ombudsman : 3108
    reform
      and semi-presidential system : 3175
      managerialism : 1679

Example 5.25. *International Political Science Abstracts* vol. 49 no. 4 (May 1999) p. 1 (subject index). Reprinted by permission of International Political Science Association © 1999.

INDEX

Numbers followed by the letter *A* refer to an abstract; other numbers refer to the additional articles listed, but not abstracted. Words in capital letters, e. g., BIOGRAPHIES, RESOURCES, are used
for listing items which are actually biographies, resources, longitudinal studies, etc., not about these
subjects. Cities with less than one million population are listed under the state if in the United States,
the province if in Canada or the country if elsewhere.

ability see spatial ability
abjection, 883A
abolitionists, 783
Aborigines (Canada) see Native Americans
    (Canada)
abortion attitudes see abortion opponents, pro-
    choice
abortion history, 964 see also U. S. history–20th
    c.–abortion
abortion opponents, 850
abortion rights see prochoice
abuse, 752A see also battered women, child
    abuse, child sexual abuse, psychological
    abuse, violence
academia, 689A, 739A see also higher educa-
    tion
academic achievement, 633A see also college
    academic achievement, educational attain-
    ment, high school academic achievement,
    junior high school academic achievement
academic progress see academic achievement
access to education, 749A
achievement see academic achievement
acquaintance rape, 755A
activism see civil disobedience, feminist activ-
    ism, militance, resistance
activism (political) see political activism
activists see INTERVIEWS WITH ACTIVISTS
Adam (Bible), 778A
Addams, Jane, 858A, 863A
addiction see substance abuse
adjustment see coping, life experiences, psycho-
    logical adjustment, stress
administrators see managers
adult age characteristics, 679A
adult children, 705A, 714A
adult development see adult age characteristics
adult education, 615A see also continuing edu-
    cation
adult women, 756A see also middle aged
    women, older women, senior women, young
    women
adventure see wilderness
advertising see periodical advertising, television
    advertising
aesthetics, 917 see also beauty
affect see emotions
affective behavior see caring
affective disorders see mental disorders
affective education, 639A
affirmative action, 944A see also college
    affirmative action, disadvantaged groups,
    occupational gender discrimination, occupa-
    tional gender segregation

Afghanistan–politics, 738
Africa, 953
age see paternal age
age characteristics see adult age characteristics
agency, 651A, 849A, 901A, 914A
aggression, 840A see also assertiveness, sexual
    aggression
aggressive behavior, 934A
aggressiveness see assertiveness
aging studies, 825A
agriculture, 847A, 961A
Aid to Families with Dependent Children,
    715A, 766A, 819A see also welfare
alcohol abuse, 827
alcohol use during pregnancy, 851A
alcoholism, 813A
Algeria–women's movement, 794
All-China Women's Federation, 606A
alliances see feminist alliances
allopathic medicine see healing
alternative medicine see folk medicine
Amazon River, 882A
American history see U. S. history
American literature, 890 see also English
    courses
American literature–17th c., 892A
American literature–19th c., 885A, 901A see
    also Gilman, Charlotte Perkins
American literature–20th c., 883A, 888, 894A,
    901A, 904 see also Gilman, Charlotte Per-
    kins, Wharton, Edith
American Society of Criminology, 733A
anatomy see bodies
ancestors, 882A
ancient history see Old Europe
Andersen, Marguerite, 887A, 905A
androcentrism see patriarchy
androgyny see femininity, masculinity
anger, 934A
Anglican Church, 873A
animal husbandry see livestock
animals, 748, 855 see also livestock
anorexia, 781A
anthropology see CROSS-CULTURAL STUDIES, eth-
    nography, folklore, prehistory
anti-essentialism see essentialism
anti-Semitism see Holocaust
antifeminists, 956A see also nonfeminists
antiracism, 945A, 957 see also race, class, and
    gender studies
antisexism education, 617A
anxiety, 647A, 673A, 808A, 843A, 845A see
    also depression (mental), guilt, stress
apes, 855

Example 5.26. *Women Studies Abstracts* vol. 27 no. 2 (Summer 1998) p. 101
(index). Reprinted by permission of Transaction Publishers. Copyright © 1998
by Transaction Publishers; all rights reserved.

SPECIAL ISSUES AND PUBLICATIONS

see also **Denial and disclosure: An analysis of selective reality as resistance to feminist curriculum, no. 601A; Curriculum transformation, no. 603A; Women's studies in Germany, no. 608A; Like Alice through the looking glass: Accomodation in academia, no. 618A; Researching women entrepreneurs, no. 664A; Inuit women: Equality and leadership, no. 770A; Dialectics of citizenship, no. 790A; Nancy Jay and a feminist psychology of sacrifice, no. 797A; Editorial: Breast cancer and *Women & Health*, no. 818A; The body as attire: The shifting meanings of footbinding in seventeenth-century China, no. 864A; L'écriture de la mémoire (Writing memory), 887A; Dating Mike Epstein, his cousin Billy, Jake Stein, Pete Diamond, Alan Freeman and the others, no. 938; Editorial [United Nations World Conference on Women (Beijing)], no. 951A; A revolution has begun [United Nations World Conference on Women (Beijing)], no. 954; What are Chinese women faced with after Beijing?, no. 961A**

596.   Coulter, Sara, Elaine Hedges and Beth Vanfossen. National Center for Curriculum Transformation: Resources on women. WOMEN'S STUDIES QUARTERLY 24 no. 3–4:215-21 Fall–Win '96.

WOMEN STUDIES

see also **World civilization [syllabus], no. 616; Integrating scholarship on women into physics, no. 621A; Women writers: Multicultural perspectives [syllabus at Cañada College, California], no. 631; Feminist pedagogy and techniques for the changing classroom, no. 637A; A note on gender and computer literacy, no. 644A; Charcot's women: Bodies of knowledge at the interface of aging studies and women's studies, no. 825A; Editorial [United Nations World Conference on Women (Beijing)], no. 951A; A revolution has begun [United Nations World Conference on Women (Beijing)], no. 954; The UN Conference, no. 955**

597A.   Arat, Necla. Women's studies in Turkey. WOMEN'S STUDIES QUARTERLY 24 no. 1–2:400-11 Sp–Su '96.
Through an account of the history of women's rights in Turkey, this essay examines the current status of Turkish women; the relationship between the women's movement and women's studies; the major achievements of women's studies thus far; and the unfinished business of women's studies in higher education. Kemalist efforts aimed at integrating women into social and political life as full citizens are still valuable and prevailing ideals to be realized. The great majority of women now want to look on the world with their very eyes, and they also want their voices to be heard. The development and success of women's studies in Turkey will contribute to this cause and to the creation of a public awareness and sensitivity to gender and women's issues. T. HOTHEM.

598.   Bollmann, Barbara, Judith McManus, E. Michelle Rabouin and Peggy Valdez-Fergason. The integration of women's studies and feminist pedagogy into the core curriculum: An annotated bibliography. WOMEN'S STUDIES QUARTERLY 24 no. 3–4:201-14 Fall–Win '96.

599A.   Bonnin, Debby. Women's studies in South Africa. WOMEN'S STUDIES QUARTERLY 24 no. 1–2:378-99 Sp–Su '96.
While South Africa is in a transition, there is a long way to go before gender equality becomes a reality. This essay considers the role of such factors as women's education and employment in the development of South African women's studies. Examined are early programs and initiatives; the rectification of sexism on campus; responses outside academe; the relationship between women's studies and the women's movement; the major achievements of women's studies (including confronting the sexual politics of tertiary institutions); and the impact of women's studies on the traditional curriculum and on educational policy. T. HOTHEM.

600.   Cascio, Carole M. Integrating scholarship on minority women into health, physical education, and dance [The author, a dance and nutrition instructor, has asked faculty to consider more fully their choice of music and movement vocabularies in order to represent the cultural differences of their students. Also Minority women and the dance curriculum: An annotated bibliography pp. 222-8.]. WOMEN'S STUDIES QUARTERLY 24 no. 3–4:81-3 Fall–Win '96.

Example 5.27. *Women Studies Abstracts* vol. 27 no. 2 (Summer 1998) p. 1 (abstracts). Reprinted by permission of Transaction Publishers. Copyright © 1998 by Transaction Publishers; all rights reserved.

00 GENERAL

00A General and miscellaneous specific topics

99i:00001   00A05 34-01 35-01 46-01

Chatterji, Srishti D. (CH-LSNP; Lausanne)

★Cours d'analyse. 3. (French. French summary) [Analysis course. 3]

Équations différentielles ordinaires et aux dérivées partielles. [Ordinary and partial differential equations]

Mathématiques. [Mathematics]

Presses Polytechniques et Universitaires Romandes, Lausanne, 1998. xxvi+755 pp. sFr. 108.00. ISBN 2-88074-350-8

This textbook is the third, and concluding, part of an analysis course; the preceding volumes are concerned with vectorial analysis [S. D. Chatterji, *Cours d'analyse. 1*, Presses Polytech. Univ. Romandes, Lausanne, 1997; MR 98g:26001] and complex analysis [S. D. Chatterji, *Cours d'analyse. 2*, Presses Polytech. Univ. Romandes, Lausanne, 1997; MR 99a:30001]. The course is intended for undergraduate students of mathematics, physics, and engineering, say, in the second academic year. In order to read the present volume it is sufficient to have a basic knowledge of linear algebra, differential and integral calculus; knowledge of the preceding volumes proves not to be essential (a few things needed are quoted in each case). This fact of being relatively self-contained even applies, to some extent, to the individual chapters themselves.

The book is divided into three main parts: I. Ordinary differential equations, II. Hilbert space theory, and III. Partial differential equations. Parts I and III each take up only about 20% of the text, whereas most of the rest is devoted to part II.

Part I consists of two chapters: Chapter 1 deals, in detail, with existence and uniqueness of solutions of ODE in $\mathbf{R}^n$, according both to the Picard-Lindelöf and to the Peano approaches, including, e.g., continuation of solutions. However, elementary solution methods are not considered here. In the second chapter, linear systems of ODE are studied extensively. Two sections treat analytic solutions and qualitative properties of solutions to second-order equations; remarks on stability, periodic solutions, first integrals, etc., are added.

Part II is divided into four chapters: The first one gives a general introduction to Hilbert spaces, up to Riesz's representation theorem. The second is devoted to orthogonal expansions, especially Fourier series, their convergence behavior (e.g., Fejér's theorem), Fourier expansions of distributions, and orthogonal polynomials. Bounded and unbounded linear operators in Hilbert spaces, and

Example 5.28. *Mathematical Reviews* issue 99 (Sept. 1999) p. 5889 (abstracts). Reprinted by permission of American Mathematical Society.

25 years of high level technical education in Arad, Vol. 1
.... ＊00043
Aachen, 1995 .... ＊0001*
Aalborg, 1998 .... ＊6800⊃
ACM Symposium:
   Principles of Database Systems, 14th
     SIGACT-SIGMOD-SIGART .... ＊6800
Advances in cryptology—CRYPTO '98 .... ＊9405*
Algebraic groups and their representations .... ＊2000.
Algorithms and theory of computing .... ＊6509
Alushta, 1996 .... ＊8100
Anniversary:
   Birth of Obreschkoff, Nikola .... ＊0003
   Birth of Smorodinskiĭ, Ya. A. .... ＊81002–＊8109
   Death of John, Fritz 01033–0103
   Division of Applied Mathematics, Brown University.
     50th .... ＊0007*
Anogia Academic Village, 1997 .... ＊6500
Approximation algorithms for combinatorial optimization
.... ＊680C
Arad, 1996 .... ＊0007*
Arad, 1997 .... ＊0001-
Beijing, 1997 .... ＊68004,＊7300
Bibliography:
   de Prony, Gaspard Clair François Marie Riche
    .... ＊0103
   Karatsuba, Anatoliĭ Alekseevich 110C
   Stasheff, James Dillon 0103
   Witt, Ernst .... ＊0103
Biography:
   Babbage, Charles 0102
   de Prony, Gaspard Clair François Marie Riche
    .... ＊0103
   Jacobi, Carl Gustav Jacob .... ＊0102.
   Schnürlein, Ludwig Christoph 0103
   Stasheff, James Dillon 0105
   Witt, Ernst .... ＊0103
Birmingham, 1997 .... ＊0001
Birthday:
   Łojasiewicz, Stanisław .... ＊0003
   Parikh, Rohit J. .... ＊0309
Boca Raton, FL, 1998 .... ＊00020–＊0002
Brisbane, 1998 .... ＊9406
Calgary, AB, 1997 .... ＊5809
Cambridge, 1997 .... ＊2002.
Campos do Jordão, 1997 .... ＊8100
Charlemagne and his heritage. 1200 years of civilization
and science in Europe, Vol. 2 .... ＊0001
Cieszyn, 1998 .... ＊110C.
Collected Works:
   Witt, Ernst .... ＊0103
Colloquium:
   Carolus Magnus: 1200 Years of Civilization and
    Science in Europe, International .... ＊0001
   Logic '96 .... ＊030C.
Conference:
   Combinatorics, Graph Theory and Computing, 29th
    Southeastern International .... ＊00020–＊0002
   Complex Geometry and Mirror Symmetry ... ＊1409
   Cryptology, 18th Annual International, CRYPTO '9‹
    .... ＊9405
   Fournier, Gilles .... ＊0003
   Information Security and Privacy, 3rd Australasian.
    ACISP '98 .... ＊9406
   Inverse Problems and Applications, International
    .... ＊0003
   Knot Theory, International .... ＊570C
   Number Theory, 2nd Czech-Polish .... ＊110C

Correspondence:
   Legendre, Adrien-Marie–Jacobi, Carl Gustav Jacob
    .... ＊01022
Current and future challenges in the applications of
   mathematics .... ＊00017
Dedicated to the memory of Fernando Serrano ... ＊00032
Dedicated to the memory of Gilles Fournier ...... ＊00033
Dedicated to the memory of Karl Weierstrass .... ＊00034
Delft, 1996 .... ＊90004
Dubna, 1997 .... ＊81002–＊81003
Dynamic decision systems in uncertain environments
.... ＊90002
Encyclopaedia of Mathematical Sciences, 34 ...... ＊35002
Errata:
   "Invariants of Hopf algebras" 16064b
Exact C*-algebras and related topics .... ＊46001
Festschrift:
   Łojasiewicz, Stanisław .... ＊00035
   Parikh, Rohit J. .... ＊03003
Fukuoka, 1998 .... ＊03025
Geometric modelling techniques . ... ＊65004
Geometry of homogeneous spaces and submanifolds
.... ＊53001
Global optimization, control, and games, 3 .... ＊90003
Hajdúszoboszló, 1997 .... ＊00036
Halifax, NS, 1997 .... ＊68007
Harmonic/analytic function spaces and linear operators
.... ＊00018
Hydrodynamics and nonlinear instabilities .... ＊76001
IEEE Symposium:
   Multiple-valued Logic, 28th International, ISMVL '98
    .... ＊03025
Information security and privacy .... ＊94060
Integrable systems and algebraic geometry .... ＊14002
Introduction to implicit surfaces .... ＊00008
Istanbul, 1997 .... ＊00019
Italian mathematics after Unity .... ＊01001
IUTAM Symposium:
   Rheology of Bodies with Defects .... ＊73001
KNOTS '96 .... ＊57002
Kobe, 1997 .... ＊14002
Kraków, 1996 .... ＊00035
Kyoto, 1997 .... ＊14002
Lecture Notes in Computer Science, 1438 .... ＊94060
Lecture Notes in Computer Science, 1444 .... ＊68002
Lecture Notes in Computer Science, 1462 .... ＊94059
Lecture Notes in Computer Science, 1471 .... ＊68003
Lecture Notes in Computer Science, 1503 .... ＊68005
Lecture Notes in Logic, 12 .... ＊03002
Lecture Notes in Mathematics, 1682 .... ＊73040
Lecture Notes in Mathematics, 1692 .... ＊81122
Lecture Notes in Statistics, 130 .... ＊62023
Lecture Notes in Statistics, 139 .... ＊60028
Linear algebra and statistics .... ＊00019
Logic programming and knowledge representation
.... ＊68003
Meeting:
   Association of Symbolic Logic, European Summer
    .... ＊03002
   Scientific Communications, 3rd "Aurel Vlaicu"
    University .... ＊00027
   Scientific Communications, University of Arad, 4th
    ... . ＊00014
Memorial Issue:
   Fournier, Gilles .... ＊00033
   Serrano, Fernando .... ＊00032
   Susarla, Vyaghreshwarudu .... ＊62003
   Weierstrass, Karl Theodor Wilhelm .... ＊00034
Mirror symmetry, 3 .... ＊14003

Example 5.29. *Mathematical Reviews* issue 99 (Sept. 1999) p. xx (key index). Reprinted by permission of American Mathematical Society.

Indexes and abstracts are rapidly entering the Information Superhighway. The following are some examples and their respective Web addresses. Again, the reader is urged to look at these electronic versions (and others) in order to be familiar with this inevitable trend.

Alcohol and Alcohol Problems Science Database
    http://etoh.niaaa.nih.gov/

Anthropological Index Online
    http://lucy.ukc.ac.uk/cgi-bin/uncgi/Search_AI/search_bib_ai/anthind

CANCERLIT
    http://cancernet.nci.nih.gov/cancerlit.shtml

Dissertation Abstracts
    http://www.lib.umi.com/dissertations/gateway

Historical Abstracts
    http://serials.abc-clio.com/

Institute for Scientific Information
    http://www.isinet.com/

International Index to the Performing Arts
    http://iipaft.chadwyck.com/

Medieval Feminist Index
    http://www.haverford.edu/library/reference/mschaus/mfi/mfi.html

Population Index on the Web
    http://popindex.princeton.edu/

U.S. Patent Citation Database
    http://patents.cos.com/

EXAMPLES OF THESAURI

Following are selected examples of thesauri to show the range of thesauri available. Again, the reader is strongly encouraged to study the many hundreds and hundreds of these tools in order to get a picture of what is available.

Sample Thesaurus Entry
Alphabetical Descriptor Display

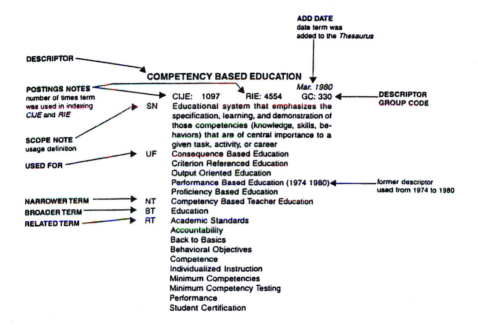

Example 5.30. *Thesaurus of ERIC Descriptors* (13th edition) (sample of alphabetical descriptor display). Reprinted from *Thesaurus of ERIC Descriptors*, 13th Edition edited by James E. Houston © 1995 by The Oryx Press. Used with permission from The Oryx Press, 4041 N. Central Ave., Suite 700, Phoenix, AZ 85012. 800-279-6799.

Descriptor Group Display

The Descriptor Groups offer a "table of contents" to the *Thesaurus*. A Descriptor Group Code appears within the main entry of each term in the Alphabetical Display of the *Thesaurus*. See the preceding Descriptor Groups section for Scope Notes about the various Descriptor Groups. Below is an alphabetical listing of all the Descriptors assigned to each Descriptor Group.

110 LEARNING AND PERCEPTION

ABILITY IDENTIFICATION
ABSTRACT REASONING
ACTIVE LEARNING
ADULT LEARNING
AROUSAL PATTERNS
ASSOCIATIVE LEARNING
ATTENTION
ATTENTION CONTROL
AUDIENCE RESPONSE
AUDITORY DISCRIMINATION
AUDITORY PERCEPTION
AUDITORY STIMULI
AURAL LEARNING
BEHAVIOR CHAINING
BEHAVIOR MODIFICATION
CLASSICAL CONDITIONING
COGNITIVE MAPPING
COGNITIVE PROCESSES
COGNITIVE PSYCHOLOGY
COGNITIVE RESTRUCTURING
COGNITIVE STRUCTURES
COGNITIVE STYLE
COMPENSATION (CONCEPT)
COMPREHENSION
CONCEPT FORMATION
CONCEPTUAL SCHEMES (1967 1980)
CONCEPTUAL TEMPO
CONDITIONING
CONSERVATION (CONCEPT)
CONSTRUCTED RESPONSE
CONSTRUCTIVISM (LEARNING)
CONTINGENCY MANAGEMENT
CONVERGENT THINKING
COVERT RESPONSE
CREATIVE THINKING
CRITICAL THINKING
CUES
DECISION MAKING
DECISION MAKING SKILLS
DEDUCTION
DEPTH PERCEPTION
DIMENSIONAL PREFERENCE
DISCOVERY LEARNING
DISCOVERY PROCESSES
DISCRIMINATION LEARNING
DIVERGENT THINKING
EIDETIC IMAGERY
ELECTRICAL STIMULI
ENCODING (PSYCHOLOGY)
EPISTEMOLOGY
EVALUATIVE THINKING
EXTINCTION (PSYCHOLOGY)
EYE FIXATIONS
EYE MOVEMENTS
FAMILIARITY
FIELD DEPENDENCE INDEPENDENCE
FIGURAL AFTEREFFECTS
FORMAL OPERATIONS
FUNDAMENTAL CONCEPTS
GENERALIZATION
HABIT FORMATION
HABITUATION

HEARING (PHYSIOLOGY)
IMITATION
INCIDENTAL LEARNING
INDUCTION
INFERENCES
INFORMATION SEEKING
INTELLECTUAL EXPERIENCE
INTENTIONAL LEARNING
INTUITION
KINESTHETIC METHODS
KINESTHETIC PERCEPTION
LEARNING
LEARNING EXPERIENCE
LEARNING MODALITIES
LEARNING MOTIVATION
LEARNING PLATEAUS
LEARNING PROBLEMS
LEARNING PROCESSES
LEARNING STRATEGIES
LISTENING COMPREHENSION
LOGICAL THINKING
LONG TERM MEMORY
MEDITATION
MEMORIZATION
MEMORY
METACOGNITION
MISCONCEPTIONS
MNEMONICS
MULTISENSORY LEARNING
NEGATIVE REINFORCEMENT
NONVERBAL LEARNING
NOVELTY (STIMULUS DIMENSION)
OBEDIENCE
OBJECT PERMANENCE
OBSERVATIONAL LEARNING
OPERANT CONDITIONING
OVERT RESPONSE
PAIRED ASSOCIATE LEARNING
PATTERNED RESPONSES
PERCEPTION
PERCEPTUAL MOTOR LEARNING
PICTORIAL STIMULI
PLANNING
POSITIVE REINFORCEMENT
PRAISE
PRESCHOOL LEARNING (1966 1980)
PRIMACY EFFECT
PRIOR LEARNING
PROBLEM SOLVING
PRODUCTIVE THINKING
PUPILLARY DILATION
READER RESPONSE
RECALL (PSYCHOLOGY)
RECOGNITION (PSYCHOLOGY)
REFERENCE GROUPS
REINFORCEMENT
REMINISCENCE
RETENTION (PSYCHOLOGY)
REVIEW (REEXAMINATION)
ROLE MODELS
ROTE LEARNING
SCHEMATA (COGNITION)
SELECTION
SENSORY DEPRIVATION

SENSORY EXPERIENCE
SENSORY INTEGRATION
SEQUENTIAL LEARNING
SERIAL LEARNING
SERIAL ORDERING
SHORT TERM MEMORY
SOCIAL COGNITION
SOCIAL REINFORCEMENT
STIMULATION
STIMULI
STIMULUS GENERALIZATION
SUGGESTOPEDIA
SYMBOLIC LEARNING
TACTILE STIMULI
TACTUAL PERCEPTION
THINKING SKILLS
TIME FACTORS (LEARNING)
TIME PERSPECTIVE
TIMEOUT
TOKEN ECONOMY
TRANSCENDENTAL MEDITATION
TRANSFER OF TRAINING
VALUE JUDGMENT
VERBAL LEARNING
VERBAL OPERANT CONDITIONING
VERBAL STIMULI
VISION
VISUAL ACUITY
VISUAL DISCRIMINATION
VISUAL LEARNING
VISUAL LITERACY
VISUAL PERCEPTION
VISUAL STIMULI
VISUALIZATION

120 INDIVIDUAL DEVELOPMENT

ABILITY
ACADEMIC ABILITY
ACADEMIC APTITUDE
ACADEMIC ASPIRATION
ACHIEVEMENT
ACHIEVEMENT NEED
ACTIVITIES
ADOLESCENT DEVELOPMENT
ADOLESCENTS
ADULT DEVELOPMENT
ADULTS
ADULTS (30 TO 45)
AFFECTION
AFFECTIVE BEHAVIOR
AFFILIATION NEED
AGE
AGE DIFFERENCES
AGE GROUPS
AGING (INDIVIDUALS)
ALTRUISM
ANDROGYNY
ANIMAL BEHAVIOR
APATHY
APTITUDE
ASPIRATION
ASSERTIVENESS
ASSOCIATION (PSYCHOLOGY)

Example 5.31. *Thesaurus of ERIC Descriptors* (13th edition) (group display). Reprinted from *Thesaurus of ERIC Descriptors*, 13th Edition edited by James E. Houston © 1995 by The Oryx Press. Used with permission from The Oryx Press, 4041 N. Central Ave., Suite 700, Phoenix, AZ 85012. 800-279-6799.

ABBREVIATIONS

ABILITY
. ACADEMIC ABILITY
. COGNITIVE ABILITY
.. THINKING SKILLS
. COMPETENCE
.. INTERPERSONAL COMPETENCE
.. MINIMUM COMPETENCIES
.. TEACHER COMPETENCIES
. LANGUAGE PROFICIENCY
.. LANGUAGE FLUENCY
.. THRESHOLD LEVEL (LANGUAGES)
. LEADERSHIP
.. BLACK LEADERSHIP
.. INFORMAL LEADERSHIP
.. INSTRUCTIONAL LEADERSHIP
.. STUDENT LEADERSHIP
. NONVERBAL ABILITY
. SKILLS
.. AGRICULTURAL SKILLS
.. BASIC SKILLS
.. ALPHABETIZING SKILLS
.. BUSINESS SKILLS
.. BOOKKEEPING
... KEYBOARDING (DATA ENTRY)
.. RECORDKEEPING
... TYPEWRITING
.. COMMUNICATION SKILLS
... COMMUNICATIVE COMPETENCE (LANGUAGES)
.... THRESHOLD LEVEL (LANGUAGES)
.. DAILY LIVING SKILLS
.. SELF CARE SKILLS
.. DECISION MAKING SKILLS
.. HOME ECONOMICS SKILLS
.. HOMEMAKING SKILLS
.. INFORMATION SKILLS
.. LIBRARY SKILLS
.. INTERPRETIVE SKILLS
.. JOB SKILLS
.. LANGUAGE SKILLS
... AUDIOLINGUAL SKILLS
... LISTENING SKILLS
... SPEECH SKILLS
... COMMUNICATIVE COMPETENCE (LANGUAGES)
.... THRESHOLD LEVEL (LANGUAGES)
... READING SKILLS
.... READING COMPREHENSION
.... READING RATE
... VOCABULARY SKILLS
... WRITING SKILLS
.. LOCATIONAL SKILLS (SOCIAL STUDIES)
... MAP SKILLS
.. MATHEMATICS SKILLS
.. MECHANICAL SKILLS
.. MINIMUM COMPETENCIES
.. PARENTING SKILLS
.. PSYCHOMOTOR SKILLS
... MARKSMANSHIP
... OBJECT MANIPULATION
.. PERCEPTUAL MOTOR COORDINATION
... EYE HAND COORDINATION
... EYE VOICE SPAN
.. RESEARCH SKILLS
.. SALESMANSHIP
.. SCIENCE PROCESS SKILLS
.. STUDY SKILLS
... WORD STUDY SKILLS
.. TEACHING SKILLS
.. THINKING SKILLS
.. VISUAL LITERACY
. SPATIAL ABILITY
. VERBAL ABILITY
.. READING ABILITY
... READING SKILLS
.... READING COMPREHENSION
..... READING RATE
.. WRITING ABILITY
... WRITING SKILLS

:::: ORGANIZATION
::: CLASSIFICATION

:: GROUPING (INSTRUCTIONAL PURPOSES)
: HOMOGENEOUS GROUPING
ABILITY GROUPING

: IDENTIFICATION
ABILITY IDENTIFICATION

ABORTIONS

:: LITERACY
:: LANGUAGE ARTS
:: WRITING (COMPOSITION)
:::: SERVICES
:: INFORMATION SERVICES
:: INFORMATION PROCESSING
: DOCUMENTATION
ABSTRACTING

: COGNITIVE PROCESSES
ABSTRACT REASONING
. GENERALIZATION
.. STIMULUS GENERALIZATION

:: PUBLICATIONS
: REFERENCE MATERIALS
ABSTRACTS

: ABILITY
ACADEMIC ABILITY

: ACHIEVEMENT
ACADEMIC ACHIEVEMENT
. EDUCATIONAL ATTAINMENT
. STUDENT PROMOTION

::: GUIDANCE
:: COUNSELING
: EDUCATIONAL COUNSELING
ACADEMIC ADVISING

:: GROUPS
: GIFTED
ACADEMICALLY GIFTED

ACADEMICALLY HANDICAPPED (1966 1980)

: APTITUDE
ACADEMIC APTITUDE

: ASPIRATION
ACADEMIC ASPIRATION

::::: GROUPS
:::: PERSONNEL
::: SCHOOL PERSONNEL
:: GROUPS
::: PERSONNEL
:: PROFESSIONAL PERSONNEL
. FACULTY
:: GROUPS
::: PERSONNEL
: ADMINISTRATORS
: DEANS
ACADEMIC DEANS

: EDUCATION
ACADEMIC EDUCATION

:: BEHAVIOR
:: PERFORMANCE
: FAILURE
ACADEMIC FAILURE
. READING FAILURE

: FREEDOM
ACADEMIC FREEDOM

: INSTITUTIONS
:: INFORMATION SOURCES
: LIBRARIES

ACADEMIC LIBRARIES
. COLLEGE LIBRARIES

:: BEHAVIOR
: PERSISTENCE
ACADEMIC PERSISTENCE

: PROBATIONARY PERIOD
ACADEMIC PROBATION

:: STATUS
: EMPLOYMENT LEVEL
ACADEMIC RANK (PROFESSIONAL)

: RECORDS (FORMS)
: STUDENT RECORDS
ACADEMIC RECORDS

: STANDARDS
ACADEMIC STANDARDS
. GRADUATION REQUIREMENTS
. DEGREE REQUIREMENTS

: FLEXIBLE PROGRESSION
ACCELERATION (EDUCATION)

:: SCIENTIFIC CONCEPTS
: MOTION
ACCELERATION (PHYSICS)

ACCESSIBILITY (FOR DISABLED)

: OPPORTUNITIES
: EDUCATIONAL OPPORTUNITIES
ACCESS TO EDUCATION

ACCESS TO INFORMATION
. FREEDOM OF INFORMATION

: PREVENTION
ACCIDENT PREVENTION

ACCIDENTS
. SCHOOL ACCIDENTS
. TRAFFIC ACCIDENTS

: RESPONSIBILITY
ACCOUNTABILITY

::: GROUPS
:: PERSONNEL
: PROFESSIONAL PERSONNEL
ACCOUNTANTS
. CERTIFIED PUBLIC ACCOUNTANTS

: TECHNOLOGY
ACCOUNTING
. PROPERTY ACCOUNTING
. SCHOOL ACCOUNTING

: CERTIFICATION
ACCREDITATION (INSTITUTIONS)

::: GROUPS
:: ORGANIZATIONS (GROUPS)
: AGENCIES
ACCREDITING AGENCIES

ACCULTURATION

ACHIEVEMENT
. ACADEMIC ACHIEVEMENT
.. EDUCATIONAL ATTAINMENT
.. STUDENT PROMOTION
. BLACK ACHIEVEMENT
. GRADUATION
. HIGH ACHIEVEMENT
. KNOWLEDGE LEVEL
. LOW ACHIEVEMENT
. MATHEMATICS ACHIEVEMENT
. OVERACHIEVEMENT
. READING ACHIEVEMENT
. SCHOLARSHIP

. UNDERACHIEVEMENT
. WRITING ACHIEVEMENT

: IMPROVEMENT
ACHIEVEMENT GAINS

::: NEEDS
:: INDIVIDUAL NEEDS
: PSYCHOLOGICAL NEEDS
: MOTIVATION
ACHIEVEMENT NEED

: MEASUREMENT
ACHIEVEMENT RATING
. GRADING
.. CREDIT NO CREDIT GRADING
.. PASS FAIL GRADING

: MEASURES (INDIVIDUALS)
: TESTS
ACHIEVEMENT TESTS
. EQUIVALENCY TESTS
. MASTERY TESTS
. NATIONAL COMPETENCY TESTS

:: POLLUTION
: WATER POLLUTION
: POLLUTION
: AIR POLLUTION
ACID RAIN

: ENVIRONMENT
: PHYSICAL ENVIRONMENT
ACOUSTICAL ENVIRONMENT
. NOISE (SOUND)

: STRUCTURAL ELEMENTS (CONSTRUCTION)
ACOUSTIC INSULATION

::: LINGUISTICS
:: PHONOLOGY
: PHONETICS
ACOUSTIC PHONETICS

:: LIBERAL ARTS
: SCIENCES
ACOUSTICS
. PSYCHOACOUSTICS

:: VIRUSES
::: DISABILITIES
:: DISEASES
: COMMUNICABLE DISEASES
ACQUIRED IMMUNE DEFICIENCY SYNDROME

:::: LIBERAL ARTS
::: HUMANITIES
:: FINE ARTS
: THEATER ARTS
ACTING

: RESEARCH
ACTION RESEARCH

: LEARNING
ACTIVE LEARNING

:: BEHAVIOR
: SOCIAL BEHAVIOR
ACTIVISM

ACTIVITIES
. ART ACTIVITIES
. CREATIVE ACTIVITIES
.. BRAINSTORMING
.. CREATIVE ART
... CREATIVE DRAMATICS
.. CREATIVE EXPRESSION
.. CREATIVE WRITING
.. IMPROVISATION
. CULTURAL ACTIVITIES
. ENRICHMENT ACTIVITIES

Example 5.32. *Thesaurus of ERIC Descriptors* (13th edition) p. 565 (two-way hierarchical term display).

```
                                  TYPE  A BEHAVIOR
DIVERSITY (CULTURAL) AS AN OBSERVATION OR  A FACT   Use CULTURAL DIFFERENCES
                HIGHER EDUCATION AS  A FIELD OF STUDY   Use POSTSECONDARY EDUCATION AS A FIELD OF STUDY
       POSTSECONDARY EDUCATION AS  A FIELD OF STUDY
                  SCHOOLS WITHIN  A SCHOOL PLAN   Use HOUSE PLAN
                       PARENT AS  A TEACHER   Use PARENTS AS TEACHERS
           DIVERSITY (CULTURAL) AS  A VALUE   Use CULTURAL PLURALISM
                          GRADE  A YEAR INTEGRATION (1966 1980)   Use SCHOOL DESEGREGATION
                                 ABBREVIATIONS
                                 ABILITY
               ACADEMIC  ABILITY
              COGNITIVE  ABILITY
               CREATIVE  ABILITY (1968 1980)   Use CREATIVITY
                                 ABILITY GROUPING
                                 ABILITY IDENTIFICATION
               LANGUAGE  ABILITY (1966 1980)
                 MENTAL  ABILITY   Use COGNITIVE ABILITY
                  MOTOR  ABILITY   Use PSYCHOMOTOR SKILLS
              NONVERBAL  ABILITY
                READING  ABILITY
             SCHOLASTIC  ABILITY   Use ACADEMIC ABILITY
                SPATIAL  ABILITY
                STUDENT  ABILITY (1966 1980)   Use ACADEMIC ABILITY
                    LOW  ABILITY STUDENTS (1967 1980)
             PREDICTIVE  ABILITY (TESTING) (1966 1980)   Use PREDICTIVE MEASUREMENT
                 VERBAL  ABILITY
            VISUOSPATIAL  ABILITY   Use SPATIAL ABILITY
                WRITING  ABILITY
                                 ABLE STUDENTS (1966 1978)   Use ACADEMICALLY GIFTED
                                 ABNORMAL PSYCHOLOGY   Use PSYCHOPATHOLOGY
              AUSTRALIAN  ABORIGINAL LANGUAGES
                                 ABORIGINAL PEOPLE   Use INDIGENOUS POPULATIONS
                                 ABORTIONS
                                 ABREACTION   Use CATHARSIS
                  STUDY  ABROAD
                WORKING  ABROAD   Use OVERSEAS EMPLOYMENT
                                 ABSENCE (EMPLOYEES)   Use EMPLOYEE ABSENTEEISM
                 FATHER  ABSENCE   Use FATHERLESS FAMILY
              LEAVE OF  ABSENCE (1968 1980)   Use LEAVES OF ABSENCE
             LEAVES OF  ABSENCE
                 MOTHER  ABSENCE   Use MOTHERLESS FAMILY
                 PARENT  ABSENCE   Use ONE PARENT FAMILY
                                 ABSENCE (STUDENTS)   Use ATTENDANCE
                                 ABSENCE (TEACHERS)   Use EMPLOYEE ABSENTEEISM and TEACHER ATTENDANCE
              EMPLOYEE  ABSENTEEISM
                                 ABSOLUTE HUMIDITY   Use HUMIDITY
                                 ABSOLUTE PRESSURE   Use PRESSURE (PHYSICS)
                                 ABSTRACT BIBLIOGRAPHIES   Use ANNOTATED BIBLIOGRAPHIES
                                 ABSTRACT REASONING
                                 ABSTRACTING
                                 ABSTRACTION LEVELS (1968 1980)   Use ABSTRACT REASONING
                                 ABSTRACTION TESTS (1967 1980)   Use COGNITIVE TESTS
                                 ABSTRACTS
                ALCOHOL  ABUSE
                  CHILD  ABUSE
           CHILD SEXUAL  ABUSE   Use CHILD ABUSE and SEXUAL ABUSE
                   DRUG  ABUSE
                  ELDER  ABUSE
              EMOTIONAL  ABUSE
          PSYCHOLOGICAL  ABUSE   Use EMOTIONAL ABUSE
                   SELF  ABUSE   Use SELF DESTRUCTIVE BEHAVIOR
                 SEXUAL  ABUSE
              SUBSTANCE  ABUSE
                   TEST  ABUSE   Use TEST USE
                 VERBAL  ABUSE
                                 ABUSED CHILDREN   Use CHILD ABUSE
                                 ABUSED ELDERLY   Use ELDER ABUSE
                                 ABUSED WOMEN   Use BATTERED WOMEN
              AGING IN  ACADEMIA
                                 ACADEMIC ABILITY
                                 ACADEMIC ACHIEVEMENT
                                 ACADEMIC ADVISING
                                 ACADEMIC ALLIANCES   Use PARTNERSHIPS IN EDUCATION
                                 ACADEMIC APTITUDE
                                 ACADEMIC ASPIRATION
                                 ACADEMIC CALENDARS   Use SCHOOL SCHEDULES
                                 ACADEMIC CURRICULUM   Use ACADEMIC EDUCATION
                                 ACADEMIC DEANS
                DEGREES  (ACADEMIC)
                                 ACADEMIC DEPARTMENTS   Use DEPARTMENTS
                                 ACADEMIC DISCIPLINES   Use INTELLECTUAL DISCIPLINES
                                 ACADEMIC EDUCATION
                                 ACADEMIC ENRICHMENT (1966 1980)   Use ENRICHMENT
                                 ACADEMIC ENVIRONMENT   Use EDUCATIONAL ENVIRONMENT
                                 ACADEMIC FAILURE
                                 ACADEMIC FREEDOM
                                 ACADEMIC GAMES   Use EDUCATIONAL GAMES
                                 ACADEMIC LEARNING TIME   Use TIME ON TASK
                                 ACADEMIC LIBRARIES
                                 ACADEMIC MALPRACTICE   Use EDUCATIONAL MALPRACTICE
                  CHIEF  ACADEMIC OFFICERS   Use ACADEMIC DEANS
                                 ACADEMIC PERFORMANCE (1966 1974)   Use ACADEMIC ACHIEVEMENT
                                 ACADEMIC PERSISTENCE
```

Example 5.33. *Thesaurus of ERIC Descriptors* (13th edition) p. 337 (rotated descriptor display).

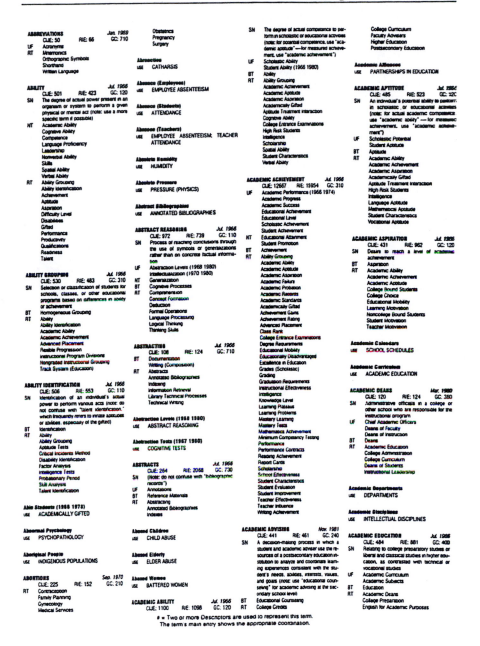

Example 5.34. *Thesaurus of ERIC Descriptors* (13th edition) p. 5 (alphabetical descriptor display).

The following are examples of thesauri available electronically:

The Art & Architecture Thesaurus
http://shiva.pub.getty.edu/aat_browser

ASIS Thesaurus of Information Science
http://www.asis.org/Publications/Thesaurus/isframe.htm

ERIC Thesaurus
http://ericae.net/scripts/ewiz/amain2.asp

The Getty Thesaurus of Geographic Names
http://tomasini.gii.getty.edu:8000/tgn_browser/

Legislative Indexing Vocabulary (LIV) Thesaurus
http://lcweb.loc.gov/lexico/liv/brsearch.html

Medical Subject Headings (MeSH)
http://www.nlm.nih.gov/mesh/meshhome.html

NASA Thesaurus
http://www.sti.nasa.gov/thesfrm1.htm

The Indexing Process

Indexing is the process of identifying information in a knowledge record (text or nontext) and organizing the pointers to that information into a searchable file. Indexing is an art, but an art that requires orderly and meticulous procedures. The outcome of the indexing process is an index that indicates topics and possible uses for the document and points to the location of the information.

When we start discussing indexing procedures, the phrase *trade-offs* always comes to mind. There are trade-offs with the use of controlled vocabulary *vs.* natural language, recall *vs.* precision, specific *vs.* generic indexing, indented format *vs.* run-in format, alphabetical *vs.* classified arrangement, conceptual *vs.* keyword indexing, and on and on. To outsiders it might appear that nobody is sure how indexing should be done. That may be true; on the other hand it is undeniable that we have developed some procedures that work, despite a lack of consensus among indexers. There are many ways to make a good index.

A good starting point for learning how to index (or maybe how *not* to index) is to study existing indexes of every type. You learn to index by indexing and studying the work of others. Success is a strong function of experience and observation.

A person who examines and uses indexes critically will gradually learn what an ideal index should be like, although indexes vary widely in their characteristics and quality. As you study indexes you will notice such things as differences in types of printing and displays, outlay of main headings and subheadings, location indicators and bibliographical information. Sometimes instructions for using the index are poor or nonexistent, so that the user must discover how to use it by trial and error. Then the real test comes by trying to find information with the index. Look up words, follow out cross-references. How many times do you have to back up and rack your brain for another synonym? Make notes of the faults you find and strive to not make the same mistakes when you index.

Good indexing is not a casual clerical job. It is the result of a professional activity carried out by people with proper training and experience. There are procedures and techniques, worked out over the years, that can be learned and followed. We will address these procedures after we discuss the fundamental concept of *aboutness*.

ABOUTNESS

A good index is the result of a careful intellectual process, involving an understanding of what an author wants to say and to whom it is said. It involves meticulous examination of the text, the discovery of topics and their particular slant, the selection of entry terms, the creating of understandable locators, and an effective and attractive display of the index.

The trouble arises when we begin deciding what the document is about. An index is an instrument for searching information stores for specific information. The user believes that she knows what her search is about, although she may have trouble expressing it. The indexer must understand beforehand what the document is about and be on the same wavelength as the user when she comes along. Otherwise there will be no information retrieval connection.

Conceiving what an item is about and then translating the concept analysis into correct index terms is a closely linked continuum, but there are distinguishable intellectual decision points in the process.

The *aboutness* of a document is not limited to the explicit keywords from the text. Indexers must learn to see both the forest and the trees. The overall purpose, scope and intended audience should be grasped first (the forest) and then there needs to be an understanding of the specific aspects and their relation to the whole (the trees).

Aboutness is not a trivial concept. It is much more than just coverage of surface content. It is concerned with the cognitive processes that involve the generator of information and the final uses of that information. A major reason that indexing fails is because the indexer superficially dealt with the *aboutness* issue.

One way to understand the concept of *aboutness* is to think of a document as having two characteristics: what the words *say* and what they *mean*. A string of words usually *say* one fairly consistent thing, but what the string *means* depends on a complexity of understandings and the variegations of language. Language is a multilayer carrier of information, with subtle messages. A sentence can convey messages that may mean different things to different people. *Aboutness* can have different interpretations according to the background and orientation of the writer of the words and the reader of the words, and, of course, the intervention of the indexer. The bottom line is that language is simultaneously expressive and vague. This is one of the reasons why computers are poor indexers. Computers do not understand expressiveness, vagueness, or *aboutness*.

The index should discriminate between major and minor treatments of topics in the document. Neophyte indexers often have an *aboutness* problem in distinguishing between primary subjects and secondary subjects in a text. Their usual solution is to index everything and thus nothing is overlooked. Experienced indexers can have this problem also. Often it is the fault of the text itself. It is not clear what is primary and what is secondary and this is a major part of the *aboutness* problem.

Finally, *aboutness* will also play a role in the exhaustivity and specificity of the indexing. An index points to all important topics in the document, but it has to work within the constraints of the exhaustivity level that may be mandated for the particular indexing environment. And specificity should be as close to the language of the document as the indexing language permits, which brings in the consideration of the *aboutness* of the document.

STEPS IN INDEXING

The task of an indexer is to provide guides to the subject content of knowledge records, the result of which is a subject index. Probably only an experienced indexer can come somewhat close to understanding the total process, which is a combination of formal rules, common sense, and an elusive thing called talent. Like people in other creative fields, indexers, even those with years of experience, often have a difficult time describing what they do. Subjective judgments play a major role.

Indexing can be done by humans, by a computer, or by a combination of the two; however, indexers have individual styles and approaches. Regardless of whether the indexer is a machine or a human being, or has this or that different style, in general these procedures are followed:

1. Decide which topics in the item are relevant to the potential user of the document.
2. Decide which topics truly capture the content of the document.
3. Determine terms that come as close as possible to the terminology used in the document.
4. Decide on index terms and the specificity of those terms.
5. Group references to information that is scattered in the text of the document.
6. Combine headings and subheadings into related multilevel headings.
7. Direct the user seeking information under terms not used to those that are being used by means of *see* references and to related terms with *see also* references.
8. Arrange the index into a systematic presentation.

The indexing process begins with deciding whether or not the document is worth indexing. What to index is decided on in two general ways. First, if you work in an organization, the organization has policies. For example, a policy might be to index editorials or letters to the editor. Second, indexers make value judgments on what material to include in the index and what to leave out. The quality of an index can be judged by what is left out as well as by what is included.

The item is scanned quickly to see if it meets the criteria for being indexed. These criteria are not necessarily a judgment of the scholarly merit of the item, but are a judgment based on the objectives and policies of the indexing environment. The policies and purposes of a large general indexing service will be geared to a large user group with a broad subject interest, while in a special library or a narrowly defined information center the users will have a distinct, more specific type of information need. In other words, the decision to index or not to index is based on the information needs of the clientele. Incidentally, needs of the clientele will also affect the indexing process proper in regards to depth and specificity of indexing.

The next decision is what parts of the document will be indexed and what parts will be passed over. Not everything in the item needs to be indexed. As an indexer reviews a document she makes decisions about inclusion and exclusion. These are value judgments based on user needs and indexing policy.

In the case of indexing periodicals, there is very likely a rigid policy guide that spells out what is to be indexed. This is necessary in order to maintain consistency when many indexers are involved across many years of journal continuation and multiple journal titles. The index should include the names of authors and co-authors to the articles. Generally, every article should be indexed. These are the centerpieces of the journal and, indeed, the reason for the journal's existence. The decision of what to index beyond this depends on the nature of the journal, its readers, and the economics involved. Some journals have only the articles indexed and others may have practically everything, including advertisements and gossip columns. The inclusion of the other material depends on the degree of pertinent information usually carried by these components in the specific journals. For example, some editorials carry weighty material and occasionally even important research analysis/synthesis. If so, this needs to be indexed. In general, conference programs, letters to the editor, professional gossip columns, and the like are not indexed.

Books also have materials that usually are not indexed. Among these are most of the up-front materials, such as title pages, dedications, prefaces, and tables of contents. All corporate, personal, and place names should be indexed.

Then the decision must be made about how exhaustively the material will be indexed. That is, will every minute aspect of the indexable material be reflected or only the applicable facets? Related to this is how specifically the material will be indexed. A good index has mechanisms (e.g., broader or narrow terms) to allow users to adjust the level of specificity in their search requests when they don't get the type of response they expected, but indexing decisions will assure that these mechanisms are adequate.

Once these decisions are made, the actual indexing begins and the following steps are suggested:

1. Record the bibliographic data.
2. Analyze the content.
3. Determine subject facets.
4. Convert to the indexing language.
5. Review what has been done.

Recording of Bibliographic Data

Good bibliographic form can be summed up simply—it includes all useful data, leaves out useless data, and is consistent in format. For example, if using only the initials of an author's given name fulfills the needs of the users and causes no ambiguity, it would be unnecessary to waste space or time verifying the full name. Care must be taken to see that the data is recorded accurately, for the obvious reason that incorrect entries cause the document to become inaccessible. Even if an error is not critical, it can be irritating.

Content Analysis

The content analysis stage can be affected by the environmental situation. For example, the process may be hurried if there is a labor shortage or other critical time factors. Also, the amount of time involved in content analysis will depend on the nature of the document and the experience of the indexer.

The major factor will be policy decisions. Indexers generally work under guidelines imposed by the agency they work for or under self-imposed guidelines if they work alone. Often these guidelines are concerned with the selection of certain content indicators and the rejection of others. For example, indexers of scientific literature may be told to concentrate on methodology, measurement, equipment used, and the results and to ignore historical material. Indexers attempt to represent every possible concept only in very general information systems. The more familiar the indexer is with the field in general, the easier content analysis.

Following the familiarization phase, indexers must decide which aspects of subjects will be emphasized and which aspects will be deemphasized. Generally, the scope of the topics of the document should be reflected in the index. Some of the facets will be basic to the needs of the index users, some will be of marginal interest, and some will be of no importance. These decisions are made at the analysis stage. As these decisions are being made, indexers jot down the concepts, either using words directly out of the text or drawing on their own vocabulary or a combination of both.

Where do the concepts come from? Formal papers can be broken down into basic units for analysis.

The Title

The use of permuted titles as indexes was discussed earlier. Surely titles (and subtitles) give important clues to subject content, but they do have certain drawbacks. In order to be concise, titles often generalize. The purpose of a title is to convey to the potential reader an understanding of the paper's major topic. Specific aspects of that topic may or may not be conveyed.

We are assuming in the foregoing that titles are indicative of document content. Unfortunately, good title writing is not always a strong point in science papers and even less so in other scholarly writings. Titles may be vague, either because they are too generalized or because the author is aiming for a *catchy* title. In too many cases, the titles, unfortunately, are simply not related at all to the subjects dealt with. Despite these drawbacks, titles are a basic indexing unit and they are the first stop in determining subject content.

The Abstract

The second important unit to be considered is the abstract. Whereas index terms simply indicate subject content, abstracts are actual information-packed miniatures of documents, and good abstracts can be fundamental indicators of subject content. Abstracts should strip away ephemeral material and deal with the key subjects in the paper. Most of the words in a good abstract will heavily convey subject content.

Extracted abstracts, that is, abstracts that simply string together sentences lifted from the text, are less useful than original abstracts. In the latter case, the abstract writer expresses concepts using words not directly used by the author. Really good abstracts of this kind come close to being all that is necessary for adequate indexing, but a wealth of studies over the years tend to show that abstracts alone are not consistently as good for indexing as using all the indexable units in a document. Unfortunately, abstracts, like titles, can be badly written and misleading.

The Text Itself

By convention, most technical and scholarly papers follow a certain pattern that gives the indexer an important shortcut to understanding subject content. First, the introduction, the summary, and the conclusion should be read. As the old saying goes, the introduction explains what is *going* to be said, and the summary and conclusion explain what *has* been said. At least the overall intent of the paper can be ascertained from these units.

Section headings should also be observed, since these are, in a sense, miniature titles to the major parts of the paper. As content indicators, they have the same strengths and weaknesses of titles.

In addition, first and last sentences of paragraphs should receive primary attention since, by convention, these sentences carry the message of the paragraphs. Numerous indexing studies have empirically demonstrated that the first sentences, especially, carry the message of the paragraph.

A number of other things in the text should be considered. The historical and theoretical background of the paper's topic should be studied, if present. The methodology and sources, if described, can be important. Charts, diagrams, graphs, photographs, and other such illustrative materials may be a key factor for understanding content. Knowing what to read and what to skim comes from experience, but these items should be helpful in examining the text of the document.

The References Section

Most technical and scholarly papers are accompanied by a list of references. In the past few decades or so there has been a growing interest in the contribution of these references to content analysis. A great deal of study has been done on references and their importance for indexing. Citation indexing and bibliographic coupling techniques are two approaches that come to mind. It is generally conceded that writers take referencing seriously and that these lists reflect the subject content of the papers. Authors cite other writers who have written on the same topic, both to support their ideas and to give the reader an opportunity to go to other works that are closely related. Of course, the subject indicator in the reference list is again the title, although the names of the authors may also be keys to subject content, especially if they are recognized as experts in particular subject areas. Although the weaknesses and strengths in title indexing are still present, the range and variety of titles in the reference list can add substantially to an understanding of subject content.

SOME KEY POINTS

Subject Determination

The indexer must determine what the document is about. The indexer, therefore, scans a knowledge record, looking at sentences, phrases, and words that reveal what the document is about. Then a subjective decision is made concerning the meaning of the document and what is relevant to the users of the index. How does an indexer make these decisions? We have little understanding of the mental processes, but there appears to be two general types of indexers. One type reads a document and understands what the paper is about. The other type may not totally understand the paper but has the talent for selecting appropriate keywords from the text.

The objective now is to form a mental picture of what the author is saying. The author is not present, and all the indexer has to go on are symbols, printed and graphic, in the knowledge record. Language is ambiguous and metaphorical, and the indexer must now make the best possible subjective decisions. For example, "The mosquitoes attack with the ferocity of a tiger" is about mosquitoes, not tigers, and tigers would be an incorrect term (with the possible exception that there might be a language professor who is studying metaphor in scientific writings).

The indexer is now making intellectual decisions—decisions that will make or break the indexing of that document. The fundamental problem here is that the concept of a subject is an elusive one. All writers in an area have a unique understanding of what that subject is and also a unique way of expressing themselves and choosing words when they write. The situation is the same when it comes to the indexer, and eventually to the reader. If we were all robots, programmed to write the same way, there would be no indexing problems.

A naïve indexing rule at this point might be to index all important subjects. But, what is important? For one thing, how often an idea is repeated may be an indication of its importance. Most of the automatic indexing techniques using computers are based in one way or another on the frequency of occurrence of words in a text, and this comes from the intuitive feeling that major ideas are repeated and minor ideas are only mentioned.

Another clue is style and grammatical structure. For example, in the sentence "The mosquitoes attacked with ferocity," the word *mosquitoes* is an important word, but in the sentence "The queen looked at me with her mosquito eyes," *mosquito* is probably not important. Also, the author will often tell us, either implicitly or explicitly, that a topic is an important point in the paper, and generally we can believe it.

Locators

A *locator* points out the place where the actual information in a text is located. Hence, the name locator. Locators can range from brief page numbers, to more detailed notations, to full bibliographic citations. Usually it is the number of a page. There can be others, e.g., columns numbers, place on an encyclopedia page, lines in a play, Scripture's book, chapter and verse. Locators for articles in periodicals are a bit more complex. Generally, they include title of the journal, year, volume number, issue number, and pages.

Term Selection

A quality index is the result of a series of good indexing decisions. Indexers must be certain that all the right terms have been selected, but also that no needed terms have been excluded. Including the wrong terms will lead the user to information not wanted or needed, and leaving out the right terms will keep needed information from being discovered. In many ways, indexers are trying to second-guess what the users need and how they will react to the index entries. If users have a particular information need, what term will they use to identify the document the indexers have in their hands? Closely related to this, if the users decide to use that term, will they be satisfied?

The ideal index term clearly reflects what the document is about. It is precise enough to locate specific information, yet it is broad enough to identify related material. It is at this point that a good thesaurus will tie terms to related terms by showing semantic and hierarchical interrelationships, through cross-references, term qualifiers, and scope notes.

Entry Points

Entry terms may be a proper term, that is, a term that was used to index, or the term may direct the user to a proper term. The relationship established by entry terms with allowed index terms is important to successful indexing and searching. The user who thinks of a possible subject term and then cannot find that term as an entry term either thinks of another term or gives up.

Entry terms are often near-synonyms of an acceptable term. They may also be permutations or pluralization. Often entry terms are colloquial and the cross-reference leads to the more formal term.

From the viewpoint of the users, entry points into the index are extremely critical, perhaps the most important aspect of an index. An ideal index would be responsive to any word users might select when they begin the information search. Such an index would probably be impractical because of construction costs and the physical size of the tool. At the same time, an index with skimpy entry points is less effective, and the burden, both in cost and time, then shifts to the user.

DEPTH OF INDEXING

Exhaustivity and *specificity* are the two sides of a coin called depth of indexing. When an item is indexed both exhaustively and specifically, then the item has been indexed in depth. Depth of indexing is the degree to which a topic is represented in detail in an index; it is related to both the exhaustivity and the specificity of the indexing.

Exhaustivity

Exhaustivity in indexing implies that possible terms have been exhausted for a particular document. Thus the document will likely have more index terms assigned, although the number of index terms is not necessarily solely a reflection of exhaustivity. The number of terms may simply reflect specificity, if many levels in a generic tree are used.

The more exhaustive the item is indexed, the more likely it will be discovered because of the wider range of subject terms. The trade-off is that the document may not be specifically pertinent to the user's need. Not only should topics be selected on the basis of their relevance to the user, but also the indexer needs to distinguish between useful information and the mere mention of a topic. For example, a 100,000-page book may have one sentence about Abraham Lincoln (e.g., "A. Lincoln was one of our Presidents"). Then an absurdly exhaustive index might have "Lincoln, A." as a term. But someone wanting substantial information on Lincoln would find that this index shortchanged him.

Complete exhaustivity covers everything including the kitchen sink. Two undesirable events may occur: too much is indexed, and too little is indexed. The lesser of the two evils is to put in too much, increasing the triviality level. This will probably irritate the user, but it is not as important as leaving out vital information. This cripples the index.

The degree of exhaustivity depends on the policy of the indexing organization, money, time and the needs of the user. Also, it can be related to topic and type of index. Scientific books usually should have exhaustive indexes that cover the contents of the book. Journal articles usually are not indexed so exhaustively.

Exhaustivity is related to how well a retrieval system pulls out all documents that are possibly related to a subject. Total exhaustivity will retrieve a high proportion of the relevant documents in a collection, but as more and more documents are retrieved, the risk of getting extraneous material rises. Therefore, when indexers are aiming for exhaustiveness they must keep in mind that at some point they may be negatively affecting the efficiency of the system.

The ideal system will give users all documents useful to them and no more. Since this ideal balance is seldom, if ever, realized in practice, the goal is to balance the two; adding more and more terms, trying to cover every facet and nuance of those facets, can throw the balance off.

Exhaustivity means that every facet of the item is described. Specificity means that the term runs the gamut out to the last twig on the generic tree.

Could deep indexing include trivial and/or slight information? Of course, and that is one of the problems. If every nut and bolt down to the last centimeter in length is indexed, that very well might include slight and trivial information and do the index user a disservice.

Specificity

The preciseness with which we describe a document is another dimension in choosing descriptors. This refers to the generic relationship between index terms. This is the extent to which a topic is identified by a precise term in a generic, hierarchical tree:

Animals

  Cats

    Lions

The more specific the term, the more precise the results, i.e., more of the retrieved items will be precisely related to the searcher's inquiry. On the other hand, more generic terms will retrieve a greater number of items that are generally related to the searcher's inquiry. If the descriptors used are parallel to the subject concepts in the documents and reflect these concepts precisely, then we say the indexing is specific. As the indexing becomes less precise and less parallel to the exact concepts, the descriptors will apply to a broader range of documents that are farther apart in informational overlap. For example, *Trees* is a more specific term than *Plants*, and if searchers use the term *Plants* they will receive a wide range of information on all kinds of plants, hopefully including their desired information about trees. *Trees* is a more precise term. A very specific indexing language will have a large vocabulary with more potential descriptors.

The problem of specificity begins at the point where the indexing language is designed and must be considered in selecting the vocabulary and designing the thesaurus. Once the thesaurus is constructed, the only way to change its specificity is to make major changes in the vocabulary. It is difficult for an indexer to be nonspecific if the language is designed for specificity.

A popular approach to the problem of specificity is simply to index to the specificity of the author. If the writer talks about cats, then the indexer has no right to post up to *Animals* as an index term, since this moves content analysis away from what the document is really about, thereby reducing the relevance of the document.

Making Choices

It should be pointed out that exhaustiveness is a decision made at the indexing stage and can be controlled by limiting the number of terms allowed for an individual document and by the indexer's decision to ignore certain facets, based on the understanding of what the user's information needs are. Choices should be made on the basis of the clientele. As a rule, an indexing agency aimed at a general user will go with the broader term approach and with more exhaustivity, whereas a specialized indexing service will use narrower terms and will decide what facets are important and what facets can be ignored.

During the first phase of the indexing process it is better to get down as many potential terms as possible, that is, the indexing should be exhaustive and specific. Every topic that may be important should be recorded. At the thesaurus filtering stage and in the final revision stage of the index, superfluous and unimportant concepts will be removed, thus reducing the depth of indexing to an effective level.

DISPLAY OF INDEXES

An index should be easily read and understood. In order to achieve this many conventions have evolved. The hard work and careful thinking that goes into the indexing process can be seriously compromised if the index is poorly displayed.

A quality display depends heavily on typographic conventions. For example, punctuation, type size, and font can quickly differentiate between units. Main entries are generally in heavy print, often in capital letters, and subheadings are in lighter print and smaller letters. *See* references are often italicized and perhaps set off with parentheses to make their appearance unique. It is also standard practice to use indentation to set off subheadings from main headings, since a straight column of words is confusing and difficult to read.

Layout is concerned with how space is used on the page, and a balance must be found between wasting space and providing easy to read entries. It is possible to have too much space. For example, if lines are too short, the reader has to read long columns. On the other hand, long, unbroken lines slow down scanning.

The printing itself can vary in quality, ranging from a beautiful work of art down to a slipshod product that convinces the user that the entire index is slovenly constructed. Quality display is the result of indexers, editors, and printers taking pride in what they are doing.

In summary, the indexing process is complex, involving many variables and points of decision. While we cannot satisfactorily mechanize the procedure, we can use informed, educated common sense to produce good indexes.

The Abstracting Process

THE PURPOSE OF AN ABSTRACT

The purpose of an abstract is to give scholars filtered access to the literature in their disciplines, and it does this in several ways. First, it is a current awareness device that allows users to scan quickly the literature in their field. Abstracts also give the user a retrospective search tool so that noncurrent literature can be examined for pertinent information. Often abstracts allow users to identify information that exists in another language because there are English language versions of the abstracts.

Abstracting and its cousin, summarizing, are as old as storytelling. The ancient peoples attached content abstracts to papyrus rolls. Runners returned from battle with summaries of the events. When we tell our friends about our vacation we select and condense what we think might be of interest. We probably will not tell about how we changed our middle seat to an aisle seat, but we probably would tell them about the plane being hijacked. The ability to summarize and abstract is important in nearly all aspects of our lives, including the bibliographic control of our literature.

Some people believe that an indexer and/or abstractor cannot know everything a user might need, and therefore everything should be indexed and abstracted. The premise of this stance is false, since all bibliographic control implies that information professionals will make decisions about what users need. This concept permeates all bibliothecal activities from start to finish, especially indexing and abstracting. Granted, the systems are far from perfect, but the professional selection responsibility, at any point, is clearly there.

Some abstracts can replace the actual articles, but not in all cases. Indicative abstracts can seldom replace the original because they are summary in nature and only alert readers to the type of information contained in the paper. Informative abstracts cannot carry all the data presented in the paper. Therefore, each and every abstract must be complete and accurate, with no exceptions. Structured abstracts have been useful in assuring that the major aspect of an abstract is covered.

COVERAGE

In an abstracting agency articles are screened before they go to an abstractor, and the abstractor will probably have guidelines for subject coverage in the abstract. The guidelines will list areas to be covered and areas to be excluded, but the abstractor will be the one making judgments during the abstracting process; the quality of those judgments will depend largely on the abstractor's experience.

Papers in referred journals are probably of better quality than conference reports; however, a large number of conference reports are published and are an important part of the literature. Special care must be taken in abstracting this type of document. In many cases the abstract will be longer than usual and will convey more details, since long after the conference is over, the abstract may be the only information available. Also, reprints and abridgments of previously published articles are generally not abstracted, and the abstractor must be on the lookout for these items.

What are some of the factors involved in deciding which materials should have abstracts?

Economic Constraints

On a priority list of items to be abstracted, the cost, in terms of time and production, may cause low priority items to be left out.

Significant Material

Notes, communications, and letters to the editor may have minimal significance. For example, a letter to the editor complaining that the journal's format is bad is probably not critical to the concerns of the investigators who read the journal.

Publication Source

Items from disreputable publishers may be ignored, whereas items from respected publishers would always be abstracted. Although it is perhaps a little unfair, items from new and unknown sources may be temporarily ignored, since no one knows if they are worthy publications. This is why indexing and abstracting services do not immediately add such publications to their database. Information professionals are taught that one way to judge the quality of a journal is to see if it is covered by a reputable indexing and abstracting service. Of course, this could develop into a vicious chick-or-egg cycle with everybody waiting for everybody else to judge the hapless journal.

Subject Interest of the Users

Some things will clearly be of interest, others clearly not, and some items will be of marginal interest. The problem arises when the abstractor does not have a clear image of the user. Again, policy guidelines are helpful. It should be emphasized that the item itself may be of value, possibly earning the author a Nobel Prize, but it may be of no interest to the users of this abstracting service.

STEPS IN ABSTRACTING

Step One

The first step is to accurately and fully record the reference. Incorrect reference entry is an unpardonable sin, since the purpose of the entry is to give exact steerage to the original paper from the abstract. Completeness and accuracy are essential. If the reference is wrong, readers will either give up and turn elsewhere or be burdened with additional work.

The type of abstract (indicative, informative, or critical) does not affect the need for full bibliographic entry because it is assumed that in all cases the abstract is only a surrogate. Indicative abstracts can seldom replace the original because they are summary in nature and only alert readers to the type of information contained in the paper. Informative abstracts cannot carry all the data presented in the paper. Each and every abstract must be completely cited with no exceptions.

The elements to be included are fairly well standardized, but the order of presentation can run the gamut and is usually an individual choice of the abstracting agency. There is a general consensus that the reference section goes at the head of the abstract, before the body, so that users can decide if they want to read further. That is, they choose on the basis of the title, much the same way they decide when using an index.

In writing the reference entry, it is not unusual to abbreviate to save space, but abbreviations should be consistent and follow established rules. A list of the abbreviations should be available to the user.

Careful attention should be given to the elements in the entry.

The Title

A good title can be a key device in identifying information for retrieval, and users have learned this. Good titles are heavily loaded with strong content-bearing words, and users will often depend on the titles to help them decide if they need the paper.

There is more to handling the title than simply copying it correctly from the paper to the work sheet. First, if the title is vague or misleading, the abstractor should take corrective action by adding modifying words in brackets. For example, the author's title might be "Controlling eating," but the abstractor's title reads "[The use of hypnosis in the] controlling [of compulsive] eating."

Occasionally, the title carries no indication of content. For example, the author's title might be "Eureka!," whereas the abstractor's title is "Eureka [the discovery of a calorieless beer]!" Too much of a title change can mislead users when they begin to look for the document itself. As a general rule, titles should be retained as they are published, with the exception of augmented titles as just described. A good title is descriptive, clear, and brief, stating exactly what the topic of the paper is, and such a title requires no augmentation by the abstractor.

In the case of a foreign language paper, many abstracting agencies will translate it. Most agencies simply use the translated English version alone, but some run both the English and foreign titles.

The Author

Some abstractors believe that the author should be the first element in the bibliographical reference, their reasons often being one of three:

1. The author's name is usually placed first and its placement any-where else would look strange.
2. Users often base their searches on authors who are leaders in the field.
3. If the user enters the file of abstracts with a citation in hand, the citation is easier to locate by author.

The last two arguments are valid, except that indexing and abstracting tools are generally subject identifying devices and if the title is given prominence, it will serve that subject need best. Most readers will be looking for subject guidance, and the title is what they are interested in first.

The form of entering the author's name varies, but a standard way is to in-vert the first name and add additional authors in the normal order. The use of initials for given names cuts down on space but can lead to ambiguity of author-ship. As we know, a number of J. Smiths write and publish. Generally, it is best not to use initials.

Author Affiliation

An author's organization is often of interest to a user because it helps in judging the author and makes communication easier if the reader wants to con-tact the author for reprints or for any other reason. Affiliation is usually located after the author's name, sometimes with an address attached. For example: Dis-raeli, Homer (Disraeli Delicatessen), or Disraeli, Homer (Disraeli Delicatessen, Muleshoe, TX).

Funding Agency

If the document is a technical report or a paper based on the results of funded research, the agency giving the money should be noted in the reference section. In the journal literature it is customary for the paper to carry an acknowledgment of funding support. The information should include the name of the agency and the grant or contract number.

Publication Source

This, of course, is the key unit in the reference because it provides the location of the paper. It is important that it be accurate and consistent and that it follows some standard conventions for citing. For journals, the following is suggested:

Journal title (abbreviated titles may be used if they are standard abbreviations and can be understood).
Volume number.
Issue number.
Inclusive pagination.
Year.

For example:

J Amer Soc Inf Science 30(5)
290-295 (1979).

Monographs and books should include:

Title.
Author.
Publisher and place of publication.
Date.
Pages.
Price.

For example:

Think Green. Thumb, Tom, Jr. and Homer Disraeli (ABCD Press, Muleshoe, TX) 1989, 250pp. $30.50.

Although these two forms will cover most material indexed, a third form, patents, should be mentioned. A patent reference might follow this order:

Title.
Inventor.
Organization.
Issuing country.
Patent number.
Issue date.

For example:

"A Sausage-stuffing Computer." Disraeli, Homer (Disraeli Delicatessen), U.S. 000000000, 1 April 2001.

Foreign Languages

Following the source, information should be given about foreign language documents. The original language should be indicated, and if it has been translated, the translation source information should be supplied. Obviously, if the paper is not available in translation, the user must be aware of this. Otherwise, if users cannot read the foreign language and the paper cannot be translated easily, their time is saved by consulting the abstract.

Other Information

Some additional information that might serve a user is descriptive notes (e.g., "available only in microfiche"), sources for obtaining the document, and price.

Step Two

When the reference section is complete, it is time for the content analysis of the document. The content analysis of a document for abstracting purposes is similar to the analysis done for indexing. Since the final purpose is different, there are some differences in the analysis procedure. When indexing, the objective is to identify key concepts with the goal of creating a word list, a column of controlled descriptors that will point to a document's content. On the other hand, the objective of the abstractor is to create a narrative of that document's content. The abstractor wants to construct a miniature surrogate of the document, which will be a skeletal representation of the document.

Abstracting is the process of expressing the ideas of other people in one's own words. It also involves reviewing all the points in a document and deciding which ones are important, keeping in mind who the readers of the abstract will be and what they will be seeking. For example, suppose we had the following simple account:

> Smith carried out the experiment on Tuesday because Monday was a holiday and on Wednesday he had a dentist appointment. Right after lunch he mixed four grams of the Red Stuff with eight grams of the Purple Stuff, put it to boil, and set the timer for exactly four minutes. While the mixture was cooking, he called the dentist's office to confirm the time of his appointment. At exactly the time that the timer rang, the mixture exploded and destroyed the lab. Smith concluded that four minutes is too long to cook the mixture.

The important points to be worked into the abstract are:

- ▲ Used four grams of the Red Stuff.
- ▲ Used eight grams of the Purple Stuff.
- ▲ Cooked the mixture exactly four minutes.

⊿ Mixture explosion resulted.

⊿ Conclusion: Do not cook the mixture for four minutes.

The unimportant points to be ignored are:

⊿ The day he did the experiment.

⊿ The time of day he did the experiment.

⊿ The dental appointment.

The trick, of course, is to know enough about the subject and to understand the paper well enough to be able to know what is important and what is not.

There are five overall indicators that the abstractor looks for first in preparing the content analysis:

1. *Objectives and scope.* Why was this document written? What purpose did the author have in mind? In most scholarly and scientific papers, the objectives and scope are discussed in the beginning of the paper.

2. *Methodology.* For papers reporting experimental work, some of the techniques and methods used should be described, but not all. Enough should be given to allow the reader to understand how the work was carried out. In analyzing documents, the abstractor should note carefully any new methods the authors have developed or used in their work. For documents that are not reporting experimental work, the abstractor should note data sources and how these data were handled. For example, attention should be given to any statistical techniques that were employed.

3. *Results.* What were the outcomes? What relationships and correlations were observed? Were the data raw, or were they adjusted? Were the results obtained from a single measurement or were they obtained from replication? Does the abstractor see any factors that might affect the validity, reliability, or accuracy of the results? All these things should be noted for inclusion in the abstract.

4. *Conclusions.* What hypotheses were accepted or rejected? What evaluations? What applications or suggestions? How are the implications related to the objectives of the paper?

5. *Other information.* Supportive information should be noted, such as results that are not directly related to the main topic but that might be important in other areas. For example, if the paper is historical, the scholar may have discovered a new source of data useful to other researchers. This type of information belongs in the abstract but should not dominate it.

These are the things abstractors will surely include in the abstract and the things they concentrate on when analyzing the document. But what does the abstractor leave out? If the purpose of an abstract is clear in the abstractor's mind, then it becomes obvious what elements in a paper can be safely ignored. The inclusion of these elements would make the abstract complete, but they would have low informational value. For example, the abstractor can usually overlook the general introduction (except if it presents objectives and scope) and historical background. Historical summary is not new to the field and is not a unique contribution of the paper being abstracted. Redundancy, old information, and a complete discussion of the methodology can also be passed over.

In the process of analysis, the abstractor should omit information a potential reader of the paper is expected to know. For example, a paper in psychology may take a paragraph to explain who Freud was, but the abstractor can safely assume that the readers of a scholarly journal in psychology do not need this information. Another example would be discussions of the author's promises of the wonderful research she is going to do in the future. This, perhaps, is acceptable in the original paper, but it has no place in the abstract.

As a rule, graphical material, such as drawings and tables, should not be worked directly into the abstracts, but the abstractor certainly should use the information in the graphics to write the abstract. If the drawings and tables are of special significance to the paper, the abstractor should note this.

Step Three

The third step is to write the annotation. At this point the abstractor has notes on the highlights of the paper and has a mental picture of the contents and concepts of the paper. Now those concepts must be constructed into a short narrative. The results of the analysis must be expressed in natural language.

For most people an outline is a useful device when writing anything, no matter what the length. Other people cannot be convinced that an explicit outline is necessary, although we would suspect that an outline exists in their head as they write. A simple model for an outline:

I. Main point
   a. Secondary point
   b. Secondary point

II. Main point
   a. Secondary point
   b. Secondary point
   c. Secondary point

III. Main point, etc.

This will not be a perfectly balanced outline, since some main points may not have secondary points or a main point may have many secondary points. A good working premise is that the abstract will be seen and read by someone who knows nothing about the existence of the original document or what it contains. Everything is in the hands of the abstract writer.

How long should an abstract be? Just exactly long enough to do a proper job and not one word more. This is not a facetious statement because the length of the abstract is determined by the length of the document, the nature of the topic, the facts discussed, the technical details, and many other factors. A key element is the quantity of information and its complexity and originality. The abstract should be a model of brevity, yet it should not read like a night letter that is costing the abstractor $500 a word. Generally, it will run less than 250 words, and less than 100 for such things as communication notes and editorials. Beyond 500 words, the abstract has possibly become a review. However, there is no law about length.

The first sentence of the abstract is critical. It should be a topic sentence that tells what the paper is all about. It is a concise, informative thesis statement and resembles the lead sentence in a news story. It should convey the type of information that allows readers to decide if they want to continue reading the abstract or not. The first sentence should not repeat words that the user has just read in the title. For example, if the title of the paper is "The History of Pecan Growing in Brown County, Texas," the abstract should not begin, "This paper is about the history of pecan growing in Brown County, Texas." The title need not be repeated and the "This paper is about" is an unnecessary space waster.

The abstract should be complete, and it should reflect the full meaning and purpose of the paper, rather than just focusing on an isolated concept. For example, an abstract of a paper that summarizes the American Civil War should cover more than the Battle of Gettysburg. This does not imply exhaustivity. The complete basic informational content of the original document is to be presented but not every detail or topic discussed. The goal is to make the abstract self-contained and understandable to readers in a way that makes it unnecessary for them to consult the original document. Readers should know what the document is about solely from reading the abstract.

Abstract writers, especially authors who abstract their own papers, constantly worry about what is being left out, but it must be remembered that an abstract, by definition, will not be as complete as the original paper. It is not supposed to be, since it serves a different purpose.

The structure of the abstract should be unified and logically developed. In other words, there should be a beginning, a middle, and an end, with the final sentences leaving the reader with the feeling that nothing more needs to be said.

Simply following the order of the paper does not ensure logical development, because not all published papers are straightforward. This does not necessarily mean that the paper is poorly written; it may simply be a reflection of the author's writing style. The author may be the type that launches a paper at the heart of the matter, and then fills in background, jumping to the next key issue, filling in background, and so forth. In the full paper this can be an acceptable presentation and is certainly logically written within its own framework. However, if the abstract is presented this way, it will be extremely difficult to follow.

Is the actual writing done with a pen in one hand and a finger of the other hand moving along the original text? It is recommended that the abstract not be written while reading for content. This will almost always guarantee a bad abstract. Definitive notes should be taken in the analysis stage and the first draft of the abstract written from the notes, thus reducing the temptation to extract; that is, to lift sentences and phrases straight out of the text. An abstract is a carefully constructed, condensed representation and interpretation of the paper, written with selected, high-content-bearing words and phrases, not simply a string of sentences taken directly from the text. If extracts were as useful as abstracts, we would simply retire all abstractors and turn the business over to a computer.

Abstract writers should try to avoid vague expressions and long, rambling sentences. In fact, complete sentences are not always necessary, because phrases can often convey the message. But a steady diet of rapid fire phrases will soon sound like a cryptogram and will be irksome to read. A phrase must convey a complete thought.

The abstract should be one paragraph only, except in the case of extraordinarily long documents. Brevity is aided by a little consideration for common sense style. For example, redundant phrases should be minimized:

Do not say: "The results of the study lead one to the conclusion that . . ."

Instead say: "The conclusion is . . ."

Do not say: "After the experiment was completed the following data were compiled . . ."

Instead say: "Resulting data were . . ."

The abstract writer should avoid using words that can have different meanings depending on the context in which they are used. Abbreviations can be used for brevity, but care must be taken to use standard ones so there will be no chance for misunderstanding.

Finally, critical abstracts should not take sides on controversial questions or preach sermons. A critical abstract is still an abstract, and it should be an objective piece of work. At the same time, bias and an author's strong opinions may be noted, but abstractors should take care that their biases do not distort what the author is *really* saying. Such items as accuracy, validity, and relationship to other works with different viewpoints should be brought out in a critical abstract.

Step Four

The last item of the abstract, the abstractor's name, gives credit (and responsibility) for the abstract. Often only initials are given, with the full name appearing elsewhere in the abstract publication, but full names are also used frequently.

Step Five

The last step is the arrangement of the abstracts. A common form is alphabetical by title, but some alternatives are alphabetical by author; alphabetical by subject descriptors; classified; and dictionary. In nearly all cases the abstracts will require indexes to support the basic file, and this is especially true of classified abstracts.

EDITING

The editing of abstracts is absolutely essential. Since abstracts are short literary pieces, they must be edited carefully, the same way any prose is edited before it is published. Abstracts have omissions, deviations from policy, errors in references, meaningless abbreviations, poor diction and grammar, punctuation absurdities, and endless other editorial nightmares. In an abstract operation, the editor's task goes beyond careless errors. The editor serves, in a sense, as a master abstractor, concerned with content analysis and quality of the abstract. Ideally, the editor assumes the position by promotion from the ranks and knows a good abstract from a bad one.

The first editing task is to check the reference section against the original paper. Author names, titles, journal names, sources, and volume and issue numbers are often incorrect. Numerical data in the abstract should be scrupulously compared with the document text because the accuracy of such data is essential and because transcribing numerical data is easily susceptible to error.

In the text itself, the editor sees to it that standardized terminology and nomenclature conform to the rules given to the abstractor. Grammar is corrected, redundancies are slashed, words are abbreviated, ambiguous abbreviations are spelled out, ephemeral subjects are eliminated, and clumsy diction is improved. The editor is not obligated to redo the abstract, and if such is required, the professional competence of the abstractor must be questioned. It is imperative that the editor work directly with the original document to determine the quality of the abstract.

The abstract editor's primary worry, like the editor of an index, is the error of omission. This is the invisible error that is difficult to detect. Most editors develop a second sense for this type of error and can sense that something is missing.

Editors are bridges between the abstract writer and the printer. On the one hand, they fuss with the content and intellectual quality of the abstract; and on the other hand, they prepare copy that conforms to the constraints of the publishing world. They must not sacrifice informational integrity or author creativity to mechanical or economical expediency, yet they know that publication practices require certain uniformities of presentation. For example, each title, cross-reference, entry, and subentry must follow a consistent pattern and appear in the same position and typeface; no exceptions can be allowed, regardless of an abstractor's creative urge.

The editor is responsible for separating the various units for publication, such as main files, various indexes, lists of abstractors, an outline of any classification scheme pertinent to the abstract, and instructions on how to use the abstracting publication. Guides to the use of the abstract are critical and are a major area of responsibility for the editor and the abstractor.

The editing process is a specialized, professional activity, involving an undefinable affinity between the abstractor and the editor.

EVALUATION OF ABSTRACTS

What is a good abstract? In the field of library and information science, evaluation has been an elusive entity. Our primary measure has been a subjective pronouncement of *good* or *bad*. We use a number of error detection devices, such as correct citations, factual description, and omission of critical points. We also criticize poor diction and grammar, redundant phrases, and obscure writing. Some additional evaluation measures are conformity to abstracting policy and rules, promptness in the publication or availability of the abstracts, the cost, the quality of supportive indexes, the authoritativeness of the abstracts, and brevity.

The cost of an abstracting operation is a quality factor in the sense that if no one can afford the service, then it is useless. Use is affected by its economic inaccessibility. Much grumbling is currently heard among librarians about how they simply can no longer afford such and such indexing and abstracting services because the price is astronomical.

Authoritativeness is closely related to the prestige of the abstracting services, and this prestige comes by performance over a period of time. It is related to the manner in which abstracts are written, edited, and published. Also correlated to this is the reputation of the people who write the abstracts. Abstractors do not win Nobel Prizes, but they do build reputations. Quality abstracting services take pride in their corps of abstractors.

In the end the ultimate test is how well the abstracts satisfy the user's information needs. Everything else is secondary.

THE WRITING PROCESS

Writing is a cognitive process that allows a reader to find out what a writer knows. Abstracts reveal what the topic is about, how the paper is structured and how relevant (or not relevant) it is to the user's information needs.

Some people question why or why not the author of the item makes a good abstractor. We assume that the author of a document knows best what a paper is about. We also assume that the author knows the audience she is targeting. The first assumption is usually true (occasionally it is not), but the second assumption is not so certain. The author may make wrong assumptions. For example, the reader may read the paper for a reason different from the reason that the author wrote it. A typical example is that the author is enthused about the results of her experiment, but a particular reader has no interest in the results. This reader is enthusiastic about new research methodologies. If the author writes the abstract with little or no attention to the techniques used, then a potential user of the document is lost. The problem lies in the author being able to be objective about his own work and being aware of the potential variation in the user's needs.

The most positive aspect to an author-constructed abstract is that the author is familiar with her paper and the subject field it is concerned with. On the negative side the author generally is not versed in the professional skills of analysis and representation of information, and does not know the principles of abstracting. The second negative aspect is that an author often cannot see the trees because of the forest. The author may not recognize that material deemed secondary in the paper may be of primary concern to a user searching for information. For example, the abstractor may consider a methodology used as being old hat and not of high interest, but a user may be seeking that particular information. Not mentioning the methodology would cause the user to not retrieve this paper. A nonauthor abstractor would routinely mention the methodology used.

Abstract writing is creative writing. A potential abstract writer should read abstracts endlessly. Read abstracts and critique them. What was good? Or bad? Did you get a feeling of what the original article was about? Go read papers and write abstracts of them. Then compare your abstract with the published ones. Did you do better? Not so good? In what ways?

Good writers, of anything, are avid readers. Some writers read the dictionary and Fowler's *Modern English Usage* just for the fun of it. Not a bad idea for abstract writers. Can you imagine a successful novelist who never read a novel? Then, how can you write a good abstract if you have not read, studied and analyzed good abstracts? Models are endlessly available in the literature.

A certain amount of background research may be appropriate. You may read an article and feel uncomfortable with certain aspects of the paper, although you are knowledgeable of the general subject area. Grab a reference book. Get on the Web. Do not write something wrong out of ignorance.

Indexing and Abstracting a Document

The purpose of this chapter is to give a practical example of how to index and abstract a technical paper. The point has been made in the previous chapters that the indexing and abstracting processes are based partly on empirical guidelines that have evolved over the centuries, but the quality of an index or an abstract is determined in large part by the talent and skills of the professional indexer and abstractor. Many decisions are made as they move through the process of appraising the document in hand and in trying to match it to the needs of a potential user. No two people would handle this paper in exactly the same way, but this example shows at least one logical and procedural way to do it.

First comes the text of a technical paper, followed by a description of the train of thought that went into the abstracting and indexing endeavor.

EXAMPLE OF
A TECHNICAL PAPER

Depth of Indexing
Using a Non-Boolean Searching Model*

Donald B. Cleveland
Ana D. Cleveland

*Originally published in *International Forum on Information and Documentation*, 8 (2), April, 1983, pp. 10–13 (This project was supported by U.S. National Library of Medicine Grant NLM-EMP (5 R01 LM 03259). Courtesy of All-Russian Institute of Scientific and Technical Information.

INTRODUCTION

The objective of the experiment reported here was to study the effect of indexing depth on retrieval effectiveness using two different searching strategies. Is there a relation between indexing depth and the particular search strategy employed?

A steady stream of discussion has appeared in the literature concerning indexing depth, but all these discussions assume one search strategy—the Boolean match of query terms with the index terms of each document in the file. There are alternative searching techniques familiar to information retrieval practitioners, but no tests of indexing depth using an alternative to the Boolean strategy have been reported.

An experiment was carried out comparing the effect of indexing depth using the direct Boolean model and Goffman's Indirect Method, which is an alternative searching strategy. The experiment was a part of a larger research project sponsored by the U.S. National Library of Medicine. The larger project was designed to test the relative effectiveness of indexing using full-text or less than full-text utilizing a non-Boolean, chaining type of file structure and searching strategy. The basic objective was to study the use of full-text and less than full-text as content surrogates for indexing using W. Goffman's Indirect Method of information retrieval as a file structuring and searching technique. The final results of this larger study will be reported in a separate paper.

In order to set the foundation for describing the experiment and its objectives, the following brief review outlines pertinent background information.

THE ELEMENTS OF INFORMATION RETRIEVAL

Information retrieval is a generic term, loosely used and meaning different things to different people. For example, to data processing people it generally means the management of unique data records as required in a data processing cycle. That is to say, exact records of data are known, are stored at specific places in a storage medium and are retrieved on demand. The only intellectual problems involved are those concerned with structuring files and developing addressing methods that will minimize time.

Information scientists call this operation data retrieval and claim that information retrieval is a more complex activity involving uncertainty as to which records are appropriate. The exact information is not known and must be inferred as closely as possible. In fact, for any given query more than one of these unknown records may be pertinent.

An information retrieval system is a mechanism for carrying out the information retrieval process. There are several basic functions involved:

1. *The creation of information.* Man's knowledge is recorded using some physical medium.
2. *The acquisition of information.* From the global mass of recorded information minute portions of it are acquired on the local level.

This is a critical step in the process, because no information system can retrieve "good" information if it does not have access to such information.

3. *Information record proxy.* No user can read all the documents in a library in order to determine what he needs. Therefore, it has become necessary to create ways of substituting documents with proxies. Abstracts are such proxies. This reduces the number of actual documents that have to be examined.

4. *Representation.* Another condensation happens in the process of representing informational content by cataloging, classifying, and indexing.

5. *Coding.* Coding is representation on another level. In its purest form coding is not concerned with representing information content. The indexing terms have already accomplished this. Coding is concerned with symbolically representing the information content tags already determined.

6. *Query formulation.* The user's needs are expressed with the same representation language and also are coded by the same process. Query formulation is an aspect of the process about which little is known.

7. *Search strategy.* Given all the above functions, the file of stored documents have to be searched. The documents (or their surrogates) are examined in order to determine which most nearly satisfy the query.

8. *Dissemination.* Finally, the results are presented to the user.

Each of the functions has been studied in order to improve retrieval systems, although indexing has always received the lion's share of attention. However, there has been a scarcity of investigations into the interdependency of these variables. Such a study was the purpose of the experiment reported here.

THE INDIRECT METHOD

This study is one in a sequence of research carried out related to Goffman's technique of the Indirect Method in information retrieval. The concept was introduced in 1968 with the publication of a paper by that name.[5]

The method is based on the ideas of communication between two objects, either living matter or machines. There are source objects and destination objects. Goffman maintains that members of the set of source objects are not necessarily independent of each other. That is to say, the relevance, or usefulness of the information sent by each source object may be affected by what was previously sent by other source objects.

Redundancy of information, or information overlap, is involved and the degree of redundancy between any two source objects constitutes a level of similarity between the objects and we may regard this as a measure of the closeness or relatedness between the objects. This allows us to order and classify the objects.

In terms of information retrieval this means that documents in a file are not independent of each other, but are related in terms of their content. This becomes the key to structuring the file for retrieval. If a given document is chosen which most nearly fulfills a query needed, then it can be determined automatically what the next most relevant document is, independently of the query at this point. The results of a query to the system are a set of ordered documents based on information already known to be relevant.

This is an alternative to the widely accepted Boolean search, which considers only the independent relation between the query and each document in the file. Goffman expresses it this way:

> The notion of treating the information retrieval process strictly as a matching procedure between the query and the documents in the file is the basis of most operating information retrieval systems. . . . One defect in the direct method (Boolean) affects the efficiency of the system in that the entire set of documents X must always be probed in order to determine the subset $A(s)$. The second and more important flaw is related to the fact that the usefulness, hence the relevance, of the information conveyed by a document relative to a query must depend upon what is already known at the time that information is conveyed. Thus, if a document X has been assessed as relevant to a query S the relevance of the other documents in the file X may be affected since the value of the information conveyed by these documents may either increase or decrease as a result of the information conveyed by the document X.[5]

The method is based on document relatedness. In order to establish this relatedness a measure was devised based on the co-occurrence of automatically derived index terms between each pair of documents in the file. The relatedness was calculated as follows:

$$P_{ij} = \frac{m(X_i \wedge X_j)}{m(X_i)}$$

where $m(X_i \wedge X_j)$ is the number of terms common to document X_i and X_j. $m(X_i)$ is the number of words representing document X_i. This gives a value $0 > P_{ij} > 1$.

The result of these calculations is a matrix showing a conditional probability of relevance between each pair of documents in the file. The matrix is used to carry out the Indirect Method search and entails the following steps:

1. From this matrix the file is partitioned into disjoint classes of related documents, based on some threshold value of equivalence relatedness.

2. A representative document is chosen at random from each class and these are in turn compared with the query. The document with the highest relatedness points to the class of documents of most importance to the query. Each document of this class is compared with the query and the document in the class with the highest relatedness value is taken to be the entry point to the file. Thus, the document of most importance is identified without checking every document in the file.

3. Chains of sequentially related documents are determined as an answer set, based on the P_{ij} matrix. Document X_i leads to document X_j based on the highest value in the X_i row of the matrix.

HYPOTHESIS OF THE PRESENT STUDY

Proposed: *The use of this type of file structuring and searching technique can stabilize the indexing depth variable.*

If this is so, it would be a significant step toward solving a variety of practical problems. For example, in-depth indexing is more time-consuming and expensive. Also, when additional index terms are added in an effort to increase recall, precision drops which is irritating to the user.

The hypothesis of this study and the decision to do the study as a part of the major study, was based on more than speculative conjecture. In the first place, the concept underlying the Indirect Method suggests that exhaustivity and specificity of indexing would be immaterial.

Professor Ana Cleveland observed in a doctoral dissertation directed by Goffman that indexing depth has negligible effect on class formations and retrieval sets using the Indirect Method in sharp contrast to Boolean search strategies. The reason lies in the fundamental concept of the Indirect Method since the file is structured independently of any query. The retrieved documents are not directly a function of query terms chosen by the user. Subsequent documents in the chain are selected by informational overlap.

The study presented here replicated Goffman's experiment with the additional procedure of varying the depth of indexing and testing the observation made by A. Cleveland.

THE EXPERIMENT

The experimental design followed Goffman's model of simulating an information retrieval system. The necessary components of such a model are:

(a) one or more queries to the system,
(b) a document file which contains answer sets to the queries,
(c) some technique of representing content and measures of the content relatedness between the documents,
(d) a search strategy
(e) a way to determine relevance.

Randomly selected scientific papers were considered as queries. The subjects of the papers were taken to be a research "question" on that topic. The references attached to the papers were considered as being relevant answer sets to the questions being asked, which were the papers themselves. The assumption here is that when a scientific paper is written the references the author dealt with are the ones he felt were relevant to his topic. They represent the previous works and authorities, out of a likely much larger set, which he thought were the most related to his topic. Hence, these references are taken to be answers to the query being posed.

The present set of data was a subset from the data set used for the primary study. The larger study had a data set of 733 documents and 38 query papers. The subset data set consisted of 100 documents with 8 query papers.

Thus, the model contained 8 queries, a document file, a method for representing content (indexing), search strategies (Boolean and the Indirect Method), and predetermined criteria of relevance (the author's choices of his references). Taken together these elements constituted a simulated retrieval system for testing depth of indexing using two different search strategies.

The following procedure was followed:

1. An alphabetical list of index terms was generated automatically from the document set. The maximum number of terms for any one document was 25.

2. Following the technique of the Indirect Method a basic document-document matrix of the relatedness between each pair of documents in the file was created, varying the number of allowable index terms. The number varied from three terms to twenty and then twenty five. In this last case, it is implied that no limit of terms was imposed, since no document was coded by the automatic word-frequency routine with more than twenty five terms. There was a matrix for each number of allowable index terms.

Thus, there were 19 matrices (100 x 100) which generated answer sets for the ensuing tests.

RESULTS

The experiment was designed to conduct tests with the following rationale: The document set consisted of 100 papers. The file could be partitioned into 8 sets of documents for each of the 8 query papers. An ideal retrieval result would partition the 100 documents into mutually exclusive sets of documents for each query paper. For exact details of the Indirect Method procedures, the reader is referred to Goffman's paper.[5]

A Boolean search strategy was applied to the system, varying the number of index terms allowed as described above. To do this a measure of relevance between each document and the query was computed using the formula presented earlier, where X_i represents the terms in the query and X_j represents the index terms of each successive document in the file.

After the measure was calculated a threshold of relatedness was set. Specifically, the threshold was determined by trial-and-error. An optimal threshold would most nearly partition the documents into the desired retrieval sets. If the threshold was too high, relevant documents were excluded. If the threshold was too low, non-relevant documents were included in the partitions. In this arbitrary way, a threshold was chosen for the purpose of each test.

The threshold was held constant for each test when the two searching strategies were used for the obvious reason that otherwise the comparisons would be meaningless. If the document relatedness value was above the threshold it was considered relevant. If below, relevance was zero.

Next, the Indirect Method search strategy was applied to the 19 matrices, under the same controlled conditions just described.

The tests were carried out with two important criteria of retrieval in mind: (1) exhaustiveness of retrieval, (2) exclusion of non-relevant documents.

Table 1 is a total summary of the results of the tests. With the Boolean search there is a drop in retrieved documents when the number of index terms reached is 15. The reason is that as recall went up, precision dropped and to avoid low precision the threshold had to be raised drastically at this point. The sharp rise also affected recall. Time and time again it has been demonstrated that, with a Boolean search, as the indexing depth increases recall goes up but precision goes down. Clearly, from the table it can been seen that no major fluctuations occurred using the Indirect Method.

Table 1
Number of relevant documents retrieved
(total number = 100 documents)

No. of terms allowed	Boolean Method	Indirect Method	No. of terms allowed	Boolean Method	Indirect Method
25	64	96	11	72	96
20	48	96	10	64	96
19	48	96	9	56	96
18	48	96	8	48	96
17	48	88	7	48	96
16	40	88	6	48	88
15	40	88	5	48	72
14	80	100	4	40	64
13	80	96	3	24	24
12	80	96			

ANALYSIS AND CONCLUSIONS

From these results the following analysis can be made:

(a)   With the Boolean search there is a significant variation in retrieval according to the number of index terms allowed per
document, but with the Indirect Method there is only a slight
variation.

(b)   The system breaks down when only three index terms are allowed. However, with 4 terms the Indirect Method still is highly
effective. Therefore, if the Indirect Method is used, as few as 4
terms could be allowed without significantly affecting retrieval.

When the Indirect Method is used, indexing depth does not seem to
be a significant factor. This is true because of the nature of the Indirect
Method. Once the file is entered, the index terms of the query are no
longer a factor because the retrieval chain is internal. The retrieval is
based on information known to be relevant to the user on the basis of informational overlap between documents and is not a function of query
terms as in the Boolean search.

The conclusion is that there seems to be a relation between indexing depth and the search strategy employed. We are suggesting that this
needs further attention in the continuing effort to understand the information retrieval process.

Especially with the rapid movement into our libraries of online bibliographic retrieval systems and the need for fully automatic indexing
methods.

REFERENCES

1. Bird, P. R. The distribution of indexing depth in documentation systems. *Journal of Documentation,* 1974, 30, 381–390.

2. Bouman, H. Optimizing information retrieval. *Revue Internationale
de la Documentation,* 1965, 32, 46–53.

3. Cleveland, A. D. *The effect of coding in information retrieval.* Ph.D.
Dissertation, Case Western Reserve University, 1976.

4. Croft, W.; van Rijsbergen, C. An evaluation of Goffman's indirect retrieval method. *Information Processing and Management,* 1976, 12,
327–331.

5. Goffman, W. An Indirect Method of information retrieval. *Information
Storage and Retrieval,* 1968, 4, 361–373.

6. Jonker, F. *Indexing theory, indexing methods and searching devices.*
New York: Scarecrow Press, 1964.

7. Lancaster, F. W.; Fayer, E. G. *Information retrieval on-line.* Los Angeles: Melville Publishing Co., 1973.

8. Meadow, Ch.T. *The analysis of information systems.* Los Angeles: Melville Publishing Co., 1973.

9. Sparck-Jones, K. Does indexing exhaustivity matter? *Journal of the American Society for Information Science,* 1973, 24, 313–316.

10. Svenonius, E. An experiment in index term frequency. *Journal of the American Society for Information Science,* 1972, 23, 109–121.

11. Watson, C. E. Information retrieval. In: *Advances in computers. Vol. 6.* (Ed. by F. L. Alt and M. Rubinoff). New York: Academic Press, 1965, p. 1–30.

ABSTRACTING THE DOCUMENT

The originally published version of this paper has with it an author-prepared abstract, but for the moment it has been left off. Let us see how we might go about writing an abstract for this paper.

The first order of business is to go over the paper and decide what it is about. Ideally, the abstractor will read the paper through several times.

Having read the paper, can we state, in one sentence, what this paper is about? It has to do with information retrieval, of course, but that is a very broad term. What specific aspect of information retrieval is dealt with here? The title gives us an immediate clue: *Depth of Indexing Using a Non-Boolean Searching Model.*

It has to do with the relationship between depth of indexing and the file structuring and searching technique used in a retrieval system. In particular, it seems to be carrying forward work done by a man named Goffman. At this point, it would be useful for the abstractor to scan the references to Goffman's work: an abstractor knowledgeable in the field would probably be somewhat familiar with Goffman's ideas. This is the kind of knowledge that supports the contention that indexers and abstractors should have subject background.

At any rate, we might now notice that in the introduction the author has stated clearly what the paper is about. We must, however, maintain a degree of caution, since it is not unheard-of for an author to say that a paper is about topic *A* when in reality it is about topic *B.* In this case it appears that the paper is about what the author says it is; so our first sentence might read:

> *Describes an experiment aimed at finding out the effect of indexing depth on retrieval effectiveness using two searching strategies.*

Having gotten this sentence on paper, we now have a launching pad.

An abstract should point out any new ideas or techniques that are presented in the paper. Review of the paper reveals that what is new here is the comparison of two searching strategies as related to depth of indexing. It

appears we should state up front what these two strategies are, so we expand
our first sentence to now read:

> *Describes an experiment aimed at finding out the effect of index-
> ing depth on retrieval effectiveness using two search strategies: the
> widely accepted Boolean search and the Indirect Method of infor-
> mation retrieval.*

A reader may be familiar with Boolean searching, but may very well not
be familiar with the Indirect Method. We should briefly state what the Indirect
Method is in order to give the abstract reader some idea of how this method differs from Boolean searching. So we add:

> *The latter was developed by W. Goffman and is based on docu-
> ment relatedness within a file in terms of their content.*

How does Goffman's model do this? The Indirect Method is aimed at showing
the relatedness (in terms of content) between each and every document in the
file in order to cluster documents around a search query. It does this by calculat-
ing the commonality of terms between documents. With this in mind we might
briefly state:

> *The related measures between pairs of documents can be calcu-
> lated according to a proposed formula, and then the values ob-
> tained are recorded in the form of matrices for each number of
> allowable index terms.*

Finally, what did the experiment demonstrate? The experiment consisted
in running a test comparing the retrieval of the results of the Boolean searching
procedure with Goffman's searching procedure and demonstrated that in-
depth indexing is not a critical issue for effective retrieval if Goffman's method
is used. This is summed up in a concluding sentence:

> *Presents the search procedure following the technique of the In-
> direct Method where in-depth indexing of every document in the
> file can be eliminated without significantly affecting retrieval
> effectiveness.*

The final abstract, as published with the paper, follows:

> *Describes an experiment aimed at finding out the effect of index-
> ing depth on retrieval effectiveness using two search strategies: the
> widely accepted Boolean search and the Indirect Method of infor-
> mation retrieval. The latter was developed by W. Goffman and is
> based on document relatedness within a file in terms of their con-
> tent. The relatedness measures between pairs of documents can be
> calculated according to a proposed formula, and then the values
> obtained are recorded in the form of matrices for each number of
> allowable index terms. Presents the search procedure following*

the technique of the Indirect Method where in-depth indexing of every document in the file can be eliminated without significantly affecting retrieval effectiveness.

The abstract tells:

1. What was studied.
2. What was new.
3. What was compared.
4. The results.

It used 102 words to accomplish this.

INDEXING THE DOCUMENT

The first step in indexing a document is to record a proper bibliographic entry. Regardless of the style followed, the entry should be consistent with the selected model. Most importantly, the indexer must carefully and accurately include all necessary information.

It is now time to read the document. First read it quickly all the way through without taking notes in order to get an understanding of what the paper is about. As an indexer you will develop your own technique, but probably you will use a pen, pencil or colored marker, or better still, computer-aided indexing software to mark up or take notes on the paper.

At this point we simply want to identify words in the text that are significant and perhaps make notes of key ideas. Keep in mind that these are not necessarily going to be the final index terms. That will come later when we filter these words through the thesaurus.

An alternative way is to check each possible term against the thesaurus as it occurs, but this is a *micro* approach. The better way is to compile a list of possible terms and then check the list against the thesaurus. This will give you a more global feeling for what is involved and will help you visualize broader, narrower, and related terms options.

Where are significant words found? First, the title itself provides a major beginning point with *Depth of Indexing and Non-Boolean Searching*. Both of these phrases carry strong indication of the subject of the paper, and they become the first words on the list.

Next comes the abstract, from which the following words are derived:

Experiment. In itself a very general word, but at this point the indexer is not overly concerned. Perhaps the paper will turn out to be important to readers interested in experimental research in information retrieval.

Search Strategy. One of the fundamental processes in an information retrieval system.

Boolean Search. Also a key concept in database searching.

Indirect Method of Information Retrieval. A specific, unique concept in the field of information retrieval.

W. Goffman. An indexing identifier.

Document Relatedness. Again a popular information retrieval concept and also a key one in this paper.

The next step is to scan the section headings, which provide the following words for our list:

Information Retrieval. This is a broad phrase, but the paper is in the field of information retrieval and the paper has an overall discussion of information in general. A decision on how to handle this will be made at the thesaurus stage of the indexing procedure.

There are several other meaningful words in the section headings, but they are already on the list.

After finishing the section headings, we turn to the text proper and scan it for additional words. The following are added:

Information Retrieval System
Information Retrieval Process

It should be pointed out that the general section called "The Element of Information Retrieval" has a number of definitions concerning the parts of an information retrieval system. However, it would not be useful to tag these definitions because the paper is not really about most of these information retrieval (IR) elements and very little information is given. The more general terms *Information Retrieval Systems* and *Information Retrieval Processes* are already on the list. It would be misleading to tag the other concepts at this point. For example, to put *Acquisition of Information* on the list would be inappropriate. These are the types of intellectual decisions that the indexer always faces.

Only one part of the text remains to be analyzed: the references. We now examine the titles in the references for significant words. The premise here is that the references will reflect what the paper is about. The following words are added:

Indexing Methods
Searching Devices

At this point the indexer may choose to add terms subjectively arrived at from personal knowledge of the subject, understanding of the *aboutness* of the paper, and the awareness of who the index users will be. Meaning cannot be totally conveyed from a list of words lifted from the text, since language is much more than a list of words. The arrangement of words, their proximity to each other, and the order of sentences and paragraphs are the proper context for words. When words are stripped away from these structures they lose much of their communication power. For this reason the exact words from the text are rarely sufficient, as naked symbols, to convey the full meaning of natural language. The indexer should understand this and try to add appropriate terms to bridge the gap as far as possible between the natural language content and bare list of *key* words. By adding a word here and there the indexer can restore, to a certain extent, the meaning lost when the text was dismembered. This allows the addition of the following words:

Index Terms
Mathematical Model
Automatic Document Retrieval
Measures of Relatedness
Retrieval Models

The final list of meaningful words looks like this:

Depth of Indexing
Non-Boolean Searching
Experiment
Search Strategy
Boolean Search
Indirect Method of Information Retrieval
W. Goffman
Document Relatedness
Information Retrieval
Information Retrieval Systems
Information Retrieval Process
Coding
Indexing Methods
Searching Devices
Index Terms
Mathematical Model
Automatic Document Retrieval
Measures of Relatedness
Retrieval Models

Now the word list must be translated into the controlled vocabulary. The thesaurus we will use to index our paper is *ASIS Thesaurus of Information Science and Librarianship*, second edition, edited by Jessica L. Milstead. Please note that in the following exercise we have not carried out every possibility with the thesaurus in order to simplify the example. You are urged to take the paper and go through it on your own, using the thesaurus.

The first word on our list is *Depth of Indexing*. On page 27 of the thesaurus we find *depth (indexing)* as an acceptable entry term. We put this down as our first indexing term.

The term has listed under it two related terms:

RT   Exhaustivity
     Specificity

There is a scope note under *depth (indexing)* that tells us that the term means "the combination of the average number of terms assigned to documents in an indexing system and the specificity of those terms." This reassures us that we are on the right track. Also, the thesaurus tells us that there are two related terms: *exhaustivity (indexing)* and *specificity (indexing)*. In fact, the scope note has just told us that these two are the components of *depth (indexing)*. So these two terms go on the list.

Now we have to carry out the chain of thinking and look up the new words, *exhaustivity* and *specificity*. On page 35 of the thesaurus we have under *exhaustivity* related terms *depth (indexing)* and *specificity*, which is where we came from, so the chain is played out with the term *depth (indexing)* and we can return to our original list of words from the text.

The next term on our list is *non-Boolean searching*. But there is no such entry term in the thesaurus. How do we deal with this? The paper emphasizes a *non-Boolean* searching idea and, in fact, has it in the title. Is this a dilemma? The solution is to be patient and remember that many roads lead to Rome. What we have here is a typical indexing situation of *opposite concepts*. An old example is the situation of the terms *employment* and *unemployment*. A searcher looking for information on either term should be able to find information either way, with one term being a *see reference* to the other. If we have statistics on the percentage of people working last year, it is a "no-brainer" to figure out how many people were not working by subtracting from 100 percent.

With this in mind we find on page 10 the term *Boolean searching*, which we add to the list. If you recall the paper, *Boolean searching* was certainly a topic. The experiment compared the Boolean method against Goffman's non-Boolean method. Under *Boolean searching*, we have two new terms to check out: *BT: searching* and *RT: Boolean logic*.

Clearly *searching* is relevant to the paper. So we add it to our list of descriptors. The broad term *Boolean logic* is a mathematical concept that is not discussed in the paper as such. So we disregard it.

Now we must continue with the term *searching*. On page 88 of the thesaurus it might appear that we have opened up a Pandora's Box, with a long list of possible descriptors. First there is a BT: *information retrieval*. This is very generic term. Should we add it? The paper is not a general paper on information retrieval, but clearly the paper is about information retrieval, and because we are indexing this paper exhaustively, we add it.

The term *searching* has a long list of narrower terms (NT):

Boolean searching
browsing
citation searching
end user searching
full-text searching
keyword searching
known item searching
proximity searching
query by example
query formulation
query refinement
range searching
string searching
subject searching
truncation

There are also seven related terms (RT):

fuzzy retrieval systems
mapping (of information)
search behavior
search strategies
search terms
search time
weighting

It turns out that only one term in the long list is descriptive of the paper. That term is *Boolean searching*, and that is already on the list. So, it was not a Pandora's Box after all.

The next word on the list from the paper is *experiment*. On page 35 of the thesaurus we find *experiments* with a broader term *research methods* and a related term *testing. Experiment* is a broad concept, but the paper does carry out an experiment, and, in fact, it uses an unusual experimental design and could be of use to someone studying experimental methods in information retrieval. Therefore, since we are indexing exhaustively, the descriptor *experiments* is selected. The attached broader term *research methods* and the related term *testing* are added for the same reason.

Now we continue on the chain of thought and find *research methods* on page 85 of the thesaurus. Under this term are:

BT: research and development
NT: case studies
      Delphi studies
      empirical studies
      experiments
      observation (research method)
      user studies

Since *experiments* has already been accepted and there are no other appropriate terms on the list, this chain has been completed and we are ready to return to our original list of words from the text of the paper.

The next term on the list is *searching strategy*. On page 88 of the thesaurus we find:

BT: (knowledge and information organization devices)
NT: hedges (online searching)
RT: online searching
      query formulation
      searching
      user profiles

No new applicable terms are found, so we return to our original list of words from the paper.

And so forth. This procedure is followed for each term on the word list extracted from the document. You examine the terms in the thesaurus, read the scope notes, consider the broader terms, narrow terms and related terms and make a professional decision. Which terms reflect what I just read in this paper? And how will my user think?

A number of words on the list from the paper had no entry term or *see reference* in the thesaurus. Let us look at two examples to see how this is handled:

Indirect Method of Information Retrieval
W. Goffman

The Indirect Method of Information Retrieval is not a well-known term, but a little common sense can solve the problem. It is a file structuring and searching technique, thus a number of terms that we have included should lead a reader interested in techniques of information retrieval to this paper where she will find the Indirect Method discussed. The name *W. Goffman* is an identifier and can be used directly as an index term.

It should be clear from this exercise that a thesaurus is more than a list of useable terms. It is an intellectual tool that guides an indexer in her decision making process. The indexer sees the relationship of words and how concepts are related to each other and these serve as guides in the selection of descriptors.

After the word list from the paper was exhausted, the following final descriptors were chosen:

depth of indexing
exhaustivity (indexing)
specificity (indexing)
Boolean searching
searching
information retrieval
experiments
W. Goffman
organization of information
retrieval effectiveness
search strategies
indexing
file structures
document surrogates
techniques
index terms
descriptors
research methods
testing

In closing, three things should be noted about this index:

1. The indexing was exhaustive.
2. The indexing was specific.
3. The influence (good and bad) of an author-prepared index is evident.

Book Indexing

THE NATURE
OF BOOK INDEXES

Modern indexing began with book indexes, and they still constitute a major portion of indexing output. A separate chapter on book indexes should not imply that these indexes are totally dissimilar to other indexes, because all indexing has the same fundamental principles, and concepts and procedures developed thus far apply to book indexes. Book indexing is a special genre, however, and this chapter will highlight certain fundamentals and point out some important differences.

Books are usually closed-ended; that is, they begin and stop. A book index is a relatively quick one-shot event, whereas with periodicals indexing continues over time, often for many decades.

Within this closure there is a set of vocabulary usage that doesn't change over time. Periodicals are open-ended systems, with dynamic vocabulary changes. A book usually has a focused topic, whereas the set of journals targeted by a particular index has numerous topics, even in specialized areas.

In terms of format, book indexes are a physical part of the book, with the exception of certain reference books. Periodical indexes cover multiple titles and therefore are separate entities.

Vocabulary control is another major difference. Book indexing usually is free-text based, with the indexer using reference books in the field. Most periodical indexing is done with a thesaurus because consistency across topics and time is paramount to such indexes. Book indexers might use thesauri in the field also, but they are used for broad guidance. The indexer maintains his/her own consistency and does not usually follow a prescribed vocabulary control device.

A book index turns the book into a random-access information store. The reader first encounters the table of contents and finds a topical outline of the book. The reader reads the book linearly, from page one to the end. In retrospect books become information databases. We go to the book to hunt specific information. When we do this, we need random access to the content of the book. That is when an index is put to use.

One of the differences between a book index and other types of indexes is that each book index is as unique as the book itself. It is a single work serving only the book in hand and generally is changed only if the book changes with a new edition. In a sense it is a more personal piece of work than other types of indexes. In most cases a single individual does it, whereas many workers create other indexes (e.g., periodical indexes) over relatively long periods of time. This means that book indexers are solely responsible for the total task, including forming their own rules and planning their own procedures. Most good indexers feel a great deal of personal responsibility for the results.

A book index rearranges the information in the text, most often into an alphabetical order. Its objective is to serve as a pointer to specific details discussed in the book, in the same way that a periodical index leads to specific details in the journal literature. A book index is not a content list, in the sense of a table of contents, although its purpose is to denote content. When authors write books, they follow a certain order, arranging their material in some sort of logical sequence, and the table of contents follows that order exactly, outlining chapters, sections, and appendix materials. The index does not follow the author's word order, but arranges it in a way that allows a reader to go directly to specific details.

Unfortunately, book indexes are too often created with less than ample commitment from the book's publisher. In a periodical indexing service the index is the product of concern, and the full operation is aimed at creating that index. In the book publishing world the index is often one of those nuisances that hold up publication. As a result, the indexer works under unreasonable time and space requirements with little appreciation from the editor for the product. In many cases the indexing task is given to a junior editor or an office clerk to be done over the weekend. Worse still, the book may be put on the market without an index.

A book index has four basic components: the main headings, subheadings, locators, and cross-references. These components give an alphabetical index a virtual hierarchical structure, providing a degree of generic searching, but the index structure is based on the structure and text of the book, not on a formal external classification system.

Usually, book indexes are alphabetical and should not be allowed to metamorphose into classified indexes; for example, letting the entries become a main index term with a string of subheadings and sub-subheadings that are a generic tree. On the other hand, any index will naturally have a degree of classification.

It should be emphasized that when we group scattered entries, that does not mean we are reverting to a classified index, but it does mean that we are pulling scattered entries together to cut down on the user's searching effort. Incidentally, scattering in an index is not all evil. In the normal course of things, scattering gives the user extra entry points into the index. Some of the scattered terms will cross-reference to the proper entry term and others will simply be double posting of a term in a variant form.

Indexing a book is not a job for an amateur. It is a demanding task requiring knowledge of the book's content, its subject, the terms and synonyms of the subject, and the basic procedures and methods of indexing.

STEPS IN INDEXING

Step One

The first formal step is to open a clear communication line with the editor of the book, who will probably have space limitations and occasionally a rigid format to be followed. In most cases publishing houses will have rules and format style that the indexer must follow. They want all their indexes to look more or less the same. If the publisher requires the index to be submitted in electronic form, it is not a major problem since they generally will accept common word processor formats. Occasionally, the publisher may want the indexer to provide codes to cut down the publisher's effort in automatic typesetting. If this is the case, the indexer's work is increased.

Publishers would like an index delivered ten minutes after the galleys arrive to the indexer. Because of the rush at the end of the book's production period, the indexer may not get a chance to edit the galley pages of the index.

Step Two

The second step is to read through the book quickly. The purpose is not to find index terms, but to get an understanding of what the book is about, who it is aimed at, and what are the major ideas. When an indexer reads the book, she reads it for a different reason and in a different way from the normal reader of the book. The indexer must understand the subject of the book and the topics being discussed and the author's use of the language and she must understand what a user might want in an index to the information in this book. The indexer should develop the ability to remember what was discussed earlier and to recognize related discussions in different parts of the book. The overall structure of the book should always be in the forefront of the indexer's mind and details should be quickly recallable. While a photographic memory would be helpful, an adequate substitute is good indexing software.

Step Three

At step three, the indexer is ready to go page-by-page and sentence-by-sentence, actually doing the indexing.

Step Four

Once the indexer has made entries for the entire text, it is time to begin the exacting task of reviewing the work.

Step Five

The last step is to prepare the finished manuscript for the editor.

Indexing is done from galleys for the obvious reason that the indexer needs to know the real page numbers. A university colleague who wanted her book indexed recently approached these authors. It turned out that the book was in unsubmitted manuscript form, but conveniently (as she put it) copied on a Zip drive disk. She wanted to impress her editor by having the index already prepared when she turned in the manuscript. We began by explaining the two basic problems facing her: we did not know what the final text would be and we did not know what the page numbers would be. She countered by saying that she did not expect any editorial changes and that she would use computer software to later match manuscript pages to the galley pages. We respectfully declined this not very attractive indexing project. She came back later when the book had been edited and typeset, and reality had settled in.

INDEX TERMS

When selecting terms the goal should be to select the first term that a user will look under. Of course, it is impossible to have an index that always does this for every user. There are many *first* choices possible according to who the user is and how information seeking is approached by that user.

Main headings should be specific to the text and should not be posted-up terms from some classification system. Likewise, subheadings should be book specific terms that qualify and subdivide the main headings. Also, words should be avoided that a user would not use. For example:

use: Cats, good skinning methods
not: Good skinning methods, cats

The user is not going to look under *good*.

Adjectives as solo words usually make bad index terms, although when used with a modified noun, they are useful to express more specific meaning. For example:

Hairy
    cats
    dogs
    monsters

would be better as:

Hairy cats
Hairy dogs
Hairy monsters

Likewise, adverbs should not be used as terms. Articles and prepositions would make meaningless index terms. In modern indexing the general practice is to retain initial articles but the entry is indexed on the first proper word. The article is not transposed nor dropped, like in indexes of the past.

The word *and* in a subheading is to be avoided in most cases. It usually adds ambiguity. For example:

Cats
    training and feeding

Does this indicate two separate aspects of raising cats or does it refer to using food as an incentive to get the cat to jump through a hoop? A better way would be:

Cats
    feeding
    training

The problem of the capitalization of terms can be generally solved by use of any number of authoritative style manuals (e.g., *The Chicago Manual of Style*). Book publishers may specify which style manual to use, or they may provide their own style manual. A popular way to handle headings is to capitalize main headings and not capitalize subheadings. For example:

Cats
    bobcats
    cheetahs
    domestic
    lions
    sabertooth tigers

Book index terms are sometimes compound headings, and one problem is knowing when to invert the terms. A compound heading is a phrase consisting of a noun with a word as a modifier. The primary noun is the generic sense of the phrase and the modifier narrows the concept to a specific subclass of meaning. Whether or not to enter compound headings directly or inverted is one topic that can make timid indexers speak up. The growing consensus is that attempts to invert compound headings lead to unnecessary trouble. If a user wants information about *hairy monsters*, then she will probably look under that phrase, not under *monsters, hairy*. The user probably doesn't conceptualize this as a *compound term*, but as a direct phrase. The basic reason for inverting is that some users think in terms of a *major* idea in the phrase and that is the way they will look it up in the index. For example:

Lou Gehrig's disease
Purple Heart
Field hand

In some cases compound headings are given double entry or are cross-referenced.

Then there is the question of singular *vs.* plural forms of the nouns. The general approach is to use plurals for countable objects. For example:

Cats
Dogs
Fleas

Use singular forms for collective terms. For example:

Sand
Water

Abstract terms are singular. For example:

Liberty
Affection
Envy

Many times index terms have to be qualified. One example is the homograph:

Bases (military)
Bases (mathematics)
Bases (Tiffany lamps)

NAME ENTRIES

Inexperienced indexers might believe that indexing names is the easiest part of indexing. If so, they are in for a surprise, because name entries are troublesome, and the seemingly endless variations thwart even experienced indexers. Certain conventions have developed over the years, influenced partly by cataloging rules and partly by the practices of book indexers and publishers.

Indexing personal names is mostly routine, but the exceptions are real headaches. Most cataloging and indexing rules on personal names deal with exceptions. (This is like Mark Twain describing the grammar of the German language: for each of the rules there are four pages of exceptions.) The problem lies in the form of the names. The names may be partial, spelled differently, differ in different languages, etc. Also, the names may change, may have pseudonyms, have prefixes, be compound, be royalty, and on and on.

There are three major categories of names: names of people, names of organizations, and names of places. The majority of the people in this world have a straightforward name (e.g., John X. Smith) but the minority of people who do not have straightforward names can be a problem; for example, John X. Smith, Jr., popularly known as Smitty "The Thug" Smith, which is an alias for Count Johann Schmidt, who is really a General in the Austrian Army.

Proper nouns are capitalized, including noun phrases:

Rockefeller Center
The Red River
Julio Iglesias

If two or more place names are the same, then they should be distinguished:

Dallas (Minnesota)
Dallas (Texas)

If more than one person is involved in an endeavor, there should be an entry under all persons, and all names are retained in each entry. For example:

Larry, Moe, and Curly
Moe, Curly, and Larry
Curly, Larry, and Moe

If government and other organizations are well known and usually addressed by an acronym, then the acronym is the preferred entry, with cross-references from the spelled out name:

IRS

WHO

OPEC

When phrases are used as names, then they should not be inverted, although there might be a cross-reference. For example:

Man, Bat *see* Bat Man

Sometimes when abbreviations or acronyms are used, the full cooperative name is cross-referenced. Government agencies often present problems because they are often long and complex and frequently change names, or to be more exact, change part of the name. The general order is generic to specific with cross-references from well-known and/or generally used, subdivisions.

Care must be taken with abbreviations. The purpose of an abbreviation is to save space, but what good is accomplished in saving space if the reader doesn't understand the abbreviation? The same can be said about using acronyms. Acronyms should not be used if they are not well known and in the index cross-references should be made from the fully spelled out form.

Indexing foreign names (e.g., Spanish, Chinese, etc.) can be a puzzle to the novice indexer. The best approach is to follow an accepted style manual, such as *The Chicago Manual of Style,* which deals with these problems.

Handling place names is relatively straightforward, but there are a few pesky points. For example, different languages may have different names for the same place. The good news is that reference sources are readily available which standardize the names (e.g., geographical sources). Of course, there is the problem of changes of name, so care must be taken to note the currency of any reference book chosen. Also, there are occasional problems with places with the same name in different geographic regions and these must be indicated. There are a lot of "Georgetowns" in the world.

SUBJECT ENTRIES

In most cases indexers do not use a formal, published thesaurus for indexing a book, although such tools certainly are consulted as aids for term selection. This does not mean that there is no vocabulary control. The indexer controls the index with her own conceptualized vocabulary structure. The most obvious example is consistency in term usage with cross-references from synonyms and related terms. Without this vocabulary control, the index is going to be a rather poor one. Consistency and structure are maintained by carefully keeping tabs on what has been done. The ultimate consistency check will come when the final index is reviewed and edited. Indexing software programs are able servants with this task.

Books are generally indexed in depth, that is, the indexing is both exhaustive and specific. Several factors influence how far to go. Readers of general mass audience books may need general terms not covered exhaustively, but highly technical books read by specialists in any area will probably need an exhaustive and specific index. In practical terms indexing depth in a book may be a moot point: time and economics may be the deciding factor.

Most book indexes do not extensively index ideas, but stick mostly to the words used by the author, trying to create vocabulary control close to the natural language of the text. As a result, a majority of the indexes are stronger in place name entries and personal names than in subject interpretation.

The problem of selecting subjects is more formidable than the problem of proper names. Establishing rules and developing a list of models to follow can control proper name selection reasonably well. The problem of subject headings is less susceptible to fixed rules and canned examples because of the elusiveness of what *aboutness* means in subject analysis. However, form of entry and internal structure can be codified well enough to be useful to an indexer.

As with any subject indexing, the indexer begins with the words of the text, scanning each sentence and underlining the key subject words used by the author. The indexer then evaluates these words within the framework of the total paragraph to determine the subject being discussed. What important topic or topics are discussed in this paragraph? What words are simply modifiers and not actually subject indicators? For example, in "the mosquitoes attacked with the ferocity of a tiger" only "mosquitoes" is a subject indicator.

How many terms should the index have? Often the editor will impose a length, but there is also a common sense limit. That is, the index covers what the reader needs and expects. Every word in the text should not be arranged alphabetically as an index. In fact, an index entry that leads to little or no information does a disservice to the user. Like cooking vegetables, an index should not be overdone.

What about indexing *extra text* (such as a table of contents, the foreword, etc.)? Primarily the indexable material in a book is in the text. The decision should be based on whether or not these materials contain important information. If the material is supplementary then it needs to be indexed. On the other hand, if the information is well covered in the main text then it probably is not necessary to index this material. For example, if a graph simply illustrates exactly a discussion in the text, then the text is indexed but not the graph.

Tables can have two basic purposes. They can be supplementary (e.g., present information not explicitly stated in the text) or they can give further breakout of such information. The other purpose is complementary. The same information is given but it is an alternative form. The question is whether or not the table alone will fulfill the user's needs, or should she simply be referred directly to the text. It is annoying if the user is referred to a table and then she must hunt down the appropriate text in order to fully understand the table. It would have been better to have sent the user to the text that refers to the table.

Some indexers believe in indexing chapter headings, but not all indexers believe this. If the table of contents lists the chapter headings, there is no sensible reason for sending the user from the index in the back of the book to the table of contents in the front of the book. Most people look at the table of contents automatically.

If a bibliography in a book is relevantly long, it is useful to index it. If the bibliography is short then the user has no problem quickly scanning it and does not have to waste time looking up items in the index.

ADDITIONAL DETAILS

Alphabetizing has always been an issue in indexing. Over the centuries alphabetization grew from the simple form of having all the A's before the B's (with a little arrangement within the letters) to very complex rules that tried to account for every possible situation. These complex rules never quite solved the problem. The advent of computers forced the return to less formulated rules because of the near-impossibility of teaching a computer to cover all the possible permutations in the existing manual rules.

Library catalogs are usually alphabetized word-by-word but most dictionaries are letter-by-letter. In practice it actually matters little which system is used as long as the reader knows how to use it and consistency is maintained.

Punctuation is another concern. The trend is to minimize punctuation. For example, instead of using commas to separate locators from subheadings, use space. About the only time to use periods in an index entry is in a name that shows hierarchy. For example:

Department of Agriculture. Domestic Animals Division. Cats Section

NINETY-NINE "DOs-AND-DON'Ts"

If one looks over the literature of indexing, there are hundreds upon hundreds of "Do-this-don't-do-thats." Some of these commands have been codified into various sets of standards and some are contradictory, and some continue to be debated. Below is a potpourri of these, culled from over seventy-five years of the indexing literature:

1. Know the target audience for the index.
2. Have a plan before beginning to index (procedures, methods for keeping track of decisions).
3. Think carefully on the rationale that you use to make your indexing decisions.
4. Learn when and for what to use the computer in indexing.
5. Use the *shoebox* method of indexing if it suits you (3x5 cards or slips of paper).
6. Use reference tools for suggestions of terms, validation of information, forms of names, spelling, etc.
7. Do not forget Internet reference resources.
8. Use accepted style manuals as general guides. Indexers are fond of citing *The Chicago Manual of Style*.
9. Begin by understanding what the document is about.
10. Visualize the meaning and purpose of the whole document.
11. Understand and appreciate the significance of what the author has written.
12. Index everything that provides *useful* information from the document—text, illustrations, front material, appendices, notes, bibliographies, etc. (note especially the word *useful*).
13. Do not index anything not related to the item's content (e.g., a thank you to the secretary who typed the manuscript).
14. Discriminate between major and minor subject treatments.
15. Do not extensively index trivial topics in the document.
16. Use the terminology of the index's users.
17. Choose terms according to what the author is trying to say.
18. Use words not in the text if these are words that user of the index will likely select.
19. Consider the relation between exhaustivity and specificity.
20. Use devices that help users adjust to the level of specificity needed.
21. When augmenting with words not in the text, do not add meanings never intended by the author; you are not a co-author.
22. Make the main headings of an index entry a noun or noun phrase.
23. Choose the most specific headings that describe the document.
24. Make lead terms in an entry terms that a user is likely to use.

25. Choose popular headings, with references from their scientific equivalents except where a specialist audience is addressed.

26. Make single terms represent a single concept.

27. Combine similar entries and give cross-references if needed.

28. Combine the word and the action that describes it where it is useful and possible, such as: *Banks* and *Banking*.

29. Index famous historical events by the names by which they are generally known, such as: *Missouri Compromise*.

30. Double post (i.e., use both terms) when there are two equally likely entry candidates.

31. Make entries as concise as possible, yet still understandable.

32. Do not use an adjective or an adverb standing alone as a main heading.

33. Minimize the use of prepositions, although sometimes they are necessary to insure clear meaning.

34. If you need to use prepositions, avoid them at the beginning or end of subheadings.

35. Do not construct main entries with unmodified subentries followed by long rows of page numbers.

36. Subheading of an index entry should bear a logical relation to the heading.

37. Make subheadings concise, informative and begin them with a keyword or phrase.

38. Arrange subheadings so they are easy to follow.

39. Use indented subheadings.

40. Use no more than eight subheadings under a main heading. If there are more, regroup ideas into more than one main heading.

41. Think twice before using sub-sub-subheadings.

42. Invert headings where necessary, to bring significant words to the front.

43. In most cases, avoid articles in index terms for the subjects.

44. Be consistent in the use of singular or plural terms.

45. Be consistent in choosing one form of spelling.

46. Link alternative spellings to the preferred spelling of the term.

47. When using abbreviations make sure the abbreviations are clear and can be understood.

48. Do not abbreviate titles of people.

49. Spell out initials and acronyms that most readers will not recognize.

50. When words of the same spelling represent different meanings, include identifying phrases in brackets, such as: *Base (military)* and *Base (mathematics)*.

51. Check for synonyms and make suitable references from forms not used.

52. Check for antonyms and combine where suitable, such as: *Employment* and *Unemployment*.

53. Subject coverage is paramount, but do not forget people, institutions, places, and events.

54. Spell people's names as they appear on the page.

55. Do not break up compound surnames, even if they are not hyphenated.

56. Do not drop articles from names of persons, places, or corporate bodies.

57. If more than one person is involved in an endeavor (such as joint authorship), establish an entry under both and put *both* names in each entry.

58. Provide personal names in the form most commonly used.

59. Enter the names of monarchs, popes, and other such people under their official titles.

60. Retain clerical titles, but in inverted form.

61. Index saints under their given names with differential tags used if there is a need for distinction from others with the same name, such as: *Thomas, Saint (the Apostle)*.

62. Do not retain academic titles like Professor and Doctor, or trailing degrees, such as M.D.

63. Index members of royal families under their given names.

64. Identify an obscure person if possible, such as: *McFeline (family veterinarian)*.

65. Use familiar forms of personal names, such as *F. Scott Fitzgerald*, not *Francis S. Fitzgerald*.

66. Make a *see* reference lead from a pseudonym to an entry under the real name. The exception is for cases when the pseudonym is paramount, such as *Mark Twain*.

67. Index married women under the way they are known best. If their names are the way the public knows them, then they should be indexed that way and *vice versa* under the married name, if that is the way they are known.

68. Decide how you are going to handle *Mc* or *Mac* (and similar constructions) and stick to your choice.

69. Make locators refer directly and clearly to the unit of information referred to.

70. Set off locators clearly from headings by spacing and punctuation.

71. Generally, do not put locators after a main heading that is modified by subheadings.

72. Make sure page numbers are correct.

73. If references are made to paragraph numbers and not to page numbers, include a note to this effect.

74. Forget about the Latin term *passim*.

75. In cumulative indexes, link changing vocabulary with old vocabulary.

76. Include most index entries in one alphabetical sequence.
77. In the case of historical and biographical works, substitute chronological for alphabetical subdivision when this will definitely assist the reader.
78. Alphabetize letter-by-letter or word-by-word. Pick one.
79. Once an alphabetizing system has been selected, stick to it consistently.
80. Alphabetize entries beginning with figures as though spelled out.
81. Capitalize the first word in main entries and make everything else lowercase.
82. Minimize punctuation without sacrificing clear understanding.
83. Do not use the same typographical device for different purposes in the same index.
84. Use cross-references when and where appropriate, but do not stick them in just to make the index look good.
85. Be sure that cross-references really do go to an actual heading.
86. While indexing, know when to strike out a previously used entry when things change.
87. Make the index easy to read.
88. Make the index easy to use.
89. Keep the index within a respectable length.
90. Remember that an index is a pointer, not a direct source of information.
91. Be as simple as possible without compromising the retrieval power of the index.
92. Check, check, check for errors in spelling, punctuation, and capitalization.
93. Avoid the use of bold type wherever possible. Use instead italics, capitals, parentheses, and any other legitimate typographical devices for distinguishing items.
94. Be consistent most of the time, but there are always exceptions.
95. When indexing, common sense and consistently go hand-in-hand.
96. Remember that consistency and simplicity are paramount to a good index.
97. Do not forget that the only purpose of an index is to retrieve information.
98. Ask someone who is qualified to review the index.
99. Do not believe that computers are on the verge of replacing human indexers.

Book indexing is not for everyone. It is something that you have an aptitude for, that you find challenging and rewarding or it is "dullsville" personified. Database indexing or Web indexing may be more appropriate for you.

Book Indexing Example

In this chapter we will present an example of indexing a book. First we present a short chapter from a book on cartooning tools that librarians might use in their work for doing publicity in their libraries. Then the chapter is indexed. As in the earlier example of indexing a journal article, we will step you through the procedures and the thinking involved.

EXAMPLE BOOK CHAPTER

CARTOONING FOR THE LIBRARIAN*

A How-To-Do-It Manual
By
Donald B. Cleveland

SERIES EDITOR'S PREFACE

Why would librarians use cartoons? Why would they draw their own? How do you incorporate original drawings and ideas if you have no artistic training? For years, Don Cleveland has answered these questions and more for students in library classes. These fortunate students come away awed by their new skill in the use of this medium. Now Cleveland shares his expertise with all of us in this new book. *Cartooning for the Librarian: A How-To-Do-It Manual* will help you liven up those memos, posters, displays, lesson plans, publicity pieces, bulletin boards, and announcements.

---

*[HOW-TO-DO-IT MANUALS FOR SCHOOL AND PUBLIC LIBRARIANS. Number 8 Series Editor: Barbara L. Stein. NEAL-SCHUMAN PUBLISHERS, INC. New York, London. Copyright 1992 by Donald B. Cleveland.] "Cartoons: The People's Art" was reprinted from *Cartooning for the Librarian: A How-To-Do-It Manual* by Donald B. Cleveland with permission of Neal-Schuman Publishers, Inc.

Cleveland has organized his instructions on "how to draw" in such a way that virtually anyone can put them to immediate use. His background material on the history of cartoons and comics provides interesting insight into this fascinating medium. The next chapters describe the materials to use for best results.

Chapter 5, "The Head Does the Talking," reveals the secret to producing good cartoon art with your very first try. Subsequent chapters lay the foundation for the maximum stretch of your abilities. Finally, "tricks of the trade" are revealed, and a wonderfully original collection of clip art is provided. . . .

Barbara L. Stein
Series Editor

Chapter 2
CARTOONS: THE PEOPLE'S ART

Al Capp, one of the masters and the creator of Li'l Abner, gave us the definitive word on cartooning: "Cartooning is fine art with a sense of humor." The word *cartoon* is applied to a wide range of humorous drawings. The word itself goes back hundreds of years to when it meant the outline or layout of a painting. The English humor magazine *Punch* first used the word in the modern sense in the 1840s, when it published drawings ("Mr. Punch's Cartoons") making fun of Prince Albert, who had commissioned fresco paintings in the new Houses of Parliament. In the years that followed, the concept of a cartoon evolved to mean a variety of humorous illustrations, usually line drawings, that highlighted the vagaries of mankind. While art in general tries to capture the full range of human experience, cartoon art focuses on humanity's foibles.

But is it art? Technically, cartooning meets any established criterion for fine art. It can be judged on such criteria as form, light and shade, perspective, composition, and color. At its best, it equals other art forms in its ability for communicate emotions and ideas, particularly because of its potential to combine visual forms with the written word. Figure 2-1, page 152, illustrates this point: neither the drawing nor the text can stand alone, if communication is going to be complete, and it is the combination of the visual and written forms that provides the impact.

In fact, cartoonists worry little about esoteric definitions of what a cartoon is. They recognize one when they draw it.

Origin and Historical Development

We know the modern cartoon primarily as a comic strip, a TV animated film or a *New Yorker* panel gag, but these forms have not been around for that long. Comic strips, for example, are only a little over a century old. The cartoon as we know it developed during the nineteenth and twentieth centuries; however, it has many diverse historical roots, which are sometimes not obvious.

sorry about the late birthday greeting....

...I had trouble inventing the alphabet

Figure 2-1   Birthday Card

Ancient Art

Although we can't exactly classify ancient cave paintings and drawings as the first cartoons, they certainly show an attempt of early people to express their feelings and observations in a clear, straightforward, and sometimes humorous picture, like cartoons. The depiction of animals, plants, and other non-human entities was often remarkably accurate. These distant ancestors had a good eye for form, correct anatomy, and sometimes for perspective. Their human figures however, were mostly distorted and exaggerated. One theory is that they were afraid to draw humans realistically because of religious or societal fears. A second theory is that they were stone-age cartoonists and they knew exactly what they were doing: satirizing their fellow human beings. The second theory isn't very plausible, but who knows?

In the kingdoms bordering the Tigris, Euphrates, and Nile rivers we find further attempts of early artists to represent reality with exaggerated and often unrealistic drawings. By the time of the Greek and Roman empires, sequential figures were appearing on pottery and tapestry.

Although these ancient artists did not call themselves comic strip artists, the idea of a sequential drawing appeared very early.

Through the Ages

During the Middle Ages, satirical drawings addressed matters of life—and death. The caricature, sometimes macabre or facetious, had its origin in the Middle Ages and came to fruition during the sixteenth and seventeenth centuries in Europe.

Humor has never been foreign to art. Hieronymous Bosch, a fifteenth-century Flemish master, is a prime example. Artists such as Albrecht Dürer and Leonardo da Vinci continually experimented in grotesque, exaggerated, and often humorous representations.

Today's Cartoon

Today's cartoon is the result of long centuries of evolution and, at times, revolution. The wide range of imaginative possibilities in comic art has always allowed the artists to branch out into new directions. The overnight development of comic books, the political editorializing in comic strips (*Pogo* and *Doonesbury*), and the popularity of off-the-wall cartoons (*The Far Side*) are good examples of imaginative new avenues.

Types of Cartoons

Cartoons come in many shapes and forms. Our first experiences were with newspaper comics and comic books. These forms are familiar to us, particularly as we recall our childhood. But there are other, less obvious types: animated Disney movies; Bugs Bunny and Sylvester shorts before the main feature; newspaper and TV advertisements; greeting cards; promotional brochures; record album covers; posters; highway signs; menus; magazine covers; and wall paper. Cartoons are by far the most universal of the visual arts.

This is truly the people's art. Let's review some of the most common forms.

MAGAZINE PANELS: In the mid-1930s large circulation magazines like the *Saturday Evening Post* and *Collier's* began to publish single panel cartoons on a large scale. Thirty to forty cartoons per issue were not unusual.

The format, of course, goes back to the nineteenth century. The *New Yorker* deserves most of the credit for refining and defining the modern panel cartoon during the late 1920s and 1930s. Early magazine panel cartoons were elaborate ink drawings with several lines of dialogue underneath. In most cases a joke was told and the drawing added little to the meaning of the joke. But with the founding of the *New Yorker*, the legendary editor Harold Ross pioneered the idea of a quick, one-sentence gag, closely dependent on the drawing for its meaning. Thus the modern magazine cartoon was born. The names of *New Yorker* cartoonists such as Peter Arno, George Price, Sydney Hoff, William Steig, George Booth, and Charles Addams are now household words.

While over the years major magazines have folded and survivors have reduced the number of panel cartoons they carry, magazines remain a showplace for this type of cartoon. The *New Yorker* and *Playboy* still publish first-class work, along with hundreds of lesser-known journals. In addition, newspaper syndicates distribute single panel gag cartoons. The long-running *Dennis the Menace* is an example.

Figure 2-2 shows an example of a typical magazine panel cartoon. Notice the interrelationship of dialogue and visual forms. One without the other would have no meaning.

"You never take me any place anymore."

Figure 2-2   A Typical One-Panel Cartoon

COMIC STRIPS: The evolution of a new art form, the comic strip, at the turn of the twentieth century was closely related to the evolution of American society in general. It was the era of socialists, women's suffragists, and Teddy Roosevelt. People were becoming assertive and rebelling against the railroad magnates and inhumane working conditions (e.g., nine-year-old "working men" slaving 14 to 16 hours a day for pennies). Labor unions were fighting for their lives and for the lives of all ordinary people.

It was a time of turmoil. The assertiveness, the righteous anger, and a surviving sense of humor gave rise to the comic strip. As Jerry Robinson so aptly put it his book, *The Comics: An Illustrated History of the*

Comic Strip, "this was the cultural stew that nourished a new American art form which proved to be of unprecedented vigor and longevity: the comic strip."[1] Foreigners have a great deal of trouble understanding American humor. They cannot understand how we take such pleasure in laughing at ourselves and our serious problems.

The early strips ranged from raw, amateur drawings to some magnificent examples of draftsmanship. Similarly, the quality of the humor ranged from crude nonsense to sophisticated humor equal to Mark Twain or any other humorist of the day.

Figure 2-3 illustrates the basic four-panel form of the comic strip.

Figure 2-3   A Typical Four-Panel Strip

Over the years the nature of the comic strip has changed. Gone are the days when the comics were printed large and covered several pages of the newspaper. In the 1930s and 1940s because of the space available, the adventure strip became popular, led by such classics as *Buz Sawyer, Prince Valiant,* and later *Steve Canyon.* In recent times the size of the comics has shrunk, and very few of the detailed comic strips exist. Most strips are now three panels, simply drawn, with a gag-per-day, rather than continuity from one day to the next. Art has been the loser.

Nevertheless comic strips remain popular. National polls show that Americans love their comic strips. Just as jazz may be the only truly original American musical form, the development of comic strips may be our only major original visual art form.

COMIC BOOKS: Comic books originated in the 1930s when newspaper strips were reprinted in pamphlet form, often with advertisements. The debut of *Superman* in 1938 launched the modern comic-book era. Kids who grew up in the 1940s had a bonanza from which to choose, and "comics swapping" with other kids on the block became a highly refined activity.

Unfortunately, by the 1950s some comic books had degenerated into gruesome violence and this deterioration, coupled with a national trend toward censorship, caused the comic-book industry to decline. In 1954 a Senate subcommittee investigated the claims of critics that reading comic books caused juvenile delinquency. The same year the major publishers of comic books attempted to head off criticism by adopting a code of ethics for comic-book publisher. They set up a Comics Code Authority to judge comics and to give a seal of approval to acceptable comic books. Many comic book publishers went out of business because they either couldn't comply with the code while remaining profitable or preferred to stop publishing rather than yielding to censorship pressure.

With the 1960s and 1970s came the underground "comix." Acceptance by the subculture movement (and others) has given "comix" a lasting place in history.

For a decade or so the comic-book industry was small, only a shell of its glorious past. Then in the 1980s a new approach brought comic books back. The new approach was to aim comic books at adult readers, employing superior drawings and stories. New drawing techniques, such as innovative page layouts and unusual perspectives, gave considerable sophistication to modern comic books.

EDITORIAL CARTOONS: Of all cartoons, editorial and political cartoons have one of the longest traceable lines of development. Throughout the ages these types of cartoons and caricatures have dealt with all the themes of life, including poking fun at authority and the pompous stupidity of public figures.

The modern editorial cartoon arose in the nineteenth century, beginning with great European masters such as William Hogarth (1697–1764), Thomas Rowlandson (1756–1817), Honere Daumier (1808–1879) and George Cruikshank (1792–1878). The development continued in the United States with such giants as Thomas Nast (1840–1902).

All cartoon types have their own character and style, but editorial cartoons are perhaps the most noticeable in this respect. Rube Goldberg put it this way:

> While basically the drawing, as in the case of illustration and comic strips, must have a feeling of reality (people and objects in them must seem real and authentic) there is a very special look necessary to the editorial cartoon. That look must convey to the reader a certain sense of power in what the cartoonist is trying to say. It must carry dignity and conviction, even though, at times it might be humorous.[2]

The importance of editorial cartoons is attested to by the awarding of a Pulitzer Prize to the best cartoon of the year and by the response of the many people who write and call a newspaper in reaction to a powerful cartoon on the editorial page.

ANIMATED FILM CARTOONS: An animated film cartoon is a series of still drawings that are photographed on film and run through a projector at 24 frames-per-second. The slight changes in the sequence of the drawings create an illusion of movement.

The animated film requires an incredible degree of precision in synchronizing drawings, dialogue, and sound effects. Adding to the challenge is the large number of drawings needed. A typical seven-minute cartoon requires approximately 10,000 drawings and a feature-length film of one and half-hours requires approximately 130,000 drawings. It is not a simple process.

Throughout time artists have tried to find a method to make a two-dimensional picture come to life. The cave drawings often included sequences of drawings with changing positions as an attempt to depict movement. The development of form, lighting, and perspective helped to give realism and a sense of depth. For many decades silhouette machines and puppets were used in an attempt to show motion.

As soon as the moving picture was developed, animated movies were created. After the turn of the century such pioneers as James Blacking and Winsor McCoy demonstrated the sophisticated possibilities of animation.

Then came the era of Paul Terry, Walt Disney, and Warner Brothers Studios. Disney, of course, brought us talking mice, full-feature films, countless developments in technology, and new artistic methods for animation.

Television picked up on animation early and now is filled with moving cartoons, not just on Saturday morning, but also in prime time with programs aimed at adults such as *The Simpsons.* And, of course, numerous commercials are animated. Animation is also still viable in the moving picture industry. Feature films such as Disney's *Little Mermaid* and *Beauty and the Beast*, continue to be popular, and most art film festivals have a prize for animation. Animation has potential as a fine art. It is a form that allows imagination and technique to flow freely, like no other art form.

ADVERTISING CARTOONS: While cartoons are certainly ubiquitous in advertising, comic drawings have also always played a role in all forms of marketing. They appear in magazines and newspaper advertisements, on posters in department stores, and, of course on the products themselves—cereal boxes, gift-wrapping paper, and appliances, just to mention a few.

Figure 2-4   An Advertising Cartoon

ENVELOPES

TV COMMERCIALS

REFRIGERATOR NOTES

Figure 2-5   Some Everyday Cartoon Images

A MULTITUDE OF OTHER CARTOON TYPES: There are many, many other places where cartoons appear: office manuals, blotters, restaurant menus, magazine and newspaper spots, children's games, travel folders, and decals, to name a few. Cartoons are one of the most common visual aspects of our modern lives.

And, of course, we haven't yet mentioned their use in libraries. But that will be coming very soon!

The Cartoonist in Everyone

If there is a people's art—that is, one that is almost universal in its appeal and one that can be learned and enjoyed by practically anyone—it is cartooning. This doesn't mean that everybody will become a successful full-time cartoonist. In this extremely competitive field, only a few make big bucks. Nevertheless, cartooning can be useful in many of our professional activities, especially in library promotion. And it can be a satisfying hobby.

Cartoonist who just learned how to draw a straight line

Figure 2-6

All of us have been cartoonists since we first picked up a pencil or crayon and began to doodle on things, including mother's new kitchen wallpaper. We doodle as we talk on the telephone and as we sit in class or in meetings.

While most of this doodling is an outlet for tension or a diversion from boredom, it also means that we have an innate skill with a potential for development. It is a skill that can be developed by practice. If you can draw a straight line, then you can learn to draw. Why don't you take the straight-line test? Take an eight-and-a-half-by-eleven-inch sheet of blank paper, a soft pencil, and a 12-inch rule, and see if you can draw a straight line. See how easy that was? There is a cartoonist in you!

That may have been your first attempt to draw. Before we get into the "advanced" techniques, we need to discuss how cartoon graphics can be useful in your daily professional activities. You will see the benefits of using cartoons in your library and classrooms in the next chapter.

Endnotes

1. Jerry Robinson. *The Comics: An Illustrated History of Comic Strip Art,* NY: G. P. Putnam's Sons, 1974.

2. Rube Goldberg In: *Famous Artist Cartooning Course,* Bridgeport, CT: Famous Artists School, 1955, v.2, p.91.

INDEXING THE CHAPTER

Now we are ready to do the indexing. But, before that we need to try to put ourselves in the shoes of the user. Who is the reader and what kind of information will be important to the reader?

The first clues are in the title and the series editor's preface. The title implies that the primary reader of this book will be a librarian and the preface says that the purpose of the book is to help librarians use cartoons for preparing memos, posters, displays, lesson plans, publicity pieces, bulletin boards and announcements. An implied secondary audience is schoolteachers, particularly those who work closely with librarians in these matters.

First, we read the chapter through twice, the second time with a highlighter in hand. We underline (and make notes, if appropriate). Our goal is to get a feel for the proportional amount of attention that is given for certain ideas and to decide which are major ideas and which are minor. We want to index everything that is relevant to the information contained in the book and to the targeted user.

Beginning with the title, we see no useable terms, since the *entire book* is about cartooning and librarians. Words in the title are usually superfluous. The reader of this book would have no need to look up these words since such words would refer to the entire book.

The first word in the chapter is *Al Capp* and it is chosen. It leads to a short, but succulent definition of the word cartooning by one of the giants in the profession. Also, we will put down *cartoon, definition.*

The second paragraph is a brief history of the evolution of the word *cartoon* and it is selected. Why select the word *cartoon* when we didn't select the word *cartooning* from the title? Because we now have a different concept. Here we have a discussion of the object itself, its background, etc. The entire book is about *cartooning*, the technique, the "how-to-do-it," thus *cartooning* is superfluous and not needed. The definition and background on a cartoon is, however, very likely to be a search objective of someone using this index.

With this in mind we examine the next paragraph and find a discussion of cartoons as art. Again this is useful information for someone unfamiliar with this debatable aspect of the cartoon art, so the term *cartoons as art* is added to the index. It occurs to us that someone might look up *art* first. So we invert and add *art, cartoons*.

So far, our list looks like this:

Al Capp
Cartoon, definition
Cartoon, history
Cartoons as art
Art, cartoons

Already it is obvious that we might want to consider collapsing our headings thus far into a main heading and subheadings, but we won't do that at this point. Instead we will plunge ahead through the text and worry about restructuring and editing after we finish this stage of getting the main concepts down.

We are now past the introductory part of the chapter. The bulk of the chapter deals with the origin and historical development of cartoons, and concentrates on the major types of cartoons. In fact, this is what the entire chapter is about.

There is a major section called "Origin and Historical Development," so we have a new page where *cartoon, history* appears. The first subsection is "Ancient Art," but this is too general and vague to be of much use. Specificity must be found. The first idea we find under this subsection is about *cave painting*, so we select that. There is also information on *sequential figures*, so we add that term. These are specific aspects of *Ancient Art*.

The next subsection is "Through the Ages" and here we find *caricature*. *Through the Ages* wouldn't be much of an index term. Also, the concept of *humor in art* is discussed, so that idea goes on the list.

The next main section is "Today's Cartoon," and from this we glean the following additional items:

Magazine panels
New Yorker magazine
Harold Ross
Modern gag-panel
Saturday Evening Post
Collier's
Playboy
Comic strips
Hieronymous Bosch
Albrecht Dürer

Leonardo da Vinci
Jerry Robinson, *The Comics: An Illustrated History of the Comic Strip*
Comic books, origin
Comic books, decline
Editorial cartoons
Animated cartoons, production
Animated cartoons, films
Animated cartoons, TV
Advertising cartoons
Ubiquity of cartoons

It should be noted that a number of cartoonists are mentioned in the text, but they are not entered on the index list because no information is given about them beyond name-dropping as examples of famous cartoonists used to illustrate a point in time. It would be misleading to direct the index user to the text if she wanted information about these individual cartoonists. Al Capp, as mentioned above, was an exception because he coined an interesting definition of cartooning.

The list has three artists known for humor in their art, so we add them, because some useful information is given about them in the context of the discussion of the historical origin of cartoons. At this point our list looks like this:

Al Capp
Cartoon, definition
Cartoon, history
Cartoon as art
Art, cartoons
Magazine panels
Harold Ross
New Yorker magazine
Modern gag-panel
Saturday Evening Post
Collier's
Playboy
Comic strips
Humor in art
Hieronymous Bosch
Albrecht Dürer
Leonardo da Vinci
Jerry Robinson, *The Comics: An Illustrated History of the Comic Strip*
Comic books, origin
Comic books, decline
Editorial cartoons
Animated cartoons, production
Animated cartoons, films
Animated cartoons, TV
Advertising cartoons
Ubiquity of cartoons

This is not our final index of this book chapter. Several steps need to be taken:

1.   Collapse repetitive headings.
2.   Eliminate headings that are unlikely to be selected.
3.   Group subheadings under proper headings.
4.   Check for ambiguous or unclear headings.
5.   Create cross-references where appropriate.
6.   Check spelling, punctuation, and capitalization.
7.   Add additional entries if needed.
8.   Alphabetize.

An example of collapsing headings is the following:

Cartoon, definition
Cartoon, history
Cartoon as art

These headings collapse to:

Cartoons
    art
    definition
    history

An example of terms a user may think of first:

Strips, Cartoon

which we put on the list as:

Strips, cartoon *see* Comic strips

The final index (page references not indicated) looks like this:

Advertising cartoons
Animated cartoons
    film
    origin
    production
    TV
Bosch, Hieronymous
Capp, Al
Caricatures
Cartoonist in everyone

Cartoons
    art
    definition
    history
    ubiquity
Cartoons, editorial *see* Editorial cartoons
Cartoons, political *see* Political cartoons
Cave paintings
Collier's
Comic books
    decline
    origin
Comic strips
    American art form
    early strips
    evolution
    popularity
    reduction in newspaper space
da Vinci, Leonardo
Drawings, cave *see* Cave paintings
Dürer, Albrecht
Editorial cartoons
Gag-panel *see also New Yorker* magazine, Magazine panels
History of cartoons *see* Cartoons
Humor in art
Humorous images
Magazine panels
New Yorker magazine
Paintings, cave *see* Cave paintings
Playboy
Political cartoons
Ross, Harold
Saturday Evening Post
Sequential drawings
Strips, cartoon *see* Comic strips
Strips, comic *see* Comic strips
Ubiquity of cartoons

The resulting index does not have page locators, due to the complications of having a book chapter within a book chapter and having to work with a manuscript. At any rate, the locators would be simple and not extensive for any index entry due to the shortness of the example chapter.

One final note. This example probably overindexed the chapter. Some of the headings are to very little information, but this was done on purpose. The example is only one short chapter of the book, thus the indexing was stretched out a bit in order to give a full example of the process the indexer goes through mentally when indexing a book.

Indexing Special Subject Areas and Formats

BACKGROUND

Do specific subjects and specific formats affect the indexing process? Or is indexing just indexing and all the rules and procedures are the same? This is an area where much more research is needed to understand how to best deal with the indexing of special subjects and different kinds of formats. Professional indexers, relying on their knowledge and experience, have differing opinions on this point, but there is a lesson to be learned from catalogers who give a lot of attention to the differences when it comes to specific subjects and to particular forms of materials.

Fundamentally, all indexing *is* the same, in the sense that content is analyzed and represented as clearly as possible to the users. The basic principles of indexing apply across special topics and formats. There are certain peculiarities with different special topics and formats. It should be emphasized that indexing is concerned with the content of the information records, and the form is a secondary concern. Form is often related to ease of storage and ease of use, and there can be a relationship between form and the index that is created. For example, users frequently express a desire to have a separate index to "what's on microform." Librarians often dismiss this as being an illogical way to approach a search, but it is not illogical to the user. The user may want to work in the microforms room with an index to the information *in that room*, then move from bound periodicals to unbound issues, then to the computer terminals room, etc. If an index on the basis of form expedites the search, then it is not illogical to create indexes based on the form and location of the material.

The field of indexing has derived some general principles, based on experience and basic research. Although it is true that we do not yet have any general theories, we have a substantial amount of empirical data and shared common sense. It is not true that some subject areas or unique formats are exempt from our general notions of indexing. At the same time, indexing must be adjusted to fit the needs of users, including any peculiarities of form or subject area.

Each information retrieval system for individual subject areas has unique aspects. For example:

1.   A defined set of people are interested in that subject and have information needs related to that subject.
2.   Each subject area has its own vocabulary.
3.   Each subject area has a variety of subspecialties, each of which has its own peculiar aspects.

The indexing process and the subsequent successful retrieval of information in that subject area depends on the attention given to the characteristics of the individual subject areas and the users interested in that subject.

In the remaining part of this chapter, several examples of special subjects and special formats have been selected in order give a flavor of what we mean by these concepts. Obviously, not all special subjects and formats can be covered, but the selected examples should be sufficient to establish the idea that certain subjects and formats have distinct aspects which should be given attention.

SPECIAL SUBJECT AREAS

Science

When a subject field has a well-defined and unambiguous vocabulary, the indexer has a strong foundation of constructing an indexing language. In some ways, the science literature meets these criteria, but not always, because the scientific literature has vocabulary problems like any other literature. Science indexes usually have a large number of descriptors and these descriptors represent a high number of precisely defined concepts. Scientific literature has its share of ambiguity. For example, the pharmacology literature contains elements of mathematics, physics, chemistry, and other basic sciences. The nomenclature is a complex combination from these areas. Acronyms, generic names, popular names, trade names, and molecular and structural formulas present problems in selecting entry terms and in constructing adequate cross-references.

The development of the scientific journal had a revolutionary effect on the communication of science, and then the relentless growth of the science literature soon presented problems of coping with the volume. Scientists tried to manage the literature by creating handbooks and encyclopedias and then, finally, indexing, abstracting, and reviewing journals and other tools.

A great deal of attention has been given over the years to the creation, storage and dissemination of information in science and technology. A large amount of time and resources have been spent in this endeavor, particularly after the fifties when a national effort was launched to close the perceived gap that the United States had with Cold War enemies.

Numerous schemes, systems, and indexing languages were developed. The literature of science and technology has a high degree of precise words for narrowly defined concepts. Unfortunately, not all scientific writing is good writing and this introduces ambiguity, which the nonscientific community may not be aware of. Fortunately for the indexer there are numerous reference resources available both in print and electronically which can render aid.

Indexers of scientific material need to use caution in deciding which synonymous terms are going to be used. Generally, in nonthesaurus indexing, indexers lean toward using the words of the author, but in science indexing there is always the ongoing effort to standardize terminology. The indexer should strive to select synonymous terms (headings or cross-references) that respect terminological standards.

A good example of the science literature is the medical field that has a large literature and well-developed systems of indexing and abstracting. Indexes to the medical literature date back to the Middle Ages. The problem in indexing the medical literature is the complexities of the vocabulary of the subject. Not only does the terminology have intrinsic subcategories, but also it is not static. The vocabulary is very large, with a great proportion of the terms derived from Greek and Latin. There are numbers, synonyms, eponyms, and specialist jargon. Medical terminology also includes terms from the supporting basic sciences, engineering, and a number of the social sciences. Drugs present special indexing problems. They have generic and brand names and they are often misspelled.

Medical works consist of: medical research, clinical applications, allied health fields (e.g., nutrition), and complementary health areas (e.g., chiropractic, acupuncture, biofeedback, and hypnosis). There are many levels of materials within these broad categories. There are materials for highly specialized medicine, broadly specialized medicine, and general medicine. There are reference works and textbooks at every level and subdivision of medicine, along with works for allied health personnel, public health and the consumer.

Journal literature is a major facet. A useful way to think of the medical journal literature is to categorize it by major function. Medical journal articles present new research data, teach with introductory essays or tutorials, and present personal viewpoints, such as comments and editorializing.

Medical journals can be grouped several ways: Some journals publish only basic research, either broadly defined across medical science or more narrowly defined by disciplines or subdisciplines. Other journals are either basic science or clinical oriented. Still other journals are aimed at specific audiences, such as the researcher, the clinician, or both.

Much of the medical literature is multiauthored and many authors of medical books have the tendency to get involved with the editing of the submitted index. This is most prevalent in the deletion of terms that the authors believe are too common and no one would look up that term, not realizing that their readers may not be quite as knowledgeable in the specific aspects of the book as is the author.

Medical indexing must deal with adjective-heavy terms, multiple very-near synonyms, internationally different nomenclature, lay language mixed with professional jargon, and, in general, a very complex and often contradictory vocabulary. Cross-references are critical in a medical index, simply because of the complex vocabulary and the wide variety of users coming from multidisciplines and from the lay public.

The National Library of Medicine (NLM) has been in the forefront of indexing for a long time, not just for the medical literature, but in basic research related to indexing. The development and application of its *UMLS Metathesaurus* is a model that all neophyte indexers should study closely.

Another example worth studying is SNOMED International, from the College of American Pathologists (CAP). Over the last thirty-five years SNOMED works have become recognized globally as a comprehensive, multi-axial, controlled terminology created for the indexing of the entire medical record.

Medicine, and science in general, have many excellent indexing, abstracting and thesaurus tools and these should be studied carefully.

Social Sciences

A good example of special subjects from the social sciences is the legal literature. Legal indexing is one of the oldest types of indexing, going back to the beginning of indexing. Lawyers cannot function without exact access to their literature. It is basic to what they do. Many techniques and index designs developed for legal indexes have carried over into modern indexes of all kinds.

A large portion of the law literature is a group of reference tools, such as dictionaries, encyclopedias, treatises, regulations, legal journals, loose-leaf services, as well as statutes, digests of cases, and judicial decisions. The main concern of an indexer in this field is that word-by-word specificity is necessary because the literature is exact and the lawyer usually is searching for a very particular case or legal precedent. Also, definitions in law are extremely important, and a law index should lead to all words in the text that are defined or described or have to do with *meaning*.

Indexes to the law literature often are a combination of types of indexes. The index has subject descriptors, which may come from a controlled vocabulary, but at the same time those descriptors may be concordance-type words or phrases. Many times the index is an annotated index, because a full citation and description will save a lawyer time.

Lawyers are often well versed in using indexes, for the simple reason that a great deal of what the lawyer does is what a reference librarian does: looks for information in the literature. Lawyers and librarians are soul brothers and sisters. Most of the publishers of law materials understand the critical necessity of an index in retrieving law information and, as a result, there are many good indexes to the law literature.

The legal literature can be divided into several categories:

1.   Collections of statutes.
2.   Collections of case laws.
3.   Collections of administrative law.
4.   Treatises on specific branches and topics of law.
5.   Legal reference works.
6.   Textbooks.

7. Works on legal aspects of commercial or professional topics for practitioners in those fields.

8. Popular accounts of legal matters for the general public.

Legal literature can be characterized by:

1. Specialized terminology.

2. Old and new terminology (ancient stuff is still used).

3. Latin and French terms.

4. No paraphrasing by indexers (words, phrases, and sentences).

5. Synonyms (listed as cross-references only if legal definitions, not general dictionary definitions, have established their equivalent meaning).

6. Citations (references to statutes and cases that are essentially a special type of locator, leading the user to previous cases and applicable laws).

7. Definitions (legal definitions of a word or phrase are of critical importance).

8. Tables of statutes and cases are compiled according to traditional set patterns and must be followed carefully.

In general, in law there is a need for high exhaustivity and specificity and over-indexing may be important, because lawyers are very specific and exact regarding the information they seek.

Humanities

The humanists have always been aware of information access problems and have created indexes, abstracts, and concordance tools since antiquity.

Models of surrogation and indexing for the humanities are not the same as those for the sciences. Humanistic scholarship needs vocabulary control structures that represent the nature of the humanities and their scholarship protocols. In the sciences an indexer looks for the usual structure of:

1. Problem statement.

2. Purpose.

3. Methodology.

4. Data analysis.

5. Summary and conclusions.

Such a structure is not usually the case in writings in the humanities.

For example, in the humanities literature "a rose is a rose is a rose," but in the scientific literature a rose is any of a *Rosa* of the family *Rosacede*, having prickly shrubs with pinnate leaves and flowers with five petals or more. Perhaps a rose is still a rose, but the vocabulary is different. Writing in the humanities goes beyond "just the facts, Ma'am" and explores the meaning of human existence. The indexing of this literature must then reflect this level of communication and *aboutness* in the writing. The writing may be elegant and expressive, but indexers have trouble finding surrogates.

There is a great deal of semantic ambiguity in the humanities literature. This is not to say that there is no consistency in terminology, although the vocabularies are much more flexible than in the sciences. There are regularities of terminology in the various humanities disciplines. Thesauri, dictionaries, encyclopedias, and other reference sources give a substantial vocabulary database for the humanities indexer.

In the humanities indexing often has to be done on several levels of analysis and meaning. For example, if the paper deals with a synthesis of the Oedipus complex in nineteenth-century literature the indexer not only has to understand the research being reported in this paper but also must understand the Oedipus symbolism being compared because this too must be brought out in the index.

The humanists enlist a variety of approaches to research, ranging from quantitative methods to a vast range of qualitative methods, using a variety of textual, graphic, and audio media. This variety of contexts presents a challenge to the indexer.

It is difficult to make general statements about the indexing needs of the humanities because each area has its own infrastructure and special materials, thus presenting individual information problems of surrogation and access. There is one major difference between the information transfer mechanisms in the sciences and the humanities: conveyance of research findings in the sciences is predominantly in the journal literature, but this is not true in the humanities. It is not unusual for a book (sometimes massive) to report detailed new research. This is very rare in the sciences.

All scholarship must be concerned with multilanguage coverage, but the humanities may be more in need of direct and immediate foreign language coverage. The humanities need abstracting and indexing in various languages.

Also, it needs to be pointed out that information in the humanities is not dated as in the sciences. Retrospective information is a main lifeline in the humanities research whereas the past is only relevantly important to the sciences. A medical student should be familiar with Madam Curie's work, but it is seldom necessary to analyze her work in modern times. This is not true in the humanities. What has gone before is still very much alive and current and is constantly studied and reanalyzed.

Vocabulary consistency is lacking in the humanities literature. A high proportion of subject words in the humanities texts is common nouns, which have many alternative free-text terms. Writers tend to use numerous synonyms to express particular concepts. This gives problems in both free-text searching and in controlled vocabulary systems in the humanities.

In the humanities literature numerous, imprecise synonyms are often used to express a single concept. This presents a problem to the user who has a huge range of choices for an entry term. And the burden then falls on the indexer to have a full repertory of entry points into the index. Due to this situation free-text searching in the humanities is more imprecise than searching with a controlled vocabulary. In a free-text system it is difficult for a user to think of all the synonyms possible for a concept.

It is commonly known that indexing and abstracting in the humanities has not been given the same attention as it has in the sciences. The most obvious reason is the proportional amounts of money devoted to information services are far greater in the sciences, but that isn't the only reason. The nature of the humanities literature, its vocabulary, its emphasis on monograph usage and the interdisciplinary nature of the humanities make it especially challenging for the professional indexer and abstractor.

There are a number of specialized areas that need addressing. One example of this is children's literature. Many publishers don't believe that indexes for children's books are necessary, but librarians, indexers, and many children's writers believe strongly in indexes and in teaching kids to use indexes early in their reading development. And children believe that books should have indexes. Children are learning to use indexes when they surf the Web, although they may not realize it. Indexes for young readers should be straightforward with a very minimum of subheadings. Cross-references are often confusing to younger readers and should be minimized and clear. Children do not have the linguistic skills to keep conjuring up synonyms and may give up when the first word or two does not yield anything.

Indexing can grow in complexity as the age groups rise. Young adult material can have indexes that are not unlike adult indexes. It should be clearly understood that children's indexes are not adult indexes that have been edited down to children. Children cannot be written down to and neither should their indexes be constructed that way. The indexes must be constructed for children, with their cognitive and emotional make-up in mind.

SPECIAL FORMATS

Special formats cover a wide range of materials, both print and nonprint. A good example of a print special format is newspapers.

Newspapers

Once the importance of newspapers as retrospective sources was established, researchers quickly realized the need for comprehensive, effective access. There are two general types of users of newspaper indexes: the news personnel and the general public. News personnel need facts, story follow-up, analysis, background material and other information that helps them on a current assignment. The public users are businesspeople, scholars, students, genealogists, writers, and trivia hunters. Local stories often cannot be indexed with the major newspaper thesauri, such as the *New York Times*. One solution is to identify keywords in the story's headline or the first few paragraphs. If the writer has followed standard journalistic practice, then most of the important words will be at the top of the story.

Few indexes exist for small local newspapers, which are important for local history research. When these indexes do exist, they usually were created *ad hoc* without any vocabulary control or with a crude list of terms. Historians make good use of newspapers and they need indexes. Before the twentieth century, the newspaper was not generally considered a legitimate source to use as a basis for writing history. The main reason for this attitude was rooted in the low regard of society for newspapers in general. Most of them were assumed to be sensational and unreliable.

The historian and the historiographer had not yet seen the newspaper as a source of information of any importance to them. The historian believed in basing the history he wrote on formal and official documents; and in telling the story as it was officially said to have happened, and in telling it once and for all. Newspapers were called ephemeral, and were scorned as a source of information.

Periodically, throughout the nineteenth century, various historians ventured to use newspapers as sources, but John B. McMaster, who wrote the extensive *History of the People of the United States,* made the first really important use of them. He relied heavily on newspapers and, in fact, this use is considered to be one of his chief contributions to American historiography. After McMaster, no historian could ignore newspapers as an important source. By 1900 historians were becoming more respectful toward newspapers as source material. The entire session of the 1909 meeting of the American Historical Society was devoted to newspapers as history sources.

The changing attitude toward newspapers was in the spirit of the changing attitude toward historiography. With the twentieth century came the rise of the interpretive approach to history. Instead of merely trying to establish historical events, the historian became interested in interpreting the spirit of a time or locality. Newspapers, with their social news, quack advertisements, letters to editors, and outspoken editorials, were recognized as a source the historian could not ignore. Indexers must realize that newspapers are used both as primary and as secondary sources. As a primary source, newspapers are consulted, first of all, for facts. The newspapers are daily records of current events. The historian and historiographer, James Ford Rhodes, who promoted newspapers as historical sources, said he often found in newspapers facts which were invaluable in the correction of *logical assumptions* which frequently appear in American historical and biographical books.

Newspapers are quoted as evidence of opinion. Again, to use Rhodes as an example, he discovered, by the use of newspapers, what a potent part public sentiment played in the repeal of the Kansas-Nebraska Act. Also, he says, the disorganization of the Democratic Party in 1856 and the rise of the Republican Party can be clearly traced in the news and editorial columns of the newspapers.

The indexer must bring out the aspects of contemporary society from the newspapers. A person needs only to read several issues of a local newspaper to form a picture of a community. Social news, advertisements, editorials, letters to the editor, all contribute to a picture of the society in which the newspaper exists.

On the other hand, the indexer should understand that newspapers are also used as secondary sources. Perhaps most often it is the historical editions of the paper, where historical items are printed, that are used as secondary sources. When users read these editions, they are accepting the secondhand opinions and verdicts of the editors and contributors to the paper, but the indexer must bring these out.

Historians and reporters have long known the drawbacks to using newspapers as resources. First, the format is discouraging. Newspapers are bulky, usually they are dirty, and the paper is brittle. If the newspapers themselves can be located, and are accessible, the information in them is hard to find. With notable exceptions, indexes to newspapers are almost nonexistent. The papers have to be plowed through, page by page, column by column, and this search may turn out to be unrewarding. The good news is that more and more newspapers are available electronically and steady progress is being made to digitize retrospective newspapers. An example of this is *Newspapers Online!* (http://www.newspaper.com), a free service for people to use to find newspaper publications all around the world. This is a comprehensive, full-text access site.

Internal criticism must be applied to the content of the paper. It takes a careful worker with a critical mind to make proper use of newspapers. Facts have to be weighed carefully. Probably, only the experienced scholar can mine the gold from the bulk of information that has come off the newspaper press during the last several hundred years.

The indexing of large, well-known newspapers is an in-house job, with several indexers using prescribed vocabulary control devices and procedures; however, doing your own local newspaper indexing is a different ball game. You create your own rules and entry control to suit the needs of the local situation.

The classical rule is to not index national or international news because people wanting that news can use the index of the famous newspaper indexes such as the *New York Times*. Does this mean that local indexes should cover everything else? No. Local newspapers should be selective. It is not necessary to include routine items such as recipes, church meetings, whose-kids-visited-who, and other such ephemeral material. Exceptions are made, such as: if the president comes to the local nursing home to visit his 107-year-old grandmother, and, of course, any local person who achieves something a little out of the ordinary.

One important aspect of newspaper indexing is the showing of related stories. Important stories are often surrounded by related stories, both in the current issue and in future and past issues. For example, a huge tornado in Oklahoma had several related stories about a deputy sheriff rescuing a mud-covered baby that had been jerked from her mother's arms and whirled away. Obituaries are also important, because people use these when trying to track down information on individuals. The same is true for local politics, sports events (settle that bet on the win/loss record in 1972?).

Vocabulary control for subject entries will probably be self-generated. One approach is the use of a skimpy subset of the headings in the *New York Times Index* or other famous models. These headings can be tailored for local needs.

Therefore, the decision process is (1) what should be indexed? and (2) how deep should the indexing be? The item can be indexed with a single keyword or many keywords, which thoroughly represents the item.

In summary, newspaper indexing is a good example of the many challenges related to dealing with special format indexing.

Nonprint Forms

The information explosion in the last two decades has taken us far beyond textual indexing. Collections of images, in many forms, covering a broad range of subjects, are becoming more and more accessible electronically. Actually, visual information is as old as civilization and came before textual information. Modern society is visually stimulated (perhaps assaulted) from every direction, day and night. In the early days of computers we punched cards and later typed commands but now we madly click on an infinite whirl of icons, cartoons, smiley faces, etc., to get our information, and then the information itself may be partially or wholly an image.

All knowledge records exist in some physical form. For example, the neurology patterns in a human brain is knowledge stored in a physical form, albeit as an electrical and chemical knowledge database. However, not all information storage is in language. Communication can be sounds and images. These types of recorded knowledge are growing exponentially and with this growth and the introduction of new media, there is an accelerating interest in how to index this material.

The list of traditional nonprint items that needs indexing is long and diverse, including: 35 mm slides, lantern slides, color/black-and-white prints, negatives, illustrations, calendars, postcards, posters, maps, charts, paintings, architectural drawings, blueprints, films, videos, casts and molds, and on and on. Indexing nonprint knowledge records has always been a nontrivial and multifaceted challenge. In the past the process was constrained by the common practice of limiting the indexing to what could be written on the item (e.g., on the slide label) or by simple cards stored in a file cabinet next to the items. This resulted in very abbreviated analysis. Fortunately, indexing systems for these materials have vastly improved in the past few decades.

Images

Modern image indexing is based on the old adage that a picture is worth a thousand words, that even a great amount of descriptive text cannot convey as much understanding as actually viewing the image.

Imaging is the process by which visual images are captured, enhanced and transformed, usually with compression, into digital form. Imaging cuts across many sections of modern society. It comes from airplanes, from satellites, from Mars land-rovers, from barcodes in the department store, from bank checks, from X-rays, and on and on. Hardly any sector of society is exempt from image processing and we encounter it throughout our day. A floodgate is opening on multimedia, brought on by new networking and multimedia technologies. Text, voice, audio, graphics, images, and animation are being integrated into heterogeneous packages and with this comes new challenges to find a way to index these packages in an effective way. As a result of the digital explosion, many major and minor museums have created their own Web sites and populated their pages with reproductions of their collections, and medical libraries are following suit. Through indexing, users have access to paintings, sculptures, and other images previously out of reach unless they could get to the museum itself. Art historians, artists, and art lovers have the chance to study works of art unattainable in the past, and perhaps to find that one piece of sculpture they saw on a special trip to the museum last year. This will work only if their search is able to retrieve the desired image.

The computer has changed many things, including a rapid rise in visual databases and digitized imaging. Now such material can be analyzed and indexed in as much depth as needed. With this came the realization that indexing was no longer a simple labeling job. The world has huge stores of image information and it is growing rapidly. As more and more organizations and institutions place this type of information on the Internet, there is a growing need for better organization, storage, and access to this material. Without adequate indexing, all the pictures of works of art, science images, etc. will be in a cyberspace black hole.

With the Web helping to usher in a new age for visual information, the rapid increase of digitized resources in libraries and beyond libraries is changing our concepts of what information storage and retrieval is. Historically indexing has been a textual based procedure and despite what outsiders may think, it has never been intellectually easy, but new challenges have to be faced with content-based image indexing. Content-based imaging is complicated by the fact that it is non-keyword based. Indexing of any kind aims at identifying the information content of knowledge records. In text indexing the source is the printed word, but in image records the source is something more inclusive: the aesthetic, textural, and cognitive attributes that come through several sensorial inputs. Then comes the task of filtering the information and turning it into content indicators in the form of an index. The nature of the wide-ranging image material is complex and requires specialized adoption of general indexing procedures.

Indexing images does not mean that we have to totally reinvent the indexing wheel. Libraries have been handling images since the birth of libraries, but what we know about indexing needs to be examined in the light of the needs of this special form of electronic data to see where old methods work, where they don't, and what new methods must be invented. There has been a convergence of intellectual problems and technical problems on a scale never faced before by the indexing profession.

As early as the 1960s information professionals discussed and researched the problems of image indexing and over the years discussion continued. In 1986, Sara Shatford (Shatford 1986) described images as existing in two different dichotomies: a picture is both *of* something and *about* something. Also, an image functions simultaneously both as a specific item and as a generic representation of a class of items. For example:

1. *of* (specific)—the Golden Gate Bridge.
2. *of* (generic)—bridge.
3. *about*—the gateway to the city itself, or a monument to one of the greatest human endeavors of its time.

There are two primary levels of image retrieval. The first is based on discrete items in the image. For example, retrieve all pictures with the Eiffel Tower or all paintings with a tree in it. At this level the indexer assigns tags similar to textual indexing. *Eiffel Tower* and *tree* are index terms in the conventional sense. At the second level image analysis is involved. For example, retrieve all paintings with hot colors dominating. In practice, user searches usually fall somewhere in between these two levels. The most desirable results meld the two levels.

Of course some images don't exist on these two levels. A picture in a computer manual may be *of* a printer cable being hooked into the processor. And it is *about* hooking up the printer to your computer. This is the same thing.

Retrieving images from databases is not a trivial problem. The difference between retrieving text and retrieving images is that in textual databases words are used as surrogates for words, but in image retrieval words are surrogates for images where aboutness and meaning exist on many levels and in many different ways. A Picasso painting carries objective data such as title, size, medium, date, general subject, etc., but it also conveys "messages" such as color subtlety and aboutness at the artistic level. A textual document *tells* us what it is about. A painting cannot. It has to be interpreted.

The physical object is described in a straightforward way. This might be a 9x12-inch black-and-white photograph with the photographer's name and the place it was taken. If the photograph is by a famous photographer, then *that physical fact* takes on an added aspect that must be dealt with in the indexing. The aboutness level deals with the content of the item, on many levels. What is the meaning, theme, or significance of the different aspects of the item? A picture of soldiers pinned down under enemy fire on the beaches of Normandy needs very few, if any, words to convey a powerful message. An architect can flip through a stack of pictures of a building from various angles, both in and outside, and he needs no words to tell him what that building is about.

Traditionally, images have been stored and retrieved in a manner based on techniques commonly used in text databases. In other words, there might be fields in the records for the artist or photographer, along with the title of the image, data produced, etc., and then some fields with descriptive text. Keyword and Boolean operators could then be used to search. Obviously, content-based image indexing has many similarities to textual based indexing. For example, normally both deal with large databases. Also, there is a high degree of uncertainty on the part of the user of image databases (usually they are browsing), requiring effective feedback of relevancy judgments, something that we have been hearing a lot about in textual retrieval in recent years.

Obviously traditional indexing is text centered, but generally images have very little textual information. The text accompanying indexes gives only a limited coverage of what the image is about. The problem is compounded by the fact that users of image material have a nontextual need of the image. They need a different approach. They are concerned about characteristics not generally structured as subject terms, such as artist's name, shape, color, time period, etc.

Shatford presented her theory for image indexing in 1986, before the Information Highway age. During the last thirteen years, the World Wide Web, CD-ROMs, and digital images have all exploded upon the scene and access to this information is a matter of primary concern. What do we index when we index an image? Should we strive for subject indexing, as Shatford recommends? Do we go just for content: color, texture, forms? Or do we search for subjects and representations of concepts? The complexity begins with the user.

For example, several people may be shown a picture of a shot bald eagle. The first person sees an eagle, the second sees a picture of an eagle and the third sees a horrible cruelty to animals. How are such items indexed to reflect this type of "content"? There may be a user who approaches an index with any of the three concepts in mind. It should be pointed out that an index to some types of non-print materials might not be verbal. An index can be displayed as a screen full of icons to be clicked on, with or without accompanying verbal representation. Or an image can be clicked on. What do we get if we click on the smile on Mona Lisa's face? Right now, maybe not a lot, but look out for the future. Art historians may put a lot of things on the image that they think Mona might be able to tell us.

Content-based image indexing begins by isolating individual units within a time span. For example, if it is a video, individual shots and scenes are pinpointed. These units are then annotated as camera positions, the effects of film editing, motion of objects, etc. Since many, many frames represent only a tiny moment in time, very few representative images are needed to summarize any particular shot. The challenge is to develop automatic methods that will identify important, content bearing frames so that users don't have to scroll through thousands of frames in order to find what they want and to best answer queries related to the video.

Furthermore, the indexer must be able to express nonverbal concepts in both verbal and icon terms. Hypermedia systems have brought us to an icon mania and with it the proposal for nonverbal searching. So far, few icons and delightful visual computer gymnastics have not come close to the power of verbal expression in an index, but times are changing and researchers are working on it.

One of the reasons we have had problems of relevance decisions in evaluating text retrieval systems is that relevance is in the eye of the beholder, that is, the relevance of a document is a unique response for each particular user. The problem is intensified in image retrieval. The meaning of an image depends on the perspective of the individual. The manifestations of an image are multilayered. For example, what information is conveyed with a photograph of Whistler painting a picture of his mother? We might begin with who took the photograph and end up with the picture of his mother's dress. The dress in the painting might differ from the dress she is wearing in the photograph, and so forth. Also, images are interdisciplinary to users. For example, a photographer may be interested in the Whistler picture as a photograph, an artist in the painter and an historian in the dress that the mother was wearing for that time period.

A common complaint of users of these systems is the lack of exhaustivity. Users often contend that the indexing must be highly exhaustive to be useful. Presently, this has not been done. Some indexers maintain that exhaustivity is not essential because browsing is a primary searching method of this material and the minute details are not necessary in the index. The user will find these as she visually browses. Another major problem is that there is no consensus of practitioners in the image retrieval area as to what kinds of information need to be indexed. This brings us the full circle back to the problem of user identity.

In the past, the purpose of the collection defined the users and vice versa. Art historians went to art museums specializing in works from various eras, historians and anthropologists went to museums of history, and art lovers visited the museum whose collection contained those pieces of art they enjoyed most. In the past, an image indexer knew her potential user and made indexing judgments based on that knowledge. However, today's image indexer has to anticipate users of every specialty and need. She is no longer indexing one isolated collection, but numerous collections, global in scope and location. This adds an entirely new layer onto the problem.

From the computing side of the issue, researchers have been developing algorithmic processing techniques that will go directly into the compressed domain of the images and seek dominant content bearing units in the images for the index. There are complexities with this approach, but given the growing size of such databases, such approaches are needed to cut both the computational and user time involved in the image retrieval process. Data compression techniques are a major area of study, since most digitized information needs to be represented in compressed formats because of the constraints to time and space involved in storage and retrieval of this type of information.

Most of the work up to this point has concentrated on similarity-based retrieval for constructing search engines that will match scientific images. These systems work well when the images are relatively stable in terms of shape, color, texture, etc., but do not work so well with videos and other streaming images, where the subjects seldom maintain these characteristics consistently over time.

What about the future? The indexing of images is not a simple process. The downside is that this field of indexing is complex, complicated by compound meanings of the images themselves and by the ambiguity of the words needed to retrieve the images. The upside is that through digitization, more and more images are more readily available to more people than ever before in our history.

As in text indexing, the professionals are in the midst of a heated discussion concerning automation in image indexing. Content indexing of images is done with software written specifically for this task and ties into Internet search tools with which the user can access files based upon criteria such as color, texture, and abstract shapes, etc. Content-based indexing works quite well in fulfilling the search attribute of perception response to a visual stimulus, but users need other attributes which content-based indexing cannot identify or retrieve, such as explanation and interpretations.

While computer scientists work toward methods for making the computer understand the difference between the *of* and *about* in an image, human indexers are working with search-tool developers, creating indexes and thesauri which will provide the Web-based user the language needed to fulfill the information need.

There is an exciting future out there.

Evaluation of Indexing

BACKGROUND

The purpose of index evaluation is to determine the effectiveness, efficiency, and value of what we have done by careful study and appraisal. We evaluate indexes to determine how good they are, and our work is not complete until such evaluations are made. A good or bad index is not the result of a single component but of many factors, ranging from human judgment to economic constraints.

Problems with indexes were known long ago. From the very beginning there were opinions on arrangement, coverage, entries, and all the issues we still discuss. We are concerned about the quality of indexes because unretrieved information is the same as nonexistent information. Evaluation of indexes, of some sort, has existed as long as indexes. These qualitative, unwritten standards slowly developed over the centuries into today's written standards. Professional indexers do excellent evaluations, based on training, knowledge, and years of experiences. Qualitative evaluation of indexes remains an important aspect of the profession.

Many things besides indexing can make an information retrieval system go wrong: file structuring, coding, faulty searching procedures, and bad computer programming are examples of other culprits. There are both system factors and human factors that affect retrieval performance. System factors include the nature of the index language, the constraints of exhaustivity, the constraints of specificity, level of coordination, and the overall structure. On the human side the indexing is constrained by its consistency, the indexer's subject expertise, her accuracy, and her level of indexing experience.

An examination of the literature shows the ubiquitous interest in index evaluation, but no totally acceptable methods of evaluation have been agreed upon. Indexing is more of an art than a science, and, as such, it depends heavily on experienced judgment.

Indexing and vocabulary decisions are concerned with a conceptual analysis and a translation of document content into index records. The subject analysis may be human or computer-based. A computer-based translation will depend upon the validity and reliability of the computer programs that attempt to duplicate the judgment of the human analyst. The resulting descriptors may be derived from a controlled vocabulary or come from the natural language of the document. The exhaustivity and specificity of term assignment, and the accuracy with which the terms reflect the document content, are all contributors, or potential inhibitors, to system performance.

The human factors associated with system performance are relevant to both input and output processes. The consistency among multiple indexing personnel in term assignments and the skill, experience, and subject-matter knowledge of the indexing personnel are as important as those of the searcher. In the output activities, searching the database relies initially upon the skilled experience of the user or intermediary. Construction of search strategies and the translation to appropriate search terms or combination of terms will increase the probability of success in the endeavor. Skill in searching and in screening the retrieved material is enhanced by in-depth knowledge of the subject matter being searched. The factors that affect the performance of an information retrieval system are many faceted.

Until such time that indexing can be based on an established theoretical body of knowledge, it is not likely that the procedures and results can be totally assessed quantitatively. At the same time, it is essential that we have some method, quantitative or not, that will help us evaluate what we are doing.

The entire information retrieval process is a series of interrelated steps, each of which is critical to the success of the total system. The indexing step itself can be broken down into a series of substeps that are similarly critical. When we attempt to evaluate indexing, we are dealing with many variables. One of the shortcomings of our quantitative methods of evaluation has been the lack of control of the many variables involved when we look at the entire process. Often, in past situations, only one, or sometimes two, variables were controlled in the so-called experiment, and the many related or intervening variables were politely ignored.

THE GENERAL PROBLEM

What is an indexer supposed to achieve? The final product is an index that works, resulting from the assignment of descriptors to identify the subject content of a knowledge record. How well the index does this determines the quality of the index as a retrieval tool.

We generally judge quality by simply saying that "the indexing is good" or "the indexing is bad," but it is difficult to define what we mean by *good* and *bad*. Attempts are then made to define good in terms of objectives, e.g., the *purpose* of the index. Does it fulfill its stated purposes? Are its scope and coverage adequate? However, once again we are not quite sure how to make those judgments. When we say purpose, for example, we are talking about how sufficient the descriptors are in meeting the information requirements of the user.

So we begin with user needs and then examine the index for accuracy, consistency, form, and internal structure. An index can be evaluated either as an individual unit or in comparison with similar units. The objective of the first approach is to rate the index in terms of the needs of the clientele, the subject areas covered, its stated purpose, and its cost. When the latter approach is used, we compare relative quality and cost. To do this, we must have made a previous judgment about the other indexes used as models.

Over the years almost every possible indexing comparison has been made. Human indexing has been inter-compared for consistency. Human indexing has been compared with machine indexing. Numerous tests have been conducted to compare the relative utility of using different parts of a document for indexing, for example, indexing only with titles, or titles and abstracts or using the full text of the document. Statistical methods and quasi-mathematical models have been proposed to ascertain the quality of indexes. The problem has not been a lack of testing models. The problem has been the subjective nature of what a *good* index is.

The evaluation methods that have been developed are not quantitatively precise and are fraught with subjective factors. A great deal of thought has gone into the problem and some workable methods exist. In the indexing endeavor the final product is an index that *works,* resulting from the assignment of proper descriptors to identify the subject content of a knowledge record. How well the indexer does this determines the quality of the index as a retrieval tool.

The serious use of empirical studies to evaluate indexing has its origins in the beginnings of computer-based information retrieval in the late 1940s and early 1950s. As soon as punched card systems went into operation, people began to criticize them and began to develop quantitative methods for evaluation.

The classical landmark in this endeavor was the Cranfield tests at the College of Aeronautics, Cranfield, United Kingdom. Numerous other tests were carried out both in the United States and in Europe. Most of the tests were focused on indexing and searching. The model was simple. Collect a set of test documents, devise a search procedure, submit artificial queries to the system, and let a panel of judges evaluate the results. The judges (hopefully experts in the field represented by the documents) looked at the results and sorted the relevant documents from the nonrelevant documents. If the results were poor, then the fault was attributed to the indexing.

Because of the constraints of early electronic storage media, these early evaluations necessarily relied on small test collections. Size limitation and the homogeneity of documents in test collections were sources of criticism of early evaluations. It is easy to look back and criticize these early attempts but we should not lose sight of the fact that we began the journey to finding an objective way to evaluate our information systems, in particular the indexing and searching components.

In the second Cranfield project (Cranfield II) some interesting results were found concerning index language that set off a continuing debate that is still ongoing. Some of these were that simple term index languages give the best results and when using a single term index language, groups of terms (that are not real synonyms) drop in retrieval performance. Also, simple coordination gives better precision than more complex devices, such as hierarchical classification. The results also promoted the idea that there is an inverse relationship between recall and precision. Despite the shortcoming of these classical tests, at least they gave a wake-up call to the complexities involved.

BEGINNING WITH THE USER

Indexing evaluation begins with who the users are. From the first moment indexing decisions must be made within the framework of who will be using the index. Neither indexers nor any set of indexing policies can assure that every user request will be anticipated, but knowing the user target can help focus and funnel the indexing process. The average user of an index is oblivious to how indexes are constructed; they use the index without any thought of how it was created, until they feel the frustration of a really bad index.

Trying to manufacture an index without knowing who the users are is like trying to manufacture kids' clothes without knowing their gender, age, culture or if they live in the tropics or the arctic. You cannot *just make* kids' clothes. Neither can you just make an index.

Although much has been said about how indexing must be aimed at the user, little is understood about the needs of the users in terms of the information conveyed by the documents and the effects of that information on the user once the document is read. Throughout the history of bibliographic control, librarians have focused on the object itself, developing content indicators according to what they conceived the document to be about. The situation did not change significantly with the advent of computer-based information retrieval.

How do users approach an information file? How do their perceptions or their problems color the interpretation of the index they use? Almost nothing is known about how users react or use the information provided. How does this use influence or change their future needs? If these questions could be answered, indexing quality would improve rather dramatically because then we would know what to do.

There is a cynical view that users approach our libraries and information retrieval systems only as a last resort when there is absolutely nowhere else to turn. When they do come in, they have low expectations, silently demanding very little more than they usually find. Therefore, we continue to operate in the same old way, never fully understanding what is meant by the phrase *use of information*. The basic problem is that the user's external expression of need may not truly express the internal need. The problem may also be that the user does know what is needed, but does not realize that she is not expressing it the way that the system requires. Then the user blames the library and the retrieval tools. Can we develop ways to evaluate our tools better so that this breakdown in interface will not occur?

A distinction should be made between the terms *use of information* and *use of materials*, although both are related to the user, of course. *Use of materials* is an objective concept that can be observed and quantified, and this kind of use is what is meant, generally, when talking about the needs of users. What we must understand is that when a user opens an index, there is no assurance that the user will find the material *useful*.

People have many objectives in mind when they approach a library. One user wants a grand sweep of a topic that pulls together every tidbit of information written about it, a second person wants only a general survey of a topic, and a third one wants to verify a single fact. To take care of all three, an index must be complete. That is, it must alert the user to everything on the topic. The index must have enough specificity for the third user to get a fact quickly, and in all cases the index must retrieve only relevant materials. Users will differ in their demands for completeness and specificity, but all of them want to avoid having to examine irrelevant materials.

The point being made is that before evaluation can be carried out, some criteria of user needs and demands concerning an index must be established. The goal of a good index is to aid the user in finding information in documents within a reasonable boundary of time and personal effort. Above all, the re-trieved information must be relevant. This is where evaluation should focus.

We are a long ways away from designing indexes tailored to each individ-ual user. Buck Rogers is still three centuries from being born, but perhaps Buck will have a computerized, totally natural language system so that all he has to do is blink an eye and the system is *exactly* tailored to his needs. In the meantime we have to design indexes in a more general way. However, this doesn't mean that we cannot direct the index at specific groups of users and their general needs.

There are three general types of user needs:

1. Overt information related to the item, such as its author or title.
2. A subject need that is specific and well-defined.
3. A vague and ill-defined need.

These three levels will directly affect the user's choice of index terms.

There are two approaches to incorporating users into the system. One ap-proach is to study the user's cognitive processes, which focuses on how people think and use feedback in searching for information. The other approach is to design rule-based systems. If the users follow the rules, then they will find what they need. The answer is the integration of these two approaches.

Although indexers will not personally know the users of the index, they will have a pretty good model in mind. If the book is a scholarly book on the Civil War, the users will generally be Civil War buffs, with a scholarly slant. A research report on chemotherapy for treating lymphomas will probably be for researchers, clinicians, and informed laypersons who are interested in lym-phoma. While it is true that there is no such thing as a perfectly manufactured average user, there are statistically valid equivalents of a *user* and this can be a very workable model.

RELEVANCE

The nemesis of information retrieval evaluation has been the problem of relevance. When a judge said a document was relevant or not relevant, what did that mean? The judge next to her might very well sort the document into the opposite stack. Those who have dedicated time and deliberation to the topic of relevance seem to agree that indexing evaluation will never be totally effec-tive until there is an understanding of the precept of relevance. It is the funda-mental notion in evaluation, not only of indexing, but also of all bibliothecal control enterprises. The problem with the concept of relevance is that human-kind is a relative animal, not an absolute one.

The notion of relevance comes about in a logical way. When users make a search of the information store, they have in their own minds an image of what information they need. Given that image, the total information file is dichotomized, with one part having the documents that they need and the other group having documents that they are not interested in. The validity of this dichotomizing depends solely on how the content of the documents matches the image that the user has. In other words, relevance is in the eye of the beholder. It follows that relevance is the crux to evaluating an index in its performance, even though relevance is clearly a relative notion. As the index points and guides the searcher to information and represents directions about what should be retrieved and what is not to be retrieved, it works under the user's personal mandate of relevance.

Relevance, as a notion, was not original with indexers and information retrieval practitioners, but has been of concern to philosophers and logicians since antiquity, and over the years extensive theories have been developed and discussed. When a logician makes an inference from *A* to *B*, it is maintained that for this to be valid, *A* must be *relevant* to *B*. Basic relationships in logic, including deduction, implication, entailment, and logical consequence, are all closely constructed around the notion of relevance. Relevance is a theoretical problem of interest to information retrieval in general and to indexing in particular.

A distinction needs to be made between the term relevance and the term pertinence. *Relevance* is the relationship between a document and a request and *pertinence* is the relationship between a document and an information need. Users base their judgment of the relevance of a document on much more than the accuracy of how the index term used pulled a particular document. The document that was retrieved might be exactly what the index term described, but the user does not find the document useful. For example, the document may not be timely, it may not be in a language the user understands, it may be written on a level of comprehensibility that is beyond the user, or it may be information the user already has. All these factors will adversely affect the user's judgment of the usefulness of the document.

Thus, relevance is most closely associated with the relationship between the document and the index, and pertinence is most closely associated with the relationship between the document and the user. Relevance is related to the general coinciding of a document with a search query. Pertinence is concerned with the immediate usefulness to a particular user. If the query is about cats and the document is about cats, then, in a general sense, the document is relevant to the topic. But that document may not give a particular user needed information at that point. It is not pertinent to the information need. At some other point in time, with different parameters, that very same document may be useful to the same user. The first aspect can be quantified by letting a subject expert evaluate the results. But, the second aspect is the reflection of a single user and is highly personal. The only way to measure pertinence is to survey users and ask them how useful they found the information. This is usually done with a scale, rather than a yes/no option since most users will find a varying degree of pertinence in the retrieved documents.

To evaluate how well an index is working, we could let three types of people make a judgment: an information intermediary, a subject specialist, and the requester of the information. The information intermediary is the one who forms the searching strategy and can judge the results within the framework of how the question was asked. The subject specialist has a more global response and is concerned with whether or not the information in the document is sufficiently close to the subject matter of the request. These first two judges are evaluating how well the index matches the document, but the third judge is judging the pertinence of the item to himself or herself.

On the surface it would appear that the only thing we can expect of an index is that it retrieves documents relevant to the information requested and expressed with an index term; we have no way to control the pertinence variable. This stance fails to recognize that, in the end, it is the pertinence of the information to the user that counts. If the index never retrieves pertinent information, the entire information system has failed, including the index. It is essential that we evaluate indexes on all levels, no matter how difficult the methodology.

Another way to look at relevance is to think of it as a measure of how well a problem is solved. If I need to find out who won the 1951 World Series and I am handed the *World Almanac* and the index leads me to the score, then my problem is solved and the reference book was relevant. People use information sources because they face a problem. An information problem can range from the trivial to the profound, can be simple or complex, but to the user it is always important. Unfortunately for the indexer these problems are seldom completely or even partly defined. Every information professional knows that the hardest part of the job is finding out exactly what the information seeker is asking. People often are not sure what they are asking for, and they approach the information professional in all stages of both problem understanding and question formulation. All of this severely complicates index evaluation.

So, one begins the task by asking the question: How do you design an index that can effectively react to any state of the searcher's problem, varying from simply a dim, obscure fancy all the way up to the scholar's well-defined information need? An index that is based on the assumption that all problems are well defined and that queries are straightforward is doomed for extinction.

RECALL AND PRECISION

Historically, information retrieval systems have been evaluated through an examination of the system's output. Databases and the indexing system employed were judged by translating user queries into search terms (using the same indexing procedure used to index the database) and then judging the relevance of the documents. Methods and algorithms were devised to track the performance of users, intermediaries, networking, and many other aspects of information retrieval (IR) systems.

Evaluation in the above context usually focuses on the indexing system and the searching strategies that are based on the indexing language. Submitting the search terms to the system causes one or more scans to occur against the previously developed index in order to ascertain the existence of indexed terms that match the terms of the search. Any matches will cause the stored document representations (title, abstracts, and indexed entries) to be returned to the information seeker for judgment. If a given representation is deemed to be of value, the corresponding source document may be obtained from the appropriate repository. Examination of the search results may indicate the need for further searching through modifications of the search criteria. By broadening or narrowing the search focus and by using synonyms or combinations of terms, along with various other strategies, the user may iteratively construct a successful search of the system. The output processes of the IR system involve a creatively designed series of entities and actions: seeker, needs, request, search strategies, search terms, document representations, and document delivery.

When users approach an information file they may find that a single document is all they need. Or they may be satisfied with several core items. At other times they want a full literature search, both current and retrospective, and they will be satisfied with nothing short of total retrieval of everything related to their search.

When users take the last option, the capability of the indexing system to identify relevant documents is known as its *recall* power. As far as these users are concerned, recall is their primary requirement of the system, since their stated goal is to find everything that the system has to offer related to the questions asked. The extent to which individuals worry more about recall or precision will depend a lot upon their particular information needs.

The recall measure is a simple quantitative ratio of the relevant documents retrieved to the total number of relevant documents potentially available. For example, if there are 100 documents in the library that are relevant to the user's needs and the indexing system retrieves 75, then the recall ratio is 75 out of 100 (75/100). Recall for this search was 75 percent effective.

Recall is not the only thing users may be concerned with, although users tend to worry about it more. If they want to be absolutely sure of total recall, they can always ignore the index and go directly to the material and read everything. They can examine the documents one by one until they have filtered out what they want.

This is the whole point of bibliographic control in general and indexing in particular—we do the filtering for the user. The index decreases the number of items users must examine, but since it is an artificial device, thrown between the user and the material, there is the risk of not getting totally everything. In the entire history of the world there probably has never been a user who walked away from a library saying to herself that absolutely everything in the library relevant to her request was retrieved. Those people surely missed something.

The recall measure is a test of the index's ability to let relevant documents through the filter. The index must not allow nonrelevant documents through the filter.

The capability of the indexing system to hold back documents not relevant to the user is known as its *precision* power. The precision measure is the ratio of the relevant documents retrieved to the total number of documents retrieved. For example, if 100 documents are retrieved and 50 of those items are relevant to the request, the precision ratio is 50 to 100 (50/100). Precision for this search was 50 percent effective.

Recall measures the completeness of the output. It is the ability of the system to retrieve all the items in its files that are relevant. Precision measures the ability of the system to select *only* the items in its files that are relevant.

EFFECTS OF EXHAUSTIVITY
AND SPECIFICITY

What effects do exhaustivity and specificity of indexing have on recall and precision? Exhaustivity and specificity are recognized as being two factors affecting the response of an indexing profile on a document.

Extensive exhaustivity gives high recall and low precision. Conversely, restricted exhaustivity gives low recall and high precision. For example, if the term *Siamese cats* is indexed for even the slightest mention in every document about cats, then documents of only minor interest will be retrieved. On the other hand, deep specificity gives low recall and high precision.

Exhaustivity is the extent to which indexing covers all the concepts in a document. Specificity is the extent to which the index terms precisely represent the subject. This is why it is believed that there is an optimum level of exhaustivity and specificity, some mystical point where recall and precision are in the best balance possible.

INDEX QUALITY

The key to a good index is the quality of its accuracy, the completeness of the entries, and its adaptability to the dynamics of language. The good index:

1.   Is easy to read.
2.   Is detailed.
3.   Reflects the user's viewpoint.
4.   Has multiple entry points for an idea.

Indexing is not an absolutely procedural activity, thus the criteria for evaluating an index cannot be absolutely procedural. However, there are legitimate ways to judge. Really bad mistakes are so glaring that it is impossible to overlook them. Three decades ago Robert L. Collison (1969) pointed out that many indexes have waste, that is, unimportant entries. He suggested one way to test an index: to scan the index for terms that you would not find useful for yourself. Do this for your own index.

Index evaluation can be objectively quantified to a certain point, but a full evaluation will also involve a degree of subjectivity. Often it is a matter of degree. For example, an objective criterion might be "Do not have circular references," such as "Dogs *see* Canines" and "Canines *see* Dogs." Subjective evaluation comes into play when we count the number of such occurrences and make a judgment. If, in a twenty-page index, circular references only occur once, then this one-time slip should not brand the index as bad. But, what if it happens forty times? Or six times?

Another example is in judging the length of the index as related to the length of the text. No quantitative ratio is always applicable. The nature of the subject, the depth of the discussion and the intended index user are all subjective factors that come into play.

More complex indexes, such as ones to cumulative periodical issues and multivolume reference sets, usually need introductory material to explain the index and its use. Typographic variations (bold, italics, etc.) should be explained. Abbreviations and what locators refer to (pages, volumes, paragraphs, etc.) should be clearly described. Limitation and scope coverage should be noted.

Some points to consider are:

1. Coverage is complete.
2. Consistency in term choices.
3. Term choices are appropriate to the nature of the users.
4. There is adequacy of cross-references, but they are not overzealously done.
5. There are not numerous strings of undifferentiated subheadings.
6. Subheadings truly reflect the main heading.
7. No incorrect or missing locators.
8. No excessive strings of undifferentiated locators.
9. No proper names missing.
10. Alphabetization is consistent throughout the text.
11. Misspellings are all corrected.
12. No indexing the same topic under different index terms without proper cross-referencing.
13. No bouncing cross-references (e.g., "cats *see* felines" and "felines *see* cats").

Certain aspects of the index that need to be evaluated, such as errors, omissions, general carelessness in construction, and poor display do not directly require the opinions of the users, although these factors are of concern to them.

There are many good indexes and their quality continues to grow, but there remains basic problems in the construction and production of indexes. No one in the field will concede that there are enough good indexes, covering adequately the vast information stores potentially available to the world. Partly responsible for this, of course, are the limited resources available for this activity. Despite dramatic changes in attitude in some quarters, the research and development enterprises in business, government, and academia still fail to accept the fact that information is a major link in their activities, and the money, personnel, facilities, and research in the information endeavor is seriously lacking. It has been observed that the lack of resources to produce an outstanding network of indexing services is analogous to the financial plight suffered by science itself until the middle of this century.

Perhaps the reason why the importance of quality indexes is not a general concern is that it has been difficult to define quality, and users have no benchmark to compare against, no sense of standards for accuracy. Consequently, users tend to believe that all is being done for them that can be done. Quite frankly, too many people are poor users of indexes and do not understand how to fully benefit from their potential. Perhaps the makers of indexes and librarians need to educate users, increasing their realization of indexing power. In turn maybe this will lead to adequate support for the activity.

EVALUATING ABSTRACTS

We also need to evaluate abstracts. Abstracts can be evaluated with several common sense criteria. A good abstract:

1. Should represent what the item is about.
2. Should exclude unimportant information.
3. Should be error free.
4. Should be brief and readable.

Modern abstracts are often expected to take the place of the document. Some users anticipate getting the essential data from the abstract rather than having to read the document itself. In recent years, disturbing studies are indicating a high level of misinformation and incorrect data in the abstracts. Information in the abstracts is inconsistent with the information in the actual document. The entire structure and processes of abstracting may well need a careful review as we enter the Information Millennium.

STANDARDS

Webster's New Collegiate Dictionary (1979) defines *standards* as:

> noun: Something established for use as a rule or basis for comparison in measuring or judging capacity, quantity, content, extent, value, quality, etc.: anything recognized as correct by common consent, by approved custom, or by those most competent to decide. adj.: having the quality or qualities of a model, gauge, pattern, or type; . . . generally recognized as excellent and authoritative; having no special or unusual features; ordinary; regular; typical.

A standard is something that has been established by an authority, or by general consent of those whom it affects. It is a basis for comparing *what is* against what *should be*, and as such is an approved model for doing something correctly.

A major purpose of standards is to increase the quality of indexes. There are several categories of standards. Those types of standards created and maintained by some national or international organization (both governmental and nongovernmental) are usually recognized as *official standards*. The types of standards most familiar to the general public are known as *proprietary standards*. These are the types of standards that assure the consumer that the lightbulb bought will fit the socket.

In many cases, institutions, consortia or other such organizations create and maintain standards for specific areas. These are generally known as *de facto* standards.

There are a number of sets of standards for indexing and abstracting. The problem is that most of these standards focus on the end results (a finished index or abstract) and not on how one goes about doing the indexing or abstracting. Some examples include:

ANSI/NISO Z39.14—1997 *Guidelines for abstracts.*

ANSI/Z39.4—1984 *Basic criteria for indexes.*

ISO 999: 1996 *Guidelines for the content, organization, and presentation of indexes.*

BS 3700: 1988 *Preparing indexes to books, periodicals, and other documents.*

BS 6529: 1984 *Examining documents, determining their subjects and selecting indexing terms.*

ANSI/NISO Z39.50—1995 *Information Retrieval (Z39.50): Application Service Definition and Protocol Specification (Version 3).*

EDITING

Indexers await the morning when they wake up to find that the *computerniks* have perfected a software package that will effectively edit an index. Until then editing is a human endeavor.

A bad index is difficult to repair without an extensive makeover. The job of the editor is not to re-do the index, but to tidy up such things as misspelling, large blocks of undifferentiated locators, too many subheading entries under a heading. Also, such things as related information spread all over without cross-references can be checked. Dead-end cross-references should be fixed and page reference accuracy should be randomly checked.

Editing is a laborious, but absolutely essential, task. Since indexers do not review most index galleys, the edit of the pre-galleys index is the final step in the process. Computers not only cannot do it, they are not a great deal of help as aids. The indexer must crawl through the index, using intellect and experience to spot the glitches.

Tasks include:

Correct alphabetizing.

Divide long multilevel headings.

Eliminate synonymous headings by consolidation under preferred term.

Recheck the editing.

Correct too many locators attached to an entry.

Correct ambiguous headings: *Base?* Is it military, or is it a Tiffany lamp?

Verify cross-references.

Correct spelling and capitalization.

Check punctuation and caps.

Check need to add entries.

Ask: Are main headings relevant and/or needed?

Ask: Are locators correct?

Ask: Is the index overdone?

Ask: Is the index underdone?

Decisions have to be made about how to lay out the index. Ease of use is the guiding principle for the layout of an index. Ease of use means that the user can quickly understand how to navigate through the index and find what is wanted without having to read extensive instructions over and over. Cross-references should be quickly and easily recognized. Punctuation, locators, and typography should be consistent. Consistency should be paramount in any index.

Index evaluation is a major concern for the professional. Research is an ongoing need in order to develop theories, methods, and practical tools for evaluation.

But the bottom line is always: Does the index work?

Indexing and Abstracting Services

CHAPTER 13

BACKGROUND

With the exception of the public catalog. the most used devices for bibliographic control in the library are the indexing and abstracting services. Access to them online by computer is growing by leaps and bounds. In most modern day libraries, electronic indexes and abstracts are frontline tools. Thousands of databases are available and sophisticated search options have expanded in the past few years.

Most of these services are aimed at the journal literature, which presently is the most extensive source of validated and reliable information. Coverage ranges from broad and general areas to highly specialized topics; however, much more than journals are covered. The services also index and abstract books, reports, pamphlets, newspapers, government documents, and even materials in collections, such as plays and poems. Although, as was pointed out earlier, much of the world's information is lost, the indexing and abstracting services in this country and around the world are an outstanding tribute to the information profession.

In the beginning, individuals did their own indexing and abstracting; then libraries and other local institutions took up the task. Individual libraries were self-sufficient, acquiring what they thought their own clientele wanted and handling whatever bibliographic control they needed themselves. The major impetus for change in this stance was the rapid growth of the journal literature in the nineteenth century. Here was a medium for spreading information throughout the scientific and scholarly world, allowing members to keep up with new developments and also providing a backup reservoir of retrospective information, all in a very handy form. With time this type of publication, along with other materials, came to be called the *primary* literature. The popularity and growth of the journal introduced a new problem, however. Any one library could not acquire all journals published, and the libraries were no longer able to index and abstract adequately all they received. Before the middle of the nineteenth century, indexing and abstracting journals were being published. A number of German journals had begun a century earlier, and in England came the *Universal Magazine of Knowledge and Pleasure* and the *Monthly Review*, which ran for almost a hundred years (1749 to 1844). By the middle of the nineteenth century there were indexing and abstracting journals covering most fields of knowledge. For example, the *Annals de Chimie et de Physique* ran from 1816 to 1913. The *New York Times Index* began in 1851. Many medical services began in the nineteenth century, such as the *Medical News and Library*, running from 1845 to 1879.

The turn of the new century brought a continuation of growth of these services, with the broad, overall scope giving way to more and more specialized services. Also, government began to get into the act, seeing the need for abstracts and indexes and perhaps realizing that the government itself is one of the main information creators. For example, *Statistical Abstracts of the United States* was started in 1878, and throughout the first half of the twentieth century numerous government information services were made available.

By the end of World War II, abstracting and indexing services had grown in every technologically advanced country. In fact, they had grown to the extent that no one could say for sure how many there were but their importance to the information access infrastructure cannot be overstated.

BRINGING IN THE COMPUTERS

In the 1950s attempts began to use computers to produce indexes, and to a lesser extent, abstracts. Citation indexes became the success story early on. Abstracting with a computer was primarily *extracting* and never became very useful.

The 1960s brought major advances in computer-assisted indexing. The complete abstract, titles, and some fulltexts could be used for computer searching. The computer could provide an index to every title word, author name, journal title, citation, etc., captured by machine-readable input.

In the 1960s, libraries began automating their acquisition and circulation functions and in the 1970s and 1980s, most went online to one degree or another. In the 1990s, we saw the advent and takeover of the CD-ROMs in the libraries. Most of the traditional services are being done by indexing and abstracting companies, such as OVID, ERIC, and CINAHL. OVID covers several indexes and abstracts, such as *INSPEC, Biological Abstracts*, and *ABI/INFORM*. ERIC is a database that is geared toward the field of education and CINAHL covers the fields of nursing and allied health. Due to the large amount of varied subjects, the indexing and abstracting services are generally subject specific. For instance, *INSPEC* is for the engineering fields, *Biological Abstracts* is just that, abstracts of biological topics, and *ABI/INFORM* is for business users. The format of these indexes and abstracts has usually been on CD-ROM. These CD-ROMs have been loaded onto the network and made available for users. Most of these databases can be costly to run. Some only allow citation access. Some databases are allowing full-text access along with the citations. With the advent of the information superhighway, this is starting to change. It is changing in ways that will be positive for users and challenging for the indexing and abstracting companies.

One of the changes that is positive for users is the availability of these databases on the Internet and as more and more become available this way, users are begin to expect this type of access.

Too much access, however, is not good for the indexing and abstracting services that are slow to change. If more and more people go straight to the Web, why use a traditional service? What is happening is that other companies are forming indexing and/or abstracting services of their own. For instance, Carl UnCover lets you search electronically from their table of contents index for hundreds of journals. Then if you find one that you are interested in, they make their money when you ask for the article through document delivery. In this case, that means they will send the article to you directly. Companies are seeing these alternative ways as a means to make money in the coming years. They sense that more and more people are starting to expect this type of service and these new companies are going to give the public what they want.

Of particular note in the past few years has been the use of computers to offer new kinds of services. For example, the citation indexes and other services from the Institute for Scientific Information have brought a whole new dimension to indexing and abstracting. Many of the abstracting/indexing (A/I) services are adjusting to these changing times, but, unfortunately, some are not.

TYPES OF DATABASES

The standard types of groupings for online databases are *bibliographic* and *nonbibliographic*. As the terms indicate, the first type deals with citations to periodical articles, books, government documents, conference papers, company research reports, directories, names, and so forth. Bibliographic databases can be citations to a document, an abstract or summary of the document or a full text of the document. A full-text database contains the complete text of each document, rather than just a reference or a reference and an abstract. Full-text searching means that every word in the text is an index term. This has advantages and disadvantages, but certainly the computer makes such an approach entirely feasible.

Nonbibliographical databases outnumber bibliographical databases, but librarianship has historically dealt with bibliographic data and has felt somewhat uneasy in dealing with nonbibliographic resources. Over the years librarians, particularly special librarians, have developed procedures for utilizing nonbibliographic databases. For example, they have assisted in analyzing data, forecasting, and generating reports from numeric databases. Numeric databases include such things as statistical data, and data on physical properties of materials, and many other types. These databases come from many sources, such as business, government agencies, professional societies, libraries, etc. These databases are major sources of information, and they must be indexed.

In recent years a new type of resource, image databases, has begun to grow rapidly. These databases have images as records and have opened up a new dimension in indexing. We do not index these databases in exactly the same way as other databases.

As indexers, we have an obvious concern about bibliographic databases, but as information professionals in general we have an equal concern about both kinds of databases. Our major concern with bibliographic databases is the validity of our indexing.

In selecting a database a primary concern is its coverage. You turn to a particular service because you know it covers the material you need in the daily operation of your library or information center. You may want to know if the entire journal is included, not just major articles. Does the service cover pamphlets and books, patents, dissertations, reports, and government documents? Does it cover only original research or more? How much overlap is there between this particular service and other services? What are the exhaustivity and specificity of its indexing? Is the service mission-oriented or discipline-oriented?

ONLINE SERVICES

One of the most profound developments in the 1970s and 1980s was the move to online access to indexing and abstracting services. The 1950s had brought the first computer retrieval systems, and the 1960s brought experimental work in online information retrieval followed by rapid developments. The 1970s gave us widespread conversion to online operations. A U.S. Senate committee report in 1960 describes in detail the status of processing systems for scientific information, with special emphasis on the economical utilization of electronic machines or equipment then available or being designed to speed up the retrieval process. Three National Science Foundation (NSF) grants had been given to Chemical Abstracts Services for projects leaning toward mechanical processing and searching of chemical information. The U.S. Air Force had contracted with Lockheed Aircraft Corporation to develop a form of English amenable to machine manipulation using an algebraic representation of syntax in English sentences.

In the 1960s two functioning automated bibliographical retrieval systems were implemented for the government. The National Library of Medicine (NLM) implemented the computerized *Index Medicus* which was a giant advancement in the field. Here was a major index now in computerized form.

As bibliographic data were routinely added to the automated files for processing *Index Medicus*, the value of the retrospective database increased. In 1965 a few search analysts on the staff of the NLM conducted about 3,000 retrospective, offline literature searches. The volume of offline searches increased with the implementation of the MEDLARS network, and by 1969 several dozen people were conducting approximately 20,000 searches per year.

In 1964 at MIT, M. M. Kessler began the first important experiments using online systems for information retrieval in a project called INTREX. About the same time, from 1965 to 1969, Lockheed designed and ran an experimental system for the National Aeronautics and Space Administration (NASA) called RECON. In 1969 it became operational, and a commercial version, called DIALOG, was put on the market.

Also in the late 1960s, System Development Corporation issued a service called ORBIT, which originally had been developed for the Air Force Foreign Technology Division as an intelligence retrieval system. It provided a number of databases and became a major competitor of DIALOG. ELHILL, another system developed during this period, was basically the ORBIT system changed to meet the needs of MEDLARS from the NLM.

In 1977 another major service was started. Bibliographic Retrieval Services (BRS) was originally designed to be cheaper than either ORBIT or DIALOG. BRS came on fast with a widespread user training program in which 600 people participated within the first six months. They also decided to limit themselves to a smaller number of carefully selected databases. One of the important services they carried early on was the databases of the NLM. In the 1980s and 1990s the A/I services began to migrate to CD-ROMs and the Internet and to slowly give up the emphasis on print form indexes and abstracts.

SEARCHING THE DATABASE

The major function of indexing and abstracting services remains the same: to facilitate retrospective literature searches and to fulfill the current awareness needs of users. In order to achieve this, journals need to have the best index coverage possible and it must be done quickly to keep the journals up-to-date.

Users often make the mistake of assuming that an online search will always give better results than a manual search because a computer is more adroit than a traditional reference librarian is. The truth is that the computer is far from being as smart as a good reference librarian is. The computer is electronically faster, but not intellectually faster. The ideal situation is when a first class reference librarian uses a well-programmed computer.

We keep hearing reports that printed indexes and abstracts will soon be a thing of the past, and then we hear others argue that there will always be a demand for hard copy. We are reminded of Jesse Shera's comment that "the paperless society is about as likely as a paperless bathroom." Jesse was probably right for our generation and maybe the next two or three. But it isn't just a matter of the world finally running out of trees to make paper. We still seem to like paper. Somehow, some things written on paper seem to be more permanent and authoritative and sometimes it can be folded and stuck into a pocket. The *New York Times* on the Web is not nearly as much fun as that great blob of newsprint that we get on Sunday morning. But the time is coming when computer literacy will be a basic education skill from kindergarten and up and people will prefer a glowing computer screen. On the other hand, kids seem to be turning away from computers a bit right now, due to the magic of Harry Potter.

Users can use printed indexes with a slow serendipity, with no sense of a ticking clock. As of yet, there is no convincing evidence that the results of a computer search are superior to a slow, thoughtful, manual search; however, we must not forget that this is the same comment that was made when John Henry challenged the rail-driving machine.

The online search is faster, so it gives users time to undertake speculative searches that they might not have tried with a printed index. Also, the online index is probably more up-to-date than the printed index. Retrieval results with either a printed index or an online system will depend primarily on the quality of the indexing and searching methodology used.

People must be trained to use these systems. Online systems are generally post-coordinated systems, whereas most of the users are acquainted with pre-coordinated printed indexes. In addition, they must learn a computer searching language. Learning the computer language is relatively simple, usually the easiest part, because most searching languages have few instructions and are simple in concept. The skill comes in learning to analyze the searching problem from service to service, although they are fundamentally similar.

Most systems are rather straightforward to use. The first step is usually a logging-on procedure. This is a password exchange that allows authorized users into the system. The second step is to select a database from the numerous ones available. The third step is to enter one or more possible index terms. The response is a tabulation of the number of documents with that index term attached. For example: *CATS (9023)* means that there are 9,023 documents in the file that have been indexed with the term *cats*.

Another command may allow a display of words in the neighborhood of the used term. For example:

CAT

CATS

CATALOGUE

CATS-AND-DOGS

Now the user may ask for the documents on *cat* and *cats* and, perhaps, *cats-and-dogs*, but not *catalogue*. Then the system may allow the user to ask for related terms.

The construction of the index is a major factor in the successful searching of an online database. A well-constructed index enhances the user's potential to choose subject terms and all the variants and to interpret the retrieval results. For example, some systems will give a user results of only exact hits, but others will automatically show related results and, in a sense, will suggest alternative strategies for the searcher. If the indexing system fully supports the searching activity, it is an expensive part of the information retrieval system.

Searchers need to know how exhaustive the indexing is. Determining how many index terms are usually used in an index will give the searcher a clue as to whether a broad search or narrow search is needed. If the index has very detailed indexing, the searcher will need to narrow the search with Boolean *AND* operators.

Related to this, the searcher needs to know how specific the indexing is and to what extent hierarchical indexing is involved. In some online indexes the documents are indexed very specifically, with little posting-up to more generic terms, while in other indexes, posting-up is very extensive. The searcher should be able to obtain this information in the documentation to the particular database. The searcher might also want to know if the index uses weighting of terms that have been designated as major or minor descriptors for a particular document.

Also, is the controlled vocabulary completely controlled or does the index have a provision for adding noncontrolled terms and tagging them as such? Can parts of compound terms be searched as single term units? Finally, the searcher should be aware of any indexing differences between the online index and printed index.

Indexers should understand certain things about online searching. First, indexers should know if the users will be general users or will be looking for highly specific information. General users will need extensive cross-references and scope notes and other such structured guides. General users will also need extensive documentation and user aids.

In addition, indexers should understand that different subject areas have different literature structures, and indexing decisions should be made on the nature of both the subject and the user. For example, the mathematics literature seldom has joint authors and usually has a short reference list, whereas the medical literature often has multiple authors and an extensive reference list. The differences in the nature of the literature will make a difference in how the document is indexed. Another example is the nature of the *language* of the subject area. In subject literatures with a high number of synonyms, a controlled vocabulary is probably preferred, whereas in a new field in which new terms are constantly being added, a controlled vocabulary may quickly be obsolete, and free-text searching is the best option.

The indexer should also remember that indexing for online systems should be highly exhaustive and very specific, for the simple reason that the computer wastes very little time and the searcher can change the general approach many times. Inappropriate retrieval results will flash on the screen, but with a computer this is a minor problem. The search can be quickly modified and reentered and the process can be repeated as long as the user's money lasts.

One problem that is concerning more and more people is the incompatibility among databases and the duplication of information in them. Indexing is one of the major stumbling blocks to compatibility among many online databases. Each database is built with its own vocabulary control devices, which makes cross searching difficult. Cross searching, or cross file searching, allows more than one file to be searched at one time.

For example, a number of the online services offer the capability to search many databases simultaneously. Users welcome this addition, but indexers see problems to be solved. The primary one is vocabulary control across the many databases produced by different indexing and abstracting services; this is a domain of professional concern to the indexer.

Multiple thesauri management in online systems is a growing concern of the profession. There is an increasing interest in creating computer software that will tie together the separate thesauri in the various databases. This in effect would standardize the indexing and searching as far as the user is concerned. Several approaches are being explored, such as integrating all the vocabularies into a master list, which would be carefully edited. Other suggestions include creating an intermediate switching language and technique for mapping vocabularies in each other.

There are, of course, problems involved. For example, a term in one language may be an index term, and the same term in other vocabularies may be a nonpostable term that refers to another term. The concept of metadata posting is currently at the forefront of research efforts.

THE FUTURE

The number of abstracting and indexing services is one indictor of growth, but the primary indicator is the number of abstracts and citations being produced. In our time this number measures in the millions per year and represents one of the most costly and extensive activities in the information handling profession.

The services offered by online vendors continue to grow rapidly, and a lot of work and thought is needed to be sure that services will continue to meet the needs of users. For example, some services are reindexing retrospective files to make them more compatible with new electronic access avenues.

One thing that is changing is that users are becoming less and less aware of a collection of databases. Now, metathesauri and cross searching are making the concept of multidatabases more transparent. The user composing a search is not too overly concerned where the computer goes to look or whose database is tapped.

Another example of new directions is the initiative to make imaging a major element in the databases. Along with bibliographic data, fulltext and full images will be routine.

Early on in the development of computers the concept of online searching was around, but the technology that enabled it did not develop until the 1960s. By the 1980s online searching was in full swing, evolving from government supported prototypes in the 1960s to commercial endeavors in the 1970s and then becoming ubiquitous in the 1980s.

The 1990s brought the realization that simply producing online bibliography files was not going to allow them to be competitive. New print services, such as full document delivery, evolved and print products still bring in meaningful income. New technology, coupled with changing user demands, is causing the services to implement new production methods for public offerings.

Traditionally, indexing and abstracting services produced print indexing and abstracting journals, and still do, but there has been a dramatic shift to electronic form. If there is a future for A/I services, then it lies in getting new services into the mainstream of the new world of Web-based electronic access.

The Use of Computers

CHAPTER 14

THE COMPUTER TOOL

Nowadays the majority of indexers use computers in one way or another. Indexers are generally computer literate and studies show that they use the latest hardware and software. They realize that computers and the complementary telecommunication technologies offer opportunities for indexers not dreamed of ten years ago.

Information technology developments continue to boggle the mind. When one of your authors left his library job in 1968 to get a graduate computer science degree at Texas A&M, computers filled large glassed-in rooms. Now we have hundreds of times the power in a little laptop we play with on an airline flight. In those days computers belonged to those elite with computer science degrees. Now they belong to the masses and there are no elite groups.

For many years people have been asking if computers can do indexing and abstracting. If the text of the documents can be converted into machine-readable form, and if the correct rules can be programmed into the computer, then, clearly, the answer is yes. The first condition is rapidly becoming less and less of a problem, but the second condition remains a difficult one. How do we write the correct rules?

It does not take very long to enumerate what makes a computer important, because it is a very specific entity, with a relatively simple mode of operation. It can find solutions only to problems that have been completely analyzed, described, and prepared in proper form by human minds. If the world is taken over by a computer in the foreseeable future, you can be sure that behind it is a diabolical human mind.

What makes computers useful? It is very simple:

1. *Computers are fast.* Everyone knows that computers are extremely fast, but the general public probably has no real concept of just how fast they are. It is common to talk about operations being done in nanoseconds (billionths of a second). How fast is a billionth of a second? Can the human mind conceive how fast that is? Speed allows computers to handle tasks that could never be done manually because it would take too long or would require an unfeasible number

of people. For the first time, problems can be solved that were too much to handle with pencil and paper or even with the aid of adding machines. The computer's speed makes these tasks ordinary. For example, let us say it takes you fifteen seconds to add up four three-digit numbers:

149

206

123

319

In that same fifteen seconds, a computer could have added many, many millions of such numbers. Or, to put it another way, in fifteen seconds the computer could do what it would take you eight or nine months to do with pencil and paper if you worked day and night without sleeping, eating, or sharpening your pencil.

2. *Computers follow instructions automatically.* Programming a computer means preparing a detailed list of instructions (a program) that tells the machine what to do in a logical progression. The program tells the computer to test certain conditions throughout the program and then take alternative routes through the program according to those conditions. After the program has been prepared, it is stored in the machine, and the computer takes over. It faithfully carries out those instructions, one after the other. The only human action is a possible input of data at various points, but the machine no longer needs any outside intervention; thus it does its duties automatically. Long ago, when one of your authors taught programming, neophyte programmers would often run a program and then keep rerunning it over and over without analyzing what was wrong, assuming that the computer would do a better job if the button was pushed again. The students had to learn that the computer was doing *exactly* what they told it to do, not necessarily what they *hoped* it would do. A computer is a very faithful, unquestioning slave and it defers to you for the correct intellectual decisions. Some indexers still need to learn this lesson.

3. *Computers are accurate.* They very seldom make mistakes. When the computer adds up the millions of numbers in fifteen seconds, it is unlikely that it will make an error in the calculation. This dependability makes the computer extremely useful in all segments of its application. Programmers and users, however, do make mistakes. If they give the computer wrong instructions and/or data, the computer executes faithfully what it is told to do with the data it is given. When we read in the paper about the little old lady on welfare who received a tax bill for $23 million, it is usually safe to assume that it was a human error and not the fault of the computer. Even the Year 2000 (Y2K) problem was not the fault of the computers. It was due to the shortsightedness of the computer elite of long-ago days.

4. *Computers promote meticulous problem analysis.* A computer can work only on a problem that has been meticulously analyzed and mapped out. A constant factor in computer system malfunction is the failure of its programmers to fully understand the problem. If the problem or the system being automated is not understood in the first place, then bringing in a computer is a mistake. This has happened over and over again in library automation. Librarians often realized that their computer was simply allowing them to make the same old mistakes—at an incredible speed.

One of the interesting attempts to use computers in library work has been given to the possibilities of applying expert systems to the traditional bibliothecal processes. This accelerating interest in the application of such systems in libraries parallels recent advances and a renewed interest in the field of artificial intelligence. Seminal work is already under way and it can be briefly summarized as follows:

1. *Online database searching.* It is not surprising that this would be one of the first areas of inquiry, since a *good* online searcher is considered to be a special expert. The work in this area has concentrated primarily on gateways and front-end systems, which appear to have the goal of allowing end users to do their own searching. One of the problems in online database searching is that the various systems have developed independently and even though they have many similarities, they have many differences in file structures, command languages, and access protocols. Only an expert intermediary is able to master the complexities across these various systems. The results of this have been an intense interest in interface systems, and this joins quite nicely with the concepts of an expert system. The early gateway software has allowed automatic dialing and log-on, offline search formulation, downloading, and other such amenities, but they are not truly expert systems; however, researchers have seen the obvious possibilities and work is well under way in this area.

2. *Indexing.* Several projects have been initiated to study the use of expert systems in indexing, including the construction and maintenance of thesauri. This is a very complex area that involves the most fundamental intellectual aspects of library and information science. The MedIndEx System at the National Library of Medicine (NLM) is probably the best example of this type of work in expert system indexing. Having medical indexers supply index terms to documents in order to construct knowledge based frames captures the expertise for the system. This system is a true expert system, not only in indexing, but also in abstracting.

3. *General reference services.* A few research projects have addressed general reference services. Most of the systems are standard *IF-THEN* types, which lead the user through an elimination sequence until the appropriate reference tool is found. An example of this type of work is ANSWERMAN, an experimental microcomputer-based expert

system at the National Agricultural Library (NAL). The system allows library users to perform their own reference work by moving through a question/answer session until they find the right book. One of the problems with most of these systems is that they are highly subject-specific and are built around actual reference tools. Since a general applications system will require a very large knowledge base, other approaches should be sought.

4. *Cataloging and classification.* Work has been done to apply expert systems to cataloging and classification. This seems natural, since expert systems and cataloging both function on the basis of knowledge expressed as a set of rules. For example, Davies and James (1984), working at the University of Exeter in England, used the PROLOG programming language in an attempt to build the use of the *Anglo-American Cataloging Rules, First Edition (AACR1)* rules into an expert system. The problems they encountered are typical of the ones researchers are having in the cataloging area, including the identification of a proper programming language. It might be suggested that the bibliographic utilities in the private sector should be more vigorous in supporting research in this area.

5. *Other areas.* Other areas include natural language information retrieval, graphic representation of information, and abstracting. This work is beginning to move out of the laboratory and exciting applications are in the making.

Although it is not possible to explain here in detail how expert systems are designed, it might be useful to give a brief example of how such a system might be designed. The example we will use is abstracting, for which an expert system would be useful for the following reasons:

1. *Quality abstracts are essential.* The need of the scientific community to have timely, well-constructed abstracts, digests, and reviews of the literature remains a critical concern. Although online searching has revolutionized reference service, it should be remembered that finding a list of computer records in nanoseconds is not the key point. What *is* important is the information in those computer records. More and more, the user is giving first priority to obtaining succinct and readable abstracts. Productive scientists and other scholars have come to value abstracts in their work, but abstracts, like all devices for bibliographic control, are imperfect. Computer-based expert systems may be useful for creating effective abstracts.

2. *Expert systems offer certain advantages.* These advantages include:

   ⌄ Financial Advantages. Once operational, an expert system can be run on a computer at far less expense than would be required for a high-priced expert.

   ⌄ Productivity Advantages. An expert system might be thought of as a clone of an expert and, as such, productivity can be increased.

    ▲ Transportability Advantages. The expert can be in many different geographical locations at the same time.

3.   *Innovative approaches are needed.* The NLM (and others) have repeatedly pointed out the need to improve abstracting services and to develop innovative methods. It has been suggested that the use of expert systems might be one such innovative method.

There is nothing mystical about the concept of an *expert system*. It simply means the designing and programming of computers to accomplish tasks that experts accomplish using their intelligence and experience. Broadly speaking, such systems have three major components. First, they have a knowledge base that captures expertise in terms of procedural knowledge. The system relies on this knowledge to work itself through a current problem. Second, expert systems have an inference engine that controls the process by making decisions needed to solve the current problem. Third, an expert system has input data about the current problem it is being asked to solve. There are a number of computer software programs designed to create expert systems, ranging from relatively easy-to-use *shells* to complex programming languages.

It should be made clear that an expert system is *not* the same thing as automatic abstracting in the traditional sense of that term, although the two could be related. *Automatic abstracting* is the generation of abstracts by the computer directly from the text of the documents, using strict, predetermined algorithms. Most automatic abstracting systems rely on statistical patterns of words in documents and are actually automatic extraction of sentences directly out of the text. Despite many years of experimental work in automatic indexing and abstracting, the writing of abstracts remains primarily a manual activity.

The objective of an expert system for abstracting would be to capture expertise and then lead a human abstractor, regardless of level of experience, through the process of writing an abstract. The objective is to create a human-machine interface where the intellectual and mechanical effort in writing an abstract is divided between the human intermediary and a computer-based support system.

The first step would be to design an initial script for the expert system. The expert would use the script to build and alter the knowledge base. Also, the interactive probing during the development of the knowledge base would cause the script itself to change.

The Script

The following is an example of what an initial script might look like at this state. The script is based on the general abstracting steps that were outlined earlier:

    System request: *Publication source?* (e.g., Should this document be rejected for abstracting because it is from a disreputable publisher? How does an expert abstractor decide? Does the abstractor have a list of "disreputable" publishers? Should the computer have such a list in its knowledge base?)

System request: *Is this document of subject interest to the users?* (e.g., Some things will clearly be of interest, others clearly not, and some items will be of marginal interest. Who is our user? The item itself may be of value, possibly earning the author a Nobel Prize, but it may be of no interest whatsoever to the users of this abstracting service. Again, what does an expert abstractor do?)

System request: *Bibliographic reference?* (e.g., Incorrect reference entry is an unpardonable sin, since the purpose of the entry is to give exact steerage to the original paper from the abstract. How is the information verified? Is there a "standard" way to enter the reference?)

System request: *Title?* (e.g., If titles are vague or misleading, does the abstractor take corrective action, like adding or modifying words in brackets? How does the abstractor decide what is "vague" or "misleading"?)

System request: *Who is the author?* (e.g., What is the author affiliation? Is it a single author or multiple authors?)

System request: *Subject indicators?* (e.g., Determination of subject, objectives, scope, methodology used, results, and conclusions.)

System request: *Begin writing?* (e.g., The results of the analysis must be expressed in natural language. How? How long? Key sentences down first? What type of abstract is to be written? How does the expert decide? How is the structure of the abstract unified and logically developed?)

System request: *Edit?* (e.g., How? On what basis are decisions made?)

System request: *Final form of the abstract?* (e.g., What is the format? If not "standard," why a different form?)

The second step in the design of the expert system would be to begin the construction of the computer programs using artificial intelligence software.

Step three would be to call upon abstracting experts to slowly build their abstracting expertise into the framework constructed by a beginning script similar to the one illustrated above. Following a standard expert system developmental approach, the program would create an internal representation of the abstractor's value judgments, and the general rules captured by the original script would evolve into less general, more microlevel rules. One of the things learned about expert systems is that often relatively few and relatively simple decision devices will work as long as there is a rich, complex knowledge base to drive the program. Consequently, a great deal of care and time must be expended at this step in the procedure.

Step four would be a run-time implementation. Now that the system has been developed, someone who is not an expert abstractor should be able to use the system and write an abstract of a quality near or at the level of an expert abstractor.

How would expert systems replace indexing and abstracting? Basically, such systems would give users a feedback loop, dialog type of help, alternating between searching, presenting results for adjustment, question answering, and resubmission. In a sense the indexing and abstracting would be customized and created in real-time thus eliminating the need for indexing and abstracting to be done ahead of time.

INDEXING WITH A COMPUTER

Computers have brought changes in indexing. And in the last two decades the improving technology has promoted interest in making the computer a more useful tool in indexing. When we think of using a computer to index we must remember that an indexer has two basic tasks: finding surrogates that represent the information in the item being indexed and clerical tasks related to producing the final index.

The question is: can a computer be given instructions to index a knowledge record? A computer has the ability to make simple decisions in the areas of number comparison, character comparison, and machine systems testing. Its most fundamental ability is to make a decision on the basis of the relative magnitude of two numbers. Essentially, this is the limit of the machine's intellectual ability. The question that immediately arises: How can computers accomplish such marvelous things if these are the only decision-making capabilities they possess? The secret lies in the skillful way a human programmer uses this simple, logical ability of the machine.

For example, suppose a company has a file of personnel information, including the number of children that each employee has. If the manager needs a list of all those people who have seven or more children, the programmer can write a program that will tell the computer to start at the front of the file and pull down the first employee's record and go to the specified block of data that has the number of children of the employee. The computer then compares the number with seven and if it equals seven or is larger, the computer is told to print out that particular personnel record and then move to the next record. When the number in the block is less than seven, the computer is told not to print out that record but to move directly to the next one.

We may look at the completed list and marvel at how smart the computer is—it knows all the families in the company and how many children each has. The truth is, the computer knows no such thing. It simply compared two numbers. Upon this elementary principle, complex systems are built. The computer has impacted every field of human activity and will probably go down in history as the most significant technological development since the invention of printing.

Human indexing is costly and can range in quality from excellent to appalling. With the rapid growth of information, the time lag between publication of a paper and the availability of indexes and abstracts to that paper has grown frightfully. Adding new people to the staff is not always a solution; it may be economically unfeasible, and professionally qualified people may not be available. This is one of the practical reasons that interest turned to the possibility of computer-based methods. Of course, there has been intellectual interest in such automatic means since the early days of information retrieval. Unfortunately, we have not been able to write programs that will allow a computer to understand natural language as well as humans do. A computing machine is an incredible device, but it is a poor substitute for the human brain.

The computer's power lies in processing mundane trivialities (humans solve a complex problem by dividing it up into a long series of mundane steps, and then the computer takes over). There is no record of any computing machine that has made a valid value judgment without human direction, and such value judgments play a major role in the creation of quality indexes and abstracts. A computer can be useful and is becoming increasingly important in indexing and abstracting. Promises and schemes have come and gone over the past few decades, but slowly we are obtaining an understanding of how to use computers in indexing and abstracting. In the last two decades considerable time and money have been spent on research in computer indexing of documents. In addition to the impetus that the information explosion provided, computer technology rapidly advanced with a shift in emphasis from strictly scientific number crunching to information processing. Computers have become available that are compatible with the needs of information professionals. Also, for a number of years considerable funds were available, principally from the federal government, for research in this area. Most of this money was aimed at information storage and retrieval systems in general, not specifically at indexing and abstracting, but it soon became clear that indexing and abstracting are at the heart of the matter, involving considerable human endeavor, both mental and physical.

TYPES OF INDEXING SOFTWARE

There are several general classes of indexing software:

Embedding software puts indexing codes into the electronic text and allows updating of locators as the text is changed. While working with a file, the indexers tag terms that should be indexed on that particular page. If there is a change in the document the tags cling to the terms wherever they go in the text. It should be pointed out that some types of software packages (e.g., word processors) come with embedded indexing capabilities. Generally speaking, indexers are a bit wary of embedded software indexing.

Stand-alone software allows the indexer to work independently of the published material. This type of software is generally used for back-of-the-book indexing. As a matter of fact, most of the indexing software has been aimed at back-of-the-book indexing, but the evolving features of current software often make it adaptable to other types of indexing, if the indexer masters the software and is creative.

Automated indexing software searches for words in the text and builds a list of words. This is useful as an aid, but to produce a true index, humans need to turn the list into a true index.

Computer-assisted indexing, as differentiated from automatic indexing, is the use of computers to do the mundane work while a human still does the intellectual task of indexing. Computers have been used quite successfully as *aids* to human indexing. For a long time they

have been taking in manual indexing, processing it, and then producing lists for index publications and the like. A three-step procedure
might be suggested for a system of computer-assisted indexing:

1. Human handler scans a document and selects portions for in-
    dexing (for example, the title, section headings, sentences cov-
    ering purpose, methods, and results, first and last sentences in
    paragraphs, and so forth). A clerk can be trained to do this with
    a reasonably high degree of skill.

2. This material is input into the computer and the machine uses
    standard automatic indexing techniques to produce index
    terms.

3. A human edits the results, making whatever changes are judged
    necessary while the computer does the tedious manipulations
    necessary to complete the indexing process.

This approach is an economic balance between unskilled labor, skilled
labor, and a computer. An example of successful semiautomatic methods was
the PRECIS system. In this system, human indexers did the intellectual work,
while the computer did the tedious manipulations necessary to complete the indexing process.

Microcomputers put a new wrinkle into the indexing task. Early on, people put the microcomputer to work to aid in indexing. They did this by using a
word processor or a database management program, or by writing a program to
do it. Indexing software for microcomputers began to hit the market in the
early 1980s, and since that time many new programs have appeared to replace
those that have quietly passed away. And slowly, the quality of the programs
has improved. This software can vary from simple word processing-type programs to complex aids for producing sophisticated back-of-the-book indexes.
Like all software, it must be evaluated carefully. The software should offer
flexible ways to organize data within database files, with a minimum capability
of keeping tabs on duplicate terms and in sorting. Data entry should be simple,
with automatic entry functions, such as repeating terms, to avoid repetitive
typing.

Linda K. Fetters (1994) outlined some useful guidelines for evaluation indexing software:

1. Formatting.

    Automatic formatting of the final index in a commonly recognized
        style (i.e., run-in or indented).

    Automatic creation of an acceptable number of subentries (three to
        seven entries).

    Suppression of repeated main entries.

    Automatic combining of page references for identical entries.

2. Entering and Edition Entries.

A reasonable length for each entry.

Easy recall of previously entered data and on-screen editing.

Method for displaying and printing entries at any point in the indexing process.

Method for storing or copying previously used headings or subheadings capability of storing the final index as a *word-processable* disk file while preserving the original records for future use.

3. Sorting.

A sort order that treats upper- and lowercase letters the same; method for marking characters or words that are not a part of the sort order, such as articles and prepositions.

Capability to sort letter-by-letter or word-by-word.

Capability to sort by main entry and each level of subentries.

4. Printing Effects.

Provision for underlining, bolding, subscripts, and superscripts.

Provision for changing or inserting the codes for printing or typesetting as needed for each publisher.

5. Cumulating or Merging of Indexes.

Capability to handle enough entries for large or multivolume projects.

Capability of cumulating or merging separately created indexes into one large index.

INDEXING SOFTWARE

Below is a brief sample of some of the more popular indexing software that is available:

Cindex™
(for DOS, Windows, and
Macintosh)
Indexing Research
Box 18609
Rochester, NY 14618
URL: http://www.indexres.com

Hierarch
Systematics
Suite 1, Level 1
189 Kent Street
Sydney, NSW 2000 Austrialia
URL: http://www.systemantics.
com.au

HTML Indexer™ (for Windows)
David M. Brown—Brown Inc.
7417 SW B-H Hwy., #524
Portland, OR 97225-2169
URL: http://www.html-indexer.com/

HyperIndex
Andre De Tienne
Peirce Edition Project, IUPUI
CA 545, 425 University Boulevard
Indianapolis, IN 46202-5140
E-mail: Adetienn@iupui.edu

IndexCheck and other utilities
Leverage Technologies, Inc.
9519 Greystone Parkway
Cleveland, OH 44141-2939
URL: http://www.LevTechInc.com

Indexer (for Interleaf)
Belsoft
55 Pleasant Street
Lexington, MA 02173-6114
URL: http://www.ileaf.com/ip.html

ISYS
Odyssey Development, Inc.
The Denver Technologic Center
8775 East Orchard Road
Suite 811
Greenwood Village, CO 80111
URL: http://www.isysdev.com

Ixgen
Frank Stearns Associates
17201 SE 38th Circle
Vancouver, WA 98683
URL: http://www.pacifier.com/
    ~ franks/ixmid.html

LEXICO
7900 Wisconsin Avenue
Suite 201
Bethesda, MD 20814
URL: http://www.pmei.com/
    info.html

Macrex™
Wise Bytes
P.O. Box 3051
Daly City, CA 95015-0051
URL: http://www.macrex.com/

ProTEXT
ETS, Inc.
1115 East Brigadoon Court
Salt Lake City, UT 84117-4969
URL: http://www.protext.com

Retriever
Dirk Djuga
Johannesstr.9a
D-70176
Germany
URL: http://www.djuga.net/
    retriever.html

ScanVue Entry
P.O. Box 178
Sparta, TN 38583
URL: http://www.scanvue.com

SKY Index™ Professional
SKY Software
6016 Oxpen Court, #303
Alexandria, VA 22315
URL: http://www.sky-software.com

wINDEX
Susan Holbert Indexing Services
24 Harris Street
Waltham, MA 02154-6105
URL: http://www.abbington.com/
    holbert/windex.html

AUTOMATIC
INDEXING AND ABSTRACTING

Indexing

In general, automated indexing can use four types of approaches:

Statistical. This is based on counts of words, statistical associations, and collation techniques that assign weights, cluster similar words.

Syntactical. This stresses grammar and parts of speech, identifying concepts found in designated grammatical combinations, such as noun phrases.

Semantic Systems. These systems are concerned with the context sensitivity of words in text. What does *cat* mean in terms of its context? House cats? Big game hunting? Heavy earthmoving equipment?

Knowledge-based. These systems go beyond thesaurus or equivalent relationships to *knowing* the relationship between words, e.g., tibia is part of a leg, thus we know to index the document under leg injuries.

The simplest level of automatic indexing is to make a list of the different words in a text and then remove stop words, such as *a, an, the*. The computer scans the text, ignoring these articles, adverbs, pronouns, prepositions, and conjunctions. These words are sentence cement words and have no content bearing meanings. What are left are the possible index terms. This scanning can be done on the fulltext or on parts of the text, such as the title.

The next step is to use an algorithm to stem words. This allows a given search term to match with different forms of a word at the searching stage. This can lead to some mismatches. After stemming, there is a count of the frequency of occurrence and a ranking of them by frequency of occurrence. The most important words are considered to be those that occur most often. This process can involve statistical weights to refine the previous frequency count.

Automatic indexing moves up the scale in complexity by introducing the idea of proximity. The premise is that if particular words keep appearing in the text in the near neighborhood of each other, then this has some sort of significance. For example, if missiles, ground, and air are close together, it indicates the topic air-to-ground missiles, or ground-to-air missiles. The situation is complicated by the fact that the order of the words can affect meaning significantly. Sophisticated automatic indexing systems contain synonym dictionaries, hierarchic terms, thesauri, and software for semantic and syntactic analysis.

The debate over automatic indexing continues, with some people on extreme ends of the discussion and most of us somewhere in between. One end of the debate includes people who see no reason to debate—the computer can do the job just fine—and on the other end of the debate are people who are almost Luddites in their thinking.

A scientist-turned-university provost once told these authors that he didn't understand what all the indexing fuss was about. He had just bought a piece of software for $29.95-plus-tax that would search the text on any word he typed in. When we asked what happens if the word he uses doesn't find anything, he said that he assumes the document has no information and he moves on. He seemed to feel that this software puts an end to human indexers for $29.95-plus-tax.

A number of studies, particularly by Gerard Salton (1989), indicate that automatic systems do at least as well as manual indexers. These carefully controlled experiments are hard to argue with and are more convincing than the counter-arguments that say such things as "a computer can index only words, not concepts." Concepts can be represented only by words, and computers can be programmed to identify concepts, albeit only with difficulty. What is implied in the above idea is that assigned indexing is better than derived indexing, but a growing body of research is seriously challenging this belief. Are the indexer's words really *better* than those of the author, who supposedly knows more about the topic than the indexer? An indexer seeing the word *cats* in the text may feel that the concept is best represented by the term *felines*, when in fact the author meant *cats*, pure and simple.

None of this means that automatic indexing presents no problems or that universal application is upon us. For one thing, most automatic indexing is still in the laboratory and we simply have not moved these techniques in any meaningful way into the real world. The information retrieval field is strewn with schemes that looked good in the wind tunnel but simply would not fly. And the so-called *automatic indexing* techniques on the Web are very far from being adequate.

Automatic methods have trouble handling synonyms, homonyms, and semantic problems in general. Conceptualizing is very crude, to say the least, and thesauri do not help very much. A thesaurus must allow conceptualization of relationships if it is to be fully utilized. So far computers have trouble with this. Human indexers go through a cognitive process that involves the indexer's background experience, education, training, intelligence, and common sense. This process allows the indexers to understand what the information item is about and how to best represent this to a known set of users. It is very difficult for a computer to reach this depth of analysis in automatic indexing.

Automatic indexing is based on the hope that in some way the computer can solve the problem of the ambiguity and variation of natural language. The human mind deals with this by utilizing complex cognitive processes that manage the mind's knowledge base and these processes are not fully understood. Expecting computers to do this is a very tall order.

Perhaps someday Intel will develop a processing chip and Bill Gates will invent a software package that together will provide failsafe indexes. But, if this happens it will because the basic principles of indexing are recognized and the project teams are headed up by indexers.

At this stage of the game perhaps an analogy could be made to the human development of tools over the millenniums. It is true that the first flint stones were crude tools; however, they were useful to primitive man. So is today's automatic indexing. In terms of machine control of natural language and thus fully automatic indexing, present day systems may be our flint stones. We must remember that nobody with any sense of the history of science will say that it can never be done.

Abstracting

Just as manual abstracting is functionally related to manual indexing, so is automatic abstracting related to automatic indexing. The basic procedure for automatic abstracting begins with word frequency counts. High frequency clusters of words indicate sentences in the text that carry important ideas.

For example, Luhn carried over his word frequency ideas from indexing to abstracting. He developed a technique for giving a priority rating to sentences in the text based on the frequency of occurrence of the words, and observed how many of the words occurred not more than four words from each other in a sentence. The computer would select sentences loaded with highly significant words, one next to the other, and print them out as a part of the automatic abstract.

Luhn's rule for assigning priority was based not merely on the word's presence in the sentence, but on the relationship of keywords within the sentence. The method involved an overall look at the sentence to break it down into phrases set off by significant words. These segments were then candidates for processing if there were no more than five nonsignificant words between the significant words. Next, the priority calculation for the sentence was made by tabulating the significant words in each isolated phrase, squaring that value, and then dividing by the total number of words in the phrase. For example: "The history of Siamese cats in Texas is written in long, rambling sentences but is of interest to the field of cat biology and its history."

Suppose that the significant words in this sentence, derived by a frequency technique, are the following:

Biology	History
Cat	Siamese
Cats	Texas

The sentence would be broken down: "The [history of Siamese cats in Texas] is written in long, rambling sentences but is of interest to the field of [cat biology and its history]."

The first cluster has four keywords and a total of six words in all, so:

$$4^2/6 = 16/6 = 2.66.$$

The second phrase has three significant words and five total words, so:

$$3^2/5 = 1.8.$$

The highest value is assigned to the sentence as its priority rating, so the sentence has a rounded score of 2.7. After all sentences in the paper have been rated, the highest ones are lifted verbatim from the text (or extracted) and are printed out in sequence. The results of this technique have been mixed, with some abstracts reading very well and others producing nonsense that gives the user a laugh and little else.

Another approach is to concentrate on certain stylistic aspects of the document. For example, the computer might be programmed to hunt for topical sentences, such as the first and last in the paragraph. Also, it has been observed that prepositional phrases tend to carry more significant words than other sentence construction parts. The computer can be easily instructed to find these phrases by using a stored list of prepositions in its memory. Such sentences are prime candidates for the extracted sentences.

Some attempts have been made to construct a thesaurus that could be stored in the computer to help identify words. The thesaurus would be a subject-oriented one, not a general type that recognizes content bearing words in a subject field. With the help of the thesaurus, significant words and sentences could be identified for extracting. The problem, of course, is that a thesaurus is expensive to construct and maintain, and it increases the use of memory space and process time.

Up to this time, automatic abstracting has had only partial success. In some cases it supplies concise, understandable information. Too often, however, the abstracts read like strings of disconnected sentences, which indeed they are. The main problems with abstracting by sentence extraction are that there is a lack of balance and cohesion.

When we have an activity that is labor intensive, we turn to machines for help. Heavy earthmoving machines are better than having hundreds of workers dig with pointed sticks. Indexing has always been labor intensive, so we have attempted to use computers to help do the work. But the problem is that real indexing is more than extracting all the nouns and noun forms from a text and putting them in alphabetical order. The reason why computers have problems creating good indexes is that indexing requires thinking, often at a complex level, and computers cannot yet do that. In the beginning, computer-aided indexing primarily mimicked manual indexing, or was limited to the printing operation of the indexes. Slowly and surely the situation changed, and as the software becomes more sophisticated, the computer is allowing us to go far beyond merely replicating the 3x5 card technique on the computer screen.

In the 1950s we began to apply computers to information retrieval (IR) with a high degree of optimism and naïveté. When things didn't work out we simply looked forward to faster computers with more storage capacity. This cycle repeated itself year after year until we began to acknowledge that this was more than a machine problem. Serious intellectual problems had to be faced in the indexing, storing, and retrieval of information with computers. Some of these intellectual problems have been solved, many have not, but steady progress has been made. At the center of this problem is the ubiquitous fact that information retrieval is probabilistic, subjective, and indeterminate. One thing is quite clear: technology will play an increasingly large role in indexing and abstracting in the new millennium.

Automatic indexing and abstracting have not quite arrived yet, but there are very strong indications that computerized processes for indexing and abstracting will be refined and widely used in the not-too-distant future.

Indexing and the Internet

BACKGROUND

The Internet is instantaneous, free, and has complete, inexhaustive, valid, and easy to find information. Correct? Not quite true for *any* of these. The Internet is an incredible phenomenon, but with its rich opportunities come a bundle of problems and issues that need to be addressed on a daily basis. A major one of these issues is: how do we organize the complex and highly diverse resources?

For indexers the Internet can be perceived in three ways:

1. It makes available incredible resources for the indexer.
2. It opens up a new frontier for indexing itself.
3. It is a rapid and inexpensive communication channel.

In the first instance, indexers are taking advantage of the resources on a daily basis. In the second instance, some indexers have plunged into the tussle of how to index the Internet, but many others are rather conservative on the issue. In addition to using the Internet as an access to stored information resources, it is also a useful communication tool for indexers and abstractors. Indexers, especially freelancers, need rapid and effective communication channels and e-mail fills the bill for this. It is faster, cheaper, and more convenient than regular mail (*snail mail*), it does not interrupt you like a telephone, and it is a lot less bothersome than using a fax machine. In addition to the one-on-one communication, e-mail offers discussion groups, where information can be posted in bulletin board form, or there can be ongoing group discussions. There are many such groups of interest to indexers and some of these are listed in the next chapter.

The Internet developed out of an experiment carried out by the United States Department of Defense in the 1960s. The objective of the experiment was to see if a national computer network could be set up that would continue to function after a national catastrophe. The network was called ARPANET and it opened the way for the development of the Internet.

The next major milestone came in 1985 when the National Science Foundation (NSF) created NSFNET. This was a service that provided a backbone for linking regional networks, which in turn linked individual institutions for free exchange of information. NSFNET quickly became popular as people discovered what it could do and began to develop a colorful potpourri of ideas. Corporations got into the act and began to build their own networks. In every sector software applications were developed and there was no turning back.

The next major development came in the 1990s with the creation and explosive growth of the World Wide Web. In less than a decade the Web grew to millions of Web sites and hundreds of millions of Web pages and the number of users and Web sites continues to grow.

Internet 2 is now online and is characterized by vast broadband potentials, which allow the transfer of data at speeds thousands of times faster than before. This is another major milestone in the development of the Internet. As the century turned the commercial world moved dramatically into the Web and now the Web has become all things to all people, both good and bad. There is no doubt that within the next ten years the Web will be highly commercial and information professionals will need to learn to work within that structure. The powerful potential of the Internet belongs to all, not just those who have dedicated their lives to making the most bucks.

The Internet brings us full circle in information access. In the past, libraries were closed stacks and we filled out forms and waited on wooden benches under soft lights for a page to bring us our stack of books or journals. Then came open stacks and we charged into the stacks where we could pull items and look at them ourselves, usually at the table of contents and the index. Many of us, after learning the general arrangement of the classification system, paid no attention to the card catalog. It seldom was necessary. No clicking back and forth through cards in frustration. Our *windows* were hundreds of time broader, faster and immediate. Now the Internet brings us back to virtual closed stacks. Once again we fill out a form (now it is a little white rectangle) and rely on browsers, search engines and not-so-good indexing to search the information store. The Internet has upset a lot of apple carts in the information world. Concepts of publishing, copyright, access to information, who the users are, personal privacy, what is a library, validation of information, what are acceptable standards, how do we best organize the information, and on and on, remain problems to be solved.

SEARCHING THE WEB

Contrary to what neophytes might believe, finding information on the Internet can be a slow and frustrating process. The lack of uniform standardization of knowledge structuring, browsing procedures, and other protocols across the search suppliers' software makes efficient use difficult and frustrating at times.

Search tools have been recognized as useful and essential in searching the Web, but the name of the game for success is serendipity, experience, and a bit of luck. It has taken the designers of search tools a long time to realize that indexing and search query strategy formulation are not trivial endeavors.

The user types in what s/he believes expresses the information need. The request is based on the information seeker's use of natural language. The response may be that there are no matches between here and the planet Pluto. The user then gets slightly more general and the response is that there are five zillion Web pages on that topic. A crazy maze of query search options exists, which most users are either unaware of or do not understand. This system is great fun for the Internet libertines, but conservative indexers cringe.

The Web has both pre-coordinate systems and post-coordinate systems. Usually when a system offers lists of subjects this is based on a directory, sometimes similar to conventional library classification systems. The keyword search tools offer post-coordinate systems and are the most common. Some system, (e.g., *Yahoo!*) permit a combination of pre- and post-coordination. In these systems, keywords can represent a hierarchically ordered classification table.

Searching the Internet is an iterative process, not a direct arrow to the bull's eye. As a matter of fact, so are most indexes, but Internet searching is an intensified version of iterative searching. In using any index, a stab is made at the index and when terms or cross-references lead down a false trail, the user backs up or else moves sideways to a suggested alternative and continues this process. A good index (paper or electronic) minimizes false starts and wrong paths.

The Web is accessed through software programs called *navigators* and *browsers*. There are a number of these, but the dominant ones are *Netscape* and *Microsoft Internet Explorer*. With navigators, the searcher decides at each stage of the search what the next step is because she has in mind the objects to be retrieved. With browsers, the searcher proceeds without having to state a specific target, and the software provides entry into the structure. They then link to distinct information retrieval mechanisms known as search tools. The searching can be instigated by clicking on buttons and going directly into a navigation mode or by typing in a traditional Boolean query. In the latter case, the tradition query leads to node-based navigation modes. Often the user has to try various queries to get on the right track.

To an individual the Web consists of three components:

1. A personal computer.
2. A Web browser.
3. A connection to an Internet service provider.

The system is called a client-server system. If you want to check the online public catalog at a university, you enter the Uniform Resource Locator (URL), or address, into your Web browser. Your browser asks for the Web pages of a Web server in that particular university and that server sends you a display of the university or the University library. Your computer is the client and the computer at the university is the server.

Searching is done with search tools. There are three general categories for search tools: search engines, directories, and metasearchers. For doing general searches, the directories are the first choice, but engines are better for finding specific pieces of data, such as who won the 1951 World Series.

Technically the term *search engine* is reserved for the keyword index type of tool and often the literature does not mention the inclusion of the subject directory and metasearch types of automated information retrieval systems.

Yahoo! is often referred to as a *directory, MetaCrawler* and others in this category are often referred to as *metasearch* engines and *Alta Vista* is an example of a search engine. Other hybrid forms of search tools are being developed that combine aspects of all the designs.

Engines are computer software that scan the Web selecting pages to be indexed for the searching system. They are often referred to as Web indexes because they examine the content of Web pages, which is different from just retrieving Web pages as a whole because they fit into a category. These engines consist of a searching mechanism (called a *robot, spider,* or *crawler*) that periodically visits sites to detect updates of information. These devices do not find all pages. Human indexers identify some of the information that is indexed. At any rate, the information is updated into a big index that is a copy of every Web page the engines know. The database most likely has indexes and related surrogates. Often the engines will present the retrieved Web page for human review or the human who gathered it may index it. Of course, there is more quality control if done by humans than if done totally automatically by robots. Typically, when a search request is received, the search engine will match user terms against surrogates from its list of Web sites and then use a ranking algorithm to present the ordered list to the user. The indexing can be automatic, manual, and/or a combination. Search engines use heuristics to prioritize pages in response to a query. These are ranking functions. In its simplest form, these functions make choices on the basis of the number of times an item contains the query terms. The constant dynamics of Web information often thwarts Web crawling-robot indexes. The robot visits a page, updates the search service's index and moves on. Then the information at the visited sites may change two minutes later.

The search engines cover:

> Full documents.
> Elements of documents.
> Specific words in the titles or URLs.
> Description of the site and its resources.
> Every component of the Web site.

Some examples of searching entry points are:

> Keywords.   Phrases.
> Subjects.   Company names.
> Proper names.   Advertising slogans.

Some shortcomings of search engines include:

> Low recall.
> Inconsistent quality.
> Wide variations in indexing depth.
> Scarcity of advanced searching tools.

Some examples of engines are:

AltaVista.　　　　　　　　*HotBot.*
Excite.　　　　　　　　　*InfoSeek.*
Goto.

Directory-based systems are usually indexed by humans and thus tend to have a higher level of quality in the indexing. They can be general or subject specific and they may include keyword searching. The indexing is not unlike any other kinds of indexing, using keyword selection or controlled vocabulary devices. This indexing may be based on fulltext or on most frequently used words. Because of the way the material is organized there is a sense of browsing that is similar to traditional library browsing.

Some examples of directories are:

Ask Jeeves.　　　　　　　*Snap.*
LookSmart.　　　　　　　*Yahoo!*
Lycos.

Metasearchers allow you to search across multiple search tools at once. These tools take a user's query and submit it to a number of other search tools. The people who prefer these tools perceive them as time-savers, because they cover cyberspace all at one time. But this brings the inherent problem of maintaining control. The problem is that we are dealing with different kinds of interfaces, structured in various ways, and it is hard to pull it all together at once in response to a user's query.

Two examples of metasearch tools are:

MetaCrawler.　　　　　　　*SavvySearcher.*

Some search tools are full-text tools and thus automatically index every word on every Web page found. These tools are comprehensive, covering every page in its Web database. In order not to be overwhelmed, the searcher must follow good searching procedures, including learning the Boolean connectors used for each system. In full-text Web databases, there may be an abstract, which either extracts descriptive parts of the Web page or simply the first few lines of the page.

On the other hand, some tools index only selected parts, such as title and a set number of initial words. Other tools are subject specific and index only records on specific subject, such as health.

Taken together, the dozens and dozens of search tools offer a wide variety of searching options. You can choose sites for their particular capabilities. For example, if you want to do image searching, *AltaVista* and *InfoSeek* are good choices. For proper name searching, first choices are *Yahoo!* and *Excite*. *Excite* and *WebCrawler* are good for Boolean searching, while concept searching is good with *Excite* and *InfoSeek*. It is possible to find the use of Boolean logic, exact phrase matching, searching by only designated parts of the record (e.g., title), word proximity searching, alphabetical lists, pre-coordinated lists of subject headings, query expansion options, and fuzzy neural network-based pattern matching. The problem is learning which tools have what and then knowing which tool to use for a particular search. The majority of search tools give results on every word in the query, so you need to be ready to qualify your query with Boolean search logic if the tool is good at this approach. The searching mechanisms often include full-text searching, Boolean and proximity searching and queries can be restricted by devices commonly used in traditional database searching (e.g., types of sources and dates).

Recall, while not totally acceptable, continues to improve with the developing sophistication of the software, but precision continues to be poor. Users typically have to click their way through dozens and dozens of sites before they get what they need.

ORGANIZATION
OF INFORMATION

The complexity of organizing the resources on the Web is mind-boggling when you realize that approximately a million electronic pages are added each day. The millions and millions of pages out there are loosely held together by more than a billion annotated connections, which are called hyperlinks. People expect instant access to a specific piece of information. That is the challenge to the information profession, especially to indexers.

What is a Web index? A Web index has the general goal of any index—to locate information—but the scope, structure, and design are different. A book index usually points to information in one file (the text of the book), periodical indexes point to information in several thousands of files (numerous journals), but Web indexes point to many millions of files, at many levels, existing in every niche and corner in the world.

And at the heart of the matter is the process of indexing hypermedia information. The advent of hypertext, hypermedia and their application to the Web introduced a new facet to indexing. For a number of years, hypermedia was touted as a powerful way to store and retrieve information. However, it existed primarily in the realm of experimentation. The Web suddenly made it a worldwide application tool. The downside of this quick move from discussion to application didn't take proper account of the need for indexing infrastructures to support the exploding navigation devices. Indexing hypertext demands both a respect for traditional principles of indexing and respect for the new information technology that is ushering in the new millennium.

The Web can be conceptualized as a gigantic database, made up of every type of knowledge imaginable, ranging from the trite to the profound, from valid information to total lies and ignorance, from the enlightening and uplifting to the most disgusting pornography, from the entertaining and educational to the dangerous.

The Web is a network of thousands of servers linking millions of resources, which are often poorly organized and unstable. Can all this ever be organized? Some professionals believe it may be an impossible mission. If we do not attempt to organize it, the system will self-destruct into chaos.

The Web is not an online public access catalog, with everything organized into one searching file. The Web has no such standardized infrastructure for bibliographic control. Given the dynamic and chaotic complexity of the Internet, a centralized, single unit access tool is extremely unlikely in the near future. Early on, the Internet employed hierarchical traditional library classification approaches with *subject trees,* such as the branching structure in the Gopher menus, and facet classification has been touted as a logical system for Internet organization. Such a system would build on the millions of existing *facets* already existing as nodes on the Internet. Attempts have been made to develop these classification structures and such systems seem to offer help, if they will be tolerated by the new world generations of surfers. Searchers appear to like a degree of hierarchical searching, rather than straightforward keyword input, but not too much library-like systems.

The average Web user assumes that library access methods are antiquated and inappropriate to Internet applications. This is based, of course, on a navïeté toward modern library classification and subject access systems. Classification systems such as the Library of Congress Classification (LCC), the Dewey Decimal Classification (DDC), and the Universal Decimal Classification (UDC) have all moved in step to adjust to the needs of the electronic era. There is nothing antiquated about modern library classification schemes. It is a matter of learning how to implement these structures on the Web when they are deemed appropriate.

While it is true that the Web is not a library in the usual sense of the word, it is true that the knowledge base and skills of librarians could be very useful in organizing the Web. This is especially true of those individuals in cataloging, classification, and indexing. A good example of using a classification approach to searching the Web is a Web site called CyberStacks, located at http://www. public.iastate.edu/ ~ CYBERSTACKS/hybrow-all.htm. This is a centralized collection of resources on the Internet, categorized with the LCC. The resources are basically monographs or serials materials, search services, and databases. The items are under one or more LCC numbers with format and subject descriptions. The classes are broken down into narrower subclasses and then into specific classification levels. The resources are fulltext or hypermedia and of a research or scholarly nature. This site is well worth looking at in order to get a feeling for the strengths and weakness of using a traditional classification approach to Web organization.

When naïve *experts* say that using traditional indexing methods on the Web is absurd, they are confusing indexing itself with format and display of indexes. An index to Web information in the form of a printed book index would indeed be absurd (or would it?), but the concept and procedures that went into the indexing are very valid. The fundamentals of indexing are universal and will always be valid no matter what form the technology takes or the output displayed.

The general public views the data files, plus the hypermedia links, plus the searching tools, to be a kind of virtual index. When they talk about indexing the Internet they seldom separate out the subject analysis and the searching mechanism. Indexing in the conventional sense does exist on the Web. Subject analysis has to be done and results organized, whether by humans or computers. There are, however, new terminologies and new challenges.

At this point in time this stampeding beast strains traditional indexing procedures. Subject access professionals, such as indexers, must play an assertive role to assure that the beast is tamed. Indexers must tackle the problem by looking for new ways to index the Internet. Perhaps radically different techniques are needed, yet to be imagined by a new generation of indexers.

The volume of material, with a minimum of control, means formidable indexing problems. How do you assign an index term to a body of content that is metamorphosing by the minute? Material accessed last week by the user may not be at the same place with the same hyperlinks and may be drastically changed in content. This is a nightmare to the traditional indexer. Do we develop metamorphic indexes? How would we do that?

Related to this is a wide range of philosophies about *what* to index. The question of what to catalog, classify, and index, and to what extent, has been around since the beginning of bibliographic control and has now become a central question with the Internet. There are two different basic philosophies: to strive for an exhaustive list of resources and to be more selective by carefully evaluating documents before linking them into the system.

In the first approach the goal is to index as many resources as possible, striving for a complete list of all documents from everywhere on all subjects and with total free speech for everyone. In the second case an attempt is made to include only valid, valuable, updated information. Both approaches fill a need. Many users want to have entertaining information and are not particularly interested in validity. The tabloid publishers are keenly aware of this.

How is this chaos to be indexed and linked together in some coherent way? One way to grasp the indexing situation on the Web is to visualize it as a gigantic, multibillion-word reference book. Then think about that big book as having every single word indexed on some pages and other pages represented with one or two words, according to the way many search tools now work. That gives a partial picture that we face if we view the issue as a very large scale traditional indexing problem. It is not. It is something vastly different.

The answer probably is not in developing a homogenous indexing structure, but rather to have a combination of heterogeneous structures. For example, it is clear that everything on the Internet will never be cataloged in the traditional sense. That would be physically and economically impossible, and a good deal of the information there may not be worth the effort anyway. On the other hand, there is a great deal of information that could best be made accessible with good, old-fashioned cataloging techniques. Librarians continue to churn away, cataloging their resources in traditional ways and there is no reason to discourage this, but at the same time we must invent ways to post this work on the Internet and integrate it into a universal search infrastructure. Many, many of those wonderful little old librarians shuffling around with 3x5 slips of paper and a pencil knew exactly that they were doing the right thing and we need to take advantage of their wisdom.

Creators of Internet documents and Web pages can help the indexers the same way as writers and publishers have traditionally helped indexers, by providing indexable clues, such as succulent titles with specific, content-bearing keywords. A number of groups and individuals are working at the problem of standardizing formats for creating Web presentations, which will help.

Some Internet authors make the indexing task more difficult, such as deliberately repeating words in order to skew the frequency counts of the automatic methods and increase the chances of a search engine pulling up the item.

This is known as *spamming*. Spamming will often interfere with the indexing validity of the item. Luckily, some search services keep on the lookout for Web sites guilty of this and will bump the sites off their list.

One of the things that librarians taught us is that standardization is a potent tool. For a number of years information professionals have been addressing the issue of standardizing data formats in electronic documents. An example of this is the Z39.50 standard. The Z39.50 standard deals with client/server protocols for information retrieval. At the heart of this standard is the concern with the search and retrieval of information in databases, which, of course, is the heart of concern for indexers. Related to this is the concept of structured metadata, which will be discussed next.

Metadata and the Web

Information on the Web is an enormous school of fish, millions of silvery flashes of light, and you click on one (if you can catch up with it), hoping it will be the right one for your information need. If it is wrong, you click again and again. The faster, the better. There are thousands and thousands of flashes of light out there to choose from. The Web has brought large amounts of information in many formats and along with it an increase in user expectations for access. Order on the Web seems to be decreasing, not increasing, and this has changed user behavior. Users no longer expect to get precise responses and they tolerate more noise, more clicking and backtracking, and more nonsense. Along with this, they are demanding simple, unobtrusive interfaces.

At the heart of information organization is the ability to uniquely identify information items. In the days of printed materials we relied on title pages, numbering systems and then International Standard Book Numbers (ISBNs) and International Standard Serial Numbers (ISSNs). Now, in the electronic age, we still rely on these systems, although new horizons have opened. Much time and resources are being expanded to develop these new methods. In recent years considerable attention has been given to the concept of metadata. At the heart of the metadata effort is the perception that Web resources are inadequately described by the existing indexing systems. The general architectural structure of the Web is generic, thus making metadata representation a reasonable approach.

Metadata is repeatedly defined as *data about data*. While this is a necessary definition, it is not quite sufficient. Metadata is data about data that is structured to describe an information object or resource. It characterizes source data and describes their relationships. Authors of resources, publishers, librarians, and other information professionals can create metadata. It can be embedded in the resource or held in separate metadata repositories.

Why should we care about metadata? Metadata is the way we describe the content of our information items, allowing us to move to precise information when we are searching. It also shows relationships between information items. Of course, the idea is not new. It is an ancient way to organize information. It goes back a very long time. An old-fashioned card in a library catalog was metadata. Librarians have been doing metadata for centuries, although they did not choose to call it that. Of course, we need to understand that the current efforts to develop these schemes are related to electronic information, so in a sense we are dealing with a new concept. The initiative of creating metadata schemes for electronic resources gives hope that librarians will be meaningfully involved in attempts to organize the Internet. We should not forget that librarians have been organizing very large collections of chaotic information for many centuries.

Not only do metadata schemes help to precisely represent information, they are also a way to protect the ownership of information. More and more publishers are having their customers ask them to make metadata representations a condition for doing business because both creators and disseminators of information are concerned with protecting intellectual properties.

When you publish something, the issue of intellectual property becomes personal. Unfortunately, there are those who do not seem to care if creators of works are justly compensated for their labors. They believe that information should be totally free and copyright is a troublesome barrier. Copyright issues have been around for a very long time, but the discussions and concerns are being intensified in the current Web environment.

The point is that the issue of intellectual property is critical. And metadata schemes offer one way to protect authors and publishers from being ripped-off. Information professionals, including indexers, need to take an active role in this. It is not just a matter of protecting writers and publishers. It is a way to organize and facilitate effective access to Internet information.

Dublin Core

In 1995 OCLC convened a meeting in Dublin, Ohio, of information specialists, for the purpose of looking at the problem of resource description records for networked information items. An objective was to reach a consensus on a core set of metadata elements to describe networked resources. The proposed set became known as the Dublin Core, which provides for indexing information for document-like sources including indicators for title, creator, subject, description, publisher, co-contributors, data, type, format, resource identifier, language, relationship to related resources, and rights management. The Dublin Core initiative is an example of the concern that we have with the concept of metadata and the Web. Although the original workshop was held in Dublin, the project soon spread and some of the subsequent meetings were held at international locations, indicating the universal interest in the evolving idea.

The concept of *core* refers to a consensus by information handlers and subject specialists of what elements are basic or fundamental to support information representation, especially for electronic forms.

The Dublin Core can be used as a convenient basis for describing information items on the Web. One purpose in the development of the Dublin Core was to create a scheme that would be an alternative to complex cataloging techniques and would be usable by catalogers, noncatalogers, and searchers of information. Creators of electronic documents could, in a sense, have *do-it-yourself* cataloging by filling in the blanks. Searchers could use it to traverse within and across disciplines, in an international environment on the Web. Hopefully, it will be more economical than the more elaborate description models such as MAchine-Readable Cataloging (MARC).

The Dublin Core is designed to be used by anyone who wants to describe information resources, such as Web pages. A number of groups, such as libraries and government entities, are using it. The system can be modified for local use, allowing the addition of elements as the case may warrant. Although the project began in order to develop a scheme for electronic resources, it has become evident that the basic idea could be medium independent.

The Dublin Core consists of 15 elements, and all elements can be repeatable and are optional. The elements are:

1. **Title**. This is the name that is given to the resource by the creator or publisher of the item.

2. **Creator**. This is the individual or organization responsible for creating the intellectual content of the item.

3. **Subject**. This is the topic under discussion and it will usually be expressed as keywords that indicate the subject of the item.

4. **Description**. This is a textual description of the content (e.g., abstracts).

5. **Publisher**. This is whoever made the resource available in its present form.

6. **Contributor**. This is the people or organizations that have made intellectual contributions to the resource, but who are not primary producers.

7. **Date**. This is the date that the present available form was created and made accessible.

8. **Type**. This indicates that it is a book, chapter, technical report, index, etc.

9. **Format**. This is the data format, presented with suggestions of possible hardware and software that might be necessary to display the resource.

10. **Identifier**. This is the tag used to uniquely identify the information item.

11. **Source**. This identifies where the item came from.

12. **Language**. This is an indication of the language of the item.

13. **Relation**. This is an indication of how and where the item is connectable to other similar resources.

14. **Coverage**. This indicates the scope, range, and depth of the item.

15. **Rights**. This is information regarding copyrights and conditions for access to the item.

There are two structural models for the system: the Simple Dublin Core and the Qualified Dublin Core. In the first case, the fifteen elements in the scheme are expressed simply, just using the elements without any further elaboration. The Qualified Core allows further refining (e.g., specification of encoding schemes or controlled vocabularies). Such qualifiers allow the augmentation of precision or specificity of the metadata information.

A number of methods can be used to post the metadata, such as Hypertext Markup Language (HTML), Extensible Markup Language (XML) and relational databases, although database management systems seem the most practical for manipulation at this point.

OCLC CORC

CORC is an acronym for *Cooperative Online Resource Catalog* and is a Web service being developed by OCLC with several hundred volunteer libraries. It is an endeavor to foster cooperation to create a catalog of Internet resources. The initiators of the cataloging effort recognized that libraries understand that they must become aggressive in organizing Web resources, otherwise the new generation will turn to other avenues. The purpose of CORC is to help libraries describe and link their resources with other information stores. It will help to give well-guided access to Web resources to their users.

This effort uses new technology to optimize metadata creation services. Currently, CORC has four databases.

CORC Resource Record Database

This is a record describing a resource and is the same record available in OCLC MARC or the Dublin Core. This makes it possible to create a new resource record by automatically extracting data from a Web site or by filling in a blank record template. It also allows searching of the current resource catalog or the archives. It is possible to use MARC or Dublin Core format to create a record that contains frequently used bibliographic information.

CORC Authority Database

When fully available, this database will have fully applicable authority information. It allows searching to find Library of Congress (LC) name or subject authority records.

CORC Pathfinder Database

The records in the Resource Database can be used to build digital pathfinders. It permits the search of the current pathfinder database or the pathfinder archive.

CORC Web Dewey

This permits searching or browsing of the DDC.

The scope of coverage of the CORC database currently focuses on creating descriptive records of Web resources, but it will evolve over time, allowing institutions to contribute records and pathfinders to the database. OCLC developed a number of templates to assist the libraries in extracting data and creating records for the catalog, including MARC and Dublin Core.

At the beginning of the new millennium, the pilot project was opened for all libraries to join. At the time the pilot project already had 170 libraries participating from around the world and the CORC database had grown to 200,000 records.

DIGITAL OBJECT IDENTIFIERS (DOIs)

In the late 1990s the publishing world launched a new system into the information and publishing world called Digital Object Identifiers (DOIs). DOIs are alphanumeric character strings that identify objects in an electronic environment.

DOIs are universal, unique, and permanent identification tags for online content that is registered in an online directory. DOIs can cover any form of digital files such as text, image, video, audio, or even software. DOIs can also cover many levels of content. For example, it might tag an entire book, a chapter in the book, illustrations, individual sentences, or perhaps the book's index. It is a system that identifies creation endeavors and uniquely marks the content of these items. It is intended to individualize information units on the Web.

DOIs can be placed in a variety of places, such as in the object itself, in an information structure that contains the object, on a Web page that describes the element, in a database, or as an entry in an indexing system.

The identifier tags have no intrinsic meaning, as a classification code does. They are content labels, each being unique and without duplicates. The identifiers are stored in a directory that allows the lookup of the current Internet address of the copyright owner and where the information now resides. The author, publisher or current owner is responsible for maintaining the response page, which presents data about the information item and the conditions of its use.

The directory of DOIs routes inquiries to the up-to-date sites on the Internet for accessing the content of the object. When addresses change, the directory will route the query to where the content is currently located or to where information is given concerning how to obtain it. Over time, when objects move around or change ownership, the directory keeps tabs on these changes.

Although the major purpose of the DOI system is the management of intellectual property, indexing and abstracting services, as well as document delivery services will find DOIs a useful tool.

SUMMARY

There is a lot of talk about organizing the Web, but due to its inherent unstableness and fluid nature, it is not clear that it will be organized, in the usual sense of the word, anytime soon.

Fully organizing and unifying the Web and its resources is still a distant dream, but such things as the Dublin Core, OCLC CORC, and the DOI system are promising steps forward. And the important thing is that librarians— the people who brought you MARC, International Standard Bibliographic Description (ISBD), ISBN, ISSN, and the *Anglo-American Cataloging Rules Second Edition* (*AACR2*)—have now asserted a role in the Web's organizational future.

Here are some useful Web sites for discussion and examples of metadata:

Copyright Clearance Center, http://www.copyright.com.

FileOpen Personal Publisher, http://www.fileopen.com.

Metadata Information Clearinghouse, http://doi.wileynpt.com.

Coalition for Networked Information, http://www.cni.org.

Dublin Core Metadata Initiative, http://purl.oclc.org/dc.

UK Office for Library and Information Networking,
     http://www.ukoln.ac.uk.

Digital Object Identifier System, http://www.doi.org.

PROMISES AND PITFALLS

Currently, there is a lot of interest in evaluating the Web, including the adequacy of its indexing, for the obvious reason that it has evolved into a major information resource and some criteria needs to be established to ascertain the quality of the systems and the information retrieved. There are three methodologies for evaluation:

1. Looking at how the systems are constructed.
2. Doing surveys of user satisfaction.
3. Running comparative search tests.

Like other aspects of the Web, reliable and valid evaluation methods are elusive.

Some of the system characteristics (as differentiated from quality of information) that have been evaluated are:

Completeness of results.

Database construction and coverage.

Interfacing.

Output duplicity.

Output options.

Response time.

Search capability and procedures.

Update frequency.

Validity of links.

There is a growing consensus that the exploding growth of the Internet is rapidly deteriorating the functionality of browsing as an effective searching method. The problem is intensified by the fact that there are over 100 million users in the world and the numbers continue to rise sharply.

Currency of information is a major problem. Very few automatic methods exist for updating site content. Outdated and no longer valid information lingers on in huge amounts.

Also, despite impressive-looking advertising numbers, most search services cover only a fraction of resources. If we add up the resources covered by a number of services it looks impressive, but the sum of the whole does not increase a lot because of overlap and duplication. But the general goals of the Internet seem to be to have 100 percent recall, regardless of pertinence or validity.

In sum, the problems are:

1. Too much information.
2. Too much duplicity.
3. Bad organization.
4. Too much invalid information.

If these current negative trends continue and gain control, then in a decade or so the Internet will be considered a quagmire for retrieving serious intellectual information. Who will trust it? It certainly will have tons of good information out there, but also tons of quicksand and alligators. Rather than being an information retrieval Neiman-Marcus it will be an incredibly gigantic five-and-dime store for triviality, dead wrong nonsense, and commercials.

Technology increases both the access to information resources and the ability to organize it. Unfortunately the Internet so far is concentrating on building up information stores and not enough effort is being put into organizing the stores. The indexing of the Internet is a Pandora's Box, and at this time is a major challenge for the indexing profession. Indexers simply must be more assertive in the Internet enterprise.

There have been good arguments promoting the usefulness of complex indexing systems for the Internet and equally good arguments for why these systems fail and that simple systems will prove adequate. Maybe the answer lies beyond complexity or simplicity of the systems. Maybe a new concept is needed, a type of indexing not quite yet conceived.

The major problem in trying to index the Internet is the sheer size of the physical systems and the information resources. It is amazing that we have done as well as we have. There are few standards (URLs are a step forward). There is no major unifying infrastructure, relatively primitive searching tools are being used, and all this is complicated with an infinite variety of individuals and organizations with their own agenda of what the Internet should be. Cooperation is manifest only when it is essential to make things work. With this kind of environment it is difficult to talk about any meaningful metaindexing system of the resources on the Internet.

Perhaps we need new terminology in order to conceptualize new approaches. *Authority control*, for example, carries a negative connotation for the freewheeling libertines who are driving the Internet. They do not want any authority. *Classification* makes them think of dusty library books and *indexing* is a way to invest in the stock market. If we are careful, we might be able to slip the word *thesaurus* past them because they have picked that up somewhere along the way. Just inventing new jargon words is no solution, but perhaps new ideas are needed which would naturally have new terminology.

The new generation of *Webbies* sees no problem with organizing the Internet. In fact, they are anxious to increase manyfold the size of the world's information store, fully confident that information technology has all the answers to the so-called information explosion. The electronic tools have developed beyond anything foreseeable twenty years ago and these tools will never let us down.

While most of us are not yet totally *true believers* that all good things must be new things, there are many reasons to be optimistic; however, some sort of new indexing theory is needed. We must find optimal ways to integrate time-tested indexing principles into the navigation mechanisms of the Internet and show the world how to do it. If, as indexers, we fail to do this, others will pick up the baton and win the gold medal.

Ninety-nine Web Resources for Indexers and Abstractors

There are hundreds, if not thousands, of Web sites that are of potential usefulness to indexers in one way or the other. General references, specialized references, thesauri, and professional societies are all examples of some general categories. This chapter lists ninety-nine examples of available Web and e-mail sources. The uniform resource locators (URLs) for these sites were current when this book went to press, but due to the volatile nature of the Web, there may be a few that have changed. Most sites listed are stable and reliable sources and can be easily found and accessed.

ONLINE BOOKSTORES

There are a number of online bookstores that offer wide coverage of books on indexing, both in print and out of print.

Amazon.com (http://www.amazon.com)
Amazon started in mid-1995 and quickly became a hit with online shoppers and soon after that became a hit with stock buyers. They have customers all around the world. Some examples of titles on indexing include:

The Art of Indexing (Wiley Technical Communication Library), Larry S. Bonura, New York: Wiley, 1994

Indexing Books (Chicago Guides to Writing, Editing, and Publishing), Nancy C. Malvany, Chicago, IL: University of Chicago Press, 1994

Handbook of Indexing Techniques: A Guide for Beginning Indexers, Linda K. Fetters, 2nd ed., Corpus Christi, TX: FinnCo Books, 1999

Barnes and Noble (http://bn.com)

Barnes and Noble came online after Amazon and gives another excellent avenue for books of interest to indexers. Some example of titles on indexing:

> *Indexing and Abstracting in Theory and Practice,* F. W. Lancaster, Champaign, IL: University of Illinois Press, 1998

> *Indexing Techniques for Advanced Database Systems,* Elisa Bertino, and others, Hingham, MA: Kluwer Academic Pub., 1997

SEARCH SERVICES

One has to be careful before recommending unequivocally that there is a *best* search service on the Internet. Just as there are many roads that lead to Rome, there are many search services that lead to information. The following is a short list of search services that the authors have found useful in their indexing endeavors, primarily for finding information that supports indexing.

SearchIQ (http://www.2dnet.com/searchiq/)

This is a great site if you do not know much about surfing the Web. It clues you in on how to run a successful search and it ranks various engines by the types of searches that they do.

AltaVista (http://www.altavista.com)

The natural language question features are useful. You do not always get a direct response from a natural language question, but you get information in the neighborhood. For example, the natural language inquiry "what is the future for indexers" brought up for its number one item *The American Society for Indexers.*

Dogpile (http://www.dogpile.com/index.gsp)

Dogpile has an appropriate name. With a click or two it checks on dozens of other search engines, newswires and newsgroups and gets you into Internet information in a hurry. In this case there is not a five-yard penalty for *piling on.*

Hotbot (http://www.hotbot.lycos.com)

Hotbot is considered by many as the best overall search engine. Its advanced capabilities let you search at many levels and depths. This provides good information for indexers needing backup information.

Yahoo! (http://www.yahoo.com)

And of course there is *Yahoo!* Its categorical capabilities are useful and indexers should study its structure. Yahoo employs indexers, and this is reflected in the search results.

MetaCrawler (http://www.metacrawler.com)

In order to get a quick view of the usefulness of this site, enter the term *thesaurus* and view the results.

About.com (http://www.about.com)

This is a network of over 600 Web sites, each of which focuses on specific topics and is managed by a human guide. Click on the *Technical Writing* link to find some useful information on indexing.

Google (http://www.google.com)
Lists the results in the order of popularity determined by the number of links from other sites.

Medical World Search (http://www.mwsearch.com)
This search engine is designed to understand medical terminology. It employs the evolving Unified Medical Language System (UMLS) thesaurus.

Search Engine Watch (http://www.searchengine.com/)
Learn how to search better and how the major search engines work from a searcher's perspective. Find all the major search engines, popular metasearch engines, etc.

INDEXING SERVICES

Web sites for indexing services are useful both because they offer services that an indexer might be interested in and because they often provide useful information about indexing in general (e.g., the discussion of indexing tools).

H. W. Wilson Home Page (http://www.hwwilson.com/)
Has indexes, indexing information, reference tools (e.g., *Famous First Facts*), etc.

Wright Information (http://mindspring.com/ ~ jancw/)
The site offers computer-based indexing services and provides interesting information for indexers and potential clients.

Index West (http://mindspring.com/ ~ indexwest/)
Kari Kells is the proprietor of this site. Service is offered to create "quality indexes for many types of publications." The site was formerly called Bero-West Indexing Services. Indexing workshops are offered.

Kingsley Indexing Services (http://indexpup.com/guidelines.html)
The site gives explicit examples of what an index from them will look like.

SunRiver Indexing Services (http://netw.com/ ~ dilworth/)
This site "will create a comprehensive, cost-effective, reader friendly index designed to locate information quickly and easily and help sell your book."

Susan Holbert Indexing Services (http://abbington.com/holbert/)
This service offers training courses for indexing and provides indexing services. The "for sale" videos of her courses are outstanding.

Marilyn Joyce Rowland (http://marisol.com)
Marilyn Joyce Rowland offers service for back-of-the-book indexing, periodical indexing, embedded indexing and Web site indexing. Consulting services "include review and editing of indexes compiled by others."

Graduate School USDA. The Government's Trainer
(http://www.grad.usda.gov/indexing.cait.htm)
The government offers correspondence and online courses in indexing.

DICTIONARIES AND
DICTIONARY DIRECTORIES

Dictionaries are a first priority tool for indexers and the Web has a great number of excellent sources for dictionaries of every type.

OneLook Dictionaries (http://www.onelook.com)
This wonderful site should be at the top of the list for all indexers. It gives an extensive list of dictionaries across many fields. Many of these dictionaries include visuals and a whole lot more.

Paderborn University (http://www-math.uni-paderborn.de/dictionaries/ Dictionaries_text.html)
This site features *one-click* access to language dictionaries, thesauri (e.g., *NASA Thesaurus*), acronym dictionaries, as well as a wonderful list of miscellaneous items (e.g., *Infomedical Dictionary for Patients and Support Groups*).

yourDictionary (http://www.yourdictionary.com)
This site provides links to more than 1,500 dictionaries in 230 different languages. Just for fun, the reader should find the definition for *indexing* on this site.

Online Medical Dictionary (http://graylab.ac.uk/omd/)
This searchable dictionary containing over 65,000 definitions. Entries include cross-referencing and related resource links.

Oxford English Dictionary (http://www.oed.com)
The online version of the *Oxford English Dictionary* is available by annual subscription. Indexers can profit by reading how they handle many problems of entry choices, word variations, etc. Each day they have a "word of the day" feature that is a delight to word lovers (as all indexers should be).

Glossary for Information Retrieval (http://www.cs.jhu.edu/ ~ weiss/ glossary.html)
This glossary attempts to give definitions for all of the terms relevant to information retrieval. This does not include names of specific projects, engines, or people.

Hypertext Webster Gateway (http://work.ucsd.edu:5141/cgi-bin/http_webster?)
Hypertext Webster Gateway provides a point-and-click client interface for accessing various dictionary services on the Internet.

MULTIREFERENCE RESOURCES
AND TOOLS

Many types of reference tools are used by indexers. While it is not possible to present an exhaustive list, the following are examples of typical resources and tools.

Information Please (http://www.infoplease.com)
   You should not leave home without it. This is an online dictionary, Internet encyclopedia, almanac reference, daily almanac, atlas and current news.

Internet Oracle (http://www.internetoracle.com/reference.htm)
   The *Online Reference & Research* portion includes a thesaurus and a phrase and quotation finder.

Medword (http://www.medword.com)
   Medical terminology galore at this site: dictionaries, atlases, spellers including tables of prefixes and suffixes.

Dictionary.com (http://www.dictionary.com)
   Contains multiple reference tools such as *Roget's Thesaurus, Word of the Day*, Strunk's *Elements of Style*, and more.

Wordsmyth English Dictionary-Thesaurus (http://www.wordsmyth.net/)
   Subtitled *The Educational Dictionary*, this is like having a number of dictionaries "rolled into one."

Web Thesaurus Compendium
   (http://www-cui.darmstadt.gmd.de/ ~ lutes/thesauri.html)
   This site has a list of a number of thesauri and classification schemes that are available on the Web with various search and browse facilities and various degrees of hypertext linking.

Pedro's Dictionaries (http://www.public.iastate.edu/ ~ pedro/
   dictionaries.html)
   Presents links to obscure terminology dictionaries as well as regular dictionaries.

Internet Public Library Standard General Reference Aids
   (http://ipl.org/ref/RR/static/ref0000.html)
   Excellent list of general reference aids.

Encyclopedia Britannica—Britannica Online (http://www.britannica.com)
   Subscriptions are no longer required for access.

HealthAnswers.com (http://www.healthanswers.com/default.asp)
   Contains an extensive patient handout database. It also has a drug information and a medical encyclopedia.

ALLExperts (http://www.allexperts.com)
   This site offers the e-mail address for online experts in a great variety of subjects. An excellent way for an indexer to get an answer.

National Geographic Map Machine
   (http://nationalgeographic.com/resources/ngo/maps/)
   This site contains comprehensive geographical information.

BigFoot free e-mail (http://www.bigfoot.com)
   Offers a free e-mail address, free e-mail forwarding and free e-mail filtering.

Hotmail free e-mail (http://www.hotmail.com)
Offers a free e-mail address and Web-based e-mail access.

AT&T 800 Directory (http://www.internet800directory.com)
Lists 800 and 888 phone numbers, regardless of long distance carrier.

Strunk, William. The Elements of Style (http://www.bartleby.com/141/index.html)
The abstract writer should have a copy of this classic of classics in front of her when she begins to write.

International Trademark Association (http://www.inta.org/)
The *Trademark Checklist* can be found at this site. This guide offers proper trademark usage including the correct spelling, punctuation, and capitalization of nearly 3000 trademarks and service marks.

The WorldWideWeb Acronym and Abbreviation Server (http://ucc.ie/info/net/acronyms/acro.html)
This gives a list of acronyms and their meanings.

Symbols.com (http://www.symbols.com/)
This site has over 2,500 western signs, arranged into 54 groups according to their graphic characteristics. Some 1,600 articles discuss their histories, uses, and meanings. The signs range from ideograms carved in mammoth teeth by Cro-Magnon men, to hobo signs and subway graffiti.

A Glossary of Literary Terms and A Handbook of Rhetorical Devices (http://www.uky.edu/ArtsSciences/Classics/Harris/rhetform.html)
Contains definitions and usage examples from more than 150 literary terms and rhetorical devices. This site is useful to both the indexer and the abstractor.

DOD Dictionary of Military Terms (http://www.dtic.mil/doctrine/jel/doddict)
This dictionary contains approved definitions of military terms used by the United States and NATO. Also, it has military acronyms and abbreviations.

BritSpeak (http://pages.prodigy.com/NY/NYC/britspk/dictLink.html)
A good site for finding the differences between American and British words.

E-MAIL REFERENCE SITES

An e-mail reference is a link to a library or other information source that allows users to post a reference question directly to a reference person. Use of some sites is restricted to the personnel of the organization, but many are open to everyone. The following are available to a general audience.

Auburn University (http://www.lib.auburn.edu/askref.html)

Boston Public Library (http://www.bpl.org/www/ReferenceForm.html)

Brigham Young University (http://www.lib.byu.edu/userhelp/libquest.html)

Ask an Expert (http://directory.netscape.com/Reference/Ask_An_Expert)
This is a list of all the other "ask an expert" links. See below (ask *the* expert) for a specific example of asking an expert.

Ask a Librarian (http://www.earl.org.uk/ask/index.html)
"Bringing the resources of United Kingdom public libraries to your home desktop."

Yahoo! Information Brokers (http://dir.yahoo.com/Business_and_Economy/
Companies/Information/Information_Brokers/)
This is Yahoo's link to many, many business resources.

University of Michigan (http://www.lib.umich.edu/libhome/askus/)
Ask-Us provides reference services via e-mail by the University of Michigan Library staff.

VIRTUAL LIBRARIES

A virtual library is a centralized access point to the many resources available on the Internet. While a virtual library is very similar to directory-type search services (e.g., *Yahoo!*), virtual libraries generally are constructed with the professional advice of librarians and therefore resemble "real" libraries.

WWW Virtual Library (http://www.ce.cmu.edu/GreenDesign/links/
virtual_libraries.html)
The World Wide Web (WWW) Virtual Library is a distributed subject catalog.

Clinical Digital Libraries Project (http://www.cdlp.org)
The Clinical Digital Libraries Project is a research, teaching and service effort led by two schools of library and information studies, that seeks to develop and test a model for health sciences libraries to adopt in order to provide professional digital library services to their offsite (including rural) clinical users.

Planet Earth (http://www.tidusa.com/index.html)
A potpourri of useful links. It includes headline news, subject-based toolboxes, and country information.

Refdesk.com–Quick Reference/Research
(http://www.refdesk.com/instant.html)
This site has the goal to be the reference librarian of the Web. Contains many links to reference tools.

SPECIAL FORMATS AND
SUBJECTS INDEXING

ASIS Thesaurus of Information Science (http://www.asis.org/Publications/
Thesaurus/isframe.htm)
Gives an alphabetical, hierarchical and expandable list of terms.

Newspaper Indexing Policies and Procedures
(http://www.ibiblio.org/indexing.html)
This excerpt from *News Media Libraries: A Management Handbook* by Barbara P. Semonche has a great deal of interesting information for newspaper indexers.

The Art and Architecture Thesaurus (http://shiva.pub.getty.edu/
aat_browser/)
This outstanding thesaurus not only can be used as an online tool, but it should be studied by those interested in thesaurus construction and use.

Getty Thesaurus of Geographic Names™ (TGN)
(http://shiva.pub.getty.edu/tgn_browser)
This tool allows searching "for place names and retrieves records of places, including vernacular and historical names, coordinates, place types, and other relevant information."

NASA Thesaurus (http://www.sti.nasa.gov/thesfrm1.htm)
This contains the authorized terms for indexing documents in NASA STI databases.

The Library of Congress Thesauri
(http://lcweb.loc.gov/pmei/lexico/liv/brsearch.html)
Includes several thesauri for use with legislative and public policy subject matter and graphic materials.

Unified Medical Language System (http://www.nlm.nih.gov/research/
umls/UMLSDOC.HTML)
The National Library of Medicine's UMLS Knowledge Sources include the Metathesaurus, the Semantic Network and the SPECIALIST lexicon. These are powerful tools for indexing.

Medical Subject Headings, MeSH (http://www.nlm.nih.gov/
mesh/meshhome.html)
It is the National Library of Medicine's controlled subject vocabulary and is a very extensive list of medical terminology.

STANDARDS

National Information Standards Organization (http://www.niso.org/)
The National Information Standards Organization (NISO) develops and promotes technical standards used in a wide variety of information services.

ANSI/NISO Z39.14-1997 Guidelines for Abstracts (http://www.ansi.org/)

ANSI/Z39.4-1984 Basic Criteria for Indexes (http://www.ansi.org/)

International Organization for Standardization Web Site (http://www.iso.ch/)

INDEXING SOFTWARE

For information regarding indexing software, see Chapter 14.

PUBLISHERS

Author's Advisory Service (http://www.lights.com/publisher/)
This site has information for authors from manuscript to print.

Publishing Associations (Go to: http://www.About.com)
Use *Search for* to link to:

Newspaper publishing associations.

Magazine publishing associations.

Canadian book publishers.

Book publishing associations.

Directory of Publishers and Vendors (http://www.library.vanderbilt.edu/law/acqs/pubr.html)
This is an international directory of publishers and vendors used by libraries.

Association of Learned and Professional Society Publishers (http://www.alpsp.org.uk/)
There are links to member pages and other sites which contain information about the book and journal industry.

Association of American Publishers, Inc. (http://www.publishers.org/home/index.htm)
This is the principal trade association of the American book publishing industry.

Editor & Publisher Interactive (http://www.mediainfo.com)
Please note classified job opportunities. Not unusual to have indexing opportunities.

Publishers Weekly (http://www.publishersweekly.com)
Publishers Weekly maintains this guide to more than 900 publishers with Web sites around the world.

Society for Scholarly Publishing (http://www.sspnet.org/)

Society for Technical Communication—Employment (http://stc.org)

INDEXING ORGANIZATIONS

These sites are gold mines for indexing information of all types.

The American Society of Indexers (http://www.asindexing.org/)

Society of Indexers (http://www.socind.demon.co.uk/)

Indexing and Abstracting Society of Canada
(http://tornade.ere.umontreal.ca/ ~ turner/iasc/home.html)

Society for Technical Communication, Indexing Special Interest Group
(http://www.stc.org/pics/indexing/)

Australian Society of Indexers (http://www.zeta.org.au/ ~ aussi)

The China Society of Indexers (http://www.yp.online.sh.cn/suoyin/sy-sy.htm)

National Federation of Abstracting and Information Sciences
(http://www.pa.utulsa.edu/nfais.html)

INDEXING-RELATED DISCUSSION GROUPS

American Society of Indexers, ASI-L (http://www.asindexing.org/asi-l.html)

American Society for Information Science, ASIS-L (http://www.asis.org/
EComm/asis-l.html)

Mac Indexers (http://www.egroups.com/group/MacIndexers)
This list is for anyone who indexes on the Mac platform.

Indexing Tech Docs (http://indexingtechdocs.listbot.com/)

IndexStudents (http://www.onelist.com/subscribe.cgi/indexstudents)

SKYIndexusers (http://www.onelist.com/subscribe.cgi/skyindexusers)

Index-L (http://listserv.unc.edu/cgi-bin/lyris.pl?enter = Index-L)
The list promotes good indexing practice.

The Freelance Network (http://members.tripod.com/ ~ fwnn)
   At this site, freelancers can register their availability for contract work. All types of freelancers and consultants (not just authors) register here.

INDEXING AND THE WEB

Indexing the Web (http://www.hypernews.org/HyperNews/get/www/
   indexing.html)

Internet Society (http://www.isoc.org)

The Dublin Core: A Bibliography (http://purl.org/metadata/DC/
   bibliography1.html)

The Profession

EDUCATION AND TRAINING

Indexing and abstracting can be a satisfying career, allowing its practitioners to develop unique skills and to work in an intellectually challenging environment. So how does one become as indexer or abstractor? There are no formal requirements. All one has to do is print up some business cards and hang out a shingle. But, becoming a *successful* indexer or abstractor requires a great deal more. There are no licensing procedures or formal education or training background required before hanging out the shingle, although there are some assumed qualifications.

How does a person acquire these qualifications? It can be by formal education, by self-education, and/or by training on the job. Formal education can be courses on the topic offered at universities, generally in schools of library and information science, or it can be short courses offered by professional associations or individuals. Self-education is accomplished by studying books and instructional manuals in the field. On-the-job training is a popular way to learn, since very few people start college with the goal of becoming an indexer. Not many job fairs in high school have a booth for indexing. Generally, the student earns a subject degree and then is trained while working.

What kind of education or training is needed? Educational preparation for an indexer or an abstractor can vary, but there are some general directions a student can take. Although a Master of Library and Information Science degree is not always a requirement, it certainly can be useful, especially if the course of study is slanted toward an indexing and abstracting career specialization, which is possible at a number of schools of library and information science. Generally, the course of study will include courses in cataloging, reference, indexing, abstracting, advanced theory of classification and indexing, online searching, information storage and retrieval, and technical writing. Most schools have a course or two in indexing, but very few have specific programs, which focus on indexing. These courses are often very useful and are an important aspect of the student's formal education. Usually the student's practical, hands-on experience is very minimal. It takes a lot of indexing and abstracting to develop into a professional.

Short courses, continuing education courses, and workshops give a quick introduction to the fundamentals of indexing and abstracting. Also, some employers give on-the-job training, although most organizations expect employees to be experienced when they are hired.

A neophyte indexer should be familiar with the professional societies and should have their Web pages bookmarked. Most of the societies pay a lot of attention to the training of indexers, both beginners and advanced professionals.

There are a number of professional indexing and abstracting organizations scattered around the world. In 1877 Henry Benjamin Wheatley formed an indexing society in England, which lasted until 1890 when it ran out of money. In 1957 the Society of Indexers was formed under the instigation of G. Norman Knight. The society has had a viable agenda of activities, including the improvement of standards for indexing and indexers, training courses, and the selection of the most outstanding index for their Wheatley Medal.

In 1968 the American Society of Indexers was formed with the goal of promoting "indexing as a professional calling." There are also indexing organizations in Canada, Australia, Japan, China, South Africa, and other countries. In addition, there are more general organizations that promote indexing, such as the National Federation of Abstracting and Information Services, which is a collective organization of individual indexing and abstracting services.

JOB OPPORTUNITIES

People enter the indexing and abstracting field from many directions, ranging from writers, editors, researchers, professors, housewives and househusbands, and, of course, from the field of library and information science. Some attempt to make a full-time career out of it and some simply want to keep the day job and supplement their incomes.

Where do indexers and abstractors get work? There are a number of different options:

1. Freelance book indexers.
2. Independent information brokers often use indexers, either on their staffs, or on an assignment basis.
3. As library staff members; this can range from indexing special materials in a research library to a wide range of special libraries.
4. Primary information publishers, such as scholarly journals.
5. Secondary information publishers, such as indexing and abstracting services.

Freelance indexing is one way to go. Successful entrepreneur and freelance indexing is still alive and mostly well. Succeeding as a freelance indexer is more than just being a good indexer. Freelance indexers have to set up and run a small business enterprise. The advantage to this is the independence of working for yourself. The disadvantage is that there are no guarantees for a steady income and job security. You need to be disciplined in your work habits, you need to have business skills, and you need to be a bit comfortable with the inherent job insecurity, especially in the beginning when you have few clients.

Also, you need to promote yourself. A major key to successful freelancing is to sell your services and the need for them. Most people in the world have never thought about how indexes are created. The indexes just *happen* to be at the end of a book, or in an online database, or as an icon on a computer screen. Likewise a lot of your potential customers are only vaguely aware that you are out there, waiting for their phone call.

You cannot be a *vague* freelancer and make a go at it. You must promote yourself and you should band together with other indexers to promote the idea of good indexes and the need of a professional indexer when an index is needed. Your publicity should go to commercial publishers, professional associations, academicians, and to any place where publishing is done and an index is needed.

As an information professional you should already know how to use reference sources to identify these potential customers. The following are a few examples:

Association of American Publishers.

Association of American University Presses.

American Medical Publishers' Association.

American Society for Information Science.

Chronicle of Higher Education.

Small Press Magazine.

There are many, many others. Always remember that freelancing is a risky business, but so are most jobs in the world.

There are many other avenues open for those who want to work in indexing and abstracting. The era of electronic information has brought indexing to the forefront as a major activity. Throughout the infrastructure of the Information Age, people who ten years ago had no idea of what indexing is, or saw no use for it, are now very much involved. Unfortunately, many of these enthusiasts are not qualified to design indexing systems and/or index.

Although the traditional publishing world will continue to need indexers, and this will remain a source of work, the real future for indexers may be elsewhere. For example, the electronic world of the Internet offers indexing opportunities in hypermedia indexing and electronic publishing. Opportunities for indexers are opening up in museums, information broker organizations, market research, on the Web, in the Silicon Valley, and beyond.

Within indexing and abstracting organizations there are a variety of positions. First, there are the indexers and abstractors themselves. Generally, these persons must be college graduates and are often expected to have studied in the subject area in which they will index and abstract. Second, there are editors, often promoted from the indexing ranks to the editorial position. It is the editor's job to see that policies are carried out and to edit the results that come from the indexing and abstracting corps. Third, there are checkers, whose responsibility is to proofread the indexes and abstracts, looking for inconsistencies and errors. These are the three groups of professionals. In libraries, information centers, research organizations, and other settings, the indexing and abstracting may turn out to be a one-person job, with the worker doing everything from indexing and abstracting to publishing the final product.

Indexes, in some form, will be necessary as long as information systems exist. And indexers will be needed to create these indexes. Roles may shift in emphasis. For example, as we move more into the use of software for indexing, who will be better able to design this software than someone who understands professional indexing? There is a jungle out there called electronic information, with full-text databases, the Web, and rapidly growing image databases. Indexers in the new millennium will need sharply honed machetes in order to lead the way into this jungle.

Where do you look for jobs? The first source is the library literature for indexing jobs both inside and outside the library, but job notices are also posted in the nonlibrarian literature as well. For example, notices are in publishing trade journals and big city newspapers. And there are a number of employment resources on the Internet. *The Internet Public Library* has a Web page called IPL located at http://www.ipl.org. Once on the site, click on *Especially for Librarians*, and then click on *Library Employment*, which gives links to job notice sources.

You do not get into indexing solely for money. Plumbers and truck drivers generally do better, but like bungee jumping, indexing either attracts you or repels you. You can find it creative and intellectually stimulating or you can see it as an unattractive way to spend the rest of your life.

THE ROLE OF RESEARCH

Research should be a prime concern to any profession. Any true profession has a research base. Research is the quest for new knowledge. New knowledge may be something never known before or it may be the dispelling of what was thought to be true, but in either case it involves discovery. It is used to find solutions to problems; therefore research in indexing should be used to solve indexing problems. Research is not an easy task in any field and indexing is certainly no exception. One of the ways we get the attention of the students in our Ph.D. seminar is to blandly state: "The major barrier to doing research in information science is the fact that there is no such thing as information science." After the storm is over, we point out that it is difficult to do research when the constructs are poorly defined. This is the problem with doing research in indexing and abstracting.

Why do people choose to do research? A cynical answer would be that it is a part of the job description for some people and in the academic setting it can help them to get tenure. Hopefully, the motivation is more profound than that. It is true that research accomplishment can give you recognition and there is nothing wrong with that motive. The recognition is especially sweet if it comes from the leaders in the field. The other principal motive is that it gives a great satisfaction to find answers to the universe mystery and to share that with others. For a professor nothing equals the pleasure of standing before a class and explaining a new discovery and when a student asks for a citation, the professor replies that there is not one yet, but her research assistant is down the hall typing up the report.

Doing research on indexing may not be as interesting to the world as discovering a cure for cancer, but the information professional can take pride in the fact that very probably an indexing system helped the medical scientist find the background material from the literature that played a vital part in the cancer research project.

What are the qualifications for being a researcher? The following are some of the qualifications:

Be curious.

Be observant.

Be educated in the subject.

Be a classifier.

Be able to analyze and synthesize.

Have perseverance.

Accept failure.

Be oblivious to jealousy-based criticism.

Be an independent thinker.

Be a hunch follower.

A good researcher must have the ability to dissect several mousetraps and then select parts from the pile of parts and assemble a "better mousetrap." Information retrieval, including indexing, is still waiting for that better mousetrap.

Over the years researchers have tried to improve retrieval systems by introducing an incredible range of schemes and complexity. These schemes come and go and then decades later, they return under different names. One wonders if when things are all said and done, the best approach is to design simple, basic retrieval systems, with an emphasis on careful, common sense indexing. You use simple search procedures and then quietly ask users if they are happy with what they got. In the long run none of the complex, super-wired, over-researched schemes have proved to be better than this.

To traditional book indexers, research has not been regarded as an essential element. It is hard to imagine a book indexer in the past being overly concerned with research in indexing. Why would we need research on something that we know how to do and that seems to be working quite well? Common sense and experience tells us what to do.

The advent of computer-based retrieval systems brought a different breed of indexer. Most of the indexing professionals involved in information retrieval (IR) systems do not have the slightest idea of how to index a book. They could, however, learn a great deal by familiarizing themselves on what book indexers have learned and refined over many centuries.

Research is essential to the future development of indexing. Indexing is no longer the esoteric, leather-binding work of ladies or gentlemen in wood paneled libraries. Indexing has moved into the workplace and will be the heart of the information superhighway. Empirical studies will be needed to transfer indexing into practical applications. The entire Web infrastructure is related to indexing and organizing information. And the compass is research.

Research is costly, much too costly to be done by an individual working alone and independently. How does it get paid for? In the business world the companies pay for it and the objective is commercial value. The business world wants practical outcomes, whereas the academic world looks for fundamental, theoretical insights. Noncommercially directed research is paid for by grants from private and public sources, often by government agencies, and is aimed at the academic world.

Over the past forty years a great deal of research in information retrieval has originated out of the academic setting and more often than not, the research has focused on the indexing problem. The researcher should begin by asking what needs to be done in the field. Indexing, like all areas of research, gets stuck on ideas and years of work are done trying to thread a camel through the eye of a needle. There is a snowball effect and every new researcher believes that that is the hot topic and jumps on it, not asking the question of what else needs to be done. A good example is the idea of relevance. Is there any more that needs to be said? We will probably not ever find anything near an absolute measure or a consensus definition, but we have workable measures and definitions that will now let us move on.

What kinds of things are researched in indexing? The range is vast, including the system components in a computer system, linguistics, human behavior, and economics and on and on. As one quick example, one area of research has been on alternatives to traditional indexing. For example, efforts have focused on citation linkages, or bibliographic coupling. The most successful of these approaches is citation indexing, which was discussed earlier. This technique identifies documents on the topic by tracing references *to* a given paper. Another one is bibliographic coupling, which clusters papers on a topic on the basis of common references.

Most of the primary work on bibliographic coupling was done by M. M. Kessler in the 1960s at MIT. He described the grouping of papers on the basis of bibliographic coupling units. Based on this unit, two criteria of coupling were defined. The idea is that articles are grouped or linked together by the references that the authors include in papers. We develop networks of papers on a topic. We do not retrieve papers by index terms but by groups based on common citations. When we use index terms we also group papers. We collect a group of papers that all include the term *cats*, for example. Bibliographic coupling would also create a group of cat papers, but on the basis of the related references. The premise is that a paper about cats will also have references related to cats.

Kessler observed that this technique is independent of words and language, since all the processing is done by a quantitative method. We thus avoid all the difficulties of language, syntax, and word habits involved in human indexing. No one reads the papers or makes intellectual decisions. As a matter of fact, the text of the paper does not even have to be present. Also, the method does not produce a static classification number for a given paper. The groupings will undergo changes that reflect the current usage and interests of the users.

Of the other studies Kessler made, one is of particular importance. He compared groups generated by bibliographic coupling with groups of papers generated by using the manually prepared analytical subject index used by the editors of *Physical Review* and found a high correlation. This study gives convincing evidence as to the validity of the technique. Bibliographic coupling works quite well in the laboratory but has not been widely implemented. This is one example of the wide-ranging areas in indexing where basic and applied research are ripe for the picking.

This type of research is part of a larger research method called *bibliometrics*. In 1969 Alan Pritchard defined bibliometrics as "the application of mathematics and statistics methods to shed light on the processes of written communication and on the nature and course of development of a discipline by means of counting and analyzing the various facets of written communication." This term replaces an earlier term, *statistical bibliography*. Bibliometric analysis has its flaws, but overall it is a useful tool for analyzing the behavioral properties of authors, journals, words, subject, and disciplines and can provide useful feedback information for an indexing operation.

What needs to be done next? Basic indexing research is still needed in linguistics. Language is at the heart of what indexing is. What are meaningful words in a text? What roles does language structures play in indexing and in searching? Research is needed that focuses on the elusive process by which humans understand what a document is about and how people select words to represent that *aboutness*. When we understand this process then we can vastly improve human indexing and take a major step toward using computers to do the task.

Some general areas of needed research are:

- How do people search for information?
- Are there better methods of human evaluation of indexing and abstracting?
- What indexing techniques are better for the Web?
- What techniques are needed to evaluate Web indexing?
- How to integrate browsing and item specific searching into the Web searching tools.
- What is the relationship between cognition and indexing?
- What are the techniques needed to effectively deal with the economics of indexing?
- What general theories of indexing are needed?

The decades of the 1960s and 1970s saw a substantial amount of research in indexing and abstracting, exemplified by the classic Cranfield experiments, Kessler, Garfield with citation indexing, and many, many others. The trauma of Sputnik brought on a serious interest in stepping up scientific output, including the access and dissemination of science information, and substantial federal funds were available for information research. A great deal of this went directly or indirectly to projects dealing in some way with indexing. The following decades brought a noticeable drop in indexing research, probably because of a dry-up of funding, but also because we saw very little of the laboratory work applied in the real world.

The Internet age is causing a dramatic return to research, but this time it is coming from private industry which realizes that at the heart of building successful, profitable information tools is the basic problem of analysis and representing information.

This is good news to all indexers. It will lead to jobs and opportunities as the new millennium progresses.

THE FUTURE

Does indexing have a future? The computer probably will never be able to index as well as a human being, but the trend seems to be to develop methods to circumvent this shortcoming by convincing publishers and readers that the computer can do a passable job and "good" indexing may not be important. The new generation seems to be content to hunt and click endlessly until they find something which, they believe, is the solution.

The Information Age has brought information retrieval to the attention of the general public and has spread all across the business, government, and educational world. Librarians, information specialists, indexers, information scientists have a very bright future in the new millennium.

Indexing in the future will be more and more tool-based. For example, embedded indexing tools are now rather primitive, but they have the potential to develop into sophisticated, useful tools. Web-based indexing is in its infancy and better tools to index the Web will surely be developed which will probably change the entire notion of indexing.

Scanners and voice-recognition related technology will bring image and sound indexing to a new high. Expert systems and progress in natural language processing are still in the early dawn of their real potential in the art of indexing.

Indexers need to find a way to put themselves in the forefront of electronic indexing in every sense of the word. They must convince the new generation that indexers have a wealth of experience and the intellectual wherewithal that will be needed. This is the way indexing will survive. Writing a beautiful manual index may win awards within the indexing profession, but this is not the way to survive.

Is there a future for indexing? The emphatic answer is *yes*.

THE FINAL WORD

Like other artists, perhaps some indexers and abstractors are born, not made. They may claim to never have studied indexing, but one day they sat down and began to index. We are assuming that you are not one of these fortunate people. We assume that you feel the need for guidance and practice. You may be talented, but you are not a natural-born indexer.

Indexing and abstracting can be satisfactory careers and we hope that this book has been useful in getting you started. However, reading a book does not make you an indexer or an abstractor. Knowing something about indexing and abstracting is not the same as knowing how to index and abstract. It takes many long hours and months of hard work and only a genuine desire will lead you to success.

We wish you well.

Glossary

Aboutness. The aboutness of a document goes beyond explicit words in the text to a higher level of meaning.

Abstract. A condensed, representative surrogate of a knowledge record. A narrative description of a document, which may include pertinent data and critical comments.

Abstractor. The person who creates an abstract. This may be the author of the original paper, a subject expert, or a full-time professional abstractor.

Access Point. An entry in an index, in which a user's chosen word matches a word in the index, giving the user a starting point in the search.

Acronym. An abbreviation that is often formed from letters within the word or phrase being abbreviated.

Added Entry. In a catalog, an entry that is in addition to the main entry. A secondary entry that allows the user to find the information with a different approach.

Alphabetic Subject Indexes. Indexes arranged in alphabetical order, containing important words that reflect subjects of interest.

Alphanumeric Display. Headings in an index that are arranged in alphanumeric order.

Alternative Title. The second part of a title that is joined by a connective word such as *or* (e.g., *Raising the Roof* or *How to Build Your Own House*).

Analytical Entry. An entry for a part of an item for which a comprehensive entry has already been made.

ANSI. The American National Standards Institute.

Arrangement. Consistent ordering of entries in an index, usually alphabetical.

Artificial Intelligence. An area of study that attempts to program computers to emulate human reasoning.

ASI. American Society of Indexers.

Assignment Indexing. Humans or computers assign index terms to represent the aboutness of a topic in a document. The terms may or may not actually appear in the text.

Associate Relationship. A relationship among terms that shows nonhierarchical relationships. Also called *related terms*.

Associative Retrieval Systems. An information retrieval system in which the indexing is based on the frequency of the co-occurrence of terms as a method of grouping.

Author Abstracts. Abstracts that are written by the authors of the original papers.

Author Affiliation. The organization to which the author is attached.

Author Indexes. Indexes arranged on the basis of the authors of the documents. Alphabetical lists of the authors of documents in a file.

Authority List. A formal list of terms to be used in cataloging or indexing. The use of terms not in the *authorized* list is prohibited.

Automatic Abstracting. Using a computer to construct abstracts.

Automatic Indexing. Using a computer to construct indexes.

Bibliographic Control. The intellectual access to public knowledge. More specifically, the processes necessary to generate and organize records of materials in libraries and other information systems for effective retrieval.

Bibliographic Coupling. The citation of two or more documents in a third one.

Book Indexes. Indexes to the content of individual monograph publications. These usually appear at the end of the book and are alphabetical, including subjects and name terms.

Boolean Operators. Connectives used to combine terms for searching in post-coordinate systems (e.g., *AND*, *OR*, and *NOT*).

Boolean Searching. The procedure of identifying information on a *yes* or *no* binary basis. For a *yes* answer, a user's request term is the same as an index term on the individual document under consideration from the file of documents.

Bound Terms. Index terms that are joined together and treated as a single concept. For example: *artificial* and *intelligence* form the concept *artificial intelligence*.

Broader Term. In a hierarchical thesaurus, broader terms and narrower terms express relationships between class and subclass. A term in a subclass would refer to class by indicating a *broader term*.

Cataloging. The preparation and maintenance of entries in a catalog.

Chain Indexes. Alphabetically arranged indexes with a separately provided entry for each term or a link for all the terms used in a classification or subject-heading scheme.

Citation Indexes. A citation index leads users to papers by citations, rather than by index terms. The entries in a citation index are the names of authors of earlier works on a subject. The index is a list of publications that have been referred to in the sources covered by the index. Citations lead the user to desired information.

Citation Order. The order in which facets are arranged (or cited) in a classified sequence of terms, headings, or entries.

Class. A set whose members share an attribute, characteristic, property, quality, or trait.

Classification. The process of bringing like things together on the basis of similarities and differences. A systematic arrangement in sets or categories according to established criteria.

Client. In a network system (e.g., the Web), the receiving end of the information retrieval procedure.

Closed-end Index. One time index. Does not continue to be published over periods of time.

Clustering. Automatic grouping of documents in an information retrieval file or the grouping terms in thesaurus construction.

Collective Title. A title proper that is an inclusive title for an item containing several works.

Colon Classification. An analytic-synthetic classification system developed in 1933 by S. R. Ranganathan, in which colons separate facets.

Compound Term. Multiword terms (e.g., *Super Bowl*).

Computer Program. A logical sequence of detailed instructions that directs a computer's operation.

Computer-aided Indexing. Human indexers use computer software, which supplements aspects of the indexing process (e.g., formatting and thesaurus checking).

Concept. Something conceived in the mind, either concrete or abstract, based on generalization from particular instances.

Concept List. A list of words representing the ideas in a knowledge record not yet translated into the formal indexing vocabulary.

Concordance. An alphabetical index of the words appearing in a text with a pointer to the precise point at which each word occurs. The index shows every contextual occurrence of a word.

Content Analysis. An attempt to infer the meaning and intent of a knowledge record in the absence of the creator of the record. A subjective interpretation of what a record is about.

Controlled Vocabulary. A vocabulary in which only an approved list of words can be used as index terms; used to manage synonyms and near-synonyms and to bring together semantically related terms.

Coordinate Indexing. An indexing scheme that combines single index terms to create composite subject concepts (e.g., the terms *eye* and *surgery* are combined to create the concept *eye surgery*). The system allows the coordination of classes either before or during searching. In pre-coordination the combinations are made at the input stage, and in post-coordination the combinations are made at the output stage.

Corporate Body. A group of people or organizations that are considered as a single entity (e.g., the IBM Corporation).

Critical Abstract. An abstract that evaluates the content of the paper.

Cross-Reference. An entry in a work that points to another entry.

Cumulative Indexes. Cumulative indexes are created by combining, at some point, a series of indexes created over a period of time.

Depth of Indexing. The result of the combined effects of exhaustivity and specificity in an index.

Derivative Indexing. Human or computers select index terms directly from the words in the document, including titles, abstracts, and text.

Descriptor. An index term chosen as the preferred representation for the aboutness of a topic in a document.

Discipline-oriented Abstract. An abstract aimed at an activity concerned with a specific area of knowledge.

Display. The final, useable form of the thesaurus or index.

Dissertation. A formal report on original research usually prepared by a graduate student at a university.

Document. The physical carrier of organized information. May be print or nonprint, including digital form.

Documentation. An activity that concerns itself with the reproduction, distribution, and utilization of documents. The movement began in Europe, spread to the United States in the 1930s, and became one of the intellectual streams leading to the information science discipline.

Double Entry. Entering an entry in two places in the index, usually done when the entry compound and several elements may be a possible lead-in term for the user.

Electronic Records. Records in a machine-readable medium.

Element. A word or phrase representing a distinct bibliographic unit of information.

Entity-oriented Index. Terms are selected on the basis of the actual topics in the document rather than on the anticipated needs and requests of users.

Entry. The point where the user is directed to the needed information. It consists of headings and subheadings with a locator, directing where to find the information.

Entry Differentiation. The practice of breaking up long, solid blocks of entry components into several, more readable lines, sometimes with additional subheadings.

Entry Redundancy. The assignment of superfluous entries.

Entry Scattering. The undesirable practice of spreading closely related entries throughout the index.

Entry Vocabulary. All the terms by which a user gains entrance into the index.

Enumerative Classification. A system in which all the elements are named and placed in fixed relationships prior to use.

Equivalent Term. A term that is used for another term. This may include synonyms, but also broader or related terms may be equivalent terms.

Exhaustivity. The range of topic coverage of an indexed document.

Expert System. A computer system that is designed and programmed to accomplish tasks that experts accomplish using their intelligence and experience.

Extract. A form of abstract which is constructed by stringing together *verbatim* sentences from the original paper.

Faceted Indexes. Indexes based on any definable aspect that makes up a subject. Composite concepts are then created in such a way that access is possible for each facet, or notion, contained in the subject composite.

False Drops. Nonrelevant documents retrieved as a result of a semantic breakdown. For example, a request for *Venetian blinds* might also result in information on *Blind Venetians*.

File. An orderly collection of similar information records.

Formula Indexes. Indexes in which the entries are listed in order, such as the symbol for the first element of a molecular formula.

Free-text Searching. Searching the entire document looking for matches of natural language terms.

Free-text Vocabulary. An uncontrolled vocabulary in which any word in the natural language is a permissible index term.

Generic Posting. The assignment of a broader term for a concept in a document.

Generic Vocabulary. A vocabulary consisting of those words that represent the basic type of an entity (e.g., *INSECTS* as generic for ants, bees, fleas, etc.). Generic terms are generally cross-reference terms.

Heading. One or more terms representing a topic in an index.

Hit. A match of query terms to a document in the information file.

Homograph. A term that has the same spelling, but different meanings, such as *Base (military)* and *Base (mathematics)*.

Hypermedia. Stored text and nontextual information with links between access points, allowing a transfer from one item to another in the file. May be a mixture of text, images, and sounds.

Hypertext. Stored text with links between access points, allowing a transfer from one document to another.

IASC/SCAD. Indexing and Abstracting Society of Canada/Société canadienne pour l'analyse des documents.

Identifier. A proper name of a person, institution, place, object, operation, or process.

Indented Layout. A form of display in which multilevel headings in an entry have each new subheading and sub-subheading beginning on a new line, progressively shifted to the right under the main headings.

Index. A guide to the contents of a knowledge record. A systematic analysis of such records, arranged in an organized way. A list of bibliographic information arranged in order according to some specified datum such as author, subject, or topic keyword.

Indexable Material. The parts of a document that are actually analyzed and indexed.

Indexing Depth. The degree to which every facet and every aspect of the facets are covered. The number of headings or descriptors assigned per unit of text.

Indexing Language. Any vocabulary, controlled or uncontrolled, used for indexing, along with the rules of usage.

Indexing Rules. A set of guidelines used for indexing a document.

Indexing Syntax. The order and structural relationships of descriptors.

Indicative Abstract. An abstract that indicates the content of the original paper without data or comment.

Information. Facts told, read, or otherwise communicated, usually previously unknown to the recipient.

Information Retrieval. The techniques of storing and retrieving recorded knowledge. Specifically, it is the process of selecting bibliographic citations from databases, using a variety of access points, such as subjects or authors. The selected recall of recorded information.

Informative Abstract. An abstract that gives key data and procedures from the paper.

Internet. Interconnected networks appearing to be a single, worldwide network.

Keyword. A word from the natural language of a document that is considered significant for indexing.

Knowledge Record. A physical object that conveys information over time by symbols, sounds, or sights. It may be printed on paper, digitized on computer storage devices, imprinted on microforms, or chiseled on stone.

KWIC. Keyword in context. A type of automatic indexing in which the significant words in a string (usually a title) are rotated and displayed, surrounded by the other words in the string.

KWOC. Keyword out of context. A type of automatic indexing in which the significant words in a string (usually a title) are rotated and displayed in a column separate from the rest of the string.

Lead term. The first nonarticle term in a heading.

Lead-in term. A term that leads, by cross-references, to an authorized index term.

Links. The tying together, at the indexing stage, of related descriptors in order to avoid syntactical error.

Literary Warrant. In the construction of authority lists, this is the justification for including a word based on the frequency of its occurrence in documents.

Locator. That part of an index entry that leads to the actual information sought (e.g., page numbers).

Machine-readable. Data that has been converted into a form that can be directly put into a computer.

Machine Translation. The conversion of text from one language into another language by a computer.

Macrothesaurus. A thesaurus with general index terms to a broad field of knowledge.

Main Heading. The first heading in multilevel headings, followed by a subheading.

Microthesaurus. A thesaurus or part of a thesaurus with terms to a delimited field of knowledge.

Mission-oriented Abstract. An abstract aimed at an activity concerned with an application assignment, not necessarily confined to any particular subject discipline.

Mission-oriented Index. An index aimed at an activity concerned with an application assignment, not necessarily confined to any particular subject discipline.

Modifier. In a compound term, one or more components that narrow the focus and specificity of one of its subclasses.

Monographic Index. An index for a single document.

Multilevel Heading. A heading in an index that has subunits.

Narrower Term. In a hierarchical thesaurus, broader terms and narrower terms express relationships between class and subclass. A term in a class would refer to a subclass by indicating a narrower term.

Natural Language. The language used by humans.

NFAIS. National Federation of Abstracting and Information Services.

Nonpreferred Terms. Terms, often synonyms, that serve as lead-ins to preferred descriptors or headings by means of a cross-reference.

Notation. Symbols representing classes and subclasses in a classification scheme.

Numeric Indexes. Indexes to numeric data (e.g., tables of statistics).

Online. Working directly with a computer through a terminal.

Open-end Index. This is a continuing index compiled over time.

Permuted Index. The representation of terms in headings by making every possible combination of terms.

Pertinence. A document that satisfies the need of an individual user.

Post-coordinate Indexing. A type of indexing where searching terms are combined at the time of searching by the user.

Posting-Up. Assigning additional terms that are higher in the hierarchy in addition to assigning the specific term.

PRECIS. Preserved Context Index System. An index created by humans and computers. A human does the content analysis and tags terms, while the computer forms the string of index terms and generates the index. The index provides the user with the context of all major indexing words.

Precision. A quantitative ratio of the number of relevant documents retrieved to the total number of documents retrieved.

Pre-coordinate Indexing. A type of indexing where terms are combined prior to searching. The combinations are not under the control of the user.

Preferred Term. An index term related to an equivalent entry term.

Probabilistic Indexing. The use of weights, usually by computer algorithms, to estimate probability that a term will lead to the retrieval of a document.

Professional Abstractors. Individuals whose livelihood is full-time abstracting.

Proximity Operator. A searching device which specifies that two or more search terms fall within a stated distance relative to each other.

Qualifier. Words or phrases used to distinguish among homographs or to clarify meaning (e.g., *Base [military]*).

Query. A formal inquiry to an information retrieval file.

Recall. A quantitative ratio of the number of retrieved relevant documents to the total number of relevant documents in a collection.

Related Term. A semantically related term to another term, but not one that is hierarchically linked.

Relevance. The measure of the degree to which retrieved informational material satisfies the needs of the user.

Request-oriented Indexing. The indexing vocabulary is based on anticipated requests from users and the vocabulary that they use for making the requests.

Roles. The modification of descriptors at the indexing stage to show their meaning for that particular document in order to avoid syntactical errors.

Run-in Layout. Multilevel headings in an entry are arranged in a single paragraph indented under a main heading. Punctuation must be used to avoid confusion.

Scope Note. A short explanation on how to use a descriptor.

Search Strategy. A plan or method for systematically identifying useful data or documents in an information storage file.

See Also **Reference**. A reference to another term or heading that is broader or narrower in the hierarchy of terms.

See **Reference**. A reference from a nonpreferred term or heading to a term or heading that is to be used in its place.

Server. In a network system (e.g., the Web), the providing end of the information retrieval procedure.

Slanted Abstract. An abstract that is aimed at a mission-oriented activity, emphasizing selected material from the original documents.

Society of Indexers. Professional indexing society of the United Kingdom.

Specificity in Indexing. The degree to which a descriptor matches the exact meaning of the subject concept.

String Indexing. The creation of multilevel headings from individual index terms by computer algorithm. Index terms may be coded by facet or role. Important terms are put in the lead position.

Subheading. A secondary heading used to subdivide headings with many entries.

Subject Specialist Abstractors. Abstractors whose primary livelihood is in a subject area, but who contribute time to abstracting.

Surrogate. A stand-in or representation of a document's topics.

Term. A word or phrase used to represent the aboutness of a topic in a document.

Thesaurofacet. A combined thesaurus and facet classification that is linked by notation and that shows the principal hierarchies in the thesaurus section.

Thesaurus. An authority file of terms that shows the full scope of each term along with its relationship to broader terms, narrower terms, and related terms.

Uncontrolled Vocabulary. A list of terms derived directly from the text of a document.

URL. Universal Resource Locator.

Vocabulary Control. A list of terms agreed on for use in indexing, along with rules of use.

Weighting. Assigning a value on some kind of scale to descriptors in order to show their relative importance for a particular document.

World Wide Web. A hypermedia-based interface to the Internet.

Bibliography

Acton, Patricia. 1986. "Indexing Is Not Classifying—and Vice Versa." *Records Management Quarterly* 20 (July): 10–15.

Addison, E. R. 1991. "Large Scale Full Text Retrieval by Concept Indexing." In *12th National Online Meeting: Proceedings—1991: New York, May 7–9, 1991*. Medford, NJ: Learned Information: 5–15.

Agnew, Brent, et al. 1997. "Multi-media Indexing over the Web." In *Storage and Retrieval for Image and Video Databases V: 13–14 February, 1997, San Jose, California*. Bellingham, WA: International Society for Optical Engineering: 72–83.

Agosti, Maristella, and Smeaton, Alan F. 1996. *Information Retrieval and Hypertext*. Boston: Kluwer Academic.

Aitchison, Jean, and Gilchrist, Alan. 1987. *Thesaurus Construction: A Practical Manual*. 2nd ed. London: Aslib.

Ajiferuke, Isola, and Chu, Clara M. 1988. "Quality of Indexing in Online Databases: An Alternative Measure for a Term Discriminating Index." *Information Processing & Management* 24 (5): 599–601.

Allen, Dennis. "Indexing Gets Smart." 1995. *Byte.com.* (January) URL: http://www.byte.com/art/9501/sec4/art9.htm (accessed February 5, 2000).

Almind, Tomas C., and Ingwersen, Peter. 1997. "Informetric Analyses on the World Wide Web: Methodological Approaches to 'Webometrics.' " *Journal of Documentation* 53 (September): 404–426.

American Society of Indexers. "Indexing the Web." URL: http://www.asindexing.org/webndx.shtml (accessed February 2, 2000).

———. "Professional Organizations of Interest." URL: http://www.asindexing.org/orgpub.htm (accessed February 2, 2000).

———. "Reference Sources on the Internet." URL: http://www.asindexing.org/refbooks.shtml (accessed February 2, 2000).

Anderson, James D. 1988. "Back-of-the-book Indexing with the Nested Phrase Indexing System (NEPHIS)." *The Indexer* 16 (October): 79–84.

———. 1997. *Guidelines for Indexes and Related Information Retrieval Devices: A Technical Report.* Bethesda, MD: NISO Press.

———. 1985. "Indexing Systems: Extensions of the Mind's Organizing Power." In *Information and Behavior. Volume 1.* Edited by Brent D. Ruben. New Brunswick, NJ: Transaction Books: 287–323.

Anderson, James D., and Rowley, Frederick A. 1992. "Building End-User Thesauri from Full-Text." In *Advances in Classification Research. Proceedings of the 2nd ASIS SIG/CR Classification Research Workshop, Held at the 54th ASIS Annual Meeting, Washington, D.C., October 27–31, 1991. Volume 2.* Medford, NJ: Learned Information, Inc. for the American Society for Information Science: 1–13.

Anderson, Margaret Dampier. 1985. *Book Indexing.* rev. ed. Cambridge, MA: Cambridge University Press.

Anglo-American Cataloging Rules, North American Text. 1967. Prepared by the American Library Association, The Library of Congress, the (British) Library Association, and the Canadian Library Association. Chicago: American Library Association.

Arents, Hans C., and Bogaerts, Walter. 1996. "Concept-based Indexing and Retrieval of Hypermedia Information." In *Encyclopedia of Library and Information Science. Volume 58, Supplement 21.* New York: Marcel Dekker: 1–29.

ASIS Thesaurus of Information Science and Librarianship. 1998. 2nd ed. Jessica L. Milstead, editor. Medford, NJ: Information Today, Inc.

Austin, Derek. 1984. *PRECIS: A Manual of Concept Analysis and Subject Indexing.* 2nd ed. London: British Library.

Bakewell, Kenneth G. B. 1987. "Reference Books for Indexers." *The Indexer* 15 (April): 131–140.

Bates, Marcia J. 1998. "Indexing and Access for Digital Libraries and the Internet: Human, Database, and Domain Actors." *Journal of the American Society for Information Science* 49 (November): 1185–1205.

———. 1977. "System Meets User: Problems in Matching Subject Search Terms." *Information Processing and Management* 13 (6): 367–375.

Bates, Marcia J., Wilde, Deborah N., and Siegfried, Susan L. 1993. "An Analysis of Search Terminology Used by Humanities Scholars: The Getty Online Searching Project Report No. 1." *Library Quarterly* 63 (January): 1–39.

Batty, C. D. 1989. "Thesaurus Construction and Maintenance: A Survival Kit." *Database* 12 (February): 13–20.

Beghtol, Clare. 1986. "Bibliographic Classification Theory and Text Linguistics: Aboutness Analysis, Inter-textuality and the Cognitive Act of Classifying Documents." *Journal of Documentation* 42 (June): 84–113.

Belkin, Nicholas J. 1980. "Anomalous States of Knowledge as a Basis for Information Retrieval." *Canadian Journal of Information Science* 5 (May): 133–143.

Bell, Hazel K. 1991. "Bias in Indexing and Loaded Language." *The Indexer* 17 (April): 173–177.

———. 1997. "History of Indexing Societies: Part I: SI: The First Ten Years." *The Indexer* 20 (April): 160–164.

———. 1998. "History of Indexing Societies: Part III: Societies of Indexers 1968–1977." *The Indexer* 21 (April): 33–36.

———. 1997. "History of Societies of Indexers: Part II: Three Affiliations." *The Indexer* 20 (October): 212–215.

Bellardo, Trudi. 1991. *Subject Indexing: An Introductory Guide.* Washington, DC: Special Libraries Association.

Bertrand, Annick, and Cellier, Jean-Marie. 1995. "Psychological Approach to Indexing: Effects of the Operators' Expertise upon Indexing Behavior." *Journal of Information Science* 21 (6): 459–472.

Besser, Howard. 1997. "Image Databases: The First Decade, the Present, and the Future." In *Digital Image Access & Retrieval.* Edited by P. B. Heidord and B. Sandore. Urbana-Champaign, IL: University of Illinois Graduate School of Library and Information Science: 11–28.

Bishop, Ann Peterson. 1990. "Index Quality Study, Part I: Quantitative Description of Back-of-the-book Indexes." In *Indexing Tradition and Innovation.* Chicago, IL: American Society of Indexers: 15–51.

Blair, David C. 1986. "Full Text Retrieval: Evaluation and Implications." *International Classification* 13 (1): 18–23.

———. 1990. *Language and Representation in Information Retrieval.* New York: Elsevier.

Blair, David C., and Maron, M. E. 1985. "An Evaluation of Retrieval Effectiveness for a Full-Text Document-Retrieval System." *Communications of the ACM* 28 (March): 289–299.

Blake, Doreen. 1990. "Indexing Medical Journals." *The Indexer* 17 (April): 33–34.

Bland, J. 1995. *Automatic Indexing in the Humanities: Full Text Versus Titles and Abstracts.* Thesis (MSLS), University of North Carolina, Chapel Hill.

Booth, Pat F. 1997. "Good Practice in Indexing: The New Edition of International Standard ISO 999." *The Indexer* 20 (April): 114.

———. 1987. "Thesauri: Their Uses for Indexers." *The Indexer* 15 (April): 141–144.

Bordogan, Gloria, Carrara, P., and Gagliardi, I. 1990. "Pictorial Indexing for an Integrated Pictorial and Textural IR Environment." *Journal of Information Science* 16 (3): 165–173.

Borgman, Christine. 1986. "Why Are Online Catalogs Hard to Use? Lessons Learned from Information-Retrieval Studies." *Journal of the American Society for Information Science* 37 (November): 387–400.

Borko, Harold, and Bernier, Charles L. 1975. *Abstracting Concepts and Methods*. New York: Academic Press.

———. 1978. *Indexing Concepts and Methods*. New York: Academic Press.

Bower, James M. 1993. "Vocabulary Control and the Virtual Database." *Knowledge Organization* 20 (1): 4–7.

Boyce, Bert R., and McLain, John P. 1989. "Entry Point Depth and Online Search Using a Controlled Vocabulary." *Journal of the American Society for Information Science* 40 (July): 273–276.

Bradley, Phillip. 1989. "Indexes to Works of Fiction: The Views of Producers and Users on the Need for Them." *The Indexer* 16 (October): 239–248.

Browne, Glenda. 1996. "Automatic Indexing and Abstracting." *LASIE* 27 (September): 58–65.

Buckland, Michael, and Gey, Fredric. 1994. "The Relationship Between Recall and Precision." *Journal of the American Society for Information Science* 45 (January): 12–19.

Buckland, Michael, Norgard, Barbara, and Plaunt, Christian. 1993. "Filing, Filtering, and the First Few Found." *Information Technology and Libraries* 12 (September): 311–320.

Burgin, Robert. 1991. "The Effect of Indexing Exhaustivity on Retrieval Performance." *Information Processing & Management* 27 (6): 623–628.

Burke, Robin, et al. 1997. "Intelligent Web Search Engines." *PC AI* 11 (January/February): 39–42.

Carey, Gordon Vero. 1963. *Making an Index*. 3rd ed. Cambridge, MA: Cambridge University Press.

Cawkell, A. E. 1994. *A Guide to Image Processing and Picture Management*. Brookfield, VT: Gower.

Chan, Lois Mai. 1989. "Inter-indexer Consistency in Subject Cataloging." *Information Technology & Libraries* 8 (December): 349–357.

———. 1988. *Thesauri Used in Online Databases: An Analytical Guide*. Westport, CT: Greenwood Press.

Chan, Lois Mai, Richmond, Phyllis A., and Svenonius, Elaine F., eds. 1985. *Theory of Subject Analysis: A Sourcebook*. Littleton, CO: Libraries Unlimited.

Chandler, Helen E., and Roper, Vincent de P. 1991. "Citation Indexing: Uses and Limitations." *The Indexer* 17 (October): 243–249.

Chicago Manual of Style, The. 14th ed. 1994. Chicago: University of Chicago Press.

Chu, Clara M., and Ajiferuke, Isola. 1989. "Quality of Indexing in Library and Information Science Databases." *Online Review* 13 (February): 11–35.

Chu, Clara M., and O'Brien, Ann. 1993. "Subject Analysis: The Critical First Stage in Indexing." *Journal of Information Science* 19 (6): 439–445.

Chu, Heting, and Rosenthal, Marilyn. 1996. "Search Engines for the World Wide Web: A Comparative Study and Evaluation Methodology." In *Proceedings of the 59th ASIS Annual Meeting. Volume 33*. Medford, NJ: Information Today, Inc. for the American Society for Information Science: 127–135.

Cleveland, Donald B. 1962. *An Analysis of Texas Local History Theses, Accepted by the University of Texas from 1909 through 1952, to Determine the Extent and Character of Usage Made of Newspapers as Sources*. Unpublished Master's Thesis, University of Texas, Austin.

———. 1992. *Cartooning for the Librarian*. New York: Neal-Shuman.

Cleveland, Donald B., and Cleveland, Ana D. 1983. "Depth of Indexing Using a Non-Boolean Searching Model." In *International Forum on Information and Documentation. Volume 8*. The Hague, Netherlands: International Federation for Documentation: 10–13.

Cleverdon, Cyril W. 1972. "On the Inverse Relationship of Recall and Precision." *Journal of Documentation* 28 (September): 195–201.

Collison, Robert Lewis. 1972. *Indexes and Indexing*. 4th ed. London: Benn.

Cousins, Garry. 1996. "Conceptual Indexing for CD-ROMs: Beyond Free Text Searching." *LASIE* 27 (September): 45–49.

Cousins, Shirley Anne. 1992. "Enhancing Subject Access to OPACs: Controlled Vocabulary vs. Natural Language." *Journal of Documentation* 48 (September): 291–309.

Cowie, Jim, and Lehnert, W. 1996. "Information Extraction." *Communications of the ACM* 39 (January): 80–91.

Craven, Timothy C. 1996. "An Experiment in the Use of Tools for Computer-assisted Abstracting." In *Proceedings of the 59th ASIS Annual Meeting. Volume 33*. Medford, NJ: Information Today, Inc. for the American Society for Information Science: 203–208.

———. 1986. *String Indexing*. Orlando, FL: Academic Press.

———. 1990. "Use of Words and Phrases from Full Text in Abstracts." *Journal of Information Science* 16 (6): 351–358.

Cremmins, Edward T. 1996. *The Art of Abstracting*. 2nd ed. Arlington, VA: Information Resources Press.

Cross, James, and McCurley, Marsha. 1994. "Clemson University Thurmond Speeches Series Indexing Project." *The American Archivist* 57 (Spring): 352–363.

Crystal, David. 1984. "Linguistics and Indexing." *The Indexer* 14 (April): 3–7.

Cunningham, Ann Marie, and Wicks, Wendy. 1992. *Guide to Careers in Abstracting and Indexing*. Philadelphia, PA: National Federation of Abstracting and Information Services.

Cutler, Anne G. 1970. *Indexing Methods and Theory*. Baltimore: Williams & Wilkins.

Davis, Roy, and James, Brian. 1984. "Toward an Expert System for Cataloguing: Some Experiments Based on AACR2." *Program* 18: 283-297.

David, Claire. 1995. "Indexing as Problem Solving: A Cognitive Approach to Consistency." In *Proceedings of the 58th ASIS Annual Meeting. Volume 32.* Medford, NJ: Information Today, Inc. for the American Society for Information Science: 49–55.

Demas, Samuel, McDonald, Peter, and Lawrence, Gregory. 1995. "The Internet and Collection Development: Mainstreaming Selection of Internet Resources." *Library Resources & Technical Services* 39 (July): 275–290.

Dempsey, Lorcan, and Heery, Rachel M. 1998. "Metadata: A Current View of Practice and Issues." *Journal of Documentation* 54 (March): 145–172.

Desai, Bipin C. 1997. "Supporting Discovery in Virtual Libraries." *Journal of the American Society for Information Science* 48 (March): 190–240.

Ding, Wie, and Marchionini, Gary. 1996. "A Comparative Study of Web Search Service Performance." In *Proceedings of the 59th ASIS Annual Meeting. Volume 33.* Medford, NJ: Information Today, Inc. for the American Society for Information Science: 136–142.

Diodato, Virgil P. 1994. "User Preferences for Features in Back of Book Indexes." *Journal of the American Society for Information Science* 45 (August): 529–536.

Diodato, Virgil P., and Gandt, Gretchen. 1991. "Back of Book Indexes and the Characteristics of Author and Nonauthor Indexing: Report of an Exploratory Study." *Journal of the American Society for Information Science* 42 (June): 341–350.

Diodato, Virgil P., and Henry, Georgianna. 1993. "The Rates of Assignment of Narrower Terms in the Thesaurus of ERIC Descriptors." *Journal of Information Science* 19 (2): 137–141.

Directory of Indexing and Abstracting Courses and Seminars. 1992. Port Aransas, TX: American Society of Indexers.

Dixon, Yvonne. 1996. "Indexing for Children." *The Indexer* 20 (April): 8–10.

Dong, Xiaoying, and Su, Louise T. 1997. "Search Engines on the World Wide Web and Information Retrieval from the Internet: A Review and Evaluation." *Online & CD-ROM Review* 21 (April): 67–81.

Dooley, Jackie M. 1992. "Subject Indexing in Context." *The American Archivist* 55 (Spring): 344–354.

"Dow Jones Unveils Knowledge Indexing System." 1997. *Advanced Technology/ Libraries* 26 (5): 2–3.

Dubois, C. P. R. 1987. "Free Text vs. Controlled Vocabulary: A Reassessment." *Online Review* 11 (August): 243–253.

Dunn, Ronald G. 1995. "Angst and Anticipation: How Will Traditional Information Services Fit in the New Information Age?" *The Indexer* 19 (April): 184–188.

Dutta, S., and Sinha, P. K. 1984. "Pragmatic Approach to Subject Indexing: A New Concept." *Journal of the American Society for Information Science* 35 (November): 325–331.

Eldredge, Jonathan D. 1993. "Accuracy of Indexing Coverage Information as Reported by Serials Sources." *Bulletin of the Medical Library Association* 81 (October): 364–370.

Ellis, David, and Ford, Nigel. 1998. "In Search of the Unknown User: Indexing, Hypertext, and the World Wide Web." *Journal of Documentation* 54 (January): 28–47.

Ellis, David, Furner, Jonathan, and Willett, Peter. 1994. "On the Creation of Hypertext Links in Full-Text Documents: Measurement of Inter-linker Consistency." *Journal of Documentation* 50 (June): 67–98.

Enser, Peter G. B. 1995. "Progress in Documentation Pictorial Information Retrieval." *Journal of Documentation* 51 (June): 126–170.

Etzioni, Oren. 1996. "The World Wide Web: Quagmire or Gold Mine?" *Communications of the ACM* 39 (November): 65–68.

"Evaluating Information Found on the Internet." URL: http://milton.mse.jhu.edu:8001/research/education/net.html (accessed February 5, 2000).

Falk, Howard. 1997. "World Wide Web Search and Retrieval." *Electronic Library* 15 (February): 49–55.

Farrow, John F. 1991. "A Cognitive Process Model of Document Indexing." *Journal of Documentation* 47 (June): 149–166.

———. 1995. "All in the Mind: Concept Analysis Indexing." *The Indexer* 19 (October): 243–247.

Fattahi, Rahmatollah. 1998. "Library Cataloguing and Abstracting and Indexing Services: Reconciliation of Principles in the Online Environment?" *Library Review* 47 (4): 211–216.

Feinberg, Hilda, ed. 1983. *Indexing Specialized Formats and Subjects*. Metuchen, NJ: Scarecrow Press.

Fetters, Linda K. 1995. *A Guide to Indexing Software*. 5th ed. Port Aransas, TX: American Society of Indexers.

———. 1999. *Handbook of Indexing Techniques: A Guide for Beginning Indexers*. 2nd ed. Corpus Christie, TX: FimCo Books.

Fidel, Raya. 1994. "User-Centered Indexing." *Journal of the American Society for Information Science* 45 (September): 572–576.

———. 1992. "Who Needs Controlled Vocabulary?" *Special Libraries* 83 (Winter): 1–9.

———. 1986. "Writing Abstracts for Free-Text Searching." *Journal of Documentation* 42 (March): 11–21.

Fidel, Raya, and others, eds. 1994. *Challenges in Indexing Electronic Text and Images*. Medford, NJ: Learned Information.

Forrester, Michael A. 1993. "Hypermedia and Indexing: Identifying Appropriate Models from User Studies." In *Online Information*. Medford, NJ: Learned Information: 313–324.

———. 1995. "Indexing in Hypertext Environments: The Role of User Models." *The Indexer* 19 (October): 249–256.

Fox, Edward Alan, et al. 1988. "Building a Large Thesaurus for Information Retrieval." In *Second Conference on Applied Natural Language Processing: Association for Computational Linguistics: Proceedings of the Conference: 9–12 February 1988, Austin-Marriott at the Capital, Austin, Texas, USA*. Morristown, NJ: Association for Computational Linguistics: 101–108.

Frame, Andrea. 1996. "Indexers and Publishers: Their Views on Indexers and Indexing." *The Indexer* 20 (October): 58–63.

———. 1997. "Indexers and Publishers: Their Views on Indexers and Indexing, Part 2." *The Indexer* 20 (April): 131–134.

Frohmann, Bernard. 1990. "Rules of Indexing: A Critique of Mentalism in Information Retrieval Theory." *Journal of Documentation* 46 (June): 81–101.

Froom, P., and Froom, J. 1993. "Deficiencies in Structured Medical Abstracts." *Journal of Clinical Epidemiology* 46 (July): 591–594.

Fugmann, Robert. 1983. *The Analytico-Synthetic Foundation for Large Indexing & Information Retrieval Systems*. Bangalore, India: Sarada Ranganathan Endowment for Library Science.

———. 1982. "The Complementarity of Natural and Indexing Languages." *International Classification* 9 (3): 140–144.

———. 1992. "Illusory Goals in Information Science Research." In *Classification Research for Knowledge Representation and Organization, Proceedings of the 5th International Study Conference on Classification Research, Toronto, Canada, June 24–28, 1991*. Amsterdam: Elsevier: 61–68.

———. 1995. *Subject Analysis and Indexing: Theoretical Foundation and Practical Advice*. Frankfurt am Main: Indeks Verlag.

Gaizauskas, Robert, and Wilks, Yorick. 1998. "Information Extraction: Beyond Document Retrieval." *Journal of Documentation* 54 (January): 70–105.

Garfield, Eugene. 1979. *Citation Indexing: Its Theory and Application in Science, Technology and Humanities*. New York: John Wiley & Sons.

Gerhard, Kristin Heidi, Jacobson, Trudi, and Williamson, Susan. 1993. "Indexing Adequacy and Interdisciplinary Journals: The Case of Women's Studies." *College & Research Libraries* 54 (March) 125–136.

Gibson, J. 1983. "The Indexing of Medical Books and Journals." *The Indexer* 13 (April): 173–175.

Green, Rebecca. 1997. "The Role of Relational Structures in Indexing for the Humanities." *Knowledge Organization* 24 (2): 72–83.

Grefenstette, Gregory. 1994. *Explorations in Automatic Thesaurus Discovery.* Boston: Kluwer Academic.

Harman, Donna. 1997. "The TREC Conferences." In *Readings in Information Retrieval.* Edited by K. Sparck Jones and P. Willet. San Francisco: Morgan Kaufan: 247–256.

Harrod, Leonard M., ed. 1978. *Indexers on Indexing: A Selection of Articles Published in* The Indexer. New York: Bowker.

Hartley, James. 1994. "Three Ways to Improve the Clarity of Journal Abstracts." *British Journal of Educational Psychology* 64 (2): 331–343.

Hartley, James, and Sydes, Matthew. 1996. "Which Layout Do You Prefer? An Analysis of Readers' Preferences for Different Typographic Layouts of Structured Abstracts." *Journal of Information Science* 22 (1): 27–37.

Hartley, James, Sydes, Matthew, and Blurton, Anthony. 1996. "Obtaining Information Accurately and Quickly: Are Structured Abstracts More Efficient?" *Journal of Information Science* 22 (5): 349–356.

Hersh, William R., et al. 1993. "Words Concepts or Both: Optimal Indexing Units for Automated Information Retrieval." In *Sixteenth Annual Symposium on Computer Applications in Medical Care.* New York: McGraw Hill: 644–648.

Hodge, Gail M. 1992. *Automated Support to Indexing.* Philadelphia: National Federation of Abstracting and Information Services.

———. 1994. "Computer-assisted Database Indexing: The State-of-the-Art." *The Indexer* 19 (April): 23–27.

Hodge, Gail M., and Milsted, Jessica L. 1998. *Computer Support to Indexing.* Philadelphia: National Federation of Abstracting and Information Services.

Holmes, Olive. 1993. "Cards to Keyboard: Indexing by Computer." *Scholarly Publishing* 24 (January): 113–117.

Holmstrom, J. 1965. "The Indexing of Scientific Books." *The Indexer* 4 (Autumn): 123–131.

Humphrey, Susanne M. "Evolution Toward Knowledge-based Indexing for Information Retrieval." In *Advances in Classification Research. Proceedings of the 2nd ASIS SIG/CR Classification Research Workshop, Held at the 54th ASIS Annual Meeting, Washington, D.C., October 27–31, 1991. Volume 2.* Medford, NJ: Learned Information, Inc. for the American Society for Information Science: 53–63.

Hutchins, W. J. "The Concept of 'Aboutness' in Subject Indexing." *Aslib Proceedings* 30 (5): 172–181.

Indexing Research. 1998. "Choosing Indexing Software." URL: http://www.indexres.com/choosing.html (accessed February 2, 2000).

Intner, Sheila S. 1984. "Censorship in Indexing." *The Indexer* 14 (October): 105–108.

Jermey, Jonathan, and Browne, Glenda. 1996. "Indexing: The Ideal Cottage Industry." *LIBRES: Library and Information Science Research Electronic Journal* 6 (June). URL: http://www.curtin.edu.au:80/curtain/dept/sils/libres/libre6n1/browne.htm (accessed February 2, 2000).

Jones, Kevin P. 1986. "Getting Started in Computerized Indexing." *The Indexer* 15 (April): 9–13.

———. 1983. "How Do We Index? A Report of Some Aslib Informatics Group Activity." *Aslib* 39 (March): 1–23.

———. 1990. "Natural-Language Processing and Automatic Indexing: A Reply." *The Indexer* 17 (October): 114–115.

Jorgensen, Corinne Lyon, and Liddy, Elizabeth. 1996. "Information Access or Information Anxiety? An Exploratory Evaluation of Book Index Features." *The Indexer* 20 (October): 64–68.

Jul, Erik. 1997. "Cataloging Internet Resources: Survey and Prospectus." *Bulletin of the American Society for Information Science* 24 (October/November): 6–9.

Kilcullen, Maureen. 1997. "Publishing a Newspaper Index on the World Wide Web Using Microsoft Access 97." *The Indexer* 20 (October): 195–196.

Kilcullen, Maureen, and Spohn, Melissa. 1996. "Indexing a Local Newspaper Using Dbase IV." *The Indexer* 20 (April): 16–17.

Kilgour, Frederick G. 1993. "The Metamorphosis of Libraries During the Foreseeable Future." In *Libraries and the Future: Essays on the Library in the Twenty-First Century*. Edited by F. W. Lancaster. New York: Haworth Press: 131–146.

King, Donald Ward. 1998. "Some Economic Aspects of the Internet." *Journal of the American Society for Information Science* 49 (September): 990–1002.

Kleinberg, Ira. 1997. "For Want of an Alphabetical Index." *The Indexer* 20 (April): 156–159.

Knight, G. Norman. 1979. *Indexing, the Art of: A Guide to the Indexing of Books and Periodicals*. London: George Allen & Unwin Ltd.

Korycinski, Chris, and Newell, Alan F. 1990. "Natural-Language Processing and Automatic Indexing." *The Indexer* 17 (April): 21–29.

Lancaster, F. W. 1998. *Indexing and Abstracting in Theory and Practice*. 2nd ed. Champaign, IL: University of Illinois.

———. 1986. *Vocabulary Control for Information Retrieval*. 2nd ed. Arlington, VA: Information Resource Press.

Langridge, Derek Wilton. 1989. *Subject Analysis: Principles and Procedures*. London: Bowker-Saur.

Lathrop, Lori. 1998. "Indexing After the Millennium 2—Existing Skills Influence Future Development." *The Indexer* 21 (April): 20–21.

Layne, Sara Shatford. 1986. "Analyzing the Subject of a Picture: A Theoretical Approach." *Cataloging & Classification Quarterly* 6 (Spring): 39–62.

———. 1994. "Some Issues in the Indexing of Images." *Journal of the American Society for Information Science* 45 (September): 583–588.

Leach, Anne, ed. 1998. *Marketing Your Indexing Services*. Medford, NJ: American Society of Indexers.

Leung, Chi-Hong C., Hibler, D., and Mwara, N. 1992. "Picture Retrieval by Content Description." *Journal of Information Science* 18 (2): 111–119.

Lopez-Hertas, Maria J. 1997. "Thesaurus Structure Design: A Conceptual Approach for Improved Interaction." *Journal of Documentation* 53 (March): 139–177.

Luhn, H. P. 1958. "The Automatic Creation of Literature Abstracts." *IBM Journal of Research and Development* 2: 159-165.

MacCall, Steven. 1998. "Fundamentals of the Information Sciences." URL: http://www.bama.ua.edu/ ~ smaccall/courses/summer1998/ls561/bibliography.html (accessed February 5, 2000).

MacDougall, Susan. 1996. "Rethinking Indexing: The Impact of the Internet." *Australian Library Journal* 45 (November): 281–285.

Mallory, Michael, and Moran, Gordon. 1994. "Scholarly Search for the Truth and Problems Associated with Indexing/Abstracting." *The Indexer* 19 (October): 99–101.

Maron, M. E. 1977. "On Indexing, Retrieval and the Meaning of About." *Journal of the American Society for Information Science* 28 (1): 38–43.

Matthews, Paula L., and Bakewell, Kenneth G. B. 1997. "Indexes to Children's Information Books." *The Indexer* 20 (October): 193–194.

McJunkin, Monica Cahill. 1995. "Precision and Recall in Title Keyword Searching." *Information Technology and Libraries* 14 (September): 161–171.

Meadow, Charles T. 1998. *Text Information Retrieval Systems*. San Diego, CA: Academic Press.

Menzel, W. 1841. "German Periodicals: A Translation from the Deutsche Viertelhahrs Schrift, *American Eclectic* 2: 13.

Miller, Elizabeth. 1995. "A Comparison of the Academic Index on CD-ROM with Four Wilson Indexes on the OPAC." *Online & CD-ROM Review* 19 (August): 207–210.

Milstead, Jessica L. 1984. *Subject Access Systems: Alternatives in Design*. Orlando, FL: Academic Press.

———. 1993. "Thesaurus Management Software." In *Encyclopedia of Library and Information Science. Volume 51, Supplement 14*. New York: Dekker: 389–407.

Moen, William E. 1998. "Accessing Distributed Cultural Heritage Information." *Communications of the ACM* 41 (April): 45–48.

Moys, Elizabeth, et al. 1993. *Indexing Legal Materials*. London: Society of Indexers.

Mulvancy, Nancy C. 1994. "Embedded Indexing Software: Users Speak Out." In *The Changing Landscapes of Indexing: The Proceedings of the 26th Annual Meeting of the American Society of Indexers, San Diego, California, May 13–14, 1999*. Port Aransas, TX: American Society of Indexers: 41–47.

———. 1994. *Indexing Books*. Chicago: University of Chicago Press.

———. 1999. "Software Tools for Indexing: Revisited." *The Indexer* 21 (October): 160–163.

———. 1990. "Software Tools for Indexing: What We Need." *The Indexer* 17 (October): 108–113.

———. 1993. *Tips for Book Indexers*. Chicago: University of Chicago Press.

Notess, Greg R. 2000. "Multiple Search Engines." URL: http://www.notess.com/search/multi/ (accessed February 2, 2000).

O'Connor, Brian C. 1996. *Exploration in Indexing and Abstracting: Pointing, Virtue, and Power*. Englewood, CO: Libraries Unlimited.

Odini, Cephas. 1997. "The Performance of Manual Indexes and Online Databases in Information Retrieval." *OCLC Systems and Services* 13 (1): 21–24.

Ornager, Susanne. 1994. "The Image Database: A Need for Innovative Indexing and Retrieval." In *Knowledge Organization and Quality Management, Advances in Knowledge Organization. Volume 4*. Frankfurt am Main: Indeks Verlag: 208–216.

Owen, P. 1994. "Structured for Success: The Continuing Role of Quality Indexing in Intelligent Information Retrieval Systems." In *Online Information*. Medford, NJ: Learned Information: 227–231.

Peek, Robin P. 1998. "Will Abstracting-and-Indexing Services Become Passe?" *Information Today* 15 (March): 46.

Pereira, Fernando, N. C., and Grosz, Barbara J. 1994. *Natural Language Processing*. Cambridge, MA: MIT Press.

Peterson, Candace. 1994. "Newspaper Indexing." In *Managing Large Indexing Projects*. Port Aransas, TX: American Society of Indexers: 11–14.

Pfaffenberger, Bryan. 1996. *Web Search Strategies*. New York: MIS Press.

Piggott, Mary. 1991. "Authors as Their Own Indexers." *The Indexer* 17 (April): 161–166.

Pinkerton, Brian. "Finding What People Want: Experiences with the WebCrawler." URL: http://info.webcrawler.com/signidr/WCOverview.html (accessed February 2, 2000).

Pollock, Annabel, and Hockley, Andrew. 1997. "What's Wrong with Internet Searching." *D-Lib Magazine* (March) URL: http://www.dlib.org/dlib/march97/bt/03pollock.html (accessed February 5, 2000).

Prasher, Ram Gopal. 1981. *Indexing and Indexing Systems.* New Delhi: Medallion Press.

Pritchard, Alan. 1969. "Statistical Bibliography or Bibliometrics?" *Journal of Documentation* 24 (4): 348-349.

Quinn, Brian A. 1994. "Recent Theoretical Approaches in Classification and Indexing." *Knowledge Organization* 21 (3): 140–147.

Ralston, Nancy M. 1995. "Controlled Vocabularies for MEDLARS Databases." *Medical Reference Services Quarterly* 14 (Summer): 25–34.

Rasmussen, Edie M. 1997. "Indexing Images." In *Annual Review of Information Science and Technology. Volume 32.* Medford, NJ: Information Today: 169–196.

Ridehalgh, Nan. 1985. "The Design of Indexes." *The Indexer* 14 (April): 165–174.

Rorvig, Mark E. 1999. "A Visual Exploration of the Orderliness of TREC Relevance Judgments." *Journal of the American Society for Information Science* 50 (August): 652–660.

Rowley, Jennifer E. 1994. "The Controlled vs. Natural Indexing Languages Debate Revisited: A Perspective on Information Retrieval Practice and Research." *Journal of Information Science* 20 (2): 108–119.

Salton, Gerald. 1989. *A Syntactic Approach to Automatic Book Indexing.* Technical Report TR 89–979. Ithaca, NY: Department of Computer Science, Cornell University.

Saracevic, Tefko. 1991. "Individual Differences in Organizing, Searching and Retrieving Information." In *Advances in Classification Research. Proceedings of the 2nd ASIS SIG/CR Classification Research Workshop, Held at the 54th ASIS Annual Meeting, Washington, D.C., October 27–31, 1991. Volume 2.* Medford, NJ: Learned Information, Inc. for the American Society for Information Science: 82–86.

Scales, B. Jane, and Felt, Elizabeth Caulfield. 1995. "Diversity on the World Wide Web: Using Robots to Search the Web." *Library Software Review* 14 (Fall): 132–136.

Schuegraf, Ernst J., and van Bommel, Martin F. 1993. "An Automatic Document Indexing System Based on Cooperating Expert Systems: Design and Development." *The Canadian Journal of Information and Library Science* 18 (July): 32–50.

Schuyler, Peri L., Hole, William T., and Tuttle, Mark S. 1993. "The UMLS Metathesaurus: Representing Different Views of Biomedical Concepts." *Bulletin of the Medical Library Association* 81 (April): 217–222.

Shannon, Claude E., and Weaver, Warren. 1949. *The Mathematical Theory of Communication.* Urbana: University of Illinois.

Shaw, W. M., Jr. 1990. "Subject Indexing and Citation Indexing." *Information Processing & Management* 26 (6): 693–718.

Sievert, M., and McKinin, E. J. 1989. "Why Full-Text Misses Some Relevant Documents: An Analysis of Documents Not Retrieved by CCML or MEDIS." In *Proceedings of the American Society of Information Science. Volume 26.* Medford, NJ: Learned Information: 34–39.

Silvester, June P., Genuardi, Michael T., and Klingbiel, Paul H. 1994. "Machine-aided Indexing at NASA." *Information Processing & Management* 30 (September): 631–645.

Simpkins, Jean. 1990. "How the Publishers Want It to Look." *The Indexer* 17 (April): 41–42.

Slott, M. 1995–1996. "Web Matrix: What's the Difference?" URL: http://www.ambrosiasw.com/ ~ fprefect/matrix/answers.html (accessed February 5, 2000).

Soergel, Dagobert. 1974. *Indexing Languages and Thesauri: Construction and Maintenance.* Los Angeles: Melville Publishing Co.

Sparck Jones, Karen. 1973. "Does Indexing Exhaustivity Matter?" *Journal of the American Society for Information Science* 24 (September/October): 313–316.

Spence, M. 1993. "How to Get Clients." *Key Words* 1 (4): 4–7, 21.

Stanley, Janet. 1995. "Reference Librarian as Cataloger: Analytical Indexing as Front-end Reference." *Art Documentation* 14 (Winter): 7–9.

Starting an Indexing Business. 1994. Port Aransas, TX: American Society of Indexers.

Stone, Alva Theresa. 1993. "That Elusive Concept of 'Aboutness': The Year's Work in Subject Analysis, 1992." *Library Research and Technical Services* 37 (July): 277–298.

Sturr, Natalie Oakes. 1995. "WAIS: An Internet Tool for Full-Text Indexing." *Computers in Libraries* 15 (June): 52–54.

Sullivan Danny. 1996. "How Search Engines Work." Mecklermedia. URL: http://www.searchenginewatch.com/webmasters/work.html (accessed February 5, 2000).

Swanson, D. R. 1960. "Searching Natural Language Text by Computer." *Science* 132 (October): 960–1104.

Swift, D. F., et al. 1978. " 'Aboutness' as a Strategy for Retrieval in the Social Sciences." *Aslib Proceedings* 30: 182–187.

Takishita, Faith. 1997. "Constructing an Electronic Library Web Page." *The Indexer* 20 (April): 125–126.

Tessier, Judith A. 1991. "Hypertext Linking as a Model of Expert Indexing." In *Advances in Classification Research. Proceedings of the 2nd ASIS SIG/CR Classification Research Workshop, Held at the 54th ASIS Annual Meeting, Washington, D.C., October 2–31, 1991. Volume 2.* Medford, NJ: Learned Information, Inc. for the American Society for Information Science: 171–178.

Text REtrieval Conference (TREC). URL: http://trec.nist.gov/ (accessed February 5, 2000).

Tibbo, Helen R. 1992. "Abstracting Across the Disciplines: A Content Analysis of Abstracts from the Natural Sciences, the Social Sciences, and the Humanities with Implications for Abstracting Standards and Online Information Retrieval." *Library and Information Science Research* 14 (January-March): 31–56.

———. 1994. "Indexing for the Humanities." *Journal of the American Society for Information Science* 45 (September): 607–619.

Tillman, Hope. 1995–1998. "Evaluating Quality on the Net." URL: http://www.tiac.net/users/hope/findqual.html (accessed February 2, 2000).

Tillotson, Joy. 1995. "Is Keyword Searching the Answer?" *College & Research Libraries* 56 (May): 199–206.

Torre, Diane S. 1995. "KRS: Keywording for Subject Retrieval." *Art Documentation* 14 (Summer): 29–35.

University of Albany Libraries. "How to Choose a Search Engine or Research Database." URL: http://www.albany.edu/library/internet/choose.html (accessed February 2, 2000).

Urdang, Laurence. 1995. "Indexing a Periodical: Verbatim." *The Indexer* 19 (April): 203–204.

Venditto, Gus. 1996. "Search Engine Showdown." *Internet World* 7 (May): 64–67.

Voorbij, Henk J. 1998. "Title Keywords and Subject Descriptors: A Comparison of Subject Search Entries of Books in the Humanities and Social Sciences." *Journal of Documentation* 54 (September): 466–476.

Walker, Dwight. 1998. "Web Indexing Prize 1997." *The Indexer* 21 (April): 15–18.

Wayne, Jean M. 1955. *Indexing with Emphasis on Its Technique: An Annotated Bibliography*. New York: Special Libraries Association.

Weinberg, Bella Hass. 1996. "Complexity in Indexing Systems—Abandonment and Failure: Implications for Organizing the Internet." In *Proceedings of the 59th ASIS Annual Meeting. Volume 33*. Medford, NJ: Information Today, Inc. for the American Society for Information Science: 84–90.

———. 1994. "Indexes: A Chapter from the *Chicago Manual of Style*, 14th Edition: A Review." *The Indexer* 19 (October): 105–109.

———. 1992. "A Theory of Relativity for Catalogers." In *Cataloging Heresy: Challenging the Standard Bibliographic Product*. Edited by Bella Hass Weinberg. Medford, NJ: Learned Information: 7–11.

———. 1988. "Why Indexing Fails the Researcher." *The Indexer* 16 (April): 3–6.

———. 1995. "Why Postcoordination Fails the Searcher." *The Indexer* 19 (April): 155–159.

Weinberg, Bella Hass, ed. 1989. *Indexing: The State of Our Knowledge and the State of Our Ignorance.* Medford, NJ: Learned Information, Inc.

Wellisch, Hans H. 1994. "Book and Periodical Indexing." *Journal of the American Society for Information Science* 45 (September): 620–627.

———. 1972. "A Flow Chart for Indexing with a Thesaurus." *Journal of the American Society for Information Science* 23 (May-June): 185–194.

———. 1992. *Indexing: A Basic Reading List.* Port Aransas, TX: American Society of Indexers.

———. 1995. *Indexing from A to Z.* 2nd ed. New York: H. W. Wilson.

Wheatley, Henry Benjamin. 1878. *What Is an Index? A Few Notes on Indexes and Indexers.* London: H. Sotheran & Co.

Wheeler, Martha Thorne. 1957. *Indexing: Principles, Rules and Examples.* 5th ed. Albany, NY: New York State Library.

Wicks, Wendy. 1997. *Careers in Electronic Information.* Philadelphia: National Federation of Abstracting and Information Service.

Wiley, Deborah Lynne. 1994. "From Print to Internet: Can the Traditional Abstracting and Indexing Services Survive?" *Database* 17 (December): 18–24.

Wilson, Patrick. 1968. *Two Kinds of Power: An Essay on Bibliographic Control.* Berkeley: University of California Press.

Wise, Mary Porter, and Gonzalez-Kirby, Diana. 1990. "Title-Keyword Indexing of Intergovernmental Organization Materials." *Computers in Libraries* 10 (November): 37–39.

Wittman, Cecelia. 1991. "Limitations of Indexing Modules in Word-Processing Software." *The Indexer* 17 (October): 235–238.

———. 1990. "Subheadings in Award-winning Book Indexes: A Quantitative Evaluation." *The Indexer* 17 (April): 3–6.

Woodward, Jeannette. 1996. "Cataloging and Classifying Information Resources on the Internet." In *Annual Review of Information Science and Technology. Volume 31.* Medford, NJ: Information Today: 189–219.

Index

ABI/INFORM, 193
Aboutness, 98
Absences of indexes, 49
Abstract journals, 8
Abstracting
  content analysis, 113–15
  recording bibliographic information,
    110–15
  steps, 110–17
Abstracting, technical paper example,
  131–36
Abstractors
  authors as, 58
  definition, 251
  education, 242
  employment, 243–44
  professional, 58
  subject-experts, 58
Abstracts
  arrangement, 117
  author-prepared, 58
  characteristics and types, 56–57
  computer generated, 213–14
  coverage, 109
  critical, 57
  current-awareness function, 25, 55
  data in, 56–57
  definition, 251
  descriptive, 56–57
  diction of, 116–17
  editing, 118
  evaluation, 119, 189
  indicative, 56–57
  informative, 57
  length of, 115
  material covered, 109–10
  purpose of, 108
  results in, 58

  signatures of, 117
  structured, 59
  use of, 33
  writing, 116–17
Abstracts in Anthropology, 74
Access points, 45, 104
Acquisition of information, 24
Acronyms, 251
Added value, 3, 4
Advertisements, 100
Affiliation of authors, 111
*Alcohol and Alcohol Problems Science
  Database*, 80
Alerting services, 25
Alphabet, 7
Alphabetic indexes, 48
Alphabetical arrangement, 7
Alphabetization, 7, 145
Alternative title, 251
American Eclectic, 8
American Society for Information
  Science, 20
American Society of Indexers, 240
American Statistics Index, 61
Annals de Chimie et de Physique, 193
Anthropological Index Online, 80
Arrangement, 48
Art & Architecture Thesaurus, The, 80
Articles
  exhaustivity of indexing, 100
  indexing techniques, 100
  locators for, 104
  specificity of indexing, 100
ASI. *See* American Society of Indexers
ASIS Thesaurus of Information Science,
  80
Assigned-terms, 37
Assignment indexing, 252

Associative retrieval systems, 252
Australian Society of Indexers, 240
Author abstracts, 58–59
Author indexes, 49
Author indexing, 49
Authority lists
   construction, 39
   defined, 38
Authors
   abstracts prepared by (*see* Author
      abstracts)
   address or affiliation of, 111
Automated indexing software, 207
Automatic abstracting
   extracting techniques, 213
   stylistic techniques, 214
Automatic indexing
   approaches, 211
   automated vs. manual, 212
   problems, 212
Automatic indexing and abstracting,
   future of, 214
Automation. *See* Computers

Back-of-the-book indexes. *See* Book
   indexes
Bates, Marcia J., 41
Beginners, 9–10
Bible, concordances of, 7
Bibliographic control, 252
Bibliographic coupling, 247–48
Bibliographic entries, 100–101
Bibliometrics, 248
Biological Abstracts, 193
Book indexes, 49
   components, 138
   depth, 144
   do's-and-don'ts, 146–49
   example, 150–64
   exhaustivity, 100
   history of, 7
   lack of, 49, 138
   name entries, 142–44
   nature of, 137
   vs. other indexes, 137–38
   selecting terms 140–42
   specificity of indexing, 100
   steps, 139–40
   subject entries, 144–45
Boolean operators, 27
Boolean searching, 27
Bound terms, 252

Broader terms (BT), 43
BRS, 196

Cancerlit, 80
Carl UnCover, 194
Carriers of information, 15
Chronological order, 48
Citation indexes, 49
Citation order, 253
Classification and indexing, 29–30
Classified indexes, 51
Claude, Shannon, 15
Cleveland, Ana, 121
Cleveland, Donald, 49, 121, 150
Closed-end index, 253
Collison, Robert L., 187
Communication Abstracts, 77
Computer-assisted indexing, 193
Computer-assisted software, 200
Computer indexing, changes in index-
   ing, 206
Computers
   accuracy of, 201
   automatic extracting, 204
   cataloging and classification, 203
   characteristics, 200
   expert systems, 203–6
   human indexing vs. automatics,
      206
   indexing with, 202, 206–7
   online databases searching, 202
   references services, 202
   speed of, 200
   use of, 200–214
Concept list, 253
Concepts, 98
Concordances, 7
Conference Papers Index, 66
Content analysis, 101
Content indicators, 131
Control, 12–13
Controlled vocabulary. *See* Vocabulary
   control
Coordinate indexes, 51
CORC (Cooperative Online Resource
   Catalog), 226–27
Corporate body, 254
Critical abstracts, 57
Cross-references, 9, 43–44, 254
Cumulative indexes, 51
Current awareness, 25
Cyber networking, 21

Data retrieval, 23, 25
Databases
    construction of indexes, 197
    multiple thesaurus management, 198
    searching, 196–99
    types of, 194
Depth of indexing, 105
Depth of indexing, books, 144
Derived-terms, 37–38
Descriptive abstracts, 56–57
Descriptors, 254
DIALOG, 195
Discipline- and mission-oriented, 58
Display, 107
Dissertation Abstracts, 80
Document delivery, 25
Documentation movement, 20
Documents
    definition, 254
    indexable concepts, 101
    subject of, 98
DOIs (Digital Object Identifiers), 227
Double entry, 254
Dubois, C. P. R., 36

Economics of information, 18–19
Editing, 190–91
Educational Administration Abstracts,
    80
E-mail, 236–37, 240
Embedding software, 207
Employment, 5
Entity-oriented index, 254
Entry differentiation, 255
Entry points, 104
Entry terms, 45
Enumerated vocabulary, 39
Equivalent term, 255
ERIC, 193
ERIC Thesaurus, 80
Evaluation of abstracts, 189
Evaluation of indexes
    Cranfield tests, 181
    effects of exhaustivity and specificity,
        187
    general problem, 180–81
    human factors, 180
    quality, 187–88
    recall and precision, 185–86
    relevance, 183–85
    use of information, 182
    users, 182
Evolutionary vocabulary, 39
Exhaustivity, 105, 187

Expert systems, 203–6
    abstracting example, 20
    advantages, 203–4
Extraction, 102

Faceted indexes, 51–52
False drops, 255
Feedback, 28
Fetters, Linda, 208
First-line indexes, 52
Formats, 4
Formula, indexes, 255
Free text, 35–36
Freelance indexing, 243–44
Frequency analysis, 213
Function of an index, 2

Garfield, Eugene, 50
Generic vocabularies, 39
Getty Thesaurus of Geographic Names,
    The, 80

Historical Abstracts, 80
Historiography, 172
History
    abstracting, 8
    alphabetical subject arrangement, 7
    book indexing (history), 9
    codex development, 7
    collecting records, 6
    computers in indexing, 9
    indexing evaluation, 9
    information explosion, 9
    language development, 6
    origin of indexing, 6
    writing, 6
History of the People of the United States,
    172
Homograph, 256
Humanities literature
    nature of, 169
    structure, 169–70
Hypermedia and hypertext, 52
Hypermedia indexes, 52

Identifiers, 45
Image indexing
    content analysis, 175–78
    development, 174–75
    future, 177
    problems, 177–78
    relevance, 177

Images, 174, 174–78
Inadequate indexes, 2
Inclusion/exclusion of material, 4
Indented layout, 256
Index Medicus, 72
Index quality, 187–88
Indexable matter
    factors for decision on, 99
    types of units, 101–3
Indexers
    as censors, 5
    education and training, 242
    job opportunities, 243–45
Indexes
    alphabetic, 48
    author, 49
    citation, 49
    classified, 51
    concordances, 7
    display, 107
    faceted, 51–52
    first-line, 52
    general purposes, 3
    hypermedia, 52
    Internet, 52
    lack of, 49
    multimedia, 53
    periodical, 53
    permuted, 53
    string, 54–55
    subject, 6, 48, 51
    use of, 33
    word, 55
Indexing
    as an art, 1, 10
    and classification, 29–30
    automatic, 211–12
    depth, 105
    evaluation, 179–80
    future of, 249
    languages, 37
    legal literature, 168
    procedures, 97, 98
    process of, 2
    as a profession, 5, 243–45
    research, 245–49
    specificity, 106
    steps, 100
    technical paper example, 121–30
Indexing and abstracting services
    computer use, 192–93
    future of, 199
    history, 192–93
    nature of, 192

Indexing and Abstracting Society of
        Canada, 240
Indexing software
    automatic, 207
    Cindex, 209
    computer-assisted, 207
    embedding, 207
    guidelines for evaluation, 208
    Hierarch Systematics, 209
    HTML Indexers, 209
    HyperIndex, 210
    IndexCheck, 210
    Indexer, 210
    Indexer's Assistant, 210
    indexTools, 210
    Ixgen, 210
    Lexico, 210
    Macrex, 210
    Protext, 210
    ScanVen Entry, 210
    SKY Index Professional, 210
    standalone, 207
    wINDEX, 210
Indicative abstracts, 56–57
Industrial society, 12
Information
    acquisition of, 24
    age of, 2, 11–13, 19–20
    basic resource, 18
    cost of, 24
    cycle, 22–23
    definition, 13–14
    explosion, 8, 12, 33
    forms of, 16
    importance of, 12
    properties of, 13
    ubiquity of, 14
Information retrieval
    basic model, 23
    changes in user needs, 20
    history of, 19–21
    information age, 19
    information cycle, 22–23
    mechanisms for, 19–21, 23
    processes, 24–29
    use of computers, 20
Information science
    definition, 18
    interdisciplinary nature, 18
    origin of term, 18
Information society, 12
Information superhighway, 2
Information systems, 15, 23–24, 25
Information theory, 15–16
Informative abstracts, 57

INSPEC, 193
Institute for Scientific Information, 80
International Index to the Performing Arts, 80
International Institute of Bibliography, 9
International Political Science Abstracts, 84
Internet. *See also* World Wide Web
  background, 215
  indexes, 52
  searching, 216
  usefulness for indexers, 215
INTREX, 195
ISBD, 223, 227
ISDN, 223, 227
Item retrieval, 25

Job opportunities, 243–45
  electronic world, 244
  Internet Public Library, 245
  publishing, 244
Journal Des Scavans, 8

Kessler, M. M., 247
Keywords, 45
KWIC (keyword in context), 38, 257
KWOC (keyword out of context), 257
Knight, G. Norman, 243

La Fontaine, Henri, 9
Language, problems, 37
Legal literature
  categories, 168
  characteristics, 169
  exhaustivity and specificity of indexing, 169
  nature, 168
Legislative Indexing Vocabulary (LIV) Thesaurus, 80
Literary warrant, 257
Locators, 104
Luhn auto-extracting, 213
Luhn, Hans Peter, 9

Macrothesaurus, 257
Marginal summaries, 7
Mathematical Reviews, 88
Mathematical Theory of Communication, The, 15
McMaster, John B., 170
Medical New and Libraries, 193

Medical Subject Headings (MeSH), 80
Medieval Feminist Index, 80
Mesopotamian Valley, 6
Metadata, 4
  defined, 223
  purpose, 223
  useful websites, 228
Microsoft Internet Explorer, 217
Microthesaurus, 257
Mission-oriented abstracts, 58
Modern information mechanisms, 21
Modifiers, 257
Monat Sextracte, 8
Monthly Review, 193
Multimedia indexes, 53

Names, 142
Narrower terms (NT), 43
NASA Thesaurus, 80
National Federation of Abstracting and Indexing Services, 240
National Information Standards Organization, 238
National Library of Medicine (NLM), 168
Natural language
  ambiguity, 35
  retrieval, 35–37
Nature of an index, 4
Need for indexes, 2–4, 7
Neophyte indexers, 9–10
Netscape, 217
New York Times Index, 173, 193
Newspapers
  historiography, 172–73
  indexing, 171, 173
  indexing policies, 173
  topics, 172–73
Newspapers Online!, 173
NFAIS. *See* National Federation of Abstracting and Indexing Services
NISO. *See* National Information Standards Organization
NLM. *See* National Library of Medicine
Notation, 258

OCLC, 224–27
Online services, 195
ORBIT, 196
Order
  alphabetic, 6
  chronological, 7

Order (*continued*)
   classified, 6
   index presentation, 6–7
Origin of indexing, 6
Otlet, Paul, 9
OVID, 193

Part-time indexing, 5
Passim, 148
Perfect index, 1
Periodical indexes, 7, 53
   compared with book indexes, 53
   exhaustivity, 100
   indexing policies, 100
   title indexes, 53
Permuted indexes, 54
Personal names, 7
Pertinence, 184
Philosophor's Index, The, 69
Place names, 45
Poole, W. F., 9
Population Index on the Web, 80
Post-coordinate indexing, 51
PRECIS, 208
Precision, 185–86
Pre-coordinate indexing, 51
Preferred terms, 45
Prichard, Alan, 248
Primary literature, 192
Probabilistic indexing, 258
Process of indexing, 2
Purpose in indexing, 1, 33–34

Readers' Guide to Periodical Literature, 9
Recall, 185–86
Reference retrieval, 25
Related terms (RT), 43
Relevance, 27, 183–85
Research in indexing
   cost, 247
   needs, 247
   purpose, 245
   types of, 247–49
Researchers, qualifications of, 246
Rhodes, James Ford, 172

Scholarly communication, 8
Scientific book indexers, 167
Scope notes, 44
Search engines, 218
Searching, 27

Searching procedures, 28
See also references, 43, 259
See references, 46, 43, 148, 259
Shatford, Sara, 175
Shepard's Citations, 50
Shera, Jesse, 196
SNOMED International, 168
Society of Indexers, 240
Special formats
   images, 174–78
   newspapers, 171–73
   nonprint, 174
Special subject areas
   humanities, 169–71
   sciences, 166–68
   social sciences, 168–69
Specificity of indexing, 106, 187
Stand-alone software, 207
Standards, 189–90
Statistics Abstracts of the United States,
   193
String indexes, 54–55
Structure of information, 15
Structured abstracts, 59
Subject determination, 103
Subject indexes
   alphabetical, 48
   classified, 51
   concordances, 7
   history, 6
Surrogates, 2, 6

Terms
   broader, 43
   forms of, 45
   narrower, 43
   post-coordinate and pre-coordinate,
      51
   preferred, 45
   related, 43
   relationships, 43
   selection, 104
Text retrieval, 25
Thesauri
   construction 41–43
   evaluation, 46
   purpose, 39
Thesaurofacet, 260
Thesaurus constraints, rules, 45–46
Thesaurus of ERIC Descriptors, 91
Title words, 9, 101, 110
Types of indexes, 4

U.S. Patent Citation Database, 80
UMLS Metathesaurus, 168
Uncontrolled vocabularies, 35–37
Uniterm systems, 38
Universal Magazine of Knowledge and Pleasure, 192
Use for references, 43–44
Use of information vs. use of materials, 182
Use references, 43–44
User needs, 20, 25
User needs, types of, 183

Virtual library, 21
Virtual libraries, 237
Vocabulary control
    authority lists, 38–39
    characteristics, 36–37
    definition, 35
    development, 35
    vs. free text, 34–35
    generic vocabularies, 39–40
    purpose, 35
    thesauri, 40–41
    trade-offs, 36

Wheatley Medal, 243
Wilson, H. W., 9
Women Studies Abstracts, 86
Word indexes, 55
World Wide Web (WWW). *See also* Internet
    browsers, 217
    components, 217
    development, 220
    directories, 218
    DOIs, 227
    Dublin Core, 224–26
    evaluation, 228
    finding information, 216
    indexes, 220
    indexing systems, 217
    library access methods, 221
    metadata, 223
    metasearchers, 218
    navigators, 217
    OCLC CORC, 226–27
    organization of information, 220
    problems, 228–30
    resources, 216
        dictionaries and dictionary directories, 234
        e-mail reference sites, 236
        indexing and the web, 241
        indexing organizations, 240
        indexing services, 233
        indexing-related discussion groups, 240
        multireference resources and tools, 234
        online bookstores, 231
        publishers, 239
        search services, 232
        special formats and subjects indexing, 238
        standards, 238
        virtual libraries, 237
    robots, 218
    search engines, 218
        searching options, 216, 219